Frank and Jesse James
"Friends and Family"

Treasured stories
from the cousins, siblings,
Friends and Family
of Frank and Jesse James

A Historical Novel
Told in the voice of
Alexander Franklin James

Freda Cruse Hardison

Library of Congress Control Number: 2015916123

ISBN: 978-0-9842111-2-8

DISCLAIMER: This is a historical novel compiled from true and believed to be true stories of the descendants of the men and women who lived them. Names, dates and places have not been changed nor have the stories or information presented. There is no intention to damage or cause harm to anyone or their ancestors through the telling of these stories. Some information has never before been told and has been shared with this author as a means of presenting a more accurate portrayal of the early life of the James and Samuel family.

Printed in the United States by Morris Publishing®
3212 East Highway 30
Kearney, NE 68847
1-800-650-7888

NOTES FROM THE AUTHOR

During research on Voices of Our People (2009) and Places of Our People (2011), I interviewed hundreds of individuals, 70 to 100 years old. It seemed everyone had a story about Frank and Jesse James. "Grandma cooked Jesse James a meal, supplied the James boys horses, hide them out at their house...." Smiling, I wrote them down tucking them away in a folder making a mental note to someday check those out. Then, fellow historian and friend Juanita Stowers learned she had terminal cancer. She wanted me to have all her research and photographs compiled over the previous decade on the James and Mims connections in Izard Co, Ark. I started running down Juanita's information and all those individual family stories, walking hundreds of cemeteries, looking through family Bibles and hearing more stories held by the descendants of the cousins, half siblings, friends and family of the James and Samuel families. I found documentation in the Official Records of the Military, census, marriage and death certificates, Quantrill Reunion stories, two War Between the States journals and newspapers supporting their stories. When put together chronologically and told together a much greater understanding of the James family both in Missouri and Arkansas was revealed.

When I ask, "Why have you never told this before?" Repeatedly the answer was a variant of, "Everyone back then had a story or a connection....Who knew what was real and what wasn't....The newspapers were only interested in Jesse." The best was "Momma said never to tell these stories until all the people were dead. 100 years is long enough."

During the Civil War, Missourians Col. Thomas Roe Freeman and Col. Joseph Orville Shelby rose to the rank of Brigadier General but to friends and family they remained Colonel Tom and Colonel Shelby. They maintained lifelong friendships not only with the James brothers, but with many of the men who served with them. It is the stories of the descendants of the men who served under these two remarkable men who have most significantly provided the links to a greater understanding of Frank and Jesse James' early lives and what Arkansas meant to them both during and after the Civil War. Arkansas was a second home to them. A place they did not talk about, a place where they could be safe among Friends and Family.

I have had the pleasure to meet some wonderful people, descendants of the James brother's half siblings, the Samuel's who made their home in Ark, first cousin's, parent's cousins and friends who knew them. The most extraordinary of all these people willing to share family photos, histories and stories has been the grandsons of Colonel Thomas Roe Freeman, brothers, John and Thomas Freeman, children of Colonel Tom's youngest son, John Fuller Freeman. And, Dr. Tom's wife, Joi Nolan Freeman, who has been an incredible researcher and facilitator in this project. I am eternally indebted to these three. I want to thank both the Emory Cantey collection, perhaps the most comprehensive collection of authentic guerilla images known and the Kansas City Public Library, Missouri Valley Special Collections, Kansas City, Missouri for use of their images. All other photographs are the property of the author, taken by the author or provided by descendants of the friends and family of the James' including John and Tom Freeman, Brian Loggains, Elvada Walker, Doug Miller and files of Juanita Stowers.

I must thank every individual whose amateur and academic research aided in this project: Sue McCluskey, Rick Dowdle, Cal Campbell, Denny Elrod and the Exploring Izard County Crew; Gloria Sanders, Director and Steven Mitchell, Board of the Calico Rock Museum Foundation; local author Rosemary Lankford whose book Encyclopedia of Quantrill's Guerilla's provided me a place to start in sorting out who's who; and, Mark Mobley and his father Freeman Mobley, author of Making Sense of the War Between the States in Batesville-Jacksonport and Northeast Arkansas who not only welcomed me into the family home but took time to discuss the intimate details of the complexities and importance of the War Between the States in the White River Valley. Without Freeman Mobley understanding the guerilla warfare of Ark would have been a much greater task if not nearly impossible. Dale Hanks always for his honest friendship and criticism, and, Dawn Young Lindsay for her friendship and tolerance of me throughout work on not only this project but so many others. And most importantly, the late Juanita Stowers for her dedication to the history of Izard Co. Thank you, one and all, for welcoming me into your homes and your lives. And, I must thank my husband, Beau Hardison, whose patience has been demonstrated daily during this project.

I have chosen to tell these stories in the voice of Frank James. They are presented in good faith as presented to this author, some are exactly, word for word, as presented, others have been used in part to represent a more accurate time line. All names, places and dates presented are real. No harm is intended to any families or their descendants through the telling of these stories. They are true and believed to be true stories of the descendants of the men and women who lived them and who provided them for use in these pages. I believe like pieces to a puzzle these stories reveal a never before told story of the early lives of the James family as they lived it. I am indebted to every person who gave me a clue, story, picture, census, referral or in any way contributed to this work.

Freda Cruse Hardison

Dedication

This book is dedicated to the men and their families who endured the American War Between the States. It is especially dedicated to the men who served under Col. Thomas Roe Freeman, Missouri Cav, Ark Partisan Rangers, protecting the White River Valley of Ark. It is the friendships of those men and the stories of their survivals and sacrifices that have brought the pieces of this puzzle together.

Brigadier General Thomas Roe Freeman
Feb 22, 1829 – Feb 23, 1893

The only known photograph of "Colonel Tom" Post War – Attorney at Law

Col. Tom's grandson's John (l) and Tom Freeman (r)
And, Tom's wife Joi Nolan Freeman

Table of Contents

Alexander Franklin James

Born Jan 10, 1843
Kearney, Missouri, Thomason home
Died Feb 18, 1915
Kearney, Missouri, James Farm
He was 72 years, 1 month and 8 days old.

He is survived by his wife Annie Ralston James, of the home
Son, Robert Franklin James and wife May Sullivan James.
Siblings: John Thomas and wife Norma Maret Samuel of Excelsior Springs, Missouri, brother in law Allen Hazard Parmer of Wichita Falls, Texas, Sarah Louisa Samuel and husband William Nicholson, Fannie Quantrill Samuel and husband Joe C. Hall all of Kearney, Missouri, and his beloved Aunt Charlotte and her son Perry Samuel and wife Susie Willis Samuel of Liberty, Missouri.
He is also survived by a host of nieces and nephews.

Preceding him in death are his
Father, Reverend Robert Sallee James
Mother, Zerelda Elizabeth Cole,
Step fathers, Benjamin Simms and Archibald Reuben Samuel,
Brothers: Robert James, Jr., Jesse Woodson James and his wife Zerelda Mims James and Archibald Peyton Samuel,
Sisters: Mary Louisa Samuel and Susan L. James Parmer

Frank James was cremated.

Annie Ralston James born Jan 25, 1853
Independence, Missouri
daughter of Samuel Ralston and Mary Catherine Hill.
Died July 6, 1944 at the James-Samuel Farm.
Annie was 91 years, 5 months and 11 days old.

Frank's ashes were laid to rest with his wife Annie Ralston.
Frank and Annie are interred at Hill Park Cemetery,
Independence, Jackson Co, Missouri

Chapter 1

Holding me at arm's length his strong hands on each shoulder, Daddy looked me straight in the eyes, "You're the man of the house now." I knew today, April 12, 1850 would be forever emblazoned on my heart and in my head. Two years before on March 5, 1848 President James Polk reported to Congress the discovery of an "abundance of gold" in the California territory. Thousands of men were heading west in hopes of making their fortunes. My Daddy, Baptist Minister and successful hemp farmer, Robert Sallee James was about to be one of them.

"You look out for your little brother Jesse and baby sister Susie, you hear. You take care of Momma. You say your prayers and you make sure to set a good example for others. People will be looking at you, son." The tears gathering in Daddy's eyes were afraid to fall. I knew this was serious. He wasn't going to be gone for a few weeks or a couple months, like when he went home to Kentucky for a visit or to finish his preacher schooling at Georgetown. I knew he was going to be gone a long time. Knowing he might never come back, fear griped my every sense. I started crying. I could feel the hot tears streaming down my face. My whole body trembled. Daddy's big warm hands squeezed my shoulders pulling me close to him, his big hands holding me tight, patting me on the back. His arms tightened into that big bear hug of his. It made me feel better, most times, but not now, I was crying like a baby. Squeezing him back as tight as I could, I gave Daddy the best little bear hug I ever gave anyone before or since. "Daddy, please don't go." I heard myself saying the words over and over begging him not to go. Jesse saw I was crying holding onto Daddy and soon both of us were squalling. On bended knee Daddy hugged us both. When he tried to stand up, Jesse grabbed hold of his leg. Daddy walked about the yard with Jesse refusing to let go holding on tight. I could see he was trying to make a game of it, trying hard to make Jesse laugh. It worked but only for a minute. "Daddy, it's a wise father that knows his own child," I said, trying hard to be the man only minutes before Daddy proclaimed me to be. "Ahh, Buck, I'm proud of you. Merchant of Venice Act II Scene II," Daddy replied. Adding, "Our Lord our God our Father in Heaven is our refuge and our strength." "Ahh Daddy, I'm proud of you. Psalm 46:1." Daddy insisted for every verse I committed to heart from Shakespeare, I must equally commit a scripture. In our house no man was greater than the Lord, our God and Savior. For a moment we both smiled.

As the local preacher man, Daddy was more popular than any preacher ever seen in these parts. I was too young to recall it, but I had been there sitting on Momma's lap the day the entire gathering recommitted their lives and new souls were saved. She could tell the story real good. People from everywhere wanted "Preacher James" to marry'em, say something over their dead and when preaching was over on Sunday, families ask him to join them in their home for dinner. That usually meant we all went along; Momma, me, Jesse and Susie. But sometimes, us kids we'd go over to Uncle Till and Aunt Lizzie's house and just Momma and Daddy would go for fixin's. The best times were when Daddy would just take me. "He was "priming" me," he's say to the family who'd offered up an invitation for dinner. I loved to go with him, hear his words and offerings to the Lord. I wanted to be like Daddy in that way, someone people looked to for help and guidance. A few months back, riding home in the wagon from church, I felt the Lord take hold of me. Sitting between Momma and Daddy, I blurted out, "I want to be a preacher, Daddy. I feel the Lord calling me to be a teacher of the Word of God." Momma heard me and with eyes wide looked straight at Daddy. He stopped the wagon pulling me in for one of his strong bear hugs. Holding me longer than usual, I could feel his tears.

I loved Daddy's books and loved it even more when he'd sit me on his lap and read to me. Momma said I picked up real fast. No matter what we were reading, the good book or one of the other 50 or so books Daddy had in his library; I didn't let them skip a page. I'd memorized the core of most of them by the time I was 5, especially Shakespeare. Momma and Daddy sometimes would read pieces out loud to us kid's right there in front of the fireplace, our own theatre. There were villains and heroes, damsels in distress and men who rescued them. Daddy made the Bible come alive when he told stories. Where the Bible and Shakespeare left off, Daddy and Momma took up adding in characters so us kids could have parts. Momma hung a piece of cloth in the doorway about waist high for our theatre. We made hand puppets and had our own plays from behind the cloth. I knew the Bible and understood the stories and now, the Lord was calling me. I know you can't see it when a person has a headache, you can't touch the pain, but you know it's there and when people look at you, they see the pain in your face. That's how I felt about the Lord as I sat there looking back and forth between Momma and Daddy. "Be true to who you are and what you believe. The Lord will lead you in the direction your life is to take." With that, Daddy handed me the reins of the team. "Let's see how ready you are to guide these two horses home." I snapped the reins and the horses continued on down the road towards home. Pride ran through me. I hoped we'd meet someone on the way who would see me at the lead. I hadn't realized it then, but those Missouri Fox Trotters already headed home needed nothing more than a little prodding. They knew the way home as sure as I knew I had been called by the Lord.

That was the first time I'd felt Daddy's tears, today, I felt them again. I was seven years old but I didn't want to be the man of the house if it meant Daddy was going to be gone. Aunt Charlotte pried Jesse loose from Daddy's leg. Hoisting him to her hip, she took my hand. "Mister Frank, your Momma needs some time."

Aunt Charlotte moved with Gramma Sallie and Gramps Bob from Kentucky. Aunt Charlotte and Gramma Sallie birthed me right here in Missouri at Gramma Sallie's house. She was both mine and Aunt Mattie's nurse maid. Gramma Sallie had Martha Ann "Mattie" Thomason, momma's half sister July 23rd, 1841. I was born 18 months later on Jan 10th, 1843. The next year, Feb 1844, her little sister, my Aunt Mary Alice "Ailsy" Thomason come along. Both Momma and Gramma Sallie with babies, Aunt Charlotte nursed and swaddled us all under one roof.

Daddy grew hemp, the stuff ropes were made of. We had a good living but I reckon 'thar was gold in them hills'. Folks all over were moving their wives and children in with family and friends, others simply leaving them behind alone as they headed west. California was calling many a good man with dreams of getting rich. The newspaper ran a story about one man who come back after only a few months with more money than Daddy made all year with his crop. Fast money, a way to get ahead, lured a lot of people, especially those surviving the Great Depression of '37. From religious men to farmers no one was exempt from the gold fever. Daddy and his friend Mister William Stigers talked it up and now they were gathered with other friends making up a full wagon train heading west.

Daddy met Momma when he was 20 years old. He was going to school at the newly established Baptist College in Georgetown, Scott Co, Kentucky just down the road from Nelson Co, where Momma was going to school. She was 15 and attending St. Catherine's Female School in New Haven. This was on the whiskey route established by the Samuel family at Samuel's Depot. Taylor William Samuel started his distillery business there. He was of kin to Momma's 3rd husband, Doctor Rueben Samuel and Doc's 3rd cousin Edward Madison Samuel the Unionist, who would come to cause us considerable headache. Doc's half brother was named for the Unionist, also Edward Madison Samuel. During the War Between the States, Confederate Genl. John Hunt Morgan raided Georgetown twice, July 15, 1862 and July 10, 1864. A year later in July 1865 I would surrender at Samuel's Depot. It was about 16 miles from there to Smiley where William Clarke Quantrill was ambushed at the farm of Jeremiah Wakefield.

Daddy and Momma were married by the Reverend Younger Rogers Pitts on Dec 28, 1841 at the home of Uncle James Lindsay in Stamping Ground, Scott Co, Kentucky. After Momma's Daddy, James Cole, died, Gramma Sallie married Gramps Robert "Bob" Thomason and moved to Missouri. Momma and her brother Jesse, Uncle J.R., for whom my little brother Jesse was named, were trusted to Gramma Sallie's brother, Judge

James Lindsay and his wife Mary Keene to complete schooling. Momma was only 15 so Uncle James had to sign for her to get married and post a $50 bond. Momma and Daddy lived in a little house on the Frankfort Pike between Lexington and Frankfort. When Momma became heavy with child, Daddy brought her to Missouri to be with her Momma. Then he went back to Kentucky to continue his education. He was ordained as a minister in 1839 but had the calling to teach and preach, additional schooling would enable him to plant churches. He was studying for his Master's. I was born in Kearney, Clay Co, Missouri at the home of my Gramma Sallie and Gramps Bob Thomason. Daddy was in Kentucky. He planned on coming at Christmas to be there when I was born but it was a cold harsh winter and travel was difficult. The Missouri River froze solid and the big Mississippi was said to have chunks of ice the size of boats floating in it. Daddy got that far and had to turn around unable to travel any further west. Momma wrote Daddy letters begging him to come as soon as he could. Along with the encouragement and support of Reverend Jeremiah Vardeman, Daddy's calling by the Lord to be in Liberty, Clay Co, Missouri was sealed when he finally made it to Missouri and he and Momma together found a house on a good size piece of land. The Lord and the Baptist Convention needed preachers to contend with the Mormon problem in Missouri. Reverend Vardeman a leader in the Flat Lick Baptist Church in Kentucky had moved to Missouri long before Daddy and was in large part responsible for many Kentucky families moving here.

Momma and Daddy acquired a lease on a 275 acre farm with the option of purchasing it. Jacob Groomer first settled the land some 20 years earlier. He built the log cabin that become our home. It was of good size, eighteen by thirty five feet with a connecting breezeway to a second cabin with an attic Mister Groomer built on in 1844. Alvah Maret helped Daddy get the farm. Uncle Jesse "J.R.", Momma's brother, married his daughter Louisa Maret, Aunt Lou. It was here we'd make our home and where my brothers and sisters would be born. Growing up, Mister Jacob's grandson Garrett Groomer was one of my friends. He married Sarah Frances "Fanny" Pence, Donnie and Bud's sister. Garrett was killed in the war and then Fanny married another of my friends, James Corum. Both Garrett and Jim rode with me under Col. Shelby then joining Quantrill and Bloody Bill.

Once at home in Missouri, Daddy rode the circuit on horseback preaching. He'd be at one church on Sunday morning and Sunday night, then move on to another place riding his horse to get there. They'd hold church whenever Daddy showed up, any day of the week. He'd stay with families along the way. They would have weddings, funerals and preaching's as soon as Preacher James showed up.

I learned early how to thaw the frozen ground in winter time. If the ground was frozen and people wanted to bury their dead, the ground would have to be thawed. Often in the winter they waited until Daddy got there to say something over the dead. They would keep the frozen body in a wooden box in the barn. They might thaw the ground and then sometimes, they'd just wait until the ground thawed itself and do the burying then. And, sometimes when Daddy came he'd be holding services for folks already in the ground, especially in hot summers. Daddy told stories about the different ways people thought about their dead, some people stayed up with the dead in their houses, someone always awake. Others covered all the windows and mirrors with cloth. He visited people who would not partake of any food and others who played music and had a party. I loved listening to Daddy. He would talk like the people he met, from Ireland, Germany and other places. I was four, in 1847, the year he finished his Master's. Momma thought that meant he was through with his long distance traveling.

Momma had been 2 years old when her daddy, James Cole, died. She had her daddy's obituary but it's been lost to time. In her Bible she carried an old newspaper from Frankfort dated June 20th, 1827. My great grandpa lost two sons in just a matter of a few months. The clipping, about the death of Momma's Uncle Amos, is in my possession now.

"The last few days have brought us news of three shocking murders within less than 100 miles of this place. On Saturday night last, the house of Richard Cole, a well known tavern keeper ten miles from this place, in Woodford Co was attacked by R. Taylor and a Mr. Gillespie of the same neighborhood, with stones. A Negro woman was struck in the face and severely wounded by one of the stones, when an affray ensued between Mr. Cole and his two sons on the other, which ended in the death of Amos Cole, who received 13 or 14 stabs from Gillespie. Gillespie and Taylor were taken into custody, and an examining court was held yesterday, the result of which we have not heard. There is said to have been an old quarrel between Taylor and the Coles."

Great Grandpa Richard Cole was a surveyor on the old road leading between Maysville and Lexington, to Frankfort and Louisville. In 1794 he was hired to work on part of the old Leestown Road, along with his son, my grandpa, Momma's daddy, James Cole. He decided to put in a tavern just down the road from Sodom. It had flour and grist mills, cotton and hemp factories, a tannery and shoe shop, carding machine and storehouse. Cole's Tavern was just a stop on the road, but lots of people stopped there. When the railroad chose its path through, Sodom was bypassed and slowly died as the trains drew business and trade to other places along its route. Cole's Tavern a much more suitable place survived.

My grandpa James Cole was only 24 years old when on April 27, 1827; he was thrown off his horse. He died from a broken neck. Momma and her brother Jesse were taken to their grandpa's house, Richard James

Cole, Jr. They were raised in Cole's Tavern. Many people have since written about Cole's Tavern mistaking it as Sodom due to its rough and rowdy, vulgar and profane type of Co, like from the Bible. However, Sodom, Kentucky according to my Momma was a community further down the way guilty of those vulgarities and because its tavern was on the road to the Cole's Tavern, sometimes Cole's tavern was thought to be Sodom Tavern. In later years, another family member bought the tavern run by a mulatto by the name of Lee and renamed it Black Horse Tavern. These are separate places in my Momma's upbringing. When Great Grandpa Cole died in 1839, Momma and Uncle J.R. went to live with their Uncle James Lindsay, their momma's brother. It was Uncle James that allowed Momma to marry Daddy. By the time my Momma 14, she no longer had her daddy or grandparents. Her Momma's mother, Grandma Alice Cole died before Momma was born and Grandpa Anthony Lindsay died when she was only six. Momma's Daddy's Momma, her grandma Sallie Yates Cole died when Momma was 11. Then when she was 14, Grandpa Richard James Cole died. Momma's family, her aunts, uncles and cousins meant everything to her. She understood loss.

Daddy lost his Daddy, John Martin James and his Momma, Mary "Polly" Poor in 1827, the year he was five. Orphaned, Daddy along with a houseful of brothers and sisters went to live with his oldest sister, 19 year old Mary and her husband John Wilson Mims. After Daddy died, Aunt Mary and Uncle John moved to Missouri to be closer to us. Daddy had been raised by them until he was grown and with him gone, Aunt Mary wanted to be close by us children. "Zee" whom my little brother Jesse would marry is Uncle John and Aunt Mary's daughter, Daddy's niece. That wasn't a happy day in our family. We were own cousins with Zee, just as Momma's momma, Gramma Sallie Lindsay and Momma's daddy, James Cole had been; children of siblings, Alice, pronounced Ah Lee Say not Al S and Richard Cole. Momma didn't like people knowing her parents were own cousins and she was dead against Zee and Jesse. Took him nigh on 10 years to get Momma to agree to them marrying, and then, well, it was more in hopes Zee would settle him down than anything else. "Maybe Zee can keep Dingus from getting killed," Momma said when she explained why she'd finally gave her permission. People always say the hardest thing in life is for a parent to lose a child. I know the hardest thing for a child is to lose a parent. Both my Momma and Daddy experienced that and us children we lost our Daddy. Momma she was not going to let anyone or anything come between her children and her, nothing short of dying. Just like Aunt Mary James Mims, a teenager herself, had taken in Daddy and all of his siblings, it was an important part of our family, being family.

I don't really know where I got my name, but my little brother Robert Sallee James, Jr born July 19, 1845 was named for Daddy. He died a month after he was born. Gramps Bob always said Daddy went back to Kentucky for more schooling because he couldn't live with the pain of Momma's tears over losing her baby. Gramps said Daddy was looking for answers from the Lord. Even before my little brother Jesse Woodson James was born on Sept 5, 1847, he was special because he lived. I was to be my brother's keeper from the day he was born. Momma had already come to terms with the fact no matter the circumstances, she was going to stand by her children and as her oldest son I was to stand by her and my brothers and sisters. Daddy, a preacher, took things to the Lord and left Momma to work it out on her own. All my life, I heard people say Momma was a tough woman, righteous and hard, but that's the hand life dealt her. By the time I was eight years old, I was beginning to think my life was going to mirror her's and Daddy's. I was more afraid of losing Momma than I was anything else my whole life.

Momma would hold me and we'd look at the Bible. She told me it was full of the greatest stories and everything we needed to know was inside its pages. At night when Daddy was home, he'd share his day or week, time he'd been gone, with Momma. He knew who was sick and who was having hard times. As they talked she would hold me on her lap gently rocking Jesse's crib with her foot. Then, we'd all hold hands, even baby Jesse's and say a prayer for all those people.

I don't recall not ever having Aunt Charlotte in our lives. After my little brother Robbie died, Aunt Charlotte never left us. She and Momma were like sisters, cooking, cleaning and working the garden and fields, more times than Daddy. He got the itch to build a church and then a college. Momma said that became his baby. Aunt Charlotte agreed saying "Mister is a gentleman farmer." Daddy he'd hire colored hands, slaves, from other farms, mostly the Hudspeth, to work our farm, putting in the crops. Then the little hands, Momma, Aunt Charlotte and us children, we'd work the fields till harvest time. I reckon Daddy was more like a Southern gentleman farmer as Aunt Charlotte said, than the rest of us. We'd be out working in the fields and when it was time to eat or break, the boss man, usually a white field hand who'd brought the workers over from whomever Daddy had hired them from, would blow a horn letting everybody know it was time to break or eat. It was kinda like Momma ringing out the iron bell announcing it was time to come in from play, time to get the chickens penned up for the night, feed the animals, eat breakfast, dinner or supper ourselves. The hands though, they called the white boss man, hornkie because he blowed the horn. One day me and some of the boys, white and black, got the boss man to show us his horn. It was made from a dried cow's horn. It took a special skill with his mouth to get it to sound out long and loud. He let us try it, most of us only got out a swoosh of air, the luckier ones a squeaking noise. Yep, I reckon Aunt Charlotte and Momma were right about Daddy being a gentleman farmer.

Reverend Jeremiah Vardeman added $20,000 to the $25,000 Mister William Jewell left for starting a college. Daddy took on the project to establish the William Jewell College. Judge J.T.V. Thompson and Alexander Doniphan worked with Daddy on the project. Judge Thompson donated the land for it to be built on. When the college opened the school of theology was named for Reverend Vardeman. Daddy was a trusted man. We are wrought with a family of ministers, both Baptist and Methodist in large part due to the influence of Reverend Vardeman, who himself was responsible for planting churches. He understood the moral crisis the Mormon's in Missouri presented long before anyone else did. Daddy helped establish churches at Mount Pisgah, Baptist Providence and New Hope. Reverend Vardeman had at one time been engaged to Miss Elizabeth James, daughter of Richard James, of daddy's kin. He had a special affinity for Daddy, somewhat like a father son relationship. Daddy missed him greatly, Reverend Vardeman died in 1842 before Daddy got fully relocated to Missouri. Momma said Daddy's sorrow was one of the reasons' the college became his priority.

The hemp we grew, used to make ropes, was sent down river to St. Louis and other Southern ports where cotton was raised, bundled and sold to the north who sold it all around the world. Daddy he'd take a seed in his hand and say, "from this tiny seed, the world will be clothed." Daddy eventually bought six black farm hands that became part of our lives and family. Children like Jesse and me, we all worked every day chopping wood, stacking and carrying it to the fireplace where it was used for heating and cooking, feeding the chickens and hogs, hoeing and pulling weeds from the garden and hemp fields. We all worked doing whatever needed doing. Aunt Charlotte and "the little hands" as both she and Momma referred to the black slave children, bedded down in the house with us, except they didn't have beds and it was their job and hers to keep the fire stoked all night. Even in summer it was needed for cooking. I'm certain now there were other things that separated us, but I couldn't say what it was.

Sunday was the best because Daddy wouldn't let anyone do any work, which only meant we didn't work the fields. All the animals still had to be fed, eggs gathered, water carried and wood chopped. When Momma read books to us, we all got to listen on Sunday. The Lord was a large part of our lives and I knew I wanted to do two things in my life, teach and preach. I knew early I'd been called by the Lord.

Most of Daddy's brothers and sisters moved to Missouri too. The lands west of the Mississippi opened up after 1803 when the new United States purchased the Chouteau Territories of France; land the United States called the Louisiana Purchase. William Clark and Meriwether Lewis made the trip to the Pacific Ocean. After returning President Thomas Jefferson made Meriwether the Second Gov. of the new Louisiana Territories. Our family believes he was murdered on Oct 11, 1809 at Grinder's Stand, Natchez Trace, Tennessee, at the hands or doin's of the first man to be Gov. of the territory, James Wilkinson. Attempting to form a new country west of the Mississippi River, Vice President Aaron Burr and Gov. Wilkinson were nearly tried for treason. Those people that come here in the Great Revolt against England, fighting to put down the colonists, had little to go back to England for. So, a lot of them married Indian women and moved into Illinois, Ohio, Ark and Missouri lands, along the great Mississippi and Ohio Rivers. Wilkinson and Burr wanted to create a new country for these people. Some say it's the marrying of whites and Indians that created the culture of the Ozarks. Half breeds weren't really accepted as Indians or whites making them a tough people and former Tories didn't really want to say they had fought against the colonists. Meriwether married an Indian woman, Sara Windwalker in 1797 just before his Great Corp of Discovery with William Clark. President Thomas Jefferson and Meriwether created a secret code using Sara's Indian language for their personal communication. Mister Meriwether was tasked by the President to find the cornstalk Indians, the blonde hair blue eyed Indians who joined with the first white explorers who arrived here, long before the first settlers. The cornstalks were called that because they were taller than most Indians and often had red or yellow hair. Wilkinson knew the President and Meriwether were communicating in secret code about possible land claims before the French. Not only did Spain have some claim, but earlier explorers, long before Jamestown and Plymouth Rock. They were worried about that. Meriwether and Sara had two boys Nathan Daniel Lewis and Joseph Lewis Desmet. Francis Boone, granddaughter of Daniel Boone, married Nathan.

William Clark, he was part Indian through his momma, Ann Rogers, sister of Chief John Hellfire Headman Rogers, children of an Indian mother and Trader John Rogers, white. While they were living in Ark, Chief John's daughter, Tiana Rogers married Sam Houston. He was Gov. of Tennessee not once but twice before moving to Ark. Then he went to Texas where he became Genl. Sam Houston and the first Gov. of Texas, President of the Republic of Texas. People don't like to talk about the fact he abandoned his wife and children when he headed off to Texas. His brother John Paxton Houston abandoned his family too. He ended up in the Missouri Territories that became Ark living among the Indians and first settlers there. Jehoiada Jeffery settled Mount Olive, Ark Territories in Sept 1816 and three years later John Houston became the first clerk. Just like Sam, he was a trained lawyer under Judge James Trimble of Nashville. Jacob Wolf built up the first courthouse in the Ark Territories at the confluence of the White River and Big North Fork at a place called Liberty. He met John Houston who was lawyering in Little Rock and told him as clerk he could have all the whiskey and Indian women he wanted. John accepted. On more than one occasion he wrecked more than a little havoc. He got into brawls with other officials including Sheriff John Adams. He was clerk for 19 years. In July of 1838 he bought his son Alford some land near Helena, Ark, the next month he died at his desk at the Athens courthouse, Izard Co, Ark.

Gravesite of John Paxton Houston 1790-1838

Aunt Lucy Poor Mims daddy's grand aunt told us:

"John paid Old Mrs. Williams to cook him up two meals a day. She took his dinner to him around 11 o'clock in the morning. When she got there, he was laid out on his desk like he fell asleep, his head on his arm. She begun rattling about local news setting down his food and when he didn't open his eyes she realized he'd passed on. She gathered up the liquor bottles strewed all over the place and discarded them. She reckoned he'd likely got on another big drunk and with his weight and all, his heart stopped. He was a very large big man, weighing about 400 pounds and standing over 6 feet tall. Nobody wanted to carry him very far so they just planted him right there."

When Daddy left headed west, I whispered another verse from The Merchant of Venice to myself "All that glistens is not gold." Jesse was barely two and a half years old. Daddy died before Jesse turned three.

Susie born Nov 25, 1849 was a baby. She'd never know Daddy, and like Jesse, never remember him. She was named for Uncle Till's Aunt Lavenia and her daughter, Oseta "Settie" Susan West Stevenson, two of Momma's favorite people. "Settie" lived in Ark near Fayetteville.

It was the middle of spring 1850 when Daddy left. Momma's daffodils and peonies were blooming. Every time I see peonies I think of that time, sometimes just for a minute and sometimes it sets about me for the entire day. Spring came early and people were gathering in throngs preparing to head west. Daddy promised Momma he would be gone less than two years. First he started out with only a year then it grew to 18 months. I think it was because the journey there and back was to take so long. In the end, it didn't matter. Momma knew something was wrong from Daddy's letters. People were sick in the wagon train. Just six days out they'd buried people in western Kansas. Then heavy snow was on the ground in the mountain passes. Horses and mules alike lost their footing and those with broke legs had to be put down. Some plunged with their wagons and riders to their deaths below. It was a treacherous trip. I think Momma knew he stood more of a chance of going to meet the Lord than coming back home to Missouri. He wrote in his letters home to Momma "should we not meet again pray we meet in Heaven."

Daddy's younger brother Drury Woodson James had gone west much earlier. He had been in the gold mines and done well enough to have him a place. I don't know if Daddy went to see him or if he come to Hangtown to see Daddy. At the Hangtown camp Daddy found many of the men sick with dysentery, cholera and measles. He didn't have time to scout out any mining. He was immediately ministering to the sick and speaking over the dead. Momma's last letter from him was full of foreboding. I remember her holding the letter in her hand, walking out to the field where the hired man, Garland Gentry was, taking into account everything happening and what 'if' Daddy didn't come back. While most women and children moved in with family when their husbands took the 'gold fever' heading west, Daddy made arrangements with our neighbor Mr. Gentry to work the hemp on a percentage and we stayed in our own home. Daddy and Momma had done well enough in the hemp farming that before Daddy left they owned the farm. Leaving Mister Gentry there on percentage in theory was a good arrangement with him using Daddy's seeds, equipment, animals and the six little farm hands. Aunt Charlotte was in charge of the house helping Momma. Whatever Momma and her decided needed doing in or outside, that's what us youngun's did.

Momma's worst fears turned to reality. In Oct a letter arrived from a neighbor Daniel Wright, who'd gone west with Daddy, informing Momma of his passing a month before from cholera, Aug 18, 1850. The letter didn't come as a means of consolation but as a fellow Missourian and debtor informing her Daddy died owing him. He wrote he took the last of Daddy's money, his wallet, boots, valise and belongings as payment but it had not been enough. He sent a letter to the paper stating his intentions of collecting what was owed him. The Tribune, a weekly newspaper, ran the announcement about a week after Momma received news from Mister Daniel herself. The paper did not ruin Daddy's reputation reporting his death. There was no mention of his debts, instead glorious accolades of his times at New Hope Church as a Revivalist "few equals in this country" filled the paper along with statements of the formation of North Liberty Baptist Association and founding of William Jewell College.

Momma waited until news of Daddy's death circulated the area and the good people of the church had had time to come by paying their respects before she ordered me and Aunt Charlotte to gather up a hog and take it to market. I can't say she asked or even told us. A change happened in Momma with news of Daddy's death. Her words were clearly an order. Momma was harsher less kindness heard in her voice. She didn't smile like she did before. There were no jokes, pranks or playing like she did before Daddy started talking of going west. She was taking charge best as she knew how. I knew I was the man of the house but when Momma said it to me in that new voice she had, "You're a man now Frank," I knew the life I imagined was gone.

Momma always called me Buck when she talked to me and Mister Frank when she talked about me or if folks were about. If she just called me Frank, I knew there was no room for discussion. And, if she called me Alexander Franklin James, that was a whole different kind of story, one usually accompanied by a switch in her hand. I knew not only was Momma different, everything was different. I was standing in the same shoes my parents had before me. Our parents lost their parents and now we'd lost Daddy. We still had Momma and she had us. Momma had always made certain we knew who our family was and that part of her became stronger than ever. Momma said, "Blood is thicker than water." Other than the Lord our God, she would prove to be my strength, my strongest advocate and the only one who stood a chance of reining in Jesse.

Momma would not be asking for credit, even from family. Monday, Nov 11, 1850, hog money in hand, Momma headed to Greenville to Uncle Till's store to purchase material needed to make our mourning clothes. While there she bought Jesse a pair of shoes. They would outlast him and be worn by Susie before they began to fall apart over a year and a half later. When done being shoes, Momma soaked them softening the leather so she could take them apart at the seams. She dried and beat them down soft finally sewing them on the knees of some britches worn first by me, then Jesse. Most everything had a second life.

When Jesse was born, Daddy said he looked like a little China man. I didn't know what a China man looked like so Daddy showed me by pulling his eyes in tight and slanted. A doctor examined Jesse and pronounced he had bad eyes. He'd be able to see alright but he would have trouble with them watering, being red and swelling. As a baby Momma told Jesse the sand man came to visit him more than the rest of us. His eyes would be caked over in the mornings sometimes so much he couldn't open them. At first we all had to help him by taking a warm wet cloth to his eyes, soaking and moistening the dried matter so he could open them. We couldn't pry them open without ripping out his eyelashes. We had to do it slow. It hurt him sometimes when he'd try to open them. His order of birth, surviving when our brother Robbie didn't and his eye affliction was cause for all of the women of the family to dote on him. People didn't really notice anything except he blinked a lot or his eyes were red like he had been crying. He said it felt like the sandman left sand in his eyes. With great distain he announced, "I do not like to sleep because I do not like the sandman to visit." He always resisted sleeping. When he got a little older and could clean his eyes without assistance rather than fretting less it seemed he became more obsessed with getting his eyes free of sand. The more he washed them the better they did a few days, but they always bothered him. The doctor called it granulated eyelids.

We were lucky children because we had business people in our family. I am eternally grateful for Uncle Till who made sure when Momma and Aunt Charlotte's potions and lotions didn't work, the doctor was called. Usually the doctor was Uncle Marc Thomason, Gramps Bob's brother. Daddy's brother Uncle John was a dentist. We weren't short on being doctored. We learned early if Momma said to open our mouths, we best comply whether it was to check our teeth or poke in a spoon of something for us to swallow. On one such occasion Momma and Aunt Charlotte were giving us our spring tonics, worming us they said. Aunt Charlotte, doctoring Jesse, told him to swallow. He held the medicine in his mouth as long as he could then blew it out all over her, coughing and sputtering. He took off running screaming it tasted horrible. Momma come out on the porch to see what the fracas was. She saw Jesse running away from the house, all the while Aunt Charlotte stamping and sputtering, trying to wipe off the stuff Jesse spewed all over her. Momma announced, "Aunt Charlotte, looks like this batch works better than the last. Jesse is all cured up, look at him go." We all ended up laughing. He made his way back to the house cautiously avoiding being seen by Aunt Charlotte. He failed to see Momma standing just inside the door, switch in hand. Momma whipped his bare legs holding onto one hand, he danced about pulling her in a circle. Jesse would be sick after that and not tell Momma or Aunt Charlotte fearing their medicines. All Jesse's life he swore himself to be a man who would die an early death. At first, Jesse's words although often repeated, didn't seem different than how we all felt. We figured we could die from what Momma and Aunt Charlotte rubbed all over us or make us drink.

Daddy had been in the middle of the slavery issue and when time came for New Hope Church to take a position, Daddy, joined those in favor of slavery. The split happening everywhere created the Southern Baptists, those favoring the position of slavery and fighting for the right of states to make their own laws free of federal intercessions and the Northern Baptists, abolitionists who supported big government rule. His choice defined our family. Suffering the Red Legs of Kansas, those harboring runaway slaves and raiding farms along the Missouri border stealing slaves, was not new to us. When the War Between the States was declared, initially it proved nothing new to us. Since the first time Momma and Daddy stepped foot in Missouri in the aftermath of the Mormon Wars, attacks from across the river in Kansas had been occurring. Jim Lane and Jim Jennison were dirty words in our house. Considered to be the force behind the Border Wars, they would fight on the side of the Union.

Momma was only 25 years old when Daddy died, with three young children in the home. She was in for a rude awakening on her rights as a widow. Missouri law left everything to Daddy's heirs; me, Jesse and Susie. Momma learned fast she didn't have rights as a parent. She couldn't be our guardian. Our world without Daddy was upon us. "The true beginning of our end" (Midsummer's Night Dream).

Ten days after having made the trip to town to buy the material to make our mourning clothes, Uncle J.R., Momma's brother and her step daddy, Gramps Bob Thomason arrived at the house in Uncle J.R.'s wagon. It was early Thursday morning Nov 21, 1850. They had come to get Momma for the ride to Liberty for the probate hearing on Daddy's estate. The court appointed James Harris as administer. Momma signed the agreement. The law was not on her side, she had no choice; the court also required Gramps and Uncle J.R. to sign the agreement. Momma fumed but when she got home, it was different. She sat in Daddy's place at the table, her face in her hands, crying. This would be the last time I ever saw my Momma like that. Aunt Charlotte kept us children back from her, taking us outside she told us Momma was heartbroken. Hungry, Susie pulled at Aunt Charlotte's blouse. Jesse understood it was not a time to be bothersome. He sat quietly trying to make a whistle from a blade of grass. Momma didn't want us children to remember her screams, her tears and pain. We sat outside, until Momma called us in. She was putting the kettle over the fire, beginning supper. She never said a word, not that evening or the rest of her life about her tears. It was 4 days until Susie's first birthday. Momma said, "Charlotte we need to make a cake."

I'm certain it was a family excuse to check on Momma but shortly after learning Daddy had died; we celebrated Nov birthdays at church. Susie and Aunt Lizzie, Daddy's sister, shared birthdays. Susie was born Nov 25th, 1849 and Aunt Lizzie in 1816. Uncle Drury Woodson James, Daddy's younger brother, born on Nov 14th, 1826 had been only a baby when their parents died. Uncle J.R.'s birthday was on Nov 29th. Momma and Aunt Charlotte made a big five layer cake dripping in fruit preserves, slathered on top and between the layers, it oozed down the sides. On Sunday Nov 24th almost everyone in our family attended New Hope Baptist Church. We sang my favorite songs and ended with a new song "I wish I was in Dixie's Land". Not exactly a church song but everyone seemed to love it. Afterwards, we ate dinner on the grounds enjoying the beautiful fall day God granted us and the birthday cake.

Coming home from church, lounging on the porch or working in the garden Momma would tell us about our people, our families. Working the Missouri soil mixing in manure, rabbit and chicken litter to make the best crop possible Momma explained that's how our family is. We come from a hearty people willing to do what it took to survive. Deep inside of us runs the blood of our ancestors, farmers, soldiers, adventurers, frontiersmen and men of the Lord. People who worked hard and cared for their families, watching their children and farms grow. We are not a people descended from Lords and Ladies, Kings or Noblemen, but of the people who work the earth. We were taught to honor and cherish each other, our family and above all the Lord. I knew Momma was a much happier person than she appeared on the outside. Life required her to appear so. Working the fields, cutting wood, whatever the work, Momma telling stories of knights of old, men of the round table and stories from the Bible, Shakespeare, Canterbury Tales and Robin Hood passed time.

Momma didn't know James Harris. She knew of him, but she'd never met him until that day in court. Three weeks later in mid Dec, Susie's little dog started barking alerting us of someone's approach. Momma recognized him immediately. Mr. Harris and three men, appointed by the court to assess Daddy's belonging, tied their horses up at the gate. With just a nod of his head, the men with ledgers in hand began to go through the house, barn and fields. They wrote down everything we owned, including that little pair of shoes Momma bought Jesse. They were sitting on the mantel above the fireplace to dry. They were counted right along with the family pictures. He said the frames gave them value. James Harris read Momma everything on the list. Two beds and stead's, two tables, one bookcase with fifty one books, one set of dinnerware, one kettle, two ovens with lids, one skillet with lid, one grindstone, the list read on. They listed every rabbit, chicken, cow, pig, horse and sheep. In order to get the hemp crop harvested, the hired man, Garland Gentry was allowed temporary use of some animals and equipment and he allowed Momma a few things for us to live on. Momma might not be entitled to anything but, we were Daddy's heirs. We kept two milk cows and a mare, one bed and a few other things. The rest he announced would have to go up for auction in order to pay for Daddy's debts, including the tablecloth Momma bought on credit before we knew Daddy died, the numerous bills Daddy amassed when preparing for his trip to California and Daniel H. Wright's remaining bill of $23.40.

Auctions are almost always held on Saturday, allowing more people to attend, to poke through the items for sale. Whispers among the crowd were not quiet enough to escape Momma's deer ears or mine: "Poor children." "It's the oldest one's birthday." It was Saturday, Jan 4th, 1851, a cold brisk wind blew across the farm, snow clouds were forming and the sky was dark. It was all very foreboding. In just six day's I would be eight years old. I asked Gramps Bob "Can we keep the rocking chair?"

As I stood there, I could feel the movement in the floorboards as Momma held me, her foot rocking Jesse in the crib. The stories she taught us from the Bible read from that chair and the fun we had acting out our own plays from the Bible and Shakespeare. Daddy gave Jesse his nickname "Dingle berry" sitting in that rocker. I didn't know what it meant until just a few days before the auction. Tending Jesse for Momma I took him for a walk out in the field where Mister Gentry was working. Jesse jerked free of my hand running off after Susie's dog. I shouted at him, "Dingle berry!" Mister Gentry got down laughing slapping his knees, "What the heck you doing calling that boy Dingle berry?" Defiant, hands on my hips, "That's his nickname," I said. My blood boiled. Thinking he was making fun of my Daddy, I wanted to hit him, "that's what our Daddy called him".

I remembered the night we were having a Shakespeare play of our own. Momma fixed Jesse a little hat making him the court jester. Daddy was rocking Jesse and Susie on his lap while Momma helped her little actor. Jesse messed his britches. Momma took Jesse from Daddy and was cleaning him up when Daddy let out that big bold laugh of his calling Jesse his little "Dingle berry." When Momma handed Jesse back to Daddy, she returned to the play and Daddy to rocking.

Mister Gentry was laughing and I was screaming at him "Stop it." Momma came out of the house to see what was going on. Aunt Charlotte was hot on her heels. Still laughing, he repeated my having called Jesse "Dingle berry" expecting them to join in the laughter. When they didn't laugh he said, "You know a dingle berry is a little piece of," he hesitated before saying "poop stuck on hair." We were stunned. Then remembering the night, Momma, Aunt Charlotte and I started laughing. Jesse was always pulling at Momma's beautiful long hair and probably he swallowed some or had gotten caught in his drawers but sure enough, we all remembered that little piece of poop she had to get off. Aunt Charlotte said, "Best we not be calling him that." Momma, she said, "If the shoe fits." Momma started shortening Dingle berry to Dingle. Aunt Charlotte and Alec and Henry they didn't say Dingle the same, it sounded more like "Dingus" and that's what stuck. It became our secret and Momma's prediction "if the shoe fits" turned out to be so very true. Remembering and smiling, tugging at Gramps coat sleeve, I begged him. "Please can we get the rocking chair?"

I am "Buck" to Momma and Daddy. I was their "young buck," they said. But whenever anyone was around, true southerners, we were Mister Frank, Mister Jesse and Miss Susie. Momma of course was Mrs. James or Missus Zerelda since she was a married woman. Daddy, he was Mister Robert or Bob, but mostly he was Preacher James. Now when Momma thought Jesse was acting wrong, she'd call him "Dingus", her way of saying, "You little shit." He rarely got the Jesse Woodson James full name treatment. Whenever Momma or any one of our aunties' called out any of our full Christian names, it brought the rest of us to full attention before it was completely out. You knew you were in trouble especially with Aunt Mary, Daddy's oldest sister, we'd come to full attention.

Having heard about the diseases rampant in the mining camps, Daddy's supplies included a large quantity of medicine, pots and pans and simple things, like buttons. He and I went to the foundry in Liberty where he had some metal buttons fashioned for the trip. It had been the last trip to town we ever took. The day he left he slipped one of those buttons into my hand. The rest of my life I carried that button with me. I grasped it tight in my hand when I needed to watch the words coming out of my mouth and when I needed guidance; I talked to Daddy or God, sometimes both. I can still feel the warmth of Daddy's hand taking mine in his. I can still see his face as he placed the button in my hand closing my fingers around it. "I'm never far away," he said. It's true. I feel closer to Daddy when I hold that button in my hand. The day of the auction I kept reaching into my coat pocket rolling it between my fingers.

Gramps Bob got the rocking chair. That chair is a part of our lives, it's been there from the beginning and comforted me the day we buried Momma. Gramps Bob, Uncle J.R. Cole and Uncle Will James helped buy some of the livestock back. When it was said and done, we had Daddy's books on the Baptist faith, the other bed, dinner table and a few odds and ends. We even had to sell Daddy's rifle leaving us without a way for me or Momma to kill anything in the woods or protect ourselves. The nearby woods provided coon, rabbit, turkey, squirrel and white tail deer with seasonal grouse, pheasant, quail and duck. I trapped a few fox, badger and bob cats for their skins. We ate the meat and Uncle Till or Uncle Will would sell the hides for me for a little pocket change. Aunt Charlotte could cook anything we killed, anything. Uncle J.R. declared it a "high priority" I learn to shoot without missing. Adding insistently, "the ability to make one's ammunition could be a matter of life and death." Gramps Bob's brother, Wild Man Bill Thomason, was a real life buffalo hunter. Gramps said when the time was right, he would make certain Jesse and I learned from the best, Wild Man himself.

That cold day in Jan of 1851 was one of those days that change a life forever. Momma was humiliated and afraid. The law was not on her side and people she didn't know, but worse, friends and neighbors, people of our church family carried off not simply our possessions, they carried off our life with Daddy. Soon afterward, my life changed again. Gramps Bob made good on his promise and my step uncle, Wild Man Bill Thomason included me along with his grandson's, Bill and Jim Anderson, leanin' how to survive in the wilderness.

Gramma Sallie ailing all summer died on Oct 12, 1851. I was 8 years old. Aunt Martha Thomason, Momma's sister, the first of Gramma Sallie's girls with Gramps Bob, was 10 years old, Alice, 7 and Susie, 5. I watched Momma waiting for her to cry like that day sitting in daddy's chair her face in her hands but tears didn't come. The girls stayed with different family for most of the next year, including us. Then on Aug 25th, 1852, Gramps Bob married Mrs. Julie. She had two sons Squire Estes, 16 and John Posey, 12. We never talked about their daddy's, not ever. Mrs. Julie didn't talk about it and Momma said we weren't to ask. Mrs. Julie liked us and was good to Momma's sisters. Reason enough for Momma to like her.

Poverty was common throughout the region. Many women whose men had gone to the gold fields were destitute without family or friends. Hordes of people died from the fever, cholera and smallpox epidemics plaguing western Missouri. Their bodies and those of their children too weak to fight off even the slightest of sickness, died. News arrived weekly of someone else having passed. Along with family, we had our church family and were not destitute. The Hudspeth boys, Rufe and Babe were always inviting us over to their house and Momma let us go. Sometimes, we'd stay on for several days, with their daddy, Joseph William Hudspeth "Mister Joe" bringing us back to Uncle Till's mercantile when it was time to come home. They'd sit and talk, "optioning" Momma, Aunt Lizzie said. I reckon Mister Joe had eyes on Momma, but she didn't look back. Mister Joe had a houseful of children with his wife, Missus Mandy who died the same year as Daddy. Aunt Lizzie said Momma was a good catch in spite of the auctions and unpaid bills; healthy, strong and with good teeth. She was considered a beauty and it wasn't uncommon for men and women who lost a husband or wife to marry again soon, especially if they had a houseful of children. We were Momma's priority along with the farm. As much as Mister Joe and Momma were friends, she didn't have time to raise someone else's children. It was years later, in 1857, when Mister Joe married Miss Louisa Brown. The next year they had Lamartine. We called him Lam. He was a happy baby and my 9 year old sister Susie loved looking after him.

Feb 27, 1852 our family endured the last of the auctions. Uncle Till, Tillman Howard West, married to Daddy's sister, Mary Elizabeth "Lizzie" James, bought back Daddy's watch and a garden hoe for us. It was $3.40 cents for the two items. Momma loved Aunt Lizzie. She was enough older than Momma to be more like a Momma to her than a sister in law. At the first probate court hearing Momma, Uncle J.R. and Gramps Bob learned Momma couldn't be legally responsible for us. Rather than let the court make all the decisions, Momma went to Uncle Till and Aunt Lizzie asking them to petition the court for guardianship of Jesse, Susie and me. It was granted and off and on, through the rest of all our lives Uncle Till and Aunt Lizzie's was home. Our family was everything. Even when we disagreed, you agreed to disagree and nobody stayed upset long. If you were family, you took care of each other.

Uncle Till's daddy, James and his brother John married sisters, Mary Mourning and Lavenia Jane Howard. Their kids were double cousins like brothers and sisters. They became our family. Jesse took to calling himself Jesse Howard, crying and throwing fits to go home with them. It generally worked. I reckon that was his affinity for calling himself Mister Howard in later years. Me, I rather liked Mister Ben Simms who Momma married and I always wanted the Woodson name, so I became Ben J. Woodson in most cases. The J. for James, in case someone called me "James" and I responded. The fella's during the war called me James as much as Frank. Alexander was saved for Momma when she was calling me to attention. No one else ever in my life called me by my given name.

We had big families and when we put the hoe down, music and food followed. Even in rough times we had plenty to eat, laughter and music. I have to admit Jesse was the best horseshoe player in the family. Most of the children would be given a distance advantage, allowed to step in a few feet. Not Jesse, he didn't need any advantage no matter who he was playing. He was a sure hitter, his aim true. You didn't want to be at the other end of a rock he might throw neither. I liked when Uncle Till and Aunt Lizzie would take us children down to Ark to visit family. Uncle Till's own cousin, Oseta Susan, "Aunt Settie" as Momma had us call her and for whom my little sister was named and her husband Samuel Stevenson lived near Fayetteville.

Aunt Settie and Uncle Sam had three boys near mine and Jesse's ages. In Aug 1854 their boy, Sammy, Uncle Sam's namesake died. It was real hard on them and our entire family packed up and went down to Ark for more than a month to help out. Missouri and Ark summers weren't all that different, but the mountain streams of the Ark Ozarks were great, beautifully clear with deep swimming holes running cold. You could see the big fish swimming just tempting you to try'en catch'em. Jesse was one year older than Aunt Settie's oldest boy Jim. They could swim like fish and were always challenging each other. I didn't mind taking them to the creek. The days seemed to stand still, listening to noises around me, the calm shattered by an old bullfrog jumping into the water and the laughter of Jesse and Jim.

Chapter 2

Daddy was an adventurous man, willing to go where other men might be afraid to go. He said the conservatives remained in the east, afraid to take a chance, the more adventurous folks moved west. He answered the call of the Lord to come to Missouri. Gramma Sallie and Gramps Bob already having moved made the decision easier when Momma and Daddy talked of marrying. But Daddy he would have chosen to make the move regardless. He had been approached by Reverend Jeremiah Vardeman and both the Baptist and Methodist Conventions about preaching in Missouri due to the Mormon crisis. In 1831 Independence, Jackson Co was targeted by Mormon founder Joseph Smith to be the new "City of Zion", the place his followers were to go to prepare "the way of the Lord for his Second Coming." The group settled into not only Jackson Co but the surrounding counties, especially Clay Co. In the years Gramma Sallie and Gramps Bob first lived here, in the decade before Momma and Daddy arrived, a religious war crept into the lives of the people of western Missouri. As early as Oct 1833 the Christian communities were openly afraid of the growing Mormon cult. They feared they were taking over religious and political control, tensions were running high. Mormons used lawsuits and petitions to settle issues in court, but the folks of Clay Co not accepting their heathen ways were intent on driving them out. In an effort to resolve things, the Missouri lawmakers created Caldwell Co just for Mormon settlement, refused to live within the county set aside for them. They were anything but law abiding citizens. Daily conflicts escalated and with 1838 came the Mormon War. Daddy, Gramps Bob and Rev. Vardeman said, "Mormons considered themselves "Soldiers of God," just not a Christian God."

Problems were reported within the Mormon ranks leading to more than one first vision by Joseph Smith as he tried to settle his Soldiers of God. Several groups broke off forming their own groups. Thomas Marsh, President of the Mormon's Quorum of Twelve was among those breaking away. Then, George M. Hinkle ordered to be the Mormon Commander of the Caldwell Co Militia left forming a new church called "The Lamb's Wife" in Liberty not far from Mister Groomer's place, which was to become our farm and home. As a result of the Mormon war, over 2,500 Missouri militia troops were called out to put down the Mormon rebellion. The Mormon businesses and banks refused service to anyone not a Mormon. Missourians took to looting and burning Mormon homes and farms. The Mormons sacked and burned Gallatin. In Ray Co south of Caldwell Co, Capt. Samuel Bogart, Commander of the Missouri Militia took Mormon hostages. The good people of Missouri wrongly believed the Mormons would stay put within the boundaries of Caldwell Co. Instead they built up a town called Far West, where the Mormon men had carnal knowledge with many "wives", one version of Joseph Smith's visions. Many of the townsfolk believed he preferred very young girls and thus had a vision allowing for multiple wives, in fact, the same girls were married to multiple men. The leaders of the church could have as many wives as they wanted, of any age, even if they were already married. This was against God's word. Capt. Bogart responded under orders from the Gov.

The Mormon militia from Far West camped on Crooked River and from there attempted to rescue the Mormon captives Capt. Bogart held. They slaughtered and massacred Capt. Bogart's militia on Crooked Creek even the ones who surrendered. Throughout the spring and summer, every barber shop, store and church was full of talk of the Mormon's invasion of Missouri and their ungodly ways. It was this environment of hostility and outrages that forced Missouri Gov. Lilburn Boggs to act.

On Oct 27, 1838, Gov. Boggs, in residence at the capitol in Jeff City, issued Missouri Executive Order 44, the Mormon Extermination Order. Joseph Smith and other church leaders were jailed in Liberty. Smith's followers were ordered to leave the state and their property seized. Alexander Doniphan argued on behalf of Joseph Smith, beseeching the Gov. 'not' to execute him instead to allow him and his followers to move away. The Christian churches, particularly the Methodists and Baptists strengthened their call for men of God to come to Missouri in hopes of balancing the scale between good and evil. It was into this world my Gramma Sarah "Sallie" Lindsay Cole, and her second husband, grandpa "Gramps Bob" Robert Thomason moved. And, it was here Rev. Vardeman said the Lord was calling Christian men, including my Daddy to preach, to bring godliness back to the people of Missouri. I'd reckon it safe to say the Mormons were directly responsible for the large number of Baptists and Methodists relocating to Missouri.

I was raised knowing in the name of God, people did horrendous things to their fellow man. I knew men's ego's, men like Joseph Smith, were often at the root of horrible imaginations and deeds.

"Every disturbed man finds righteousness in his acts, glory to himself. And for men like him, there will be followers, believers that he is somehow above the law of the land and in some cases even God. There will be those who will act on his word, followers who need to belong, to believe." Daddy said these words to the New Hope congregation as we sat there on the hard wooden benches in that little 20x20 building. Jesse was only a baby. As he grew, I found it no less true in my little brother Jesse than in Joseph Smith. Thirty years later, in 1869, Missouri Gov. Thomas Crittenden offered the first of many rewards for our capture.

In 1838, Gov. Boggs directed "the Mormons be treated as enemies and must be exterminated or driven from the state if necessary for the public peace and safety as their outrages are beyond all description."

In 1839, due to Alexander Doniphan, the Mormons moved east to Commerce, Illinois. They bought the entire town renaming it Nauvoo. A group of men upset over Joseph Smith marrying their wives just to have relations with them attacked him by publishing word of his and his followers actions in the newspaper. Smith was arrested and jailed. Shortly afterwards a mob of men with painted faces attacked the jail killing him and his brother. Most people said Brigham Young jockeying to become the new Mormon leader, orchestrated the "Indian attack" with intentions of killing him. After Joseph Smith was killed, the Mormons left Illinois under Brigham Young and moved west, settling in Utah. In 1857, less than 20 years later, again dressed as Indians, with painted faces, the Mormons, under Young, killed an entire wagon train of people from Ark and Missouri, including children older than the age of seven. The people of Missouri knew just as Brigham Young played a part in the death of Joseph Smith he orchestrated the revenge killing, attack and murder of innocent people on the Baker wagon train at Mountain Meadows.

After the auctions were over, we lived with Uncle Till and Aunt Lizzie. With Momma and us kids all under one roof things became difficult. Learning of Daddy's death, Cousin Davis Mims wrote Momma of his wife, Elizabeth dying and prospects of moving to Missouri. The next thing we heard he was living at Hesstown, Ark , north of Batesville on the White River, with his boys: Byron Otho, John Marcellus, Linah, Robert and Davis Russell Mims. When his five year old granddaughter Marcella died, they renamed it after her. Davis' wife Elizabeth Cresap had died and a lot of people just can't continue living in the same house, sleeping in the same bed where a loved one dies. His son, John Marcellus and cousin Samuel Mims who was living near Athens, south of Calico Bluffs Landing, enlisted with the Confederacy in Ark the same time I joined in Liberty, May 1861.

Momma needed to go home to the farm and to do that she needed an income. She needed security for herself and us children. Because of Missouri laws, she needed a husband to do so. Two years after Daddy died, Jesse turned five years old on Sept. 5th, twenty five days later on Thursday Sept. 30th, 1852 Momma married widower Benjamin Simms. He was an older man, but a good man. His wife Missus Martha died the same year Daddy had. She died of a different fever than the Gold Fever that led to Daddy dying. Mister Ben's children were 'older', Momma said. I reckon she was thinking of Mister Hudspeth. Missus Martha's brother James George lived in Ark.

Benjamin "Mister Ben" Simms, he and Missus Martha, had Elizabeth, the oldest and only girl. Momma was only 3 years older than her. Then they had boys, Francis, Richard, Strother, James and Charles. Charlie was 14 when Momma and Mr. Ben married; I was nine. While Momma needed a man about the house, Mr. Ben didn't need for anything. Uncle Till said Mr. Ben was "a rich old 'fart". Momma insisted they had more in common than people thought. At first it was okay, me and Charlie we got along real good. We played draw, dominoes and jacks. I liked Mr. Ben. He was teaching me to ride English style, jumping fences and how to fancy walk the horses. He loved to race them and us boys, we provided all the encouragement he needed to hold such an event. But, he didn't much take to having Jesse and Susie afoot. Momma and him, they had lots of friends and family of the same standing from Kentucky now in Missouri and then, they both lost someone to the 'Gold Fever.' Mr. Ben and Mrs. Martha's son Richard "Dick" had been on the trip with Daddy. And like Daddy, he died in a California gold mining camp in 1850. The Liberty newspaper, The Tribune reported their passing in the same issue. Momma told us, she and Mr. Ben understood each other.

"Things will be alright Buck," she told me that cold Jan day when we had to leave Mr. Ben's place. I'd celebrated my 10th birthday two days earlier. "You have to go with Jesse and Susie. You're the man of the house." I got along real good with Mr. Ben and his children but Momma explained in her condition she couldn't care for Jesse and Susie the way she needed and keep Mr. Ben content. Uncle Till and Aunt Lizzie who still had guardianship of us came to get us and our belongings. We didn't get to see Momma much that winter. She was sick much of the time. On March 8th, 1853 Momma had another baby die, another son. Dr. Absalom Kerns, Momma's doctor, said he was a "blue baby." I thought for a long time that meant he was blue in skin color but I found out it meant he was too young to breathe on his own and turned blue like when you can't breathe. About a week after the baby died, Dr. Kerns came and checked on Momma making sure her body and mind were okay. Momma stayed another month before coming to Uncle Till and Aunt Lizzie's to see us. We were hers and people talked, saying if she didn't start "being a mother her own children will forget her." They certainly didn't know our mother or us. Mr. Ben understood Momma needed to see us. She came home to Uncle Till and Aunt Lizzie's for most of the late spring and summer, going back to Mr. Ben's house a week or two at a time.

In the early summer of 1853, Momma, Uncle Till, Aunt Lizzie and us children took a ride home to the farm. Coming into the yard, we saw James Harris loading up the farm hands to take them to auction. That was the straw that broke the camels back for Momma. I heard her tell Aunt

Lizzie, "there'll be no going back to Mr. Ben." She made excuses when he came to fetch her, first Jesse was sick, then Susie. In the fall after Susie's birthday she did go back to Mr. Ben's for a few weeks but was home with us at Uncle Till and Aunt Lizzie's by Christmas. Then we got word Mr. Ben died Jan 2, 1854. He was out riding his horse, something spooked it and he was thrown. We know that's what happened. He was an excellent horseman and something had to upset the horse for him to be thrown off. Uncle Till said his heart might have give out on him. He died right there where he lay. We knew Momma had chosen us over Mr. Ben and now no divorce was needed. Momma was just a girl, a young woman of 26 and already buried two babies and now, two husbands.

Pulling the wagon to a stop, Momma and Uncle Till were quick to have words with James Harris, the man appointed overseer of the farm, "harsh ugly words" I must say. Not the kind of words you would expect to hear out of the mouth of a young woman, a lady. Words Daddy said should never come out of any person's mouth. Alec was only twelve years old, not even two years older than me. We worked side by side in the fields. Alec played soldier in the fields with us, carrying cornstalks as rifles when Uncle Wild Man first taught us how to march and fight. Upset Aunt Charlotte screamed, crying and begging somebody to do something to stop him. James Harris was taking things from the house and he was taking Alec.

Daddy bought babies, black babies. We called them little hands. They cost $200 maybe $250 dollars when a grown farm hand cost as much as $600 or even $800. To Aunt Charlotte, they were her babies even more so than we were. She nursed us all, cared for and swaddled us and be sold off like that, it was the same as dying. In some ways being sold off was worse because you rarely knew what happened to them. James Harris left taking only one little hand, Alec. I had my hands deep in my pockets, gripping Daddy's button tight, watching the wagon pull away with Alec tied to the back. He wasn't crying but Jesse and Susie were. I fought back tears.

With James Harris gone, Momma consoled Aunt Charlotte. Finally we began packing up the house. Momma was talking to Aunt Charlotte when I saw her turn white. I turned following the direction of her eyes. Ike Wells, one of the men who'd gone west with daddy stood before us hat in hand. He and Uncle Till shook hands, nodding at each other then talking in a quiet whisper. Mister Ike walked toward Momma and hugged her. "I'm sorry, Missus James," we heard him say. He told Momma how Daddy held onto the picture of her he'd taken with him. He had been there when Daddy was buried. When they crossed his arms and rolled him in the sheeting, Mr. Ike said the picture of Momma was in his pocket right where he kept it. We sat in the back of the wagon listening to Mr. Ike tell how Daddy came down ill caring for the other men, ministering to them and every night praying for his family, his wife and children, always ending with "Let God's will be done." Mr. Ike came back from California to "marry his sweetheart, Missus Sallie, Sarah Shepherd Flannery", he said. He was done with gold. They talked a while longer then he got back on his horse and rode off toward Raytown. Headed back to Uncle Till's, I listened as best I could over the rattle of the wheels on the old road as Momma and Uncle Till talked about how grateful they were Mr. Ike come to speak to them of this.

Missus Sallie Shepherd married John Flannery and had one son, my friend Ike. We were the same age. Ike and his Momma were making do, mostly living at home with her Momma but Mr. Ike Wells was gonna marry Mrs. Sallie he said and have a family. As Momma and Uncle Till talked it was clear Momma was more at ease now. I think she laid Daddy to rest that day. We didn't make it to Mr. Ben's funeral. His place was near 100 miles distant of us and by the time they laid him out and in the ground was about the time we got word. Soon after, Uncle Till got word Momma was to appear in Clinton Co court regarding Mister Ben's estate. When time come, he and Uncle J.R. went with her. Mister Ben owned 380 acres of land in Clinton Co and Momma learned she was entitled to a portion of it. The Probate Court of Clinton Co determined his heirs were: "Nancy Clark, Betsey Sims, Frances Price, Strother Sims, Charles Sims, all of Clinton Co and James Sims, of Tulome Co, California and wife Zerilda Simms." "Having established her right of dower in the land, she sold that right to Joseph Baxter who later sold it to Mister William Brown in 1856."

After Mr. Ben died, Momma lived with us at Uncle Till and Aunt Lizzie's until I was 12, Jesse 7 and Susie 5. Aunt Charlotte lived between our farm and theirs making sure things were kept up. Uncle Till was in charge of everything having to do with us as Daddy's farm belonged to Jesse, Susie and me, not Momma. The only way for circumstances to change for Momma was to find another husband. I heard Momma, Aunt Lizzie, Uncle Till and Uncle J.R talking about Missouri laws in regards to women and marriages. Women were not allowed to vote, couldn't own land and should they divorce, they couldn't have their own children. Mister Ben's dying had prevented that, however, Uncle Till and Aunt Lizzie continued to have guardianship over us. It was still many years until I would be of age. Momma needed a husband.

Momma carried a newspaper clipping in her Bible from the Jefferson City Inquirer: July 20, 1843:

"Horrible. - We are informed by an acquaintance of ours from Springfield, of a horrid transaction which occurred in Barry Co one day last week. A man whose name our informant had forgotten had been in the habit of treating his wife in a manner too brutal and shocking to think of. On the morning of the day mentioned, he told his wife to get up and get breakfast for himself and her two children and then to commence saying her prayers, for she should die, he swore before sunset.

She got up and made a fire, and returned to the room where her unnatural husband slept, he was lying on his back in a sound sleep. She took the ax with she had been chopping wood, and with one blow sunken deep into his head, just through the eyes. She immediately went to the house of a neighbor and related the circumstances as they occurred, given it the reason that she was certain he would kill her that day and concluded that it was his life or hers."

Momma said Martha Curnutt had been sentenced to five years in prison for killing her husband, clearly a man not worth killing. He beat and abused her until fearing for her life she killed him. She was only the second woman to ever be sentenced to prison in Missouri. They had no place for her so Missus Martha was housed in jail with the men in Jeff City. The monsters guarding the prisoners molested her. She had a little baby girl in prison. They wanted her and the baby, the evidence to die, so they refused her wood for heat and clothing. In 1844 the Gov. pardoned her. Momma said, "I ain't gonna be no killer but I ain't goin' through this again." Her children and the farm were hers. They began talking about what they needed to do to make that happen. We didn't have lawyers but we had doctors and a wagon load of preachers and all of them knew people.

Uncle Will, Daddy's brother had joined the Revivalist Movement sweeping the country along with Daddy. Except, Uncle Will, instead of Baptist, he was a Methodist preacher like cousin, Burwell Lee, down in Batesville, Ark. The Lee's, James' and Mims along with other family and friends come up from Ark to Missouri when I was just a boy, for Daddy's last great revival. I was too young to remember much of them but I remember people staying on at the farm for days.

In 1832, Uncle Will was ordained as a Methodist minister. He operated a mercantile store and pastured a church near LaGrange, Kentucky. He married Miss Mary Ann Varble Dec 2, 1843. Daddy's baby brother, Uncle Drury Woodson James born in 1826 was one when their Momma and Daddy died. When old enough Uncle Drury moved to Missouri establishing a Genl. Store in Greenville, about three miles from our farm. He talked Uncle Will into going into business with him, so they moved to Missouri. When they were able to open a second store, Uncle Drury headed west to California. As I got older I worked in the store at Greenville stocking shelves and helping customers carry out purchases. A great many people came to Watkin's Mill and Uncle Will's store. Greenville was a busy place. Me and some of the boys cut wood, hauling it down to the river where the steam boats came up. If they needed wood they stopped, downed an anchor sending a yawl to the shore where a man would buy our wood, and then haul it back to the steamer. And, we could make a little money tasseling corn.

Then a new man entered our lives, Archibald Reuben Samuel. He helped his daddy, Fielding Samuel move to a farm a few miles from our place then left out for medical school in Ohio. We knew Mister Fielding and the rest of the family real good, but not Mister Reuben. When he finished his schooling he come back home to his Daddy's place. After a few weeks, he rented out a space in Uncle Will's store in Greenville for his office. Uncle Will arranged for Momma and him to meet. Mister Reuben bought himself a little piece of land not far from his daddy's and began courting Momma. On Sept 25, 1855 they married. For the first time since Daddy died 5 years before, things felt right. We were a family. We all liked Mr. Rueben and there was no mistaken how he felt about Momma.

At first we called him Doc. Then on April 17, 1858 Sarah "Sallie" Louisa Samuel was born, named for her grandma's, the Doc's Momma Louisa Bond and Momma's momma, Sarah Lindsay. We called our new baby sister Sallie Lou. Momma started referring to Doc as Pappy, so, as time wore on and other children came along, Doc became Pappy to the younger children even Jesse and Susie. To me, I called him Pappy around them but when it was just me and him, man to man, I called him Doc. He liked that. And, Doc he called Momma "Ma" and soon Jesse and Susie were both calling her Ma, but to me, she was always Momma.

It was during those early years Momma learned one of life's hardest lessons. Women didn't have any rights in the state of Missouri. Everything belonged to the husband whether it was acquired or inherited by the wife. Land that might have been Momma's would belong to her husband. It would be over a year later before we were legally allowed to live with Momma and Doc. In fact, it was Nov 3rd, 1856 when the courts gave legal guardianship of us not to Momma, but her husband, Reuben Samuel. Momma had endured much in the six years since Daddy died, and us children. By the time winter really set in and Christmas was upon us, we were home, together on the farm, now referred to by friends, family and neighbors as "Missus Samuel's place." That came about due to Gramps Bob Thomason and my Uncle's Will James, J.R. Cole and Till West. And, since I was the "man of the house" I had gotten to go along when they consulted lawyer Alexander Doniphan about the situation.

A young attorney by the name of Thomas Freeman was present at Doniphan's when they discussed how to "get around the law" of Momma standing to lose everything should something happen to her new husband before us children came of age. This young lawyer, Thomas Roe Freeman, born in Benton Co, Missouri, on Feb 22, 1829 moved to Crawford Co with his family and grew up there. He attended community subscription schools and in 1848 married Miss Mary Lamb. He supported his family through blacksmithing and raising livestock. At night he read law books and was admitted to the bar in St. Louis. After passing the required examinations he lawyered like Daddy preached. He rode from town to town offering services to people. Every little settlement, every town had a place where the men met. And, in Greenville, that was Uncle Will's store. They discussed the options available to women in Momma's circumstance, which wasn't many. He advised them of new attitudes emerging in the cities especially after what had happened with Missus Curnutt in prison. He suggested a legal agreement be drawn up regarding the farm and children. Mr. Reuben had his doctor office in the back of the store and when he wasn't doctoring folks, he enjoyed talking with the men at the store. Unbeknownst to him he had been discussing what would become his own prenuptial agreement. I just remember Mister Freeman as a large man, tall and strong, like he might be able to carry the world on his shoulders. His horse looked small under him. Uncle Till ask him along during the discussions with Doniphan.

Thomas Freeman and his wife continued living around St. Louis but home was to be western Missouri. He made extended trips visiting the courthouses, talking to people in the rural western counties, making plans to move. Mrs. Mary bore him seven children in ten years. Then on Feb 16, 1861 just before the War Between the States was declared, Mrs. Mary died. Mr. Tom's daddy, Rev. James Freeman, was a Kentucky ex pat who had been among those coming to Missouri to fight the Mormon Wars through the word of the Lord. Reverend Freeman died three months after Mrs. Mary. Mr. Tom's momma, Rebecca Roberts Freeman, died the next year in Sept. Mr. Tom bore a great deal of hurt and had much responsibility descend on him that first year of the war. Mrs. Mary's brother, James married Mr. Tom's sister Nancy Freeman. Along with his in laws, John and Catherine Adams Lamb, his sister Nancy and her husband cared for the children during the war years. They lived on Spring Creek and Dry Forks in Dent Co, in south central Missouri, much closer to the Ark border. The Lamb's were also Kentucky ex pats. Some of them moved down into Ark on the White River below Rapp's Barren.

Doc signed what very well might have been the first 'prenuptial agreement' in the United States. Not only did the agreement guarantee Momma us children, it guaranteed her any children they might have and ownership of the farm and slaves. I understood if something happened to Momma or Doc, as the oldest, I would legally be the man of the house with all the rights, privileges, headaches and heart aches that entailed. And, like Aunt Mary, who at 19 years old took Daddy and the other children in, I too would be my brother's keeper, caring for not only Jesse and Susie but any other children Momma and Doc would have. And should I remain in the great state of Missouri, as the oldest, the farm would someday be mine.

Chapter 3

Border ruffians and jayhawkers were coming into Missouri, destroying crops, farms, burning homes, murdering slave owners and taking their slaves back into Kansas. Northerners formed the Republican Party to oppose slavery's extension anywhere it didn't exist. Both pro and anti slavery forces starting paying settlers to move into the Kansas Territory. Both in the east and here in Missouri it was being called the "Border Wars." At the heart of the conflict was whether Kansas would be a free or slave state. Between 1854 and 1861 it was a proxy war over the issue of slavery in the United States, with both sides pushing people to move into Kansas to sway the vote. Some people said it would be the only thing that could save the country from a war on itself while others said it was the very thing that would bring on a war. With certainty, the Border Wars impacted how our family and friends, hemp farmers mostly, came to be who we were in the War Between the States. In 1855 most of the men of our church family, friends and neighbors, pro Southerners, went to Lawrence, Kansas to vote for territorial legislators. Uncle Till took leave of us to join them, including a number of hemp farmers from across the state. More than forty men rode to Lawrence, Kansas for the vote. It didn't go well as Genl. Atchison had it in mind all along to attack Lawrence, headquarters for the growing population of abolitionists. The attack was averted by sane minds on all sides, including my uncles and Jo Shelby, who would become a strong friend and supporter of our family the rest of our lives.

Capt. Joseph Orville Shelby
Missouri Valley Special Collections

George Sequoyah Gist
By Charles Bird King 1836

Jo Shelby's grandma Judith Bell Gist was the daughter of Nathaniel Gist and niece of Chief George Sequoyah Gist, half brother of her mother.

We learned from our teacher, Mister Bird, Sequoyah created the Cherokee alphabet and written language. Christopher Gist, father of Nathaniel, was a surveyor for the new United States. As a boy George Washington worked for him and the Gist's and Genl. Washington remained close. Orville Shelby, Jo's daddy was so wealthy he set up a trust for him as a baby. He'd never have to work a day in his life so the coming war was a different matter to him, a cause. Jo's aunt Eliza Gist was mother of Missouri Representative Francis Preston Blair, Jo's own cousin. He offered Jo a commission in the Federal Army but he refused and joined the Confederacy. He was among the men Genl. Hindman chose to recruit with the authority to commission officers in Missouri.

While Momma had been trying to figure out a future, marrying and burying Benjamin Simms and a baby, we had been living with Uncle Till and Aunt Lizzie. It was the church, who approached Daddy's brother Methodist minister, Uncle Will first, then Momma's brother Uncle J.R. and finally Uncle Till about our schooling. Momma made certain not only her boys, but her daughter would learn their 3 R's, Readin, Ritin and Rithmatic. And, we learned about war.

My 8th birthday was celebrated at New Hope church with a singing school performance. I whispered to Uncle Till and Aunt Lizzie that Momma's birthday, her 26th was on Jan 29th. They called me and Momma up to the front of the church and everyone came by shaking our hands, hugging Momma and wishing us well. I held her hand tight, thinking about the happy times with Daddy. It was then, about six months after Daddy died the church took up a love offering for Momma. They heard Preacher James' boy was no longer attending school.

With schooling paid for I attended a subscription school. My teacher, Mister Bird Price Smith was born in Kentucky. All of us students loved him. He was older more like a daddy or big brother to us. He'd stay with different families for a week at a time. It was then many of the women learned their letters, to write their names and read a little, many men too. Most people just wanted to be able to read the good book and sign their name. The Bible was most often the only book people had or needed.

Now five years later when Momma married Doc, life was normal again. All of us children went to school, played and rode horses. I loved watching my little sister Susie and her friends play hopscotch and jump rope. We played red rover, tag and hide and seek. Us boys, we especially liked horseshoes and King of the Mountain, a game of push and shove trying to get the "King" off his spot.

I loved to go with my friends Carroll Wood, Bill and Jim Anderson, Jim Cummins, Babe and Rufe Hudspeth, Alvis Dagley, Doc's cousins, the Bond brothers and always Uncle Wild Man, camping, fishing and hunting.

We grew up with family living close by, knowing everyone around us, cousins, cousins of cousins, aunts and uncles who became everyone's aunt and uncle whether you were related by blood or marriage or not at all. We pretty much lived close by each other and were family one way or another. You could walk to someone's house to play in half an hour or run the distance in a quarter hour. Uncle Wild Man was Bill and Jim Anderson's grandfather, Daddy to their momma Martha Thomason and brother to Gramma Sallie's second husband, Gramps Bob. Unc would take as many of us that could go hunting, fishing, camping and swimming. His number one rule was we had to know how to swim. That was easy for me and Jesse, we swam like fish. Jesse was especially good swimming underwater. Unc wasn't going to be watching after no babies who couldn't swim. On one occasion several of us were out in the boat with Unc on the Missouri River when it sprung a leak. Unc said "We're going down boys, jump out and swim to the bank while you can." We all jumped in except little Jim Cummins. I reckon Unc had had his suspicions he couldn't swim. Jim held his own saying he was going to help Unc make sure the boat got in safe and so on. Unc stood up in the boat and started for Jim saying, "You either jump in or I'm gonna throw you in." Jim yelled out "I can't swim." Unc said, "I don't reckon I care if you swim to shore or drown. I'm the only one going down with this boat." And with that, he picked up little Jim and threw him in. He wasn't much bigger than a fly and as pesky as one too. Most of us were making it to the bank by now. We heard and saw what was going on. Some of the boys were treading water, not knowing if they needed to go back to rescue Jim or swim for the bank. Unc shouted "You boys get on," pointing toward the bank. Jim sputtered around and went under a few times then started swimming, dog paddling his way towards us. We cheered him on yelling out so much no one realized Unc plugged that hole and was paddling his way right behind Jim. He could have just reached down in the water and plucked him out of it if he'd wanted. Jim just beaded in on the shore line. Unc never had much respect for Jim after that day, being Jim wasn't willing to jump in on his own. When Jim reached the shore he collapsed on the ground and us boys slapped him on the back making sure he hadn't swallowed too much water and congratulating him on swimming.

Everybody knew everybody and so when there was a social function everybody went. And, when we were at our respective farms, everybody worked. It's how we survived. Tensions were growing as talk of a war between the states became everybody's interest. In Clay Co we continued suffering the raids from across the river in Kansas where the abolitionists lived. At first they would come in the middle of the night, sneaking in and stealing the slaves, helping them escape across the river where they could live "free." Then as the reality of the looming war raised fear in all of us, the Red Legs became outright brazen, crossing during the day, raiding farms, stealing livestock, burning barns and homes, running people out if they didn't kill them first. Jim Lane was behind it all, a name those of us true to the South came to hate. He wasn't a kind man with the intention of freeing a race of people, he was a looter, robber and thief, slavery his excuse. He was the first of the "Jayhawkers" and represented everything the North believed including that Southerners deserved to be shot on sight for owning slaves.

Abolitionist John Brown moved to Kansas along with several of his sons. He had for all intents and purposes declared war on Missouri slave owners. With the coming War Between the States and the Border Wars we were suffering, cotton was at an all time low forcing many of the farmers to convert from growing hemp to tobacco. With Doc on the farm we turned to tobacco farming as well. During the years from, 1856 to 1861, ages 13 to 18 for me life was again 'normal', we were a family. I taught Jesse the finer skills of patience in fishing and talked to him about Daddy. Only two years old when Daddy left, Jesse no longer remembered running after Daddy as he was leaving, clinging to his legs crying. I didn't remind him. In fact, for the most part, Jesse didn't remember Daddy at all. I told him of his voice, how kind and strong he was. Between hunting, fishing and riding horses, we went to school together. This was probably the best times of our lives. Crops were bountiful, Momma and Doc were happy. We saw her smile again. We were at home and we were a family.

Outside of our farm, life was anything but happy. The Border Wars were raging. On May 21, 1856 Sheriff Sam Jones, Doc, Uncle Till, and most of momma's brothers, along with as many as 800 Missouri men armed with guns, hoes, mauls and axes rode out to attack the town of Lawrence, Kansas, I wanted bad to join them. I had turned 13 in Jan and pleaded with Momma to let me go. But as expected, Momma put her foot down and I stayed home. John Brown had made Lawrence his anti slavery headquarters. Three days after the attack, Brown and his sons hacked five pro slavery settlers to death at Pottawatomie Creek in Kansas. We started hearing how they branded men like cattle, hot irons on their face or head so the whole would know they were slave owners. It was then "Unc" Wild Man Bill Thomason came for an extended visit.

He'd been teaching me for awhile but the growing problems with Kansas and talk of the coming war, Unc said it was time to "get serious." He was a real adventurer. He had lived with the Indians, primarily the Cheyenne who taught him to hunt and kill buffalo, trap and survive and to ride a horse like no white man had ever seen or done. He was friends with Christopher "Kit" Carson and William Bent, fellow Missourians who moved west to the frontier and were living with the Indians. One of Unc's best skills they'd learned him was the ability to ride while hanging on the side of his horse undetected by prey, man or beast. It looked like a horse running by, if'en there was no saddle or blanket. Bareback was how most of the Indians rode guiding their horses by their manes. You could slip by an enemy this way then fire upon them from the underbelly of the horse.

His stories of living with the Indians were exciting, full of beauty and respect for the earth. The Indians didn't understand how white people could own land. Unc fearing for his family should talk of war become a reality had come home to Missouri. He told us how the Indians were fighting to hold onto their way of life. He explained in war, you must kill or be killed. This coming war he said was no different than the Indians. We were fighting for freedom of self government, for a way of life.

Unc wore his hair long, sometimes platted like a woman's, Indian style folks said. He stood less than 6 ft tall in his moccasin feet clad in a suit of beaded dyed buckskin. He had an air of a wild man about him. As Gramma Sallie's brother in law, he was our grand uncle and demanded respect. He was mild mannered and courteous, something he said often gained him more than a club or rifle. "Generally easier to win a man over with a little honey rather than brine," he'd said. He wore his long hair tucked inside his belt. He had the greatest respect for the people who had settled this land, his home. And, he had great respect for the Indians. He was torn between the two but clearly had chosen the Indian life style over living in houses, choosing the open plains over city streets.

Unc was just a year or two older than Gramps Bob. He stayed around for most of the warm months of 1856 and 1857. He kept us boys occupied and well, I figure that's how Doc and Momma had found time for the first addition to our family, our little baby sister Sallie Lou. Unc was teaching me to ride a horse "Indian style" hanging on the side, mounting and dismounting and remounting while you were moving, running alongside the horse. We used different horses and even mules so you learned the skill and not the animal. We lined up soft wood in key places then shot them with guns and bows and arrows. We learned to throw knives and tomahawks. Unc would call out the mark we were to hit just before we let loose. It was never the same, a limb, rock or tree called out just before we let loose, like a surprise enemy might lunge out just as you were about to let loose on someone else. Your target would change that fast. Unc always said, "You got to think quick and react quicker, you never know what just might save your life." Unc would let out a whoop and holler every time he was about to let go with a shot, regardless if he was firing a gun, shooting an arrow or throwing a knife or tomahawk. He learned these wild blood curdling screams jarring your soul, not just hiya's, from the Indians.

After watching me practice one afternoon, Bill and Jim, 17 and 14 took a hankering to join in, challenging me. They lived nearby and as his grandchildren he'd been learning them all their lives, especially Bill who was the oldest. There's always something special about being the oldest Unc told me and Bill, and a family responsibility that comes with it. I was a little bit jealous of Jesse named for Uncle Jesse "J.R" Cole, Momma's brother and he carried the Woodson name. There were no Alexander's nor Franklin's in our family and no connection to family friends so it was always just a name to me. Bill was named for his daddy William Anderson and carried his Momma's maiden name, William Thomason Anderson. I thought the first born should have those privileges. Unc was the man in our lives, our role model. He never lacked in something to say on almost any subject. He was particularly fond of me quoting Shakespeare. He likened our duels and battles to the knights of old protecting the kingdom.

We should always remember we are the working class, a good stock of people and it's our responsibility, mine and Bill's he said, to honor those people, our people. He told us about Robin Hood and his merry band of gentlemen of England old. The legend of Robyn Hode as an early freedom fighter originated over 600 years ago in England. He was faced with a corrupt system committing wrongs against him, his family, friends and townspeople. He tried to balance the scale by challenging the system. As hero he committed crimes but the people who understood and supported him, kept him safe. His crimes were committed through outwitting his enemy and not simply for the sake of committing the crime itself. He robbed from the rich and gave to the poor. Over the centuries men have risen to the cause of righting wrongs both continuing and expanding the legend, Earl of Huntington, Robin of Loxley, Robin of Wakefield and Robin of York. Others simply used Robin Hood as an alias and for Jesse, the legend became his own hero. Unc said Robin Hood was one of the earliest known independent fighters, other than of course Jesus.

I was the Friar because I wanted to preach like Daddy. When Bill wanted to be Sheriff, Unc told him, he's the bad guy, robbing from the poor. "Rob from the rich and give to the poor," Jesse said asserting himself and the idea he was Robin Hood and we were his band of merry men. Unc would make us follow him, telling me and Bill that's what older brothers do. Momma chastised him for indulging Jesse again to which Unc would just say he was making me and Bill responsible. They were both right. Leaving the least one, the youngest in charge had a way of exacting truth out of everyone, "Out of the mouths of babes." We got in trouble more than once with our Momma's because one of the younger ones spoke up.

Unc was always reading the paper and talking to the men in town at "the round table" Momma called wherever they might gather. She said the men met up discussing the news and events, watching the crop markets and whatever else was necessary to keep people informed. Doc and Uncle Till met up at Uncle Will's store where there was the men gathered usually hanging around playing cards, tiles and dice. I didn't know what Unc was talking about but he told us about Elisha Otis having installed in a New York City building an elevator. It would carry people in a box on a cable up and down stairs so's they didn't have to walk up on their own. Try as I might, I couldn't imagine how it worked and everything I suggested, Unc found comical. I will just have to see that contraption for myself.

March 6, 1857, the United States Supreme Court ruled in the Dred Scott case, 6-3, declaring a slave did not become free when transported into a free state. It also ruled slavery could not be banned by the U.S. Congress in a territory and blacks were not eligible to be awarded citizenship. The newspapers carried the decision and everybody had an opinion about it, be it for or against, people spoke up. Unc said the Dred Scott decision had declared us a slave nation. He had lived with the Indians and said every man, no matter what color they were, where they lived, had someone who they treated less than themselves. And yet he believed every man had a right to be free. It went back to the days of the Bible. As much as Unc loved the Cheyenne with whom he had lived and with whom his friends Kit Carson and George Bent had both married into, they too were fighting with other Indian groups for hunting grounds. Even the great Tecumseh couldn't reunite the Indians against a common enemy, land hungry white man.

Unc explained to us we were children of frontiersmen, warriors who had fought as both British and Colonists in the Great Revolt. The new United States didn't have a leader, a President until 1789, after Unc was born. His parents remembered the war and what it had done to this nation. It was the first war between whites on this soil. He said so in that way because the whites warred against the Indians and enlisted them in their own wars, France, Great Britain and Spain. The new country acquired the Louisiana Purchase in 1803, fought the Indians forcing their removal for their lands in the 1830's and the Mexicans, in the Mexican American War, securing even more land in the Mexican Cessation of 1848. Unc said the new country had added almost 2 million square miles of land west of the Mississippi by the time the Mormon Wars and Border Wars erupted. East of the Mississippi, the thirteen colonies and the land they had fought for was less than 400,000 square miles, a fourth the size of the new lands. They really didn't know how to govern these lands. The issue of slavery was one that had been debated over all those years, but had never risen to the level of a cabin burning fight. The Missouri Compromise of 1820 allowed no slaves north of a certain point, except for the state of Missouri. California had been admitted as a free state, New Mexico and Utah were allowed to decide the issue by vote of the people and no new states were to be admitted allowing slavery without a vote of the people. Washington, D.C. allowed slavery. Then the Kansas Nebraska Act of 1854 had thrown Missouri and Kansas into the vicious and bloody wars along our borders. Things had seemed to be going along pretty well; the north lived off the labor of the southern slaves supporting their textile industry and really didn't want to rock that financial boat. But, Unc he had been telling us there was a war coming. A war like the border states that would pit the north who wanted control of the cotton industry against the southern growers. If the north couldn't control them and have first shot at their cotton, then nobody would have it.

Anything Unc showed him, Bill could do, better than me and his little brother Jim first try. Of course we said it was because he was older and been learnin' longer. Daring us, Bill ask Jesse to be his partner. "He's only 9", I said. "Almost 10," Jesse said correcting me as he stepped out from behind a big tree. He was getting really good at hiding, sneaking about. He had been completely unnoticed by any of us watching silently almost every day, thinking, planning and learning. He and Bill beat me and Jim down; so much Unc challenged us to a weeklong camp out in the woods. We couldn't take anything but the clothes on our back and a knife. He'd been showing us how to throw spears we made out of long slender limbs. Those with nubs had to be skinned down smooth. Most momma's would hesitate to allow their children to do this, but our Momma was all for it. She encouraged everything Unc suggested. And this time it was more than the other campouts and she understood. Jim and Bill were moving to Kansas. This was a good bye campout. We might not see them again for awhile. Unc chose a location in the woods behind the farm; far enough away we couldn't smell supper cooking or hear people talking. Unc said it was important to be able to recognize the sounds of the night and more importantly the sounds interrupting the night. Sounds that didn't belong. It might be other wild animals out on the hunt for food, but it could be the jayhawkers from across the river in Kansas. He wasn't much on the idea of them moving to Kansas but balancing the vote over there was becoming every Missouri slaveholders concern. Jim and me, we were quick making our spears but getting any fish with them seemed impossible. I had to sharpen mine twice after plunging it into the rocky bottoms of the creek.

It might have been a hot summer day but I'm telling you when that sun went down it started getting cold. Unc showed us how to make a fire. We had learned the easy way first, by hitting flint rock making sparks, then the harder but quieter safer way, by using a stick and string. Unc had a special lens you could catch the sun in which was the easiest and fastest way but you had to catch the sun just right. Unc said having fire and water could mean the difference between life and death. He made us practice fire building over and over until we could get a fire started with any method in one or two tries, even with damp tinder.

I have to admit, I sure did feel a lot better with a fire going, even if we hadn't had anything to eat. Bill and Jesse hadn't come back. Me and Jim started nagging Unc he ought to go look for them. He told us if we were so worried maybe we should do the looking. We were pulling our wet boots back on when up walks Bill and Jesse, both of them with rabbits slung over their shoulders. They had gutted them and used the blood to draw all over their faces. Illuminated in the light of the roaring fire, they looked wild, really wild, like Indians or something. Unc was delighted, slapping his knees with approval he let out one of those blood curdling yells announcing his job was done "with at least two of you boys". Although it stung me and Jim a little, soon we joined in, hooping, hollering and jumping around dancing about the fire like wild men, how I imagined young Indian boys reaching manhood might do.

Unc taught us it was important in being leaders to never drink, keep a clear head watching over your home, camp and men who were to be treated like your family. It wasn't because of God he felt that way. It was because he was teaching us what it took to survive in the worst of circumstances. We spit the rabbits over the fire. There was one for each of us. Unc had shown us how to spit our meat and watch it cook. How to be responsible for getting the food cooked right so it was safe to eat was another lesson. We'd done that many times with squirrels. He'd even shown us how to skin a snake keeping the skin in one solid piece so it could be used or "sold for coin or traded for goods", Unc said rubbing his thumb and a finger together. Unc made us practice on some old river eels first because he said we had to learn to skin them before we learned to kill'em. We hung them up in a tree; a small sisal rope around their bodies just below their mouth and eyes tied tight enough it made their eyes bulge. Then we'd make a good clean cut all the way around below the rope. Slowly with a good sharp knife you'd work down under the skin a few inches so you could get a good grasp. Then taking hold with your hands, with a good downward pull you could take off the skin without taking any meat with it. Unc he could do it really fast, then he'd sling the old ell out over a stump for cutting up. He'd cut it into pieces ready to drop into hot grease if we had any, and if not, larger hunks perfect for skewering and cooking over the fire.

To distract our grumbling bellies while the rabbit's cooked, Unc told us stories. We were really hungry by the time they were fully cooked. I never tasted anything so good. Enjoying the evening, the smells and the taste in my mouth, I looked around at Bill, Jim, Jesse and Unc eating. It occurred to me there was only one really big rabbit, the rest were small. I jumped up angry, "You robbed a rabbit hole. You killed the momma and her babies," I said looking straight at Bill and Jesse. I'd been so hungry when they showed up with something to eat and distracted by their blood stained faces, I hadn't noticed before. Unc made me sit down and listen. He said Bill had earned an Indian name, he called it out in Indian words none of us knew, then announced, "You shall be known as Bloody Bill."

Bill had hit every mark during our challenges earlier in the day and clearly was able to kill anything that crossed his path. Unc said it was critical to survival to be able to kill your enemy without a second thought and to kill what you needed to eat even if it meant killing a momma rabbit. He told us Bill done the right thing by killing the babies. They would have died without a momma and the momma would have cried without her babies and that would have called predators to where she was. None of them would've survived the night. "She too would have been eaten just not by us," he said. I understood. I mean I understood but I still had a problem with it. Jesse was hanging on Unc's every word, taking it to heart. Bloody Bill as Unc instructed us to call him now, for the rest of his life, and Jesse, went into excited detail about how they got the rabbits. It was abundantly clear how proud Unc was of them. They cut a young tender strong branch, split the end down about 4 or 5 inches, pushed it down in the hole and started twisting. The ends got caught in the momma rabbit's fur as she struggled and they twisted. They pulled her out holding her like a momma cat holds a kitten at the nap of its neck, keeping her alive near the entrance until all the little ones ventured out, each one caught and killed right before their momma's eyes. She fought with her paws. Jesse showed the scratches on his arms where she tried to get away. After killing her and her babies, they split the tendons in the hind legs skewering a limb through it to carry them back. Jesse wanted an Indian name too but Unc told him he hadn't fully earned one. I was almost sick at my stomach, as was Jim. I saw Jesse and Bloody Bill hanging on Unc's every word, forgetting to eat. Their interest greater than their hungry stomachs. It was the first night of our weeklong camp out, but with the War Between the States looming, it would not be our last adventure in the woods. For "Unc", Uncle Wild Bill Thomason who had been our teacher and keeper over the last 8 years, it was his last. He soon fell ill.

In Aug, Unc come back from one of his round table discussions, upset. His friend Col. Isaac Neff Ebey had been killed. Friends in Missouri, he and Unc had gone west seven years earlier to the new territories on the Pacific Ocean. Unc was mostly upset because not only had a group of local warring Indians shot him, they cut his head off. As a result, we got a lesson in scalping and cutting off heads. As much as Unc hated his friend had been beheaded, he told us this act was a statement about the courage of the man himself. He told us how in the days of the Bible they didn't just kill their enemies; they took time, often burying them alive in the earth. The more feared an enemy was the more they needed to watch him die a slow death. Other times they would actually make a sport of it with chariots racing around and over them as the players lobbed their heads off. Making certain your enemy understood your intention of not simply killing but decimating them was crucial to the end game of war, even Christian wars. He explained Jesus having died on the cross was torture. His arms had been outstretched and a spike driven through his wrists, his feet crossed and drawn up with a single spike driven through both of his feet. He died amongst criminals hung on crosses in the same manner. Unc explained some of the means by which people tortured other people who didn't believe as they did. People didn't have to be criminals and outlaws. They could be entirely innocent. The longer it took for someone to die, the more valuable they were, the more feared.

A few months later we learned the United States had sent two companies of soldiers of the 1st Cav under Capt. Samuel Sturgis to Fort Scott, Kansas to intervene. The fighting and killing of the border wars, fighting over the issue of slavery had reached President Buchanan. Whether he intended to stop the wars or was playing a part in the escalation of the coming War Between the States wasn't clear to us in Missouri.

Chapter 4

It was all too common for someone at church to announce the deaths of folks in another wagon train, succumbing to the elements or attacked and killed by bandits or warring Indians. But when stories about the Sept massacre in Utah started, people simply didn't want to believe what they were hearing. Even if it was the Mormons who had proven they were ungodly and violent, willing to do whatever they wanted in the "name of God" even to their own followers. I knew they didn't worship the same God I did. I thought it was a funny when someone told me that the Mormon god lived on Kolob. Really, they think they know where God lives and it's not Heaven? I was far too Baptist for this.

Born in North Carolina, Squire Beaver moved his family to the Ozark Mountains of Ark. He ran a trading post and supply depot in North West Ark. The Baker wagon train purchased supplies from him making ready for their journey west. This is where Doc's daddy, Fielding Samuel was talking about moving. As word started coming in about the massacre, people who knew anything were riding through the night to family and friends alerting them, seemed everyone knew someone killed. Squire Beaver referred many of the families to Absalom Rorie to have their wagons and barrels made for the trip west. The Rorie's had settled on a creek with a source of clear clean water coming right out of the bottom of the mountain. They first built a grist mill supplying their large family and community with ground meal. Then Mister Rorie built a lumber mill part of their wagon making business. That portion of the Sylamore creek became known as Mill Creek and was a thriving community by 1857 when the wagon train was making its final plans to head west. The Baker family was mostly from nearby Campbell Valley in Ark along the Batesville to Harrison Road. They purchased wagons built by the Rorie's knowing they would be the strongest and surest, able to make the torturous trek west. Outfitting a wagon for a cross country trek was a special order, costing around $5,000. One of the wagons was trimmed out with carved roses. The purchaser's wife thought she might never see roses again so he'd special ordered the wagon with roses carved into it. Of kin to Squire Beaver, Jesse Beaver would ride with us under Col. Tom, in the White River Valley during the War Between the States. Squire Beaver's niece, Sarah Elizabeth Beaver, daughter of his brother Samuel Johnson Beaver and Mary Cargill, would marry Mister Absalom Rorie's grandson, Newton Rorie, son of Hezekiah, tortured and killed by the Union.

In March 1857, the Baker wagon train met up with other families from Ark and Missouri at Caravan Springs near Rolling Prairie in Ark to begin the journey. It got its name from the many wagon trains that used the place both as a starting and resting place, heading west. Squire Beaver's trading post was the last and most important stop the wagon train made before beginning their trek west. Squire wrote down everything they purchased and his list became critical when the U.S. government got around to investigating the Sept 11, 1857, Mountain Meadows Massacre.

Earlier in the year on May 13, 1857, in Ark, Parley Parker Pratt, one of the twelve Mormon apostles was killed by Hector McLean. Pratt ignored the fact, Eleanor McLean was married and took her to be his 12th wife. This was done by the Mormon men who wanted to have carnal knowledge with women. Most times the women would stay with their first husband but be married to other men, especially the apostles who wanted to be with them that way. Her husband Hector McLean was outraged. When he caught up with Pratt trying to leave with his wife, he stabbed him several times then shot him. Pratt died two and a half hours later from loss of blood. Word arrived to Utah making Pratt another martyr to the Mormons who by now had been chased out of Missouri and Illinois.

It had been nearly twenty years since the 1838, Executive Order #44, the Mormon Extermination Order, issued by Gov Lilburn Boggs which stated was a result of "open and avowed defiance of the laws, and of having made war upon the people of this State. The Mormons must be treated as enemies, and must be exterminated or driven from the State if necessary for the public peace—their outrages are beyond all description." After leaving west Missouri the Mormons moved east to Illinois. It was there Joseph Smith was killed and Brigham Young became their leader moving them west to Utah.

With talk of war looming, Brigham Young was made Gov. of the Utah Territories. The Mormons established the Nauvoo Legion, their own militia. The Great Salt Lake Valley and Utah Territories were home to only Mormons and Indians. Young's fiery rants told of ongoing persecutions leading him to declare martial law in Utah; issuing a command they would not provide any supplies to passers through. He directed his followers to cache supplies of food, grain and munitions in the hills and caves in order to fend off aggressors. It was clear the Mormons held every Arkansan accountable for Pratt's death, as every Missourian was hated due to the expulsion order. The Utah Territorial Militia by order of Utah Gov. Mormon Brigham Young attacked the Baker Fauncher wagon train disguised as Indians. Then under the ruse of aide and protection from "the Indians", they slaughtered them.

The wagon train camped at Mountain Meadows south of Salt Lake City in the first week of Sept 1857. Brigham Young said nothing happens without my authorization. The attacks lasted five days during which time the settlers began to suspicion it was not Indians but white men. In order to cover up what they had done, the Mormons believed they had to kill all of the people in the wagon train. Final word means Brigham Young must have authorized the attack, which is what most non Mormon residents of Missouri and Ark, if not the world believe. The Mormon Wars that had first brought our family to Missouri were still being fought.

Stories circulated throughout Clay Co: the wagon train run out of water and food, exhausted all ammunition and out of desperation allowed members of the Mormons to come into their camp. The Mormons were said to have assured the emigrants they would protect them as they escorted them out of their circled wagons to safety past the "Indians." They even agreed to turn over their guns to the Mormons and walk out unarmed. The Mormons separated men, women and children over the age of eight into groups. We heard the littlest children were spared. Then we heard it was only the children under the age of eight, too young to tell what happened. Seventeen had been spared and taken in by Mormon families to be raised as their own. Stories of one hundred and twenty unarmed men, women and children eight and older slaughtered by the Mormons filled the walls of every home, church and business across the nation, but especially in Missouri and Ark. News came in slow but it was said the heathen Mormons didn't bury the dead, leaving their bodies exposed to the elements, possibly so the wild animals would eat the evidence. Worried about the reality of the War Between the States and daily dealing with reports of the increasing violence between Missouri and Kansas, President James Buchanan did not investigate the Mormon Massacre fully until after things settled down. That "settling down" would turn out to be after the War Between the States ended, after Abraham Lincoln was elected, served and was assassinated with Vice President Andrew Johnson thrust into the position of President.

When the United States did investigate, the newspapers ran the children's testimonies: Martha Elizabeth Baker and her brother, William Twiddy Baker, from Burrowsville, Searcy Co, Ark:

"My father, George Baker, mother, Minerva Beller Baker, grandfather, John Twiddy Baker, several uncles and aunts were among those killed." Martha testified. "My brother, sister and I were kept in the family of John D. Lee," leader of the Mormon sect who attacked the wagon train, "until the soldiers came a year later upon the insistence of families here, to retrieve the survivors." "Only seventeen children under the age of eight, who were deemed "too young to tell", were spared. The wagon train was under attack for five days." "We ran out of water with people dying in the hot sun from thirst as much as from wounds. There really was no choice but to surrender to John Lee who said he had worked out with the attacking Indians to allow safe passage," "but the men had to give up their guns. They loaded us children into a wagon."

In her testimony, Martha said the last time she saw her mother alive was as she was being placed into a wagon. She saw her mother lining up with the other women and older children. Seeing the men wash the Indian paint from their faces, they realized these were white men, dressed as Indians. But it was too late. Given a signal by Lee, the Mormon's turned and shot each unarmed person, men, women and children with whom they were walking point blank. Those that immediately survived or managed to flee were chased down and beaten with the butts of their gunstocks, some shot repeatedly. More than 120 innocent men, women and children over eight years old were savagely murdered. The survivors recalled seeing their "mother's dresses worn by the Mormon women, their daddy's guns used by the men and Brigham Young himself riding around in one of the fine carriages" made by Absalom Rorie, easy to recall by the beautiful hand carved roses. When the soldiers came to retrieve the children over a year later, they found the remains of the slaughtered and stopped to bury the bodies the Mormons left exposed. Most had been ravaged by animals and weather, many only portions of a body remained. Martha Elizabeth, Sally Ann and William's grandma Mary came from Ark to claim them. While their ages made them too young to be able to save their own souls, the age of reason, it certainly hadn't stopped the horrors of what they witnessed and would remember the rest of their lives. Their story struck close to my heart and in my mind. Unc explained good people will do horrible things when they believe themselves righteous, when they believe they are doing God's will. And, some, they will claim righteousness when they know it is the devil and not the Lord leading them.

I was haunted by the acts of the Mormons. I found little to celebrate as my 15th birthday came and went. I would have been among those killed. My dreams were filled with screams of children, boys and girls trying to run from their attackers. Their atrocities filled my heart and soul. I was still having dreams when on Feb 17, 1858, Uncle Wild Man, William McGehee Thomason died. As we sat at his services I thought about the times we had together. Before Alec was sold Unc taught us to march like soldiers, to hide and most importantly how to listen to everything and everyone around us. How to know if a man was scared by the way his body talked to you, or if a man was lying by the way he looked at you or couldn't look at you. I had not had the opportunity to talk to Unc about the Mormon's massacre of men, women and children, now I never would. I knew he would have helped me make sense of it. I'd have to say this man we called Unc he was the "grand" father of the men we were to become. He'd taught the core of our group everything we knew about survival out in the woods. When we joined the Partisan Rangers, we would teach and train all of the boys. And, Unc's wild yell, now Bloody Bill's, would become our trademark battle cry. We would believe ourselves righteous in our acts upon our enemy.

At church on Sunday, the preacher talked about Psalm 23. He said in the south, men working in the fields eat dinner mid day, and their last meal of the day, when their work is done, is supper. Just as the Lord did. He said when a person dies, whether he has known the Lord or not, as Christian people we should repeat the 23rd Psalms and John 3:16. It matters not if we love this person who lays dead or dying before us, the Lord does. We should always remember our last supper just as we remember the Lord. After church services talk turned to the Mormons. Everyone was trying to make sense of the atrocities committed, trying to find forgiveness.

In May 1858, a group of men from Missouri including my uncles killed nine anti slavery farmers in Kansas. I had insisted on going as the man of the house, but Momma had the last word. I think she knew I wasn't ready. John Brown increased attacks, stealing slaves and burning homes, barns and farms. The closest he came to our place was on Dec 20, 1858. He attacked two neighbors taking 11 slaves. People said they walked over 1,000 miles to freedom. Antoine Barada a mixed breed hulk of a man on the Nemaha Reservation near Rouleau, Nebraska was reported to be aiding him. They called moving blacks from slave states to free states, the Underground Railroad. Righteous and justified, Brown took the law into his own hands, burning homes, killing people and looting in order to have goods to travel with. He was terrifying people on both sides of the river. In Oct 1859 John Brown led a raid on the federal armory at Harper's Ferry in Virginia. He was caught and convicted. On Dec 2, 1859 he was hung for treason by the State of Virginia for his leadership role in the raid on the armory and attempt to spur revolt among Virginia slaves. Just as one day John D. Lee would be the sacrificial lamb hung for the crimes of every Mormon there on Sept 11, 1857.

We knew it was coming, we understood when the newspapers started hailing John Brown as a hero, southern states had no choice but respond. The newspapers were depicting him as the abolitionist grandfather to slaves, benevolent and kind, risking his life for their freedom when in fact this was the same man who hacked men to death in Missouri. The men arresting Brown found an invitation from Frederick Douglas, a free black man, which made Douglas one of the most wanted men alive. It was not the issue of slavery in itself; it was an issue of Northern Aggression against the South. The North heralded the acts of John Brown, making him a martyr for treasonous acts against the State of Virginia. Applauding his intentions of freeing and arming slaves in a revolt against white men, women and children set the stage for war. We were fighting against Northern oppression and aggression. This was what Unc had prepared us for and what Daddy had preached from the pulpit. The Northerners were making John Brown out to be the sacrificial lamb on the Christian alters of slavery.

Chapter 5

In 1959, Illinoisan Abraham Lincoln ran for Senator against Senator Stephen Douglas famous for the Missouri Compromise. Lincoln lost but the debates between them did more to gain Lincoln national attention than anything he could have done on his own. All the politicians, elected and campaigning avoided talking about the Mormon's killings or slavery. Clay Co and counties along the border of Kansas and Missouri were still suffering our own war and they didn't talk about it either. The Border Wars were violent and deadly, people who supported slavery and those against it were taking the law into their own hands, pitting neighbor against neighbor.

Any time there was a wedding and often funerals, folks made a celebration of it. A new life beginning when two people joined together and a commemoration of their lives when they passed. It was at the wedding of Nathan Kerr and Charity McCorkle on Jan 26, 1860 I first laid eyes on Thomas Coleman Younger. Charity was a beautiful girl with skin as pretty as cream. Nathan was a tall fella sporting a mustache and the beginnings of a beard. Cole was the nephew of Augusta Peters Younger, niece of Momma's second husband, the late Mr. Ben Simms. She was the daughter of his sister Francis Simms and John Peters, and her husband Coleman Purcell Lee Younger was a brother to Cole's daddy Henry Washington Younger. Cole had been named for his Uncle Coleman and to sort the two, Thomas Coleman Younger was called "Bud." Like I was Daddy's little Buck, Cole was his Daddy's little Buddy. No one ever called him Cole in his family, but with his later years of "fame", the world would know him as Cole Younger. He and Charity were own cousins, children of sisters, grand children of Judge Richard Marshall Fristoe. He had been one of the first judges appointed in Missouri. The great grandson of Chief Justice John Marshall of Virginia, the Fristoe family were our own real lords and ladies in Missouri. The wedding was one of those large gatherings of friends and family throughout the area. On her daddy's side Charity was a cousin to Nathan Bedford Forrest. He was establishing a group called the Knights of the Golden Circle supporting the south.

Gatherings such as this provided opportunities for politicians of every persuasion and to not be invited considered an insult. When Abraham Lincoln came through Missouri campaigning for President entire communities filled wagons headed to hear him speak. Afterwards he dined with the Younger and Fristoe families, Unionists. I never heard of him one time talking on the issue of ending slavery. All's he said was he intended to stop the expansion of it, no more states would be admitted as slave holding states. He was a slave owning man himself and I reckon that spoke for him on the subject. He would be elected President in Nov 1860. Even though

Congress passed an amendment to keep slavery, supported by the new President, in Dec, South Carolina was the first of the Southern States to secede from the Union. Even when the war changed in 1863 with the Emancipation Act, President Lincoln allowed some of the northern states to maintain slavery. Maryland kept their slaves as a bargaining tool for staying in the Union and only slaves in the states of rebellion, southern states, were declared 'free'. In the North, they were not 'free' but could earn or buy their freedom, and freedom of their families.

Everyone that could looked for anything to keep their minds off the fact war was coming. When news of the new "Pony Express" exploded in the papers, everyone who could made plans to go to the big to do in St. Joseph, Missouri on April 3, 1860. William Russell, Alexander Majs and William B. Waddell partners in a freighting Co were extending service of the Pony Express, the mail delivery system between Fort Leavenworth and Colorado. It would run from St. Joseph, Missouri across the Plains and Rocky Mountains to Sacramento, California. They run advertisements of the opening for weeks and the huge crowds proved the success of them. Uncle Will planned his journey to Kansas City for mercantile supplies with the opening, allowing time to go to St. Joseph. I was thrilled when invited to go with him. Someone Uncle Will knew told him a few miles out of St. Joseph the rider leaving was replaced by young boys. Seems the partners were looking for young boys, especially orphans of any color 12 and older to ride for them. They were younger and would be less likely to be stopped, killed or hurt by whites and Indians alike. And, they weighed less so the horse could carry rider and mail with greater ease. I thought about what Aunt Charlotte told me about the warring villages in Africa, rounding up men, women and children selling them to the merchant ships. It seemed to me, white or black, people were willing to do horrendous things to people for money and power.

Sallie Lou was turning two years old on April 15th, born the day before Daddy's brother, William "Bill" Harvey James. On April 16th, 1860 Uncle Bill turned 41. He and Aunt Lindy lived in Indiana and didn't visit much. Daddy's youngest brother Thomas Martin James was 37 on April 8th. Seems about every month we had a family gathering for a wedding, funeral, birthing or birthdays. Uncle Will allowed me to buy Sallie a doll from one of the tents in St. Joseph. It was like a carnival, people were set up selling food and hawking goods and games. I was glad for time with Uncle Will. We talked about many things but mostly family. Momma made certain we knew who our family was and where they lived. Who was whose daughters and sons, who had lived and died where and whether deaths had been from natural causes, sickness, illness or come at the hands of foul play. Family was important to both Momma and Daddy who taught us, trust in the Lord, protect your family and honor your ancestors.

Doc's daddy, Fielding "Pappy" Samuel's farm was a few miles from ours. After Momma and Doc married, he sold his little piece of land to his brother. Pappy Fielding was talking of moving to Ark and had been down to scout out some places. He wasn't happy with anyone, north or south and feared for his family. He was a war objector. He and 10 year old Ed, Doc's youngest half brother had gone to visit Aunt Lucy Poor Mims, our cousin Zee's grandmother and our great grand aunt looking for a new place to live. With the rivers the highways, he hadn't taken a likening to Aunt Lucy's location on the White River. Doc wanted him to stay in Missouri anyways. When Doc was ten years old, his Momma, Louisa Bond died. Her parents, William and Charity Hinds Bonds, helped Doc's Daddy, Fielding care for Doc and his siblings. Doc had been raised near the Ohio Kentucky border in Owenton, Owen Co, Kentucky before his Daddy and grandparents moved to Missouri. Owen Co was named for Abram Owen who fought at the Battle of Tippecanoe in 1811 under William Henry Harrison who became our 9th President and Genl. James Wilkinson who was the first Gov. of the Missouri Territories. Gov. Wilkinson and Vice President Aaron Burr created the Wilkinson Agreement which was signed by Abraham Ruddell, one of the first people to settle Batesville, Ark. Captured as a six year old child at Fort Ruddell, Kentucky in 1780, Abe and his older brother Stephen lived nearly 20 years with the Shawnee as brothers to Tecumseh. Burr and Wilkinson wanted to create a new country west of the Mississippi that remained allied with the British and the Indians. They were nearly tried for treason. Then at the conclusion of the War of 1812, it was discovered Wilkinson had been a spy allied with the Spanish all the way back to the Great War of Revolt.

Pappy Fielding, like Daddy, knew the politics and history of these new United States. Pappy was born on May 26, 1803 in Frankfort, Kentucky, about 30 miles from Owenton. Ruddell's Fort had been located on the Licking River in north east Kentucky, not far from where Pappy and Doc were born. Pappy knew the Boone's and loved to tell how the great frontiersman Daniel Boone was buried in Frankfort right close to where he himself had been born. When we got together with Doc's family, it was a homecoming. There were a lot of children and grandchildren to visit and for us to play with. And, there was exciting stories of our families. Most of all, I loved the music. Jesse learned to play the banjo and Susie the mountain dulcimer. I could sing but never learned to play anything well although I liked the mouth harp. Momma said I didn't have enough patience. Perhaps not, I couldn't wait to see the look on Sallie Lou's face when she saw her little doll, so I gave it to her early.

June rolled in with thick black heavy rain clouds. The creeks and rivers overflowed and ran muddy. The Missouri humidity was so thick you could cut it with a knife. Aunt Charlotte loved to fish. She always said fishing in muddy water was the best. The fish couldn't see far and they'd be gettin' hungry. She'd tie a little piece of bright cloth to her string right near the hook and dang it all, bait or no bait, she'd out catch us all. We'd have fish fry's. The kettles were put up over the open fires and the hog lard heated real hot. The fish was cut up into filets with no bones in them, coated in corn meal and dropped into the hot grease. It only took a minute or two and the cooked pieces would have to be fished out. Us children we'd be lined up waiting for the first pieces. Hot in our hands we'd jump about burning our mouths trying to eat. The cooks took turns over the kettle. It spit hot grease as each piece was dropped in. They dropped in spoons of corn meal batter. Someone said the little balls of hot fried cornpone was called hush puppies. What was in the bottom of the kettle was fed to the dogs keeping them quiet. Pappy Fielding said us children were the puppies that needed kept quiet. I reckon he meant me and Martha Ann Thomason. We had lots of fun, we were real close. I called her Mattie. She called me Frankie. Susan Alice "Alsey", born in 1846 was a year and a half younger than me. We were all very close, especially after Gramma Sallie died in 1851 a year after Daddy.

It had been five years since Momma and Doc married on Sept 25, 1855. They celebrated their fifth anniversary with a hoe down. People come with guitars, banjos, fiddles, mandolins and dulcimers. Some of the women played spoons and fiddle sticks. The dancing dolls were entertaining and musical. The dolls were puppets on strings that when held over a board danced as the board was tapped. Aunt Charlotte had her own set of dancing dolls she made like field hands with walnut wood so they would be darker like her. "Fiddle sticks," Aunt Charlotte said, "came from the field hands." They carried two good sticks in their back pockets and when the day was done, they could tap out music on the hoe, rake or shovel if need be. But the best was when they could find a fiddle player tapping the strings as the fiddle was being played making it sound like two instruments. I learned to play the mandolin just a little but I didn't have the ear or as Momma said, the patience. Jesse became good at the banjo and when at church or hoe downs, people ask him to play. He loved being up in front at any gathering. When we went to singing schools, Jesse would play while the girls and us boys sang. There were big people singings and little people taught by Uncle Will, Daddy's brother, the Methodist.

The weather was good and for Daddy's oldest sister, Aunt Mary's birthday Sept 28th, we had a hoedown on her birthday Friday evening at our house. It lasted all weekend. We celebrated Jesse turning 13. Our Aunt

Nancy Gardner James' birthday was in Sept as well. She was married to George Hite and they had a houseful of children, all my own cousins. They lived on the south side of Kentucky on the Tennessee border.

An early fall came bringing a light snow in Nov. Momma and Aunt Charlotte picked baskets of paw paws and persimmons. They cooked them into a mush then spread them out to dry on the roof. In the winter time we'd have dried fruit to eat. They laid out all the persimmon seeds and compared them. If the persimmon kernel was spoon shaped it was a prediction of heavy wet snow fall. The spoon meaning you was going to need a shovel for the snow. If the kernel was fork shaped it was a prediction of a powdery light snow and a mild winter. You didn't want to see kernels knife shaped, which meant cold icy cutting winds. At least you didn't want to see them in equal numbers with the other two, especially the spoon. That meant the worst kind of winter.

Doc was standing watching Momma, Aunt Charlotte and the girls. He said he had a sure way of predicting the weather, one hundred per cent accurate, all the time, every day using only a cow. He went on about it until finally all us children were hounding him to tell us. "Okay", he said. "If the cow is wet, it's raining. If there's ice or snow on her back, it's bad weather, snowing or coming an ice storm. If she's dry, it ain't snowing or raining. But, most of all, if she ain't out there, it's come a tornado." With that, Momma started chasing him with her dish towel. She rolled it, twisting it where it would snap when she slung it trying to pop Doc. She got him once on the arm and he yelped. Laughing he said she'd hurt him. They both were laughing and all us children joined in. Such were our fall and winter months, and those persimmon seeds were right, but so was Doc and the cow. I think about those times and a smile creeps over my face.

At family gatherings talk was always about the Border Wars and whether or not the President was gonna get us into a war. We didn't think anyone east of the Mississippi remembered what war meant. We had been living it all our lives, and our parents before us. War with the Mormons and the Border Wars, people in western Missouri had a solid understanding of what a War Between the States would mean. Most of us felt we were stronger as part of the United States, but when South Carolina seceded people had to take sides. On Feb 4th, 1861, the new Confederate States of America formed in Montgomery, Alabama. Jefferson Davis was elected President. Missouri hesitated, wanting mostly to avoid war. This was what Daddy preached and Unc learned us, war was upon us. When Lincoln was inaugurated as President of the United States on March 4, 1861, a convention assembled in St. Louis to decide whether Missouri should secede. Despite support from pro slavery Missouri Gov. Claiborne Jackson, the decision to secede was rejected by a vote of 98 to one.

Harper's Weekly reported extensively on a plot to assassinate the President elect, Abraham Lincoln being fouled by Allan Pinkerton. Pinkerton was the first detective in Chicago where he partnered with Edward Rucker, an attorney there, forming the Pinkerton Agency. They were hired to protect rail transportation and solve crimes. It was then Pinkerton first came into contact with George McClellan, Chief Engineer and Vice President of the Illinois Central Railroad and the Co's lawyer, Abraham Lincoln. When war was declared he was hired to protect Lincoln.

Allan Pinkerton, President Abraham Lincoln and Maj Gen John McClernand

A month later on April 4th, 1861 secessionists captured the federal arsenal in Liberty, Clay Co, yet another war at our front door. A week later on April 12th, Confederates fired on Fort Sumter, Charleston, South Carolina. Two days later President Lincoln called for 75,000 troops to put down the rebellion. Most of the people in Missouri felt differently about succession at that point. Momma told us even the President's family was split, his wife, Mary Todd, had four of her brothers' join the Confederacy. For Southerner's this was a War of Northern Aggression, a War Between the States brought on by the North's approval of the acts of a mad man, John Brown. A man whose goal was to free and arm Southern slaves in a revolt against their white owners, free to murder men, women and children supported by the North. Those acts, his intentions, were supported by the North against the South. Within a year, in 1862, President Lincoln signed an Income Tax bill, imposing a 3% tax on incomes between $600 and $10,000 and a 5% tax on higher incomes to pay for the Union war effort. After the war was over, everybody, north and south, had to pay the new Federal Income Tax to finance "reconstruction".

The wars fought in our homes and churches, on the farms along the Missouri and Kansas Border had been a surrogate war between the North and South. Before war had been declared between the states, on Dec 10th, 1860, William Clarke Quantrill joined some Quakers on a mission to steal Missouri slaves freeing them. They planned to raid Morgan Walker's farm near Blue Springs. The Walker's had a large successful farm with 2,000 acres and 25 to 30 slaves. Quantrill and four men were to attack the farm freeing Walker's slaves. Instead, he found Andy Walker out squirrel hunting. He rode up to Andy telling him he'd got word Montgomery was planning to attack their farm that night. Andy was on foot not far from neighbors. Quantrill offered him a ride but cautious, Andy declined. They hightailed it the neighbor's house. Together they went to Lee Koger's who lived about three miles west of Fort Osage and Sibley, then on to Dick Williams, Marcus Gill and John Tatum's. With Quantrill they planned an ambush for the Kansas men.

Nancy Elizabethjane "Annie" Walker 1841-1884

Andy and his brother in law Doctor William Ryland Slaughter, husband of his sister Nancy Jane "Annie", and several neighbors were ready when the attack came. Quantrill had returned to the Jayhawkers and as dark fell he led them straight to the Walker farm. Going to the door he was admitted in. Once out of the line of fire, Andy Walker and his neighbors fired on the men outside. Ed Morrison was shot dead. Chalkey Lipsey was seriously wounded and John Dean was hit. Charles Ball and Dean fled on their horses. Ball returned under fire and carried Chalkey to the woods. Within a few days, Andy and Quantrill along with some of the neighbors managed to hunt them down and kill them. Andy had proof of all this from the Kansas City newspapers hailing the men for fowling an attack. It reported the attackers as part of Montgomery's gang, Quantrill had told them it was Jennison's Jayhawkers, but Andy learned later it had been four Quakers. The paper simply referred a stranger who learned of the raid giving the Walker's a timely warning. The Southern Quantrill was born. He stayed the rest of Dec and part of Jan 1861 at the Walker farm. Morgan and Andy were happy to have Quantrill around, grateful he warned them, thus changing the outcome of the attack. He became involved with Annie, leading to a split between her and her husband Doctor Slaughter.

Their neighbor Marcus Gill was growing more concerned about the growing attacks by Jennison's men, especially after his friend and neighbor Emmett Goss joined him. His older son Enoch Gill living in Texas was urging his father to bring the family south. Gill owned a prosperous mill, was a boat builder, cattleman and lumber baron. He owned several slaves. Gill purchased a herd of hogs from neighbor Jacob Teaford Palmer and was preparing to drive them to Gill's farm when Jennison's men under Goss attacked him. They stole the hogs and some of his horses, broke into his house, smashed windows, chopped furniture to bits and took what they wanted. Quantrill, Palmer and Gill went after Goss skirmishing near Westport. Quantrill's quick ability with a pistol and riding skill was well demonstrated when he saved Gill's life by killing one of the men who had his gun aimed directly at Gill. Turning, seeing the dead man, Gill knew Quantrill saved his life. Marcus Gill was telling Andy of Enoch's insistence he move to Texas but he was fearful of traveling with his wife and young children. Andy Walker saw this as the perfect opportunity to get Quantrill away from his sister. Quantrill was hired to escort Marcus Gill, his wife Mary Jane and six daughters, Leah, Sarah, Susan, Sallie, Mary, Louella and son, William along with twenty slaves to Texas. After Annie and her husband Dr. Slaughter split she married Joseph Vaughn in April. During the winter while Quantrill was gone to Texas, Andy Walker formed his own band. They made a name for themselves recovering cattle, horses and slaves taken by the Jayhawkers.

Jan 1861 came on hard, bitter cold. The creeks and edges of the rivers were frozen solid. We had to bust open holes in the ice for the animals to get water. I thought about the winter I was born and how Daddy couldn't get home to Missouri because of the frozen rivers. By early April the Gill family escorted by Quantrill arrived safe to Texas. When Quantrill heard about Fort Sumter, along with their son, Enoch Gill, he hightailed it back to Missouri. Shortly after arriving back, William Gregg, Aide de Camp Adjunct to William Haller riding with Andy, brought Quantrill some food and horses he stole from local farmers convincing him he needed to start his own band. Gregg was his first recruit. Within a few days Quantrill had the first of the men to ride with him: William Gregg, William Haller, George Todd, Joseph Gilchrest, John and James Little, James Hendricks, Joseph Vaughn, Perry Hoy and John William Koger.

Chapter 6

Spring came on beautiful, that perfect kind of weather after a long winter that finds young and old alike heading to the creek for a little fishing. Momma announced she was pregnant. John Thomas was to be Momma and Doc's Christmas present. Then life changed. War was upon us. But just like it had not started for people of Missouri with that shot at Fort Sumter, it didn't end with Lee's surrender at Appomattox.

Our neighbor, Lt. Colonel Calhoun "Coon" Thornton held the first recruitment meeting in April. It was then several joined the Missouri Volunteers under Capt. Thurston. Most of us officially joined May 4, 1861 after another meeting at neighbor George Claybrook's house. That day, 20 of us boys having grown up as friends and neighbors, joined up including brothers Brantley and John Harrison Bond, Thomas Anderson Gill and his brother Enoch, Colly, Dick and Kit Chiles, Nate, Bill and Jim Anderson, George "Clell" and Oliver "Ol" Shepherd, George and John Tyler Burns and Jim Griffin. My friend Carroll Wood joined at the first meeting. Donnie Pence joined too, his daddy Adam was among our folks having migrated from Kentucky. I wished Unc could have been there. Knowing war was coming, he'd trained us good. I reckon he knew life would change for us when it did. Ten days later along with my family, we gathered at Haynesville with neighbor boys waiting on other new recruits. The Shepherd's lived just north of Liberty; we joined them near their place. Boys were from Holt, in Kearney Township, about a mile and a half south of Haynesville, Converse about 3 miles to the north east, Lathrop a whopping 6 miles as was Lawson. Kearney itself was almost 7 miles south and Excelsior on the Fishing River in Ray Co was 7 miles to the south and east. We rode into Centerville, proud, for our official enlistment in the Missouri State Guard under Genl. Sterling Price.

The Wood family was part of our New Hope Baptist church family. Carroll Wood, seven years older than me, was one of my best friends, along with Frank Gregg and James Corum. After Daddy died, Carroll was like my big brother. He took me under his wing. I could talk to Carroll about anything. Us boys even made a raft and crossed the river on it. I was proud to be a friend of these boys. They say if you sit in one place long enough everyone you have ever known will pass by. Thomas Roe Freeman had been one of the lawyers to help Momma with what may be the first prenuptial agreement in the United States, or at least Missouri. Acting as legal counsel for the group, he was among those at that first meeting to decide if we should fight for the North or South. Carroll and me, and most of the other boys had decided right then on joining up, just some momma's had more say so than others, mine among them. It had taken me another month to convince her, after all I had turned 18 in January.

Archie Clements Jim Cummins
Missouri Valley Special Collections, Kansas City Public Library, Kansas City, Missouri

Peyton Long was in Capt. Tom McCarty's Co of John T. Hughes regiment. We'd see Peyton fighting at Oak Hill on Wilson's Creek and Elk Horn Tavern before their unit went east to Corinth, Mississippi. After getting back he joined Si Gordon for a year then in 1863 he joined with us riding with Quantrill in time to attack Lawrence, Kansas. When I made the decision to ride with Bloody Bill, most of the boys went with me, including Peyton. I had said my goodbyes to family and friends alike that day. Some I would not see again until the war was over, some never again.

Little Jim Cummins didn't immediately join up, his momma, a widow woman didn't want him to leave her alone. His daddy, Samuel Cummins died in 1854. His Momma, Eleanor "Ellie" Crossett Cummins, was named for her grandma Eleanor "Nellie" Lindsay. Missus Nellie and Momma's grandpa Anthony Lindsay were own cousins, children of siblings. Me and Jim were cousins, enough family he was always underfoot. When Momma give me that sideways look, cutting her eyes, I knew I had to be the bigger person, "family" come first. Cousin Wirt Woodson married Jim's daddy's kin, Clarissa Cummins, so there was nothing doing but to put up with him. Things were in heated conflict where we lived and no woman was safe alone. He later joined Col. Calhoun Thornton recruiting at the home of his Uncle Robert Ferrell, in Clay Co. Union troops under Capt. Bigelow hung Jim's uncle for recruiting rebels. They wouldn't let anyone cut him down. After Bigelow's men left some of their hired hands cut the rope. Jim got his due in 1864 when he was among the men to capture Bigelow and his brother. "Resisting" they were shot.

Jim was always a cowardly sort of person who liked to tell tall tales about the things he done, like killing four armed men when he was just a boy. If that was true, I think we would have known it. He started a lot of that kind of talk after Unc threw him in the water. He was a feisty little fellow you didn't want to challenge. He would get mad as a wet hornet. He always said, "I may not kill you but I'm gonna make you wish you was dead." Just like the day Unc taught him to swim. When he finally quit spitting out water and got his breath, he jumped up mad, daring and shouting at not only us boys but Unc.

Momma always said we need not ever lie especially to her. If you do, you have to remember the first lie because it always calls for a second and third and another until you don't know where the truth starts and ends. She said she better always know what the truth was and she always did. And, she knew it before anyone else. You best never blindside Momma. She'd still be there to defend us but if she was to have ever been caught not knowing the truth; I wouldn't have wanted to be the subject of Momma's wrath. And, thankfully, "I" never was. Jim, he'd just soon tell a lie when the truth was a better story.

Jesse was jealous when I left home as a new enlistee for the Southern cause, but for me, it was the only time I wasn't directly responsible for him. It was a time when he had a chance to be the man of the house and I could be my own man. While he was home it was his job to oversee and work the tobacco crops. We converted from hemp to tobacco due to the War. Tobacco work is hard. Plants have to be started inside and can't be put out until the last killing frost has past. Sometimes that's hard to know. Should it appear a frost is coming after they have been put out, then it's everybody's job to protect the plants with smoke fires, keeping the low ground warmer so the plants stay safe. Up all night, everyone's dancing and waving cloth sheeting in the fields to move the warm air. It's fun at first, then weary and by morning light, a person is bone tired. The plants are about half a foot tall when planted in the ground. It's best to wait until the ground is wet from rain as it makes planting a whole lot easier. After you work the ground a bit, you make a hole with a tobacco peg, a curved wooden tool or as Unc had shown us, a deer antler would do. They generally have the perfect curve and are strong. You work two rows at once, making a hole on either side as you walk, get a plant from the bag carried across your shoulder, drop them in, and tap the ground with your foot to cover the roots, then step ahead a couple feet and do it all over again. This is really pretty boring, but Aunt Charlotte she always had a way of making things easier, fun almost. We would play games. One of the best was a kind of soldiering and we'd sing. At harvest time the entire stalk would be cut off at ground level with a tobacco knife, then speared in the same manner you cut the tendons in a rabbit or squirrels hind legs putting a stick through to carry them, or string up a deer, hog or cow to bleed them before butchering. You can get four or five plants on a stick; then they're hung in the barn to cure.

It was in the overseeing of the tobacco crops that Jesse took off the end of his finger with a tobacco knife. It makes for better reading, especially by our later friend newspaperman John Edwards Newman that Jesse lost it in battle. But the truth is Jesse made up the story himself because whacking off the tip of his finger in a careless motion with a tobacco knife didn't tell well. He'd clean and pack our guns and I think somewhere along the line someone ask him if that's how he'd lost his finger tip and that was it. Eureka, he had his story. That was the beginning of the cover up of how his fingertip got shot off. When us boys would ride in with our stories of battle, Jesse learned to tell a good story himself. And, Momma she indulged him, a lie and a story were two different things. And, besides, she was in on most all of it when it come to Jesse. Doc said it was because he was a sickly boy cause of his eyes and all. I knew his eyes watered but he could conjure up tears whenever he wanted.

On April 20, 1861 when the Liberty arsenal was raided, the guns and ammo were hidden at Ephraim "Junior" Murray's farm. Junior and his sons Plunk and Thomas were among the first to join up. On April 22, Gov. Claiborne Jackson ordered the militia into encampments. Over 800 men reported to Camp Jackson near St. Louis. The Gov. tried to arm the men with guns and ammunitions taken from the Federal arsenal. After the boys took the arsenal at Liberty, Union Genl. Nathaniel Lyon knew the St. Louis arsenal was at risk. Unionists Genl. Lyon and Lt Gov. Francis Blair, Jo Shelby's kin rounded up all the Missouri State Guard now loyal to the Confederacy under former Gov. and Genl., Sterling Price in Camp Jackson, surrounding them with 3,000 troops and volunteer militia. Marching the prisoners into St. Louis the people in the streets watching fired on them. A street riot erupted with a number of men, women and children killed and 20 soldiers. Among those witnessing the events was the President of the St. Louis Street Railway, William Tecumseh Sherman, Lt. Gov. Blair's kinsmen Joseph Orville Shelby and Ulysses S. Grant. This was their introduction to the War Between the States.

Some of the boys who signed up from home made it back from St. Louis after swearing the oath of allegiance to the Union. They told of Lyon having been kicked in the stomach by his own horse. "Even his horse was a Southerner." "His horse tried to kick sense into him," and the like brought all ages to laughter. People had to leave out, including the Southerners who were holding office. Genl. Sterling Price had to vacate declaring his loyalty to the South. We had been marching toward St. Louis to meet up with Genl. Price when we heard Genl. Lyon had taken Jeff City. Suddenly sides changed with nothing more than one man's say so. We didn't know what to do. Some of the boys went home. I waited with others to join Genl. Price.

A good many of the boys didn't think we were part of the regular Confederate Army so they took off to sign up. The Missouri State Militia (MSM), Union, formed on May 11 due to the massacre in Saint Louis on May 10th. The military bill outlawed other militia groups from forming without authorization from district commanders. They were trying to prevent what was happening south in Ark and across Missouri. They were faced with vigilante groups calling themselves home guards, reportedly to protect those at home, Union or Southern, Union and Southern. These home guards quickly become nothing more than looters and pillagers, vigilantes, like the Kansans. People didn't know if they were southern bushwhackers or northern jayhawkers. Either way, Genl. Sterling Price was our commander, under the Missouri State Guard and I stayed with him. We heard the boys who made it to Jeff City were taken prisoner and forced to join the Union. On June 2 we got word Gov. Jackson called for 50,000 volunteers to defend Missouri from the Union. Genl. Price made us his boys, his men, his troops, we were his militia. With him from the beginning, he would come to rely on those of us who stood by him that day.

Some practiced at home, others in small groups of neighbor boys while most joined camps of upwards of 100 recruits under a single Col.. As soon as somebody showed promise, leadership abilities, they made ranks through promotion or by being elected by the boys. I shied away from that. I knew I was the man of our house even if Momma did have Doc. I knew I always had to be able to go home. We enlisted for 30 to 90 days. We were fighting neighbors and knowing how to navigate sides became crucial. Some of the older ones, men, were members of the Freemasons. There were signs developed allowing us to know if a home was safe. A kitty cat meant a nice lady and a hat a nice man. We had ways to draw on the fence for Federalists or Secessionists, or just wanted to stay out of it, messages to those who came after us. The signs changed as life around us changed.

Genl. Lyon set out to destroy the Missouri State Guard, those of us remaining loyal to the Confederacy. After St. Louis, Lyon started for the capital, Jefferson City. Genl. Price had already moved toward Boonville. Genl. Lyon was determined to take control of the Missouri River by taking Boonville for the Union. They came in on steamboats from below, marched into town and attacked. We engaged on June 17, 1861, defeated we retreated southwest. Two days later at a place called Cole Camp we skirmished and defeated a pro Union Home Guard, killing at least 35 men.

Capt. Joseph "JoeC" Porter gathered together a unit of men made up of Missouri farm boys. They captured a unit of Union MSM, took their equipment and released them. By July boys and men were flocking to join him. Later in the month JoeC was promoted to Lt. Col. under Genl. Martin Green. Genl. Hindman approached a number of men about recruiting in Missouri to form commands with the goal of causing trouble for the Union through the disruption of rail, supply and communication lines, JoeC was among the most successful. As soon as the recruiters raised 100 volunteers they were promoted to Col. with their recruits making up their regiments. Elections determined position of Lt. Col., Maj, Capt., First Lt. and Second Lt. in descending order or position, then Sgts and Corp.s. A Sgt. was placed in charge of units of men under the Lt. Our teacher Mister Bird taught us a regiment is a large body of men coming together with a single leader. We learned a unit is the most basic of soldiers with three to five men. A squad is comprised of eight to sixteen men, then platoon of two to four squads ranging from twenty five to sixty men. Two to six platoons make up a Co, numbering 70 to 250 men. Two to six companies make up a battalion, 300 to 1000 men, and two to five battalions make up a brigade totaling from 3,000 to 5,000 men. A division is made up of two to four brigades or 10,000 to 20,000 men. These leaders were Brigadier Generals.

Genl. Robert E. Lee had been to the U.S. Military Academy and was a Col. in the regular army of the U.S. When he chose to fight with the south and was promoted to Genl., he continued to wear his three star insignia for Col. on his collar stating he wouldn't wear the Genl. insignia until the South won. When John Brown attacked the arsenal in Virginia, it had been Robert E. Lee, from the Virginia Military Academy who led the troops to find and capture him. And, Stonewall Jackson, a half brother of our cousin Wirt Woodson, was in charge of crowd control at his hanging.

At Carthage with Gov. Jackson and Genl. Price leading the troops, we matched the Feds 4 to 1, with over 4,000 men. Most of us, 30, 60 and 90 dayers were assigned to ride with Jo Shelby. We had demonstrated skills and had our own guns and horses. Us boys who trained with Unc could ride and shoot noticeably better than the others. Shelby assigned Bloody Bill and me to teach the other boys, pairing us with two or three, then they would teach others; mostly how to shoot and ride using our horses for protection. We were mostly called by our last names; Bloody Bill was "Anderson" and me "James". Cowskill Prairie was our main camp and training grounds. It had been a sale barn before the war. What none of us, enlistees or commanders was prepared for were the boys coming with no shoes on, carrying hoes, pitchforks and fishing gigs as their weapons. A great many more that did have guns had no ammunition. Many of the guns they did have were old and in need of cleaning if not some kind of repair.

Confederate President Jefferson Davis as Secretary of War in 1855 for the United States had purchased the Springfield rifle and Enfield Rifles arming the entire U.S. Army, now the Union, with them. Using the same bullets they would be the main arms used against the South. The minie ball was created to destroy bones, shattering them, passing through the body rather than imbedding in the flesh. The result was huge numbers of amputations taking place in the field. We quickly realized how important the ammunition efforts in southern Missouri and north Ark were.

When I got a chance I ask Momma where 'green horns' came from, I'd been too embarrassed at not knowing to ask anyone in camp. She said in the spring time when the first green plants of spring emerge they are so fresh and new the cattle go straight for them, rooting them out with their horns. The green horns are a result of the fresh and new but underneath is the strong bone that's tough. At least that was her version. I thought about what Unc would have said. Even if it had been the same story his version would have been elaborate, filled with snorts and chomps, bulls fighting making their way to the best of the new grass. He'd of told a bigger story.

Walking among the recruits it was easy to understand the shock on Genl. Price's face when he looked at the shotguns and squirrel rifles the boys brought from home. I know what I felt; I can't imagine how he felt. But, he knew spirits were high and every one of them was itching to fight. The boys were anxious. And, I say boys, because a lot of them were just that, boys, 15 years old. Momma hadn't seen fit to allow Jesse to join and the Missouri State Guard wouldn't have taken him if they had of known his age. He looked like a girl; all our aunts and cousins said he was a "pretty" boy. But these country boys anxious to defend their homes and farms, their size denied their ages. I think the youngest boy I saw was 10 or 11. David Dearien come with his daddy, Gus, from Ark. It was his job to carry the drum or fife and do odd jobs around the camp. He would go home with his daddy after the 90 days. He aided the Quartermaster as a gopher, going for this and going for that. Worst was should his daddy be killed, as young as he was, it would be his job to make it home breaking the news to the family. I reckon father and son went east and both survived the war.

With all this going on our new President, Abraham Lincoln suspended the Writ of Habeas Corpus. The writ allowed arrests and imprisonment had to be lawful, now without it, the northern military tribunals could issue the death penalty without a trial. Us Southerners, boys and men alike, could be shot for any reason and that was that. We'd been hearing about a number of men, different groups trying to defend against the Kansas Jayhawkers forming their own independent groups; Dick Kitchen, James Cason, Ki Harrison, Bill Marchbanks, Cliff Holtzclaw, Alf Bolin, Indian Bowles, Andy Walker, Doc Himes, Joe Kirk and more. Genl. Price called them guerilla warriors. They fought frontier style, a do or die attitude, take no prisoners. He seemed to have an appreciation for them. He and Unc would have liked each other.

John Jarrette Dick Burns

Missouri Valley Special Collections, Kansas City Public Library, Kansas City, Missouri

Some men rode alone, others in groups of up to fifty men, burning bridges, pulling down telegraph lines, creating all kinds of problems for the Union even before being acknowledged by the Confederacy. They destroyed the Salt River Bridge and tore out culverts near Centralia on the North Missouri line. It was a solid defeat at Dry Forks which was good news for us. Some of the guerillas were; Dick Burns, Sol Basham, Bill Gregg brother of my friend Frank, George Shepherd, Dave Poole, James and John Little, George Todd, John Koger, John Hampton and John Jarrette. The guerillas were growing in numbers and having great successes. Farming men who couldn't commit to 3 to 6 months or to regular service were joining these irregulars staying close to home. They could watch out after their farms and family and still manage to fight the Union.

Missouri wasn't safe at all. People didn't always understand the difference between a bushwhacker and a jayhawker. Maybe because men would wear the uniforms of North or South robbing people, they come to not know or care which was which, their victims were getting the worst end of it whoever they were. Bushwhackers were for the most part Southerners who learned to fight in the dense woods and undergrowth and Jayhawkers and the Red Legs of Kansas were Northerners. You couldn't ride very far into the flat lands of Kansas without seeing some kind of hawk perched on fence posts, lone trees and buildings. Maybe they were actually Jaw

Hawks. I don't know but the fella's from there were called Jayhawkers and were always looking to prey on something.

Bill Marchbanks joined the Missouri State Militia in April. When Genl. Price made it clear he was staying with the south and maintaining command Bill stayed with him. Bill and me, we'd fight together at Wilson's Creek. Ordered to recruit in Missouri a number of boys joined him. He rode with Sydney Drake Jackman, was captured and sent to Alton Prison then exchanged at Vicksburg. He come back in the spring of 64 with a raging vengeance. Riding under Fletch Taylor he joined us for Genl. Price's Raid into Missouri.

William Thomas Wilson, called Bill by Missourians and Tom by those who met him due to the war, was one of the first and worst of the independent fighters. When the Border Wars were going on, if someone said bushwhacker they first thought of him. His daddy, Sol Wilson was a rich man, a slave owning man. They say he freed his slaves prior to the war mostly because he wanted his family to survive and remain neutral. When I first met Bill I was impressed by his stature, over 6 ft tall, a head full of jet black curly hair and bright blue eyes. He was a jokester, playing pranks on the young ones and women. Momma sat in a chair listening as our family and neighbors discussed joining the fight. Tom got behind her with a strand of winter grass, fox tail, tickling her neck. Thinking it was a fly or bug crawling she'd reach back and swat at it. Most everyone in the room saw what he was up to and finally, someone giggled. Mind you, my Momma could be a jokester. But there was nothing funny about Momma ever when it came to discussing war. She turned giving him one of those ice cold stares of hers and the room fell silent. Then she slapped her knees laughing, "You got me." The whole room relaxed joining in the laughter. Must say, I liked him from that moment on. Bill was a fine fiddler player. He could play a waltz or a hoe down. He was always in great demand for parties and weddings but he never took off his guns, two 44 caliber six shooters, no matter the occasion. Even in high society, they understood a man didn't remove his guns, whether preaching, teaching, weddings or funerals, it didn't happen. He was never wounded, not once. I had Uncle Wild Man Bill Thomason as my mentor and Bloody Bill, Jim, Jesse, me, we were all better than most, but all of us took hits.

Shortly after meeting in May 1861 we heard of Union horses taken by a guerilla gang, no one thought of Wilson. He rode alone. His neighbor Mary Arthur Case near the Little Piney in Phelps Co told him four uniformed Union men come looking for him. Knowing which trail they'd take back to their camp, Bill hid waiting until he saw them riding up. He urged his horse out onto the trail facing them, without hesitating he drew his guns killing all four. He rode over to Mrs. Mary's pulled her up behind him and rode back to the bodies so she could identify them. She assured him it was the same men who come looking for him. He took their valuables and rode away with four Union horses. A few days later the Jayhawkers looted his place burning the house, barn and outbuildings. His family had to move into a slave house on his Momma and Daddy's place. Tom, like most of us, went home when he could. When he got home and found everything burnt, it was then he began his fighting campaign with a vengeance.

I went home in July making sure Momma was okay. Federal troops were looting and stealing, killing animals and people. For every place or person they attacked, a dozen signed up for the South. When I returned to camp, talk was of attacking the garrison at Springfield. Genl. Price gathered us at Oak Hill on Wilson's Creek on Saturday, Aug 10th, 1861, about 10 miles outside Springfield. With Genl. Ben McCulloch and his Ark troops our numbers were over 13,000. By my own assessment I'd reckon that one out of every four of them had no arms, no shoes or blankets. Growing up we always knew we had a little more than other folks, "Blessed by the Lord", Daddy said. Even in those darkest days after Daddy died we never went without something to eat, clothes on our backs and food to eat. I was stunned at the number of men coming to fight with nothing but the clothes on their backs. It was summer and that might be fine now but it would turn cold before we knew it. I wondered if the 6,000 men under Union Genl. Nathaniel Lyon faired any better as Union. We heard they were getting a new kind of saddle Genl George B. McClellan had designed. All the boys were talking about it. Most of us who had horses had saddles, but not everyone. Some of the boys rode with blankets and bare back pads. Unc taught us how to ride bare back, with pads and with a saddle and to shoot from each. He'd said it was in us, not the animal. The South couldn't afford to issue arms to the boys, saddles were certainly lower on the list of needs. Summers in Missouri, July and Aug can be filled with drenching humidity that suffocates you but the nights are perfect for sleeping. I lay awake thinking. I didn't know what we could do except take it off the dead.

It was five o'clock in the morning when Union commanders Lyon and Sigel attacked. Coming on us from two sides cannonballs and shots tore through the air, ripping tents. We scrambled pulling ourselves together. The whoops and hollers turned to screams as we charged up the hill situated above our camp. This was the first real war action, first battle for most. This was no skirmish and no matter what Uncle Wild Man had taught us, Bloody Bill and I were scared. Genl. Lyon had secured most of his men on the ridge and we were easy pickin's. The hill was almost instantly slick with the blood of the wounded. Blood ran like fresh rain through the grass trickling downwards. We were slipping and sliding in it like water on Missouri's red clay. We saw the faces of boys like us. It was quickly kill or be killed. Us Missourians fought each other to hold our ground, our positions of Northerners or Southerners determined by where we went to church and where we lived. Patches on the hill thick with green briar and brush, ripped skin. There were attacks and counterattacks for hours. The other side of our camp faired better, wiping out Union troops to the south. We attacked three times that day without breaking the Union line.

Genl. Price ordered some of the boys with long rifles to take pot shots, sniping he called it. I'd grown up talking about snipe hunting. It was a game where we'd take our cousins who'd grown up in the city or younger cousins who just didn't know better, out into the fields at night, looking for snipe birds. We'd tell scary stories and all, but we never did find those snipes. I wondered if the word snipe might come from the shooter not easily being found. My thoughts were interrupted when one of the boys shot Genl. Lyon dead bringing on whoops and hollers heard above the screams as the Union army retreated.

Genl. Isaac Stand Watie

War Chief Joel Bryan Mayes

We were joined by other regiments including the Cherokee Brigade under Genl. McCulloch led by War Chief Joel Mayes. In Missouri, most of our contacts with Indians were those who spoke a little English. They came into the port towns to trade. Kansas City was a melting pot of emigrants and Indians with about any skin color you wanted. St. Louis, people called the gateway to the West was said to be the same, but I've never been there. I'd never met any Indians, but from time to time growing up, no matter where we'd be, I'd sit and watch the activities, the comings and goings of all the varied sort of people. Even in Greenville from the front porch of Uncle Will's store, there was an abundant variety of people.

Col.s John Hughes and Jo Shelby had their commands under Genl. Price. I felt like the fighting was slow costing more lives than need be. It was a hard fought battle. This wasn't how Unc had taught us to fight. Both the Union and us lost over 200 men killed, 800 wounded. One might say we suffered less because we had more men, but when it comes down to watching a man die, it doesn't matter if he's one of 10,000 or 100. He's one man and you're watching him die. Some boys ripped off their shirts shredding them into strips of cloth tying them around their own arms and legs others pushing them into the stomachs of the wounded, anything to stop the bleeding, to offer hope. I walked from man to man, saying the Lord's Prayer, at first I didn't stop at the Union men, but then, it didn't matter, they were boys mostly, like us, and they had given their lives.

"Our Father who art in heaven, hallowed be thy name. Thy kingdom come. Thy will be done on earth as it is in heaven. Give us this day our daily bread, and forgive us our trespasses, as we forgive those who trespass against us, and lead us not into temptation, but deliver us from evil. For thine is the kingdom, and the power, and the glory, forever and ever."

I hear myself saying it in my sleep, see myself holding that bloody hand, looking at a boy's face covered in dirt and blood, tears leaving a clean streak as they asked for their Momma's. I asked if they are alright with God, knowing they weren't long for this life. One of the boys asked me how it was I wasn't afraid. I told him I hadn't been hit. He looked at the blood all over me. I shook my head and said, "It's not mine." "Aren't you afraid of dying?" I looked about me, dead bodies of men and animals scattered across the field, groans of the wounded and dying, screams. I reached for his hand. "Are you alright with God?" He nodded his head yes. I couldn't admit I was scared, not really of dying but of being wounded. Of life being lived without a leg, or arm or half of my head, no wits about me. "My daddy was a preacher who went west to California and died alone in the mining camps. He told me before he left the Bible teaches us that every man is appointed a time to die and we know not when that is. If death comes in the night when we sleep or by the hand of our enemy, why fear what only God knows. I am thankful every day in everything I do. I talk to God all day long. I thank him for the beautiful day, for the clean water and clothes on my back. I thank him for the meal I am provided and the step I take without faltering. The Lord is by my side. Where two or more are gathered in his name, there I will be also. He is here with us." I could see the comfort my words gave to these men, boys who breathed their last breathes, others as they were loaded onto gurney's and wagons headed to the Presbyterian church at Mount Vernon which had been set up as a hospital for the severely injured.

This was one of those battles that strip's away all that was once innocent, jerking a boy straight into being a man. I thought about Daddy and his lessons on the 23rd Psalms of King David. "The Lord is my Shepherd; I shall not want." With the Lord as our guide through life, we should not want for anything. "He maketh me to lie down in green pastures: he leadeth me beside the still waters." The Shepherd watches over his sheep in the green pastures, and with his rod and his staff he guides them through the desert to find water. Sheep will not drink from running water so the shepherd must take his rod making a pool at the water's edge that is calm from which they will drink. "He restoreth my soul: he leadeth me in the paths of righteousness for his name's sake. Yea, though I walk through the valley of the shadow of death, I will fear no evil for thou art with me; they rod and thy staff they comfort me." I wished I could talk to Daddy, remember his words. I wanted to comfort those around me and myself.

I'd been a pall bearer, carrying the casket of the dead but I'd never had to dig a grave before, that was left for the elder men. There dead and dying all around on both sides. Genl. Price ordered mass graves dug. They couldn't lay there in the Aug heat. Each unit sorted through finding the ones we knew were from our homes. We loaded at least 3 wagons with dead, one headed to Clay Co. A rider went ahead to notify the community they were coming. Those whose faces we didn't know were confined to the mass graves dug in the Missouri hillside. The bodies of the Unionists, Genl. Price said to leave them. He knew they would be back retrieving those they could and burying those they couldn't. This wasn't what my imagination held when I thought of war. It was a scene no young man could ever imagine and once seen could forget. Sabers of the Union were so sharp they sliced arms completely off, severed legs and heads. The smell of men gutted was worse than the blood. I'd grown up killing hogs. I knew what a punctured gut smelled like. I'd seen some of the women turn green with the smell. This was worse. Blood was spattered across the living who checked themselves to make sure they weren't injured. This was hand to hand combat where you looked the other person in the face then rammed your gun into their belly and fired. You saw the change as they drew their last breath; life, gone in an instant. We had no time to react; no time to do the right thing, no time to wonder, more often than not, as soon as that person fell, another had stood before us just as eager to kill us, each of us afraid of not becoming the killer. Prayers were said and almost no looting occurred. But that would change as we changed. Some men feigned illness, others were really sick and other's fought wounded, sick and dying. There were all types of men and battles. The boys were silent in camp that night. Memory can be a monster with a will of its own. You think you have control of your memories, but really it has you.

Chapter 7

Early on the morning of Sept 2nd we fought the Battle of the Mules on Big Dry Wood Creek in Vernon Co. Jim Lane now a Union Col. in charge of the Kansas Cav Brigade had some 500 men. We knew they were in the area and sent men out to lure them to us. Face to face, we heavily outnumbered them, Jim Lane might be blood thirsty and a lunatic but he didn't want to be killed. They fled. We captured their mules and continued on our way to Lexington. While making our way another group under guerilla leader, Capt. James Cason joined us. I'd heard about his group of fighters. I watched them closely recognizing much of what Unc taught us in the way they rode, watching their surroundings, attention being paid to what was going on. They had ambushed Union Maj Hunter on the 17th at Boonslick Hills, near Lisbon.

We headed north towards Lexington. Those of us that could marched giving our horses to those who couldn't. It was imperative we take Lexington on the Missouri River back. We faced Col. James Mulligan with 3,000 soldiers. We numbered over 12,000. We didn't think Mulligan would fight but by the time we got there on Sept 13th, he had dug earthworks and fortifications with trenches along the hill providing a good view of the town. For over a week, we took aim at the Union on the hill. Southerners joined us from throughout the countryside. It became a show. Men and women sat at a distance and watched us fight. Other's brought food and supplies, tended to the wounded and sick. One old man brought his lunch and an old flintlock he might have used in the Mexican War. He would find himself a stand and all day he would blast away. Then as night fell he'd go home. We all took to waving at him and watching his back. We all wanted to be him, a fighter and survivor to the end. Genl. Price walked among the men talking to us, asking our take on the situation, especially the boys that knew the area. I thought about not being home for Jesse's 14th birthday. He was changing from a boy into a young man more slowly than I had. He still looked like a runt and acted like a little "Dingle berry."

On Sept 15th, 1861 arriving reinforcements needed to cross the Platte River to reach Genl. Price at Lexington. We knew the Union was heavily guarding all rail crossings and bridges after the destruction of the Platte River Bridge. Caught in a heavy fall rain storm movement toward Liberty where we planned to cross the river was difficult. The Union sent Lt. Col. John Scott to stop us from crossing, his men camped near Centerville, ten miles north on the 16th. Around two in the morning they broke camp reaching Liberty by seven. He sent out scouts to reconnoiter. Our boys engaged with the Union advance, around eleven o'clock. Scott, hearing the fire, marched his men toward it and Blue Mills Landing. Genl.

David Rice Atchison, a resident of Liberty and the same man who in 1856 had wanted to attack the abolitionists' at Lawrence was prepared with an ambush. Men were on each side of the river road hidden in the brush. They attacked scattering and killing most of the front line and gunners. The Union fell back to the bluffs and cliffs in Liberty.

Jesse Woodson James 1861, age 14
Emory Cantey Collection

It was well after sunset before they returned to retrieve their dead and wounded. One of our scouts reported Scott set up a hospital unit on the campus of William Jewell College and was burying their dead in the lawn of the campus. We lost about 70 from the Missouri State Guard, including Theodore Duncan who had been promoted from Capt. to Col. that very day, and Uncle Harry, Doc's older brother, Harrison Bond Samuel. At thirty four years old, he was one of the oldest of the troops.

We'd been with Genl. Price at Lexington since the 13th. The Federal's were well defended in their position. Press Webb advised Genl. Price to make a flank movement. We moved forward under heavy Union fire pushing the Union back into their inner works. James Welby's left arm was shattered with a minie ball. Dr. Meng found Welby but before he could tend to him, the Federalists were all over them. Meng hide Welby then drew the Feds after him. Genl. Stand Watie and his Cherokee Mounted Rifles were impressive to watch. I missed Unc. I wished I could write home and tell him of all the things he taught us and how it was him who gave us the skills to survive.

Someone made Press the softest of soft red shirts. Huett Preston "Press" had fine skin that didn't require much shaving. He wore his hair very neat, trimmed short. He had a pair of suspenders he wore instead of a belt, sometimes wearing them with no shirt when it was hot. He didn't have a hair on his chest. Genl. Price and Col. Shelby trusted him. He tried his best to order about the men getting the wounded picked up and carried to wagons. Soon others among us were aiding him. It's just what you did.

Matthias Splitlog was a rather famous steamboat man not simply because he had built and operated his own steamboat but because he was a Seneca Indian. Most everyone in these parts knew of Splitlog. He was carrying freight for George Nelson between Wyandotte and Atchison, Kansas on the Missouri River. During the battle, one of the Union men took command of his steamboat in an effort to get support to Mulligan. Genl. Price ordered Col. Rives to capture any Union boats and to keep the Union away from the river so it couldn't be used as a means of escape nor a supply source. On the 19^{th,} the pilot of Splitlog's steamboat, George Schreiner, lost an arm due during the bombard by Rives and his men. They captured the steamer and a number of Union soldiers. Schreiner and Splitlog were paroled and had to walk all the way back to Wyandotte.

Whether it was illness, wounds or the heart, there were times, going home was the only answer. I didn't consider myself a boy. I'd been man of the house since I was seven. However most of the troops were just boys. Any time we neared places someone was from, we made detours making camp nearby affording them the opportunity of going home which included a good night's sleep, visiting, clothes and food. There was an expectation they would return and most times they did. Sometimes, units of three or four would go along, getting a night's sleep in the barn, maybe a meal.

Union Col. Mulligan begged for reinforcements from Fremont but he sent none. Very early in the morning hours of the 20th Genl. Price set out an advance behind the breast works. Mulligan had use of an old building up on the hill. We were determined to burn it down. We could see a young boy in the light of the cannon fire running with a shovel inside throwing the cannonballs back out through the window. We were starting to get into real trouble and knew sooner or later, Union reinforcements would show up. I don't know whose idea it was. I'd like to lay claim to it, and it should have been my idea, the son of a hemp farmer, but it wasn't. The docks on the river port were full of bales of hemp ready to be shipped south. The idea was to dunk'em in the river soaking them so they wouldn't catch fire, then a wall of reinforcement was prepared. We started moving up the hill, rolling those bales as a solid line of cover. They were bullet proof. The hot lead shot couldn't penetrate nor set the wet bales on fire. The cannon balls only knocked them over. We got close enough we started getting better shots. Cut off, low on water and without reinforcements, they surrendered. We captured over 3500 men. The stuff of ropes won a victory for the Confederacy. Fremont was an arrogant man, word was circulating he had refused to obey orders of the President, even sending him a letter stating if there was an election today it would be he, who was elected, not Lincoln.

Learning Fremont was advancing Genl. Price withdrew. Heading south out of Lexington there was no choice but to leave me and a dozen others behind. Measles, chicken pox and mumps could kill and were highly contagious. It seemed all of us were sick with something, Jabez McCorkle and me were so sick we thought we were going to die. Jabez was Charity's brother, wife of Nathan Kerr, own cousins with Cole Younger. I'm not sure but I think I heard Jabez praying to die. We begged his brother John to go for a doctor. Finally, he saddled up one of the mules left behind and headed out; "Bring'em back at gunpoint if necessary," Jabez told him. It had been a week since Genl. Price had moved south. The day after John left the Union captured us. We were too sick to resist. We were required to take the oath of loyalty to the Union. Those of us who were sick and could make everyone else sick were told to go home, promising not to take up arms. It seemed a better option for the Union to kill us or let us go than hold us prisoners. I had given my horse over to the cause so I walked most of the way home stopping at farmhouses, hollering from a distance I had chicken pox but would appreciate a bite of something to eat.

Those true to the Southern Cause had developed a means of people knowing each other through better signs; some say those led to the signs used by railroad hobos. A round rock by the gate or front door meant that there were plenty of friends there. If there was a flat rock, it meant that they were without or enemies suspected them and best to go on. This led to snide talk of Union being flat heads because it brought out the flat rocks with a head on them. On the way home one old man come on out to the fence where we could talk. I ate some cold biscuits and honey while we talked. He told me two days after Lexington, Jim Lane of Kansas attacked the town of Osceola. He offered me some dried meat which I readily accepted for the walk home. I chewed it almost as slow as I walked. I was almost dead from exhaustion when I made it home but thankfully, my illness had passed. I was no longer contagious. My frame of 6 foot looked fragile and ghastly to Momma. She and Aunt Charlotte cooked and cared for me while Doc made sure I was healed up. Although Doc was a certified doctor, it was Momma and Aunt Charlotte who cooked up the salves, potions and lotions. They worked. One way or the other cause sick or not, you did your work, went to school and whatever else to not have to live through what they were gonna rub all over you or make you drink. Doc told me even if the Union had killed us, we could still have infected the men near us. They couldn't have buried us or burned our bodies without risking infecting their men. Their only choice had been to release us. I thought about that a lot. Thought about ideas of puffing out my cheeks and ways to feign the mumps or other contagions should I be caught again.

When caught and paroled we were supposed to go home and not take up arms, unless joining the Union. Every Missourian not joining the ranks of Union troops was guilty of being Southerner's and anti-Union. With Southern troops moved east, Missouri was left to the hands of the drunken Union officers, whose men were pillaging and destroying farms and property, stealing and plundering and raping women. What the Union didn't perpetrate, Jim Lane, Charles Jennison and James Montgomery along with their men did. Lane was every kind of sorry, rather than fight, he and his men followed behind Genl. Price and other leaders, punishing people who offered support. He was known as the leader of the Looting Brigade. Nothing was spared, including the homes and farms of men in the service of the Union. Lane avowed there was no loyal Missourian. Having ridden with him before the war, Quantrill, Bloody Bill and Jim knew Lane's tactics. Quantrill was making himself well known in Missouri aiding Missourians who had suffered at the hands of the Red Legs, Jennison and Lane. Charles Jennison urged President Lincoln to guard and protect the capitol and its building earning him favor with the north. Col. Shelby considered Jennison pond scum.

William Clarke Quantrill and Bloody Bill would become their own worst enemies. They brought out the best of their fighting tactics and the worst of what some called plain craziness, both mentored by Jim Lane. But nothing they would do could compare to what the men of Kansas were doing. Now duly authorized by the Union, the acts they committed were "acts of war". Word circulated the Union was taking no prisoners. Taking full advantage of President Lincoln's suspension of the writ the Union executed anyone they captured or considered "suspicious." Lincoln had given them the license to kill at random.

On Sunday at New Hope Church, we got the full account of Lane's attack on Osceola, a town of 2,000 people and the Co seat of St. Clair Co. Genl. Price headquartered there on more than one occasion. On Sept 22, 1861, Lane's looters found ammunition and guns in a warehouse. This was their excuse to destroy the town. Nine locals were accused, tried, court-martialed and shot. Lane and his looters burned businesses, homes and buildings including the courthouse. They confiscated teams and wagons, filling them with all the valuables and goods they'd looted including several kegs of whiskey which they drank during their rampage. People wanted to believe it was because they were drunk the women were violated and raped, but we knew better from people who suffered at their hands when no alcohol was involved. When they left, they took 200 blacks and 350 mules. On their way back to Kansas they burned homes, barns, outbuildings and crops along their path. Once back in Lawrence, they divided the loot among the three of them. They were stealing their wealth, which is what Bloody Bill's daddy intended for himself. I watched Col. Shelby's face as Bloody Bill explained the intent with great detail him. Col. Shelby was beginning to understand the length to which these men would go and now, they were authorized. But for now, Col. Shelby would have none of it from his men.

Jim Montgomery was the kind of man Daddy preached about, a man considering himself called by the Lord to strike down slavery believing himself righteous in his acts. Jennison was not only Montgomery's best friend but an equally demented religious maniac. Then there was Jim Lane and his band the Seventh Kansas Volunteer Cav, we called them Jennison's Jayhawkers. Later on we learned one of their first Maj forays had been to the home of another Union man Col. Henry Younger, Cole Younger's daddy. This changed the Younger family into fighting for the South. Two months before Jennison had been engaged as advance guard for Union Maj Van Horn near Harrisonville in Cass Co. They arrived first to assess the situation military style but instead went to looting and burning, robbing the stores and banks. By the time Maj Van Horn arrived, Jennison and his men had packed most of the items into wagons. Col. Younger, a wealthy farmer, raised stock and ran a livery in the town. He lost 40 horses and $4,000 in wagons and carriages during their raid. Jennison and Lane were nothing more than looters, robbers and thieves commissioned by the Union.

Given Horn come from to enlist. He told us they found men who had formed a secret peace society, men like Pappy Samuel, objectors to the war but these men really Unionists, were raiding and looting in the name of "peace." Ark Gov. Henry Massie Rector ordered Col. Samuel Leslie to go north into the Boston Mountains to round them up. A lawyer, Gov. Rector had seen a lot of men sentenced to prison for their misdeeds. He had taken it upon himself to get these murderers, thieves and ner do well's released in exchange for fighting for the south. One of the murderers was Bill Dark. Horn reckoned he was just the kind they wanted to round up the Union, had no scruples. Rector had been the lawyer for Dark who had been sentenced to five years in prison. Rector got him out giving him the rank of Capt. He put together his band, choosing his own Lt.'s. He sent Dark over to meet with Col John Jacob Kemp at Sylamore, a port on the White River. Pronounced SealAMor after the Isyllamo tribe of Creek Indians. His instructions were to round up dissenters, loyalists and Federalists.

West of Sylamore, in Searcy Co, Col. Leslie rooted out and arrested about 100 men, 87 were chained and marched to Little Rock. The Searcy Co investigation under Col. Leslie produced the list Given brought north to the commanders. If found north enlisted with the Union they were to be shot. Their leader was Christopher Denton. One of the names, Benjamin Franklin Brantley and his son Frank, caught my eye. I wondered if they were of any kin to Brantley York Bond, son of our neighbors John and Hannah York Bond. Most southerners took to naming their children with their momma's maiden names or grandparents, so I figured they might be kin, but Brantley had joined the Missouri State Guards with us. He was no Northerner. Given said Benjamin Brantley was one of the most notorious of the jayhawkers in the foothills of the Ozarks along the White River. While Christopher Denton's men ran the area from Burrowsville to Meadowcreek, Ben Brantley ran the area above Sylamore and was determined to find and destroy the Confederate powder works. Sylamore lay about 25 miles across the hills from Leslie and Burrowsville in Searcy Co. He was married to Elizabeth Hicks, daughter of Cherokee Chief George Augustus Hicks and wife Lucy Brown Fields. Chief Hicks led a group of the Cherokee being forced from their homelands through Dwight Mission and Fort Smith. One of his wives was Mary Arkansas "Arky" Ulusquatogu Rogers, daughter of Chief John Hellfire Rogers and Elizabeth Emory. Chief James Emory, a great nephew of Arky, would be sent by Genl. Sam Houston, husband of her sister, Tiana Rogers Houston, to aid the Confederacy in the White River Valley. The Cherokee just like Missourians were split over north and south.

At Sylamore Col. Kemp rooted out about the same number but Brantley wasn't among them. These men were not marched off as prisoners of war, instead, those not immediately joining the South were shot. They hung one fella because he begged not to be shot. I wondered if he thought they might not kill him or if he just preferred hanging. They held their investigations and trials at the home of Judge Henry Hill Harris who Gov. Rector appointed for that purpose. Given Horn was ordered to go north into Missouri to find supporters there. Learning where Genl. Price was said to be, he found us. The men arrested under Col. Leslie were marched to Little Rock to be shot or hung if they didn't enlist. He reckoned they all enlisted in Col. John Marmaduke's Ark Infantry. Given carried copies of the list for the commanders because Col. Marmaduke said he figured when these boys had served their time, those surviving would not simply head home to the mountains, they would head north to Missouri to enlist with the Union.

These men who called themselves a peace society were anything but neutral. Called Mountain Boomers according to Given Horn, they were as guilty as the jayhawkers of looting and stealing. They were to be shot without question if found in Missouri.

Missouri Gov. Claiborne convened in Neosho with members of the legislature passing an Ordinance of Secession signed Oct 31. Missouri was officially admitted as the 12th Confederate State on Nov 28, 1861 but the Unionists controlling the state refused to recognize the secession. On Dec 22, 1861, the Union issued Genl. Order Number 32 giving the right to Union troops and supporters to kill 'anyone suspected of Southern sympathies, aiding or riding with Southerners'. They had the right of the law on their side to kill anyone they wanted. Even if he wanted to, which he didn't, Genl. Price couldn't have stopped what the Union set in motion. Southern response would be of like kind.

News of Turner Ashby crucifying Union captives spread quickly among the ranks. Ashby was operating under Col. Thomas J. "Stonewall" Jackson, our cousin Wirt Woodson's half brother. Shortly after learning of Order Number 32, Ashby captured four Union soldiers which he and his men proceeded to strip down to complete nakedness. Then they nailed one of the men to a tree crucifying him alive with the other prisoners watching. They were killed one by one and finally the last man was killed with a saber to his side, stretched out on the ground in the stance of the crucifix. Ashby was acting out his personal anger and vengeance. Shortly after war was declared, he and his brother Richard joined the 7th Virginia Cav. They were men of substance with mighty horses cutting a dashing figure. Ashby considered the Black Knight of the Confederacy was said to be one of the finest horsemen in the South, astute and accurate in battle. A few months earlier in June 1861 he and his brother Richard were engaging Union in the Shenandoah Valley of Virginia when Richard was hit with a saber taking off half his head and a portion of his face. Knocked from his saddle his Union attacker ran upon him plunging his saber into his side, and then stole his boots, horse and other personals while Richard anguished upon the ground still alive. Ashby found his brother with blood gurgling from his mouth begging for water. He languished with exposed brains and an eye hanging from its socket for nearly a week with his brother by his side.

War changes people, young boys laughing, fishing, heading off for schooling, working on their farms, singing in church, were jerked into a new state of being coming face to face with death, kill or be killed. Ashby became a man on a mission, hating the Union with a passion, his methods were known throughout the Virginia's if not the entire Confederacy. He was a killer, unorthodox and effective. I thought of Robert Roger's independent fighters, Queen's Rangers, during the Great War of Revolt

Momma and Mister Bird Smith Price told us about. They learned the skills of the woodsmen and lived off the land. They were used to keep the colonists' distracted and acted as spies, much as Col. Shelby and Genl. Price used the irregulars and Partisan Rangers. I thought of Abe Ruddell, captured as a child in 1780, living 20 years with the Indians, then in the War of 1812, acting as a British scout and spy.

Stonewall Jackson might not approve of the atrocities committed by Turner Ashby but he understood the necessity. Col. Jackson had lost his home at Clarksburg, Jackson's Mill. His roots ripped from the earth beneath him when the northern part of the state decided to remain with the Union. Losing the war would mean he could never go home. Like it or not, the independent fighting units, guerillas and partisans were made up of men who had come face to face with the atrocities of the Union and were critical to the southern war effort. There was a sense of independence among the irregulars who operated within limits they set for themselves. The result was no leader really had control, always subject to jockeying within the ranks, men breaking off forming their own irregular command.

Andrew Jackson Grigsby, Commander of Stonewall's Brigade
Cousin of James Grigsby husband of Margaret Houston
Grigsby's Ferry, Independence Co

Surviving the winter was hard on the Ark boys. The weather was a little warmer, less harsh down there, so Genl. Price sent most of'em home. While men were enlisting on one side or the other for 30 days, maybe 90, the war was turning out to be much longer and brutal than anyone expected. Seems both sides thought it would be done and over quickly with few actual engagements. No one expected it to last into the winter and no one was prepared for wintering the troops. Fatigue and hunger was rampant. And to make matters worse, Jayhawkers and Red Legs were pillaging and plundering farms and homes, molesting women and girls and killing young boys and old men at home. Momma got word through Uncle Till having received a letter from cousin Wirt, of news from his half brother Thomas "Stonewall" Jackson. Seems some of his men finished their year of service and laid down their arms, threatening mutiny if not discharged. Col. Andrew Jackson Grigsby, Commander of Stonewall's Brigade come to him telling him of the men's actions. His anger directed at Col. Grigsby for bringing the news to him prompted an authoritative response to kill them all if they did not pick up their arms. "Given a choice, they responded by returning to camp for further service," Stonewall wrote Wirt, reporting there had been no additional cause of concern over mutiny within the ranks.

News at church was always full of what the boys were doing. Nothing had changed since New Hope Church had been firmly planted on the side of the South. If a new face showed up we'd be a little quieter until we made heads or tails about them. The need for clandestine warfare was growing as neighbors turned in neighbors. Almost everyone was carrying an oath of allegiance to the Union. Knowing who your friends were could mean life or death. True in the war it would remain so throughout our lives. Daddy had instilled in everyone at New Hope, "We fight because we believe." Tonight, my thoughts are of the Christians who slaughtered people in the olden days, the Mormons and us. We all believe God is with us, on our side. Men among us said their prayers daily, some more, talking with God throughout the day. Thinking of Daddy, I twisted my button in my pocket. I missed him and so wished he was here to talk to.

Chapter 8

Friday last, Quantrill met up with Lt. Haller and his men at the home of one of the irregulars, Tom Flannery's daddy, John not too far from us. Union Capt. Albert Peabody from Kansas, Co D First Missouri Cav cornered them at Flannery's house. In an effort to drive them out, they set the house on fire with everyone inside. Some of the boys had melted enough ice and snow to take a bath. Cole Younger told everyone to get wet, dunk themselves in the water. I can see it, fully clothed men jumping and splashing water all over themselves before running through the burning house escaping the flames. It was as exciting a story as any the old Bard himself might have put to paper. As stories of Quantrill and his men, and the other bands filtered through the area, the loins of young men like me wanted to be part of it, more than a foot soldier that had to eat his own horse to keep from starving, feeding the starving men around him. Frank Gregg, six years younger than his older brother Bill, was my age, and had joined the Missouri State Guard under Genl. Price. Momma listened to us talking shushing us to keep quiet around Jesse. Frank heard Sol Basham captured at a ball given at Riley Alley was sent to Rock Island Prison.

William Clarke Quantrill

William "Bill" Gregg

Missouri Valley Special Collections, Kansas City Public Library, Kansas City, Missouri

During 1861 even though most folks had never met William Clarke Quantrill, they heard the stories and took to calling him "old Bill", felt he was a brother, of kin somehow. More and more men were looking to him and other guerillas and irregulars for leadership. Most everyone had not only heard the story how Bill Quantrill was to attack the farm of James Morgan Walker in Dec of 1860 but knew with each telling the story got bigger. Most of us never really knew until after the war, until after Quantrill was killed he had himself raided Missouri before the war broke out. Bloody Bill knew him and that he had been a Kansas jayhawker riding with the abolitionists. Some of the boys never believed anything but what Quantrill told them. He told a tale of how he and his brother were attacked by Montgomery's raiders and his brother killed. He joined them as a ruse waiting until he had the opportunity to avenge his death. He told this to assuage the doubts of the boys who'd heard he was a jayhawker. I reckon him and his brother Thomas did ride with Jennison, but when his brother showed up in '63, Quantrill acted like it was a different brother killed. Thomas went along and the boys were no wiser. Then when war broke out, Joe Vaughn and Quantrill rode with Stand Watie's Cherokee before joining Genl. Price. Quantrill fought at Wilson's Creek under Capt. Stewart's Cav riding with the Cherokee before forming his band of men.

At church on Sunday Jan 5th, 1862 we heard John L Brown, son of abolitionist John Brown had joined Quantrill. People said it was a set up but turned out he didn't abide by his daddy's beliefs.

On Jan 16, Si Gordon's band of men was sworn in at Springfield as the 9th Co of Col. Gates Regiment Brigade of the Missouri Volunteers. The Union was hearing more and more about the independent leaders growing in strength and the Confederacy commissioning them. They had heard about Si but couldn't locate him. I didn't know what land north looked like, expected it looked a lot like the plains of Kansas and Nebraska as those Northern boys were all but lost in the greenbriers and creek bottoms. When they'd run upon a cliff on horseback they tended to get a little spooked. Si and his boys were good at running the hills of Missouri on those Fox Trotters. Those horses could do anything. When the Union did get what they thought was reliable information they sent forces to the camp on Silver Creek about 14 miles north and west of Fayette. They took the boys by surprise killing, wounding and capturing most, destroying the camp. Made no difference, the boys just found a new place, in fact, several of them. Camps and safe houses, farms where shelter and rest were provided were never more than 10 miles distant. It was necessary to never use the same place twice close together, space it out, especially when being pursued.

On Jan 27th, 1862 in the Sni a Bar Township in Jackson Co at Noah McAlexander's house, William Gregg and Harrison Trow, riding under Andy Walker were attacked by more than a dozen of Jennison's Jayhawker's. Crockett Ralston, John Frisby and John Barnhill were in the house with them but had no guns. Trying to escape Ralston and Frisby were captured and shot on site. Gregg and Haller escaped. They had been trying to recruit the boys. John Barnhill figured he was safer to join up with two guys who could out shoot a dozen.

Bill Gregg's sister Mary was married to Samuel Ralston a brother of Crockett's. Bill had to take Crockett home to be buried. When he came by the house, Momma wasn't happy about Bill riding by himself. She sent me with him to take Crockett's body home. We headed to his sister Mary's house thinking it might be easier to tell Samuel the news first. Losing someone this way could turn a person, most wanted revenge but some grew weak, afraid to fight, afraid of losing some other loved one. When we got to Mary's house, she was the first to see Crockett slung across the horse. "Tell me, please, he's not dead," she said. Bill didn't say a word, just shook his head "No." Samuel came from around the side of the barn. Not sure who was approaching he'd taken cover not only for his safety but to protect his family. He laid his head on his brother never shedding a tear. We took Crockett from the horse, laid him on the bed covering him with sheeting. Annie Ralston, a cousin of Samuel and Crockett was there, she immediately attended to Mary and Samuel's young children, Willie, Albert and little Mary. We had our supper in almost complete silence then retired for the night. I lay thinking about the day trying to fall asleep. I thought about Annie, a beautiful young girl, barely 10 year old, reading to her young cousins earlier, taking charge. I was twice her age but drawn to her. I missed my momma and sister's when I'd be away from home. I knew they worried after me. Annie's eyes had been wet with tears when she saw Crockett, but she hadn't broken down. At ten years old, the war had already changed her. I fell asleep thinking about Momma and my own family. The next morning Samuel said he would take Crockett home for burial.

As we rode, walking our horses, Bill filled my head with exciting stories daring and successful. Momma's everywhere both admired and feared the talk while us boys becoming young men, anxiously awaited another chapter. Bill and I rode together most of the way, then I headed back to Momma's and he rode toward the new camp at Walker's farm. Bill had given me a taste of guerilla life. I'd repeat the stories over and over to friends and family alike, each time getting bolder in how I'd tell them. Just as I had hung on as Bill spoke, Jesse hung on my every word.

Directions were given not by the names of roads, but by markers. The big "Black Oak" hit by lightening, or "Blue Cut" the big dip in the Independence to Harrisonville Road where you see the stars or "Lone Jack" from the big oak that stood alone out in a field more than 100 yards away from the nearest scrub. Then there's cross the creek two times, look for the jutting rock, watch for the grove of pine, or little rock which could really mean the big rock and whatever else became our landmarks, our road signs. We used old Indian traces and animal routes through the undergrowth. We followed hog trails and deer runs. Those boys, men, soldiers from the North East, they were settled. They had towns, townships, roads and highways all with names of prominent people and landmarks but rarely did they know how to get from place to place following the stars and descriptions. They had forgotten how the Great War of Revolt had been won. This would serve us bushwhackers, us boys fighting for the south. Everyday, I was more and more thankful for Unc.

As stories came in, it was clear the Border Wars had served as a training ground for Union killers. A group of 30 Jayhawkers and soldiers stopped by Amos Blythes house while he was away fighting. His son tried to tell them he wasn't at home but they weren't gonna have that. They drug him out to the barn intent on hanging him. Blythe's old slave man found Cole Younger and told him what was happening. The boy wiggled free escaping as they tried to get the barn doors open. He ran to the house and got an old pistol. Running toward a wooded area, they shot him in the back. He got off two shots, killing two of the soldiers. When Cole and the boys got to the Blythe home, they found the boy had been shot in the back seventeen times. They hadn't just shot him, they massacred him. With the battle cry, "Remember Young Blythe," Cole and the boys with him prepared an ambush for the men responsible. Retribution was swift and deadly, they killed half of the 40 men. Amos was a cousin to Andy Blythe. Neighbors in Ark, Andy was friends with Given Horn.

Stories were repeated at night. No one really wanted to talk about the truth of what was happening. Andy Blythe told us a story from the War of 1812. Shawnee Chief John Lewis and his wife Mary Succopanous moved out of the Ohio River Valley into Missouri with 4,000 of his tribe after Andrew Jackson destroyed Lewis's village, Lewistown, Ohio. They made their way through the Missouri Cape moving south, settling between the confluence of the Buffalo and White Rivers in Ark in 1815. They had upper, middle and lower villages making Shawneetown, now Yellville, in Marion Co. Andy was full of tales of the exciting times growing up in the river valley and mountains. Most of the Indians' hadn't left when the reservation ended in 1828. They married with whites and stayed.

He told us a story of the Wood family. A story he said every child was told growing up. President Andrew Jackson might of have been a hero to many but to the people of Shawneetown, who had lost their homelands in Ohio because of him, to the Indians who had been forced from their lands east of the Mississippi to Indian Territory west of Ark and to Revolutionary Bill Wood who had fought in the War of 1812, Andrew Jackson was evil incarnate. When the War of 1812 broke out Revolutionary Bill enlisted in Tennessee along with two of his sons, young John and Big Bill. Andrew Jackson was their commander. He was having trouble keeping his men in line, especially the recruits fresh from the country. Andy laughed at that point. We all nodded knowing he was talking about the squabbles so frequent in the camps.

The younger son, John, 16, was on picket duty and left his post. Since Jackson had been having trouble controlling the men he told them there would be no more reprieves. John was court marital and sentenced to be shot. He was the first to come up after Jackson's order of no more reprieves. He was recommended for mercy, but Jackson wouldn't give. John's brother Big Bill and his daddy stayed with him. When the soldiers came to get young John they said their goodbyes. They left refusing to see him shot. They deserted the army and left Tennessee making their way to the Ozarks. They first settled on the south banks of the White River across from Mount Olive near where our Uncle J.R. and Aunt Lucy Poor Mims lived. No one ever came after them. Revolutionary Bill could never talk of it without tears and any mention of Andrew Jackson brought forth swearing and oaths. The Old Man Revolutionary Bill died in 1845 in the newly named town of Yellville. I hung on Andy's every word. There were always two sides, sometimes more, to every story.

I thought about our teacher, Mister Bird. He had family that fought on both sides in the Revolutionary War and in the War of 1812. He told us what his grandpa told him about those wars. It didn't seem much had changed. People loyal to Great Britain escaped to Canada. Colonists remaining loyal to the crown were called Tories. The nation was torn and it was the first War Between the States for white people who settled here. People burned each other out, looted, plundered and did horrible things to those who differed from them. Women were terrified and violated at will by the soldiers, unable to seek intervention, assistance or retribution. Great Britain offered 200 acres of land to people who could make their way from the colonies to Canada. One side of Mister Bird's family had gone to Canada and hadn't come back until the War of 1812 when they again fought on the side of the British. After the war, they made their home up north on the lakes before finally making their way south. He told us, the other side of his family may have been the very people who burned them out. This war was not the first war for people here, not even the first war since becoming a new nation, free from Great Britain.

Momma told us her Grandpa Dick Cole fought in the War of 1812. He answered the call to defend the southern seas at New Orleans. His Daddy, Richard Cole, Sr. fought in the Great War of Revolt. When we learned about these from our teacher, Momma corrected some of what he learned us. Daddy's grandfather William James had been a young man when the Great War of Revolt broke out and his son, Daddy's daddy, John Martin James, had been called to preach and served as a chaplain for the army. He said words over many a dying and dead man. The War of 1812 ended in 1815. Momma said, her daddy recalled watching his daddy leave in 1814. "He was only 9 years old. Many a boy went with their daddy's. It was their job to get the news back home if their father's didn't survive. Both sides did this and so you didn't kill the children." Momma and Mister Bird were right, things weren't much different now. I'd seen father's with young sons, uncles and brothers joining up together increasing their chances of someone surviving, returning home to tell their story.

Si Gordon and his boys were successful enough in their guerilla tactics the Union went after him with a vengeance. A month earlier on Dec 16th, trying to catch Si, the Union burned Platte City, Missouri to the ground. One of the boys with Si recognized his neighbor old man Jacob Cogdill among the Union. He thought he might try to talk to him, but Si threatened him explaining he would get the wrong end of the gun one way or the other if he talked to Cogdill. Platte City was only about 20 miles from where the Cogdill's moved, closer to St. Joseph in Buchanan Co. It was Si and his boys that had planned and carried out the destruction of the Platte Bridge on Sept 3 and Cogdill knew it. Si hadn't anticipated the crash of the Hannibal & St. Joe Railroad which killed nearly 20 civilians injuring five times that number. The railroad was a critical communication and supply line for the Union. It was the first railroad to completely cross the state of Missouri. Union Col. Ulysses S. Grant served with the Army of Engineers and was in charge of guarding the train. Si and his boys burned the support timbers of the bridge leaving the top of the bridge looking as if everything was fine. When the train started to cross the bridge, the supports gave way flipping the train. At midnight the entire train including two passenger cars loaded with men, women and children, plunged thirty feet into the river below. Folks hearing the crash came out of their houses to aid the passengers. Bodies of the dead and injured were taken to the Patee House, a hotel near the St. Joseph depot. The Union was immediately ordered to hunt down and kill any person involved, directly Si Gordon. The newspapers blamed it on Genl. Price. He supported guerilla warfare in Missouri and wrote to Union Commander Genl. Henry Halleck protesting the sabotage was both lawful and proper and within the rules of war. The bridge was a military target and there had been soldiers on it bound for Fort Leavenworth, Kansas. Therefore, any man captured should be treated as a prisoner of war. Halleck used the rhetoric that would define irregulars the remainder of the war; "spies, marauders, robbers, incendiaries, guerrilla bands...in the garb of peaceful citizens." In Nov, the Union troops caught up with Si at Bee Creek. He and his boys killed two Feds before running out of ammunition forcing them into retreat.

Early Dec, Si was camped on the lawn of the Platte Co Courthouse in Platte City. The Union issued an order for Platte City to deliver Gordon or the city would be burned. A native of Platte City, Si Gordon would never be turned over to the Union. Si aided the locals in securing the Co records from the courthouse and hiding them. Union Col. James Morgan of the 18th Missouri Infantry was ordered to march the thirty miles from St. Joseph to Platte City and there set fire to the city and courthouse. He captured three Confederate soldiers who were at home, Black Triplett, George Case and William Kuykendall. On Tuesday, Dec 17th, 1861, Col. Morgan ignored the pleas of Bill Triplett to speak to his son, 13 year old Black Triplett. Morgan took Black and another boy, 14 year old Case to Bee Creek where the Federal soldiers had been killed. He shot and killed Black in front of his daddy. Col. Morgan himself was said to have scrawled the letters "U.S." on the Bee Creek Bridge using young Black's blood. George Case had his arms tied behind his back. He ran. Jumping from the bridge, he got stuck in the loose mud. The Union soldiers caught him and bayoneted him to death. Union soldiers held his father refusing to let him go to his son. People gathered protesting, saving William Kuykendall.

Polly Levisay and her sister Cecilia, daughters of George "Jerry" Levisay and Peggy Hackler of Green Township, northwest of Miller, north of Mount Vernon, was arrested for aiding the South. Polly was married to one of our boys, Squire Callaway. Polly and Cecilia had gathered what produce they could from the farm and were headed into town with their horse and hack to trade for staples when they were stopped and questioned by Unionists. Their horse and hack were taken and Polly and her 17 year old sister Cecilia jailed. The Union stole whatever they desired or needed, making up accusations sufficient to secure their end. Although they brokered deals, they paid for little, jailing those they weren't certain were loyal to the Union justifying their actions providing them with what they needed to subsist on.

We heard Genl. Thomas J. "Stonewall" Jackson had been promoted to Brigadier Genl. and was advocating the 'black flag' policy. I didn't know with certainty what that meant but I didn't have to wait long before one of the other fella's ask its meaning. The black flag was opposite of the white flag of safe surrender. Supporting the black flag meant Jackson was promoting the idea of neither giving nor accepting quarter, prisoners were to be killed. He had gained the name Stonewall because he had kept fighting at Bull Run in July, winning what seemed an impossible battle.

We sat around in the heavy Missouri winter telling stories, reliving what had happened. Several of the boys at home were getting cabin fever. It had been a really hard winter coming on top of the fall drought. Word came help was needed on the Missouri Ark border below Springfield. I was fully recovered from the chicken pox and had put some meat on my bones, due to Momma and Aunt Charlotte constantly feeding me. I headed out alone. Within a few miles, Alvis Dagley joined me and then a few more until six of us were riding together. Alvis Dagley's family had been threatened but hadn't been burned out. "Yet," he said. We arrived at the Yocum place learning of several more boys having left the day before headed to Northwest Ark. In Taney Co, we saw a regiment of Union camped on the White River. We stopped, broke off a cedar limb tying pieces to our horses tails dragging behind covering our path. We led them away until we were safe enough to toss the limb, mount and ride on. We later learned we had seen the advance guard of Maj Samuel Curtis' troops.

We caught up with Genl. Price's rear guard. Most of the boys not seriously wounded were back. We were riding with the First Missouri Cav under James Little when we were joined by about 100 young men and boys from the surrounding area. Maj Samuel Curtis was after them. We told them about seeing a group of men earlier, bedraggled and exhausted near the White River. We camped only 4 hours that night on a ridge overlooking a beautiful vista. There was no time to rest, eat, or sleep, Curtis, taking leadership decisions from Stonewall Jackson, was forcing his men to march without rest. The Union commanders were becoming exasperated at Curtis, ordered to eliminate 'the nuisance' and having little to no success.

On Feb 16th, 1862 coming down Telegraph Road into Ark, at Potts Hill on Big Sugar Creek, Curtis advance guard caught up with us. Familiar once again in the greenbriers and undergrowth we knew how to use it to our advantage. We continued retreating south coming upon a detachment of Capt. Churchill Clark's Missouri Battery. The Capt. wanted to stand our ground having the advantage on top of the ridge. Ellis and the Union's First Missouri Cav charged along the mountainside coming out from the west of Cross Timber Hollow, they caught us in the Big Sugar Creek valley. We were at once engaged in hand to hand and horse to horse combat with double barreled shot guns firing all around us. I was thankful Unc and Gramps Bob had insisted us boys learn to shoot pistols and that we carry at least two. Those on horses could maneuver better than the ones on foot but in doing so, we left our artillery men surrounded. Word reached Little as to what was happening to us on the rear guard. He ordered a counter attack but his men were more exhausted and offered little help. Everyone was ordered to fall back to Big Sugar Creek. The Union was as exhausted, hungry and freezing as we were. The fighting lasted less than an hour with the worst of it only 20 minutes. We fell back into the undergrowth around Big Sugar Creek and the Union men, just stopped, watching us. Exhausted, they moved back north over the Missouri line and made camp. Everyone was alert on both sides knowing either could attack, exhaustion kept everyone in camp. We moved south before daybreak.

Feb 22 was a nasty winter day. For those of us growing up in Missouri and North Ark this wasn't anything new. We grew up knowing the weather could change in a day's time. Col. Shelby and us boys saw the beauty in the low fog hanging over everything. The roads were covered with freezing mud and ice. Walking or riding in this muck was nigh on impossible, this didn't deter Quantrill from fighting. He was in Independence when several of the Federal troops camped outside of town rode in to get bread for their meal at Uhlinger's Bakery. It was there in front of the bakery where they ran into each other and the shooting started. Even with several wounded they managed to capture ammunition and kill a number of the Union militia. Quantrill never ask any of the boys to do anything he wasn't willing to do. He would ride in first just as he quick as he would leave in the rear guard. Men from the Union camp run to town when they heard gunfire and their numbers forced the boys retreat. Quantrill made it safe to the woods. Retreating along Spring Branch Rd they were attacked by Genl. Abner Doubleday and 15 men with the Ohio Cav. Hop Wood was killed shot dead in his saddle. George Shepherd said he grabbed the reins of his horse but Hop fell dead on the road.

Men were coming into our camp on Big Sugar Creek cold and hungry. Several of the boys were cooking up some provisions while others gathered around open fires. They were anxiously repeating their tales of the day and stories of the successes and defeats. Bill Gregg leaned close to me and said, "Look here at this." He showed me his arm which had several cuts on it. He said, "I drew my gun on this Federal and when I pulled the trigger, it snapped. He drew his saber as I pulled again and it snapped again. I knew it couldn't happen again but just as he hit my arm, I pulled the trigger again. Seconds passed but it seemed like hours, my revolver snapped again and he cut me. As he drew back for what I know would have severed my head from my body, I pulled the trigger and this time, it fired. He fell from his horse dead upon the ground." All of us listening to the more experienced of our leaders, especially Gregg, were at once encouraged, enraged and excited by their stories. When we broke camp, those of us with Shelby made our way back to Cove Creek setting up camp at Devil's Den in Ark. Word came in on Feb 14, at Crane Creek, during the Pea Ridge Campaign, Col. Thomas Roe Freeman was among those captured along with twenty-nine of his men by Maj William D. Bowen's Missouri Cav Battalion. The loss of Col. Freeman left many of his men riding with us uncertain of what they were to do. Shelby received orders from Price to put Capt.'s William Osby "Os" Dillard, Huddleston and William "Bill" Chitwood in charge and send them back to Ark. Lt. Col. Joseph B. Love was dispatched with men to Rolling Prairie. Dex Webb was discharged from service at Cove Creek. He had ridden to enlist with Shelby in Dec and served his three months. He informed us he was going to go ride with Quantrill. Bill Gregg gave him directions and passwords.

During late Feb and March, 1862, the Union troops were intent on driving Genl. Price out of Missouri. It was then the real bushwhacking began full on, the guerilla war. War isn't pretty "to the victors go the spoils" has been true since the days of the House of Caesar and before. News spread fast when boys were caught and taken to prison camps. Such was the case with Col. Freeman's capture. It was over three months before he swore "the Oath of Loyalty" to the Union and another 30 days before he was paroled on June 18, 1862. He returned and went right back to work for the Confederacy. This time with most of his efforts solely dedicated to the protection of the ammunition efforts in southern Missouri and north Ark. I had returned to fight just in time to go to Pea Ridge, Ark.

We had been hearing rumblings from Ark. all winter long. Of course, to me, the most important area was where family was along the middle White River around Batesville and in the hills of North West Ark. Uncle Till's Aunt Settie lived near Van Buren, south of Fayetteville. Grand Aunt Lucy lived upriver from Sylamore at Athens. It was there in Nov 1861 the first significant military action in the White River Valley occurred when the Izard Co Investigative Committee arrested, detained, shot and forced enlistment of members of the Mill Creek Peace Society. Another group Given Horn told us about, a group of rough shod locals who were mostly vigilantes and Mountain Boomers, east of the White River. In order to be ready to put down a possible insurrection, the Ark State Militia under Col. John Jacob Kemp remained near Kickapoo Bottoms from Dec 1861 through Feb 1862. According to Judge Henry Hill Harris, his slaves, and several of the Lancaster's, Hinkle's, Dillard's and Beckham's were hiding in the hills around Sylamore waiting for the Feds. William Hill Dillard was a known slave trader and a number of his slaves were among those hiding. Groups of local men, loyal to the Confederacy had rooted out a group of the Peace Society Mountain Boomers near Big Flats; they had been taken to Col. Leslie at Burrowsville. The weaker of the men disclosed of a group of the boomers meeting in secret at the farm of Henry Bradshaw near Campbell Valley. Col. Leslie himself led the attack on the farm, securing and capturing all of the men. They were brought to Burrowsville where they were held with other captives at the courthouse, a wooden log structure with only two armed guards. Col. Leslie called a local meeting forming the 45th Reg Ark Militia for the purpose of escorting prisoners to Little Rock.

Report of Albert W. Bishop, Lt. Col.: "The seventy-seven were chained together two and two, with an ordinary log chain fastened about the neck of each, and for twenty-four hours prior to their departure from Burroughville were thus guarded, in two ranks, as it were, with a long chain running down the centre of the column." Realizing movement would be impeded walking in such a manner, the men were "fastened together by twos only, the odd man bringing up the rear with a chain encircling his neck and thrown over a shoulder, that his walking might not be impeded."

The walk would take six days and the men knew, they would be required to enlist or face death, by execution, hanging or firing squad. The men of the 45th Regiment escorting the prisoners would become part of Genl. Marmaduke's army upon return to Burrowsville in Dec.

Home of Judge Henry Hill Harris and Lucy Dillard junction of 5, 9 & 14, survived.

Richard Carol Gravelly, one of Judge Henry Hill Harris' most trusted slaves, was said to be the leader of the escaped slaves. He later joined the Union at Batesville and the first colored troops of Ark. He had been born in 1834 at Riggsville, the son of his white owner, Thomas Augustus Riggs and Carolina Gravelly, a slave. His momma had belonged to the Gravelly family of Pickens, Alabama. Riggs bought her before making the move to Mississippi with his family, then brought her and two male slaves west with him to help establish what would become Riggsville. When Richard was four years old, Missus Riggs was moving to Riggsville with the children. Richard was sold to William Hill Dillard. He lived and worked with the Dillard's on Round Bottom until Mister Will's sister, Lucy married Henry Hill Harris. Richard was a wedding gift to Miss Lucy.

Batesville fell to the Union on May 4th, 1862. Col. Kemp headquartered at Riggsville had been put in charge of securing munitions for Ark' troops. Munitions were being made from the saltpeter and bat guano found in the numerous caves throughout the region. One of the primary locations for the state lay in the heavily forested and protected area above Sylamore. The location took on the name Gunner Pool. With the port of Sylamore nearby, protecting these efforts for the Confederacy was the duty of Col. Freeman's First Missouri Cav. His being a prisoner of war had not dampened the spirits of his men. Over two-thirds of his men were local from the White River valley and eager to be home doing their service.

Talk of the successes in both warfare and recruitment of the independent guerilla leaders was on every one's tongue. On Feb 28th, Quantrill and John McCorkle were at Warrensburg in Johnson Co going to the homes of trusted people setting up safe places for the boys and recruiting. William Davenport joined Quantrill during that recruiting trip. John Brinker was elected Capt. and had 85-100 men under him. His sister was arrested for carrying Confederate information to the guerillas. The Union took her and made her ride in front as they rode looking for the guerillas. We learned later they put her in prison. The women's prison in St. Louis was disease ridden. The Union put many of the women in charge of tending to the wounded, sick and dying in the men's prison camps. They returned and infected the healthy women.

Following Pea Ridge, on March 17, 1862 Genl. Price merged the Missouri State Guard into the Confederate Army of the West, more than 300 of us were re-registered during this time. His reputation in Missouri was strong among us Southern boys and over time, it was Missourians who made up the core of his army.

Whilst we fought at Pea Ridge, Ark, March 7, 1862, Quantrill was in Aubry, Johnson Co, Kansas. He shot a man, Abrahm Ellis looking out the window of a local inn. Greenbury Trekle, Washington Tullis, John Brody and Mr. Whitaker were also at the Inn. Mr. Ellis was the superintendent of schools when Quantrill had been a teacher there. When Quantrill realized he'd shot an old friend he got Ellis medical help. Even though he was shot between the eyes, Ellis lived over it and was called ole Bullet Hole Ellis. One of the new recruits, William Davenport had gone with the boys. He captured Second Lt Reuben Randlett of Co A 5th Kansas. Quantrill wanted to trade Randlett for Perry Hoy who was awaiting execution at Fort Leavenworth. Randlett was allowed the freedom of the camp and didn't try to escape. On March 18th, Quantrill ordered him to go to Leavenworth to see about an exchange and report back to him. While Randlett was gone, Quantrill with about forty boys hit the Union recruiting post in Liberty, there wounding Union Capt. Hubbard. Afterwards Momma and Doc, along with Pappy Fielding, Doc's daddy, provided a safe place; half went to the Corum place and half a dozen more to the Gregg's farm.

On March 19, 1962 camped at the Little Blue Baptist Church near Independence, Quantrill read Special Order Num 47 to the boys. It ordered guerrillas to be treated as outlaws, shot by the Union. Four days later on the 22nd, in Jackson Co they burned the bridge over the Blue River near Independence. Quantrill was so angry over Halleck's order he pistol whipped a Union Sgt. before shooting and killing him. Then he shot and killed the toll keeper, Mr. Allison, in front of his young son. Quantrill then headed to the home of Alexander Maj's the manager of the Pony Express and a partner in the freighting Co of Russell, Majs and Waddell, another safe place for the guerillas. From there with 20 men, they headed to David Tate's house about 3 miles from the Little Santa Fe in Jackson Co.

Bill Gregg returned north couriering information from Col. Shelby to Quantrill. He, George Todd and the boys were at the Wyatt and Kerr homes further south. The Union was hot after Quantrill. They were questioning local citizens about the guerilla band but with little success. People that were southern weren't going to turn him in and the northerner's were afraid to. There had been a public gathering where a Col. with the Union offered safety to anyone who provided information. The people were gathered on the court square to hear him. Quantrill and a half dozen of the boys were there in the crowd and no one was willing to point him out. David Tate was a very tall lean man with a well trimmed head. His mutton chops he'd allowed to grow long joining his mustache made them look like peaks and points, a mountain top. His chin he shaved clean.

Union Prisoner of War Randlett returned to camp just as he promised. He brought word the Union was unwilling to make an exchange stating they considered them guerillas and not to be treated as soldiers. Quantrill asked Randlett what he thought about the order and decision. He said he wouldn't blame them if they shot him right then and there. Quantrill told him he would not be harmed and released him to return home. Perry Hoy, 25 year old son of Samuel and Ruth Turner Hoy, was found guilty of killing toll keeper Allison. Hoy was executed on July 25th, 1862.

Thomas Little and Andy Walker surrendered to Col. Burris at Wyandotte. They were paroled and signed oaths of allegiance. Col. Penick arrested Andy in Independence and put him in prison even though he had his protection papers given to him by Burris. Penick wanted to hang him. Andy joined the Feds to get out of prison. When he was given a 10 day furlough, he left and never returned. Later Penick found Andy with John Koger, William Cox, and Alf Ketchum. Andy and William Cox were able to escape but Alf Ketchum was shot down. John William Koger was severely wounded and captured. Andy walked home, barefoot, in four inches of snow. He found a pair of pants belonging to Fletch Taylor which only went to his knees, a boy's hat, woman's shoes and a blanket which he wrapped around him. Then he left to join George Todd. Word came in daily with each new recruit of what was happening around us, ranked or not we wanted to know what was happening, especially with the irregulars.

On the night of March 22, around 10 o'clock, a squadron of Feds was dispatched to the Tate farm. They had heard guerillas were holed up there. They had orders to arrest Richard Calvin Tate. He and his wife Bessie Hamblin, daughter of John Hamblin and Lucy Boone, ex pats from Kentucky, had had a houseful of children with several still at home; Julia was the oldest at 14, then Sallie, Annie, Albert, Jesse, Missy and two year old Billy. Maj James Pomeroy arrived with his men surrounding the house. Cole Younger and Quantrill were sharing a bed and the rest of the boys were asleep on the floor. It was raining hard and around 1:00 in the morning the picket stationed by the road dashed by the house firing his gun shouting they were surrounded by Feds. One of the boys shouted out there were women and children inside. The Feds let Missus Bessie and the children come outside to safety. Then one of the soldier's went to the front door and demanded to be let in. Richard Tate had stayed in the house with them, fearing for himself and his son John serving the Confederacy in Woods Co. He fired through a portal in the door hitting the Fed in the right leg with a minie ball. One of the boys, Bud, started crying alligator tears wanting to surrender. Quantrill had several men help him out a window, shouting "He's surrendering." They told him to tell Pomeroy he held been held against his will until they realized he was just a boy. He told Pomeroy at least 25 men were inside with Quantrill and would fight to the death. Maj Pomeroy was more concerned with the information and let the boy go. He believed this was his chance to wipe out a significant number of guerillas. He didn't realize the Tate house was constructed of logs with a wooden ell in the back. The Union set the house on fire and within minutes, the entire house was on fire, the blazes lighting up the night. Two more men went to the door telling the boys to surrender, both were shot dead. Pomeroy and his men were cocky, leaning back on their rifles expecting to pick off the escaping guerillas or simply watch and listen as they burned to death.

Upstairs walking on the roof of the second story ell, Quantrill ordered the boys to stoop low and go in two lines each firing to the sides with their backs to each other. As the ell fell, they emerged through the blazing timbers stooping low which provided safety as the soldiers fired over the boys heads right into each other. Breaking through the Union line bursting through the garden railing, running through blackberry and gooseberry vines within seconds the boys were safe in the woods. Two of the boys, brothers John and Ben Rollin were hit. John was killed instantly and Ben died the next day. There were five bodies found in the house, including Mister Richard Tate. Four of the boys were taken prisoner. Most everyone had thorns imbedded and rips in their skin from running through the briars. Cole Younger was teased about having run out of the house without his boots on. About 40 Union soldiers had been killed, most in the crossfire. When we heard this story, I could see it in the eyes of the troops. They wanted to be there with them. And, every time the story got told, it got bigger. Some boys were natural story tellers like Unc making swooshing sounds like wind and rain, guns firing and lightening flashes.

The next morning the Feds went to the farm of Al Wyatt, capturing two more of the guerillas riding under George Todd. The prisoners were taken to Fort Leavenworth, Kansas to be executed. With the increase in guerilla successes, the Union had mud on their faces and were intent on wiping it clean by burning houses, barns and outbuildings in the neighborhood, arresting anyone they caught, subject to being sent to Leavenworth or killed on the spot. Quantrill struck back with over 200 men hitting the Union post at Warrensburg on March 26th.

On March 30th, Quantrill held a rendezvous with his Lt.s at Samuel Clark's farm located about 3 miles southeast of Stony Point near Pink Hill in Jackson Co. The Union scout had seen some of the boys headed in that direction and lead the troops to the house. The boys were able to flee aided by over 100 of Sam Clark's family, friends and neighbors using their long range Sharps rifles. The Union set fire to Sam's home, his barn and outbuildings, burning everything to the ground.

Newspapers were running accounts of his actions, the effect, good or bad; his name was becoming known in every household in Missouri.

SEDALIA, March 29.—The notorious brigand Quantril, with 200 of his guerilla band, made a sudden and unexpected attack on a detachment of Col. Phillips's regiment of Missouri militia under Major Foster at Warrensburg Wednesday last, but after a spirited skirmish they were driven from the town with a loss of 9 killed, 17 wounded and 20 horses captured.

Our loss is 2 killed and 9 wounded.

Quantril made another attack on the town the following day, the result of which was not known.

Lieut. Col. Crittenden had left Georgetown with reinforcements for Foster.

Scouting parties of this regiment have captured over 200 kegs rebel powder in Pettis county within the past few days.

Chapter 9

A year after the war started, April 1862 numerous families along the western border of Missouri were preparing to vacate their homes, most heading south. Samuel Wells, also known as Charlie Pitts, was the great grandson of James Shepherd and Rachel Gault, grandson of Elizabeth Shepherd and Robert Wells, son of George Wells and Margaret Umberger. His siblings were Henderson "Hugh" Wells, Mary Jane, Franklin, Robert, Sarah Bell and the youngest Valerie Lou born in 1860. Frank, Ol, and Clell Shepherd were the grandsons of James and Rachel, sons of John P Shepherd and Eleanor Boggs. Elizabeth Shepherd Wells was their aunt and George Wells, Charlie's Daddy, their own cousin. Sixteen year old Charlie, his Momma and the other children aided his aunts and uncles as they prepared to go south. With his Daddy away fighting his Momma chose to remain in Missouri against the wishes of her family.

On April 12, 1862, the wagon train departed from Strother. The road took them south through Lone Jack to Pleasant Hill, Johnson and Cass Counties, toward Joplin into Ark. Made up of mostly of war widows and their children, there was an older man Buck Murie and his son who joined them each with a wagon and team. Sarah Shepherd Flannery Wells and six children filled one wagon loaded with all of their belongings and cooking provisions along with one older girl Margaret Baker whom the Wells were raising. Like everyone else, they had to pick and chose what to take. They knew as soon as they left, carpet baggers from the north would move into their abandoned homes. But only if they got there before the jayhawkers looted them, taking whatever they wanted then burning it to the ground.

Mrs. Sallie had a decent horse and an old blind one. Sarah "Sallie" Shepherd had married John William Flannery. They had one son Ike before John died in 1847. Then she married Isaac "Ike" Wells. When Mister Ike come home from California, he'd come by the farm telling Momma about Daddy and his burial at Hangtown. John's extended family, sisters, and brother's families joined the wagon train: Mrs. Rebecca and six children with their team, Mrs. Laura Flannery with one child and Duke Flannery's wife Nancy and children. Travel was risky, especially for women and children. Both troops and vigilantes from the north and south stopped folks, demanding to go through the wagons. Searching for possible arms and ammunition, wagon trains could be stopped several times a day. The first night shortly after they made camp, Union soldiers rode into the camp stating they were in need of their horses, even Mrs. Sallie's old blind horse. Then seeing they were driving a few head of stock, they rounded them up. The women begged and pleaded holding onto the ropes of the horses. The Unionists cut the ropes and led them away. After they realized one of the animals was blind, they cut it loose. The next morning the women went into town begging the Union to return their stock and horses. The Union relented offering some of their worn down horses, one of them blind as well and a yoke of steer. Nothing of their own was returned. Returning they found Mrs. Sallie's old blind horse.

They made it into Cherokee Territory where they encountered men headed to join Genl. Price in Missouri. Southerner's these men understood the risk the women and children faced. They provided them with some decent horses and good mules. Sgt. Calvin "Cave" Wyatt came upon them. He returned to camp and relayed the situation. Sarah's son, Ike Flannery was among the men in the camp with us. When he heard what his Momma and the women were attempting, he and Cave got a team and took it to them. Ike and Cave rode south at a distance from the wagon, escorting it and every night making sure they were safe until they reached Texas. Both Ike and Cave told the story on more than one occasion. It was the same story over and over as family after family had to leave all they owned behind in Missouri. At church, every Sunday there was word of another family burned out or leaving. Although the risk to move was great, the risk to remain was greater, especially in the absence of the men. Folks who had been close friends and supporters, moved their families anywhere they thought them safe, away from the border counties where conflict was great.

Quantrill had secured the area east of Kansas City as his territory. He had safe houses located throughout the area. The farm of Reuben Harris was one of those. He was Cole Younger's uncle, married to Laura Fristoe, Cole's aunt, sister to his Momma, Bersheba Fristoe Younger. On April 16th, the boys rendezvoused there, then headed to Job Crabtree's to rest before moving on to Jordon Lowe's abandoned house where they planned to stay. The Lowe House was located east of Independence in Jackson Co, Missouri. Union Lt GW Nash 1st Missouri Cav quietly surrounded the house. They gathered all the horses capturing them before they ever fired a shot. Anderson Scrivener pushed out a window and started firing back. All but three of the boys were able to escape. Bill Carr, Joe Gilchrist and James Lytle were killed. James Vaughn was wounded. He captured a horse then took off his hat waving it at the soldiers who were shooting at him. Vaughn dismounted twice to adjust his saddle. His luck ran out and he was shot in the right breast, the bullet passed through his lung out the back near his spine. Andy Blunt was captured by Nash but escaped and joined back up at William Bledsoe's house. Escaping they headed toward the Little Blue River. Bill Toler, one of the boys from Jackson Co, was waiting with a boat to take them across. Lt. Nash would have caught up with Quantrill and the boys there and killed them dead if not for Toler.

Bill Gregg and about 40 men headed back to north Ark to meet up with men under Col. Freeman to discuss extending troops farther north. Given Horn went with them as scout, guide and escort as this was his home ground. They camped on the south side of the White River near Talbot's Ferry. One of the pickets got off a warning shot alerting them of Union approaching. A Lt. from the 4th Iowa Cav asked to parlay. Bill Gregg with several of the boys holding aim on the Union spoke with him. When his demand for surrender of the powder works was not accepted the Iowa Cav began firing across the river at the boys. Capt Jesse Mooney jumped his horse into the floodwaters of the White River making his way to safety. The Lt. was struck in the head and killed, with this the Union retreated. Gregg and the men took cover in the Davis cabin near the river but the Union didn't advance. Sim Whitsett volunteered to go with Given Horn to patrol and report back. Men of Bowen's Co who had been pursuing Col. Freeman's men had killed one of Capt Mooney's men and captured several others. Given knew there was a powder works nearby at Talbert's Ferry. They circled back down river alerting Gregg the Union returned and Ed Cockrum leader of the local Mountain Boomer gang was with them. The Union set fire to the buildings destroying the munitions efforts. Gun fire was exchanged for 10 minutes then the Union unlimbered their howitzer cannon bringing it into position firing on them. Rather than engage further, Gregg moved the boys south to a point on the river where they could climb the ridge. From there they rode to the rendezvous at Big Flats joining about 100 of Col. Freeman's men on the farm of John Calhoun Freeman.

Momma was certain there would be no joining the guerillas for me, not as long as Jo Shelby was willing and able to keep me an enlisted man. But, I knew I was talking her down. I had occasions to engage in battles and skirmishes with the boys since they frequently rode with Col. Shelby and I knew I was better suited to the frontier Indian fighting than this regimented marching and drilling. Besides, I had Bill Gregg on my side and Momma liked him and Frank. I'd go with then whenever I could to their sister's, Mary Francis and Sam Ralston's house. And sometimes, I got to spend time with Sam's young cousin Annie. She was a brilliant girl. Educated to read and write she volunteered to write letters home for the boys. Sometimes, she would write letters to their girls but I think mostly the boys thought her too young to write those kinds of letters for them. I liked talking to her. She liked to read books as much as I did. We always had something to talk about other than the war that engulfed out lives.

I walked home after being captured and released. I'd made a couple trips south to Ark fighting with Col. Shelby riding back north with Bill Gregg. On April 26th, I signed the Oath of Allegiance to the Union. The newspapers picked up the news of the Confederate Congress passing the Partisan Ranger Act on Monday, April 21st, just five days earlier. The Act would enable President Jefferson Davis of the Confederates States of America to "commission officers to form bands of partisan rangers." Momma agreed I needed to sign the oath. We both knew it wouldn't be long before Genl. Thomas Hindman would commission the boys as Partisan Rangers. She was satisfied they would operating under orders of President Jefferson Davis. Hindman believed in their military significance, this was what Momma had been waiting for. Thirty of us signed oaths of allegiance gaining at least a temporary reprieve could be fully paroled now. Of course, each of us had to have parents, family or friends able and willing to sign a surety bond in the amount of $1,000, for each of us. The bond could be forfeited with the possibility of arrest for any act deemed against the Union. They listed our names in the May 2, 1862 Liberty newspaper, the Tribune.

Union Genl. Curtis was operating on orders to take Little Rock securing Ark for the Union. They were headed down through West Plains, Missouri toward Salem, Ark where they were headquartered. At West Plains, they learned Col.s W.O. Coleman, Jo Shelby and Tom Freeman were at Batesville with over 400 men; among them was Bill Gregg who had returned back south with 25 men. Curtis's army moved out of Salem south to Batesville on May 1. They were instructed to move as quickly as possible toward Batesville. On May 2, they rested about 15 miles out of Batesville close to the Little farm. Bill Gregg and James Little were alerted of their presence and rode to Batesville to warn Col. Coleman. They were barely ahead of the Union who marched all night entering into Batesville at five o'clock in the morning. The Union circled the town entering on the west side of the city rather than keeping to a direct march from the north. They took the pickets by surprise capturing half a dozen men along River Road, along with supplies of sugar and rice. In order to keep the fighting out of the streets of Batesville, Col. Coleman moved his men and horses to the south side of the river leaving the Union stranded on the north banks. Each side fired at the other but was out of range. The Union moved a howitzer cannon into place and began shelling. Col. Coleman and his men moved west along the river headed to the war conference at Hesstown. There along with Col. Freeman's men, they could hide in Ennis Cave sufficiently large enough to hold them and their horses.

Bill Gregg told how people in Batesville came out to watch the event. We experienced this throughout the war when the terrain and proximity to a town allowed. Union Genl. Curtis occupied Batesville, a strategic city only 90 miles north of Little Rock for the next couple of months. Curtis believed transport of supplies and provisions would be easy in the river town, but Col.s Coleman and Freeman instructed their men to maintain constant attacks. Using long range rifles, a number of the local boys proved their worth many times over.

When James Little and Bill Gregg reached Buckhorn they spent the night with Armistead Younger and wife Rebecca Crews. Her brother Jim Crews and nephew Tom were fighting with us. The Younger's had three boys who enlisted in regular service but were now fighting with the irregulars: Williamson Armistead Younger called "Son" was the oldest at 21, John Bomar called Cole, 20 and 18 year old, James Williamson, called Jims. Mister Younger had one of the largest and most successful mercantile stores in the area, along with a tavern and hotel. He started the first bank in that part of the Co and was one of its most influential men. He and Thomas Gist Ivey financed the construction of a rampart wall running along the edge of the mountain directly across from Penter's Bluff north and west to the river's edge at the holler, nearly two miles in length. Mister Ivey supplied the slaves and Mister Younger supplied the materials and feed the laborers. They knew should Batesville fall to the Union, they would best be able to defend Buckhorn from this point on the White River. Armistead Younger had moved his family to the area nearly 30 years before, shortly after the end of the Cherokee Reservation here. Thomas Gist Ivey was an own cousin to Col. Shelby's grandma, Judith Bell Gist, wife of Joseph Boswell. Col. Shelby was the great grandson of Genl. Nathaniel Gist. Thomas Gist Ivey was the son of James Ivey and Elizabeth Gist, sister of Genl. Nathaniel Gist. Col. Shelby instructed our boys any time safety was needed, seek out the Ivey's and Younger's.

Rampart Wall on river bottom near Buckhorn

After a hearty breakfast of fat back and eggs, Missus Rebecca gave James Little and Bill Gregg biscuits filled with fried potatoes and salted pork for eatin' later. They were directed up river along the ridge road past the newly built mill of Joel Foster at Cagen Landing, passing to the south of Wild Haws Landing, to Rocky Bayou, Herpel, Round Bottom and Sylamore, there crossing the creek moving north until they reached the next creek, there moving back east to the river at Jeffery Island. There crossing the White River to Mount Olive they rode to Aunt Lucy's at Athens. Arriving at Aunt Lucy's they caught her and neighbors up on news, both local and at home in Missouri.

Jennison made Jude Hall's momma set fire to her own house burning it to the ground. She ran in managing to get out with a few items which they made her throw back into the fire. While wiping away her tears, they jerked her hands away from her face cursing her. There were four other neighbors' homes burned in the same way that day. Many of the sons and fathers had to flee for safety chose to join Quantrill, including Ike and his brother. One of the women made her way to the home of a church lady. She had been beaten and violated by Jennison's men. No matter where Jennison himself might be, these men acted in his name with his authority and blessings. Not unlike it was becoming for Quantrill. Jude's daddy, Isaac Jude Hall hailed from Virginia and had gone home to join up with the Confederacy there. He hadn't wanted to fight against neighbors in Missouri. Missus Martha was on her own without a home. Then his momma and some of the other women were raped. They could do nothing but watch as the Jayhawkers drove their livestock away. The Halls' were of kin to Richard Hall, Cole Younger's brother in law, husband of his sister Belle. The women made a pact amongst themselves to speak carefully if at all about what the Union and jayhawkers did. They feared what their men would do if they knew all of it.

On the 26th after leaving Aunt Lucy's, Gregg met up with some of Col. Tom Freeman's boys, camped at the springs, south of Calico Bluffs. The scout located a group of a dozen Unionists made up of the Hall boys, of no known kin to Jude. They laid out a plan of ambush, attacking them just before they reached Calico Bluff Landing. There killing sixteen year old Robert Joseph "Joe" Hall who had just been riding with his brothers as far as the river intending to return back home. The family lived north of town and brothers, William, Ben and John Hall were headed to join the Union. They were men of faith, boys who had been trying to stay out of the war. William was married to Martha Ellen King, Ben to Margaret Hutcheson and John to Matilda Trimble. Daddy made decisions that set us on a path that guided our future. I saw families split. People took sides, hate and revenge spewed forth. I wondered if Daddy could see what was happening from Heaven. Boys like Joe Hall killed this way, no side really wins in war.

That same day Quantrill and his men were skirmishing with Union soldiers near Fred Farmer's house about 8 miles south of Independence. Dave Poole was wounded. Bill Toler was with James Tucker behind his horse when Tucker's horse was killed. Toler and Tucker escaped. 2nd Sgt. Cole Younger ordered they would not be abandoning anyone. Kit Chiles horse was shot, falling, pinning him down. Cole Younger pulled him out from under the dead horse. They mounted Cole's horse and fled. Peabody continued his pursuit then tried to corner them on Swearingen's farm. Joe Hart was saved by Andy Blunt who pulled him up behind him on his horse. John Moore was wounded. James Morris was wounded trying to escape. His horse was killed and he fought his way out on foot. John Jarrette's horse was killed and Frank Ogden pulled him up behind him carrying him out. After Henry Ogden's horse was killed, him, Billy Ogden and their brothers were captured and took to Kansas. Bloody Bill exchanged a Union militia man for Billy July 15, 1863. Billy said, after the war was over he was moving to Wichita Falls, Texas. Bill Haller sent a message to Col Albert Peabody telling him to send out 8 of his best men, 4 of his men, John Brinker, Cole Younger, William Haller, and David Poole would fight them. Peabody refused. They stalled Peabody long enough for Quantrill to get away. Peabody pursued them. Haller and Brinker were wounded. Poole pulled Haller up behind him on his horse. They fled escaping. They set up camp in the woods near Indian Creek. Some months later Bill Gregg said he rode by there and the stench of dead rotting horses was everywhere. You couldn't escape it, breathing it in, the smell got on your clothes.

Union Capt's Neugent and Irvin Walley next found them at Indian Creek, blasting the woods with two cannons. The boys held on through the night. Cole Younger and Jim Haller snuck into a nearby herd of cattle stampeding them into the midst of the Union camp. The startled Union jumped and run around not certain what to make of it all. It created enough confusion the boys got away. The following morning, thinking the guerillas were still hiding in the woods, the Union began blasting, but the boys had already gone. They were firing into nothing but trees.

John Shepherd's farm, father of Oliver and George "Clell," north of Liberty, was a safe place for the boys. The family left Strother in the wagon train headed to Texas on April 12. There were four guerillas at the abandoned Shepherd home when the Federal's first attacked. Theodore Blythe was standing as picket when a Federal scouting party found and killed him, nearly cutting his head completely off. Martin Shepherd, son of John Shepherd and Ruth Harris, cousins to both the Harris' and Shepherd's was a scout and spy for Quantrill. He climbed a tree and saw the Feds approaching on the Harrisonville Independence Road. All of these goings on happened near our farm and everyday there was new stories. Whenever I could be at home, Jesse and I talked while working the tobacco fields, hunted and tried to sleep at night, listening to the sounds as Unc taught us. Whether we were inside the house listening to the night or taking a break under the warm spring sun, we listened. Our lives depended on it. And, the crop of 1862 would be our last successful tobacco harvest.

May 8th, 1862, a few days after the Liberty Tribune ran the list of those signing the Oath and just after the Partisan Ranger's Act had been enacted, Gramps Bob Thomason drove his carriage into the yard halting the horses in a way we knew he was upset. I wondered what news of such urgency he had learned at the round table. He disappeared into the house talking to Momma and Doc first, then sat on the porch telling us Bloody Bill and Jim's Daddy was dead, shot and killed the day before. I sat silent on front stoop while Gramps related the details.

Paroled, Jim Griffen was at home same as me. Jim, Gramps said, stole some horses from Ira Segur. Judge Baker, a son in law of Ira Segur's went to talk to Mister Bill about Jim having stolen the horses. They were saying Judge Baker shot and killed him in self defense. Momma told us to get things ready we were going to the Anderson's house. Bloody Bill and Jim's momma, Martha Ann Thomason, was Gramps Bob's niece, daughter of his brother Uncle Wild Man. Momma took her famous apple pie she'd cooked up using the last of the winter apples along with some curds and whey and hard cheeses. When we got there, Missus Martha was dressed in black along with the rest of the women and girls. The men had on their suits. Mister Bill was laid out in the main room. All the furniture had been pushed around to make room for the casket. People brought food and were sitting and standing, talking and eating. The women were cleaning, cooking and caring for the younger children. Every now and then, someone would laugh about something Mister Bill said or done. The weather permitted sitting outside on the porch for those that chewed or smoked. Others joined them just to hear another version of the killing, catch up on the war or other news of the day. People didn't just show up and leave, they stayed, sleeping in their wagons or makeshift tents. The children were allowed to play late into the evening, wearing themselves down for a good night's sleep. The adults stayed up late, talking about what might need to be done for the family. Bloody Bill was the oldest at 22. Then Eli, 21, Jim 18, Mollie 15, Josie 14, Mattie 13 and Charlie 10. It would not be easy for Mrs. Martha to care for her children without the boys. Eli and Jim were both at home with her, but the war was pulling Jim to join up with Bloody Bill. He'd always shadowed him where Eli had favored remaining at the farm working. For two whole days, people kept showing up, arriving to pay their respects and nobody came empty handed. As we sat around talking it was clear, not only was I was going to join Quantrill but so were a lot of others. We knew Bill Gregg wasn't there recruiting us. He was there, as neighbor and friend of the family but it didn't make no matter. The day after the services of Mister Bill, along with a dozen others, I joined the now famed band of William Clarke Quantrill. There had been no need for discussion with Momma. She had seen me preparing my things readying to return to service before we'd left home. And, with the Partisan Ranger Act, and Bill Gregg, there was nothing more to be said.

We met up with Bill Gregg in Clay Co at the Missouri River then took boats rowing across. Our horses tied to ropes swam behind us. We made our way to the Webb place near Blackwater Ford of the Sni close to Blue Springs. Although we had been at the same place at the same time, both at Wilson's Creek and Lexington and I had ridden with some of the boys on different raids, I had never really met Quantrill but like others, I felt I knew him. This was the first time I laid good eyes on him. He was everything I'd imagined, over six feet tall, thin with sandy brown hair and thick mustache. He was laughing seemingly happy surrounded by his closest men, his Lt.s, Sgt.s, and Capts. Because I came in with men he knew, he shook my hand and introduced himself. Momma would like that. She'd already met him with some of the boys when they'd come by the farm. Maybe he already knowed who I was.

Bill and Martha Thomason Anderson

Bloody Bill and Jim arrived the following morning after Mister Bill's services. That night they told about having been part of Jim Lane's jayhawkers along with Quantrill. For them it has been a ruse created by their daddy to gain information on Lane and Jennison and to add horses and cattle to their own inventory. They needed to talk so mostly the rest of us sat around the fire swatting off the first of the season's no seeum's and mosquitoes listening. Quantrill heard every word, never interrupting, never correcting anything they said. If the men understood what they were saying about him and themselves, it made no difference.

Their story began after their move to Kansas before our Unc, their grandpa "Wild Man" Bill Thomason died. A man by the name of Arthur Ingram Baker of Agnes City was hit hard by the drought and depression that followed. Baker was Agnes City. He founded it in 1856 naming it for his momma, Agnes Miller. He owned the entire town and all of its buildings. His home, a two story stone house, was one of the finest around. Baker was the postmaster, store keep, justice of the peace and judge. He had large land holdings stocked with cattle. The town, eight miles east of Council Grove, Kansas was located on the Rock Creek crossing of the Santa Fe Trail. Baker owned the town's only newspaper the Council Grove Press and the only hotel in Council Grove. In 1861, things began to go downhill in a hurry for him, neither the newspaper nor hotel had successful years, then the drought came. He lost most of his crops and cattle. His wife Susan died leaving him a widower with a young daughter. The rug had been pulled out from under him. Bloody Bill and Jim said they went into a pony business with him. We knew without clarifying this meant they joined him on raids to steal horses. Jayhawking was a means of Kansans stealing themselves rich. Their Daddy said it was a means to an end serving both for gaining information and making money.

Bloody Bill continued, "It ended badly. We were camped along Drywood Creek when a Union patrol came along. They musta thought us bushwhackers because they attacked hard. We all managed to escape except for one fella John Radcliffe. They killed Radcliffe and captured Baker. Accusing him of trying to join up with Genl. Price's army. They took him to the military prison over near Fort Scott, Kansas holding him for nearly a year before taking him before a military tribunal. Who knows what took place to cause it to happen, some say it was because he was close friends with Senator James "Jim" Lane, but they let him go, no charges against him. Daddy he knew something dirty was at hand. Jim Lane, "King of the Jayhawkers," was the political boss of Kansas. Baker needed himself a wife to help care for his little girl. He'd been over to the house on a number of occasions. We only lived 5 miles from him."

"Daddy knew Baker was more than interested in our little sister Mary Ellen. She was only 14 but that was alright since Baker could provide a good life for her. We all knew that they were going to marry. He'd been visiting almost daily and staying late into the night. Then word came he was engaged to Annis Segur, a 17 year old school teacher. Daddy and Momma were outraged knowing he'd defiled Mary Ellen. Adding insult to the whole thing, Baker himself formed a posse to go after Bert Griffin. He'd been accused of stealing two horses from Ira Segar, Annis' daddy. He tracked Bert to the Chavez place, 90 miles west of Council Grove. He rounded up the horses and old man Chavez dragging him back to Agnes City. Then, he got a warrant to arrest Bert. He'd been working on our place. We knew Bert to be solid. Outraged, we rode over to Baker's and threatened him." "Just a little," Jim interjected.

Bloody Bill continued, "Daddy wanted him to drop the charges against Bert but Baker refused. He had a whole posse of friends and employees backing him so we knew we'd best just get back on home. Daddy, I reckon was thinking about Mary Ellen and Bert. He sat up drinking most of the night. When morning light came, he picked up his double barrel shot gun and rode back over to Bakers'. We weren't far behind him. We heard him yelling before we got there and saw him kick down the door of the house going in after Baker. He was headed up the stairs when Baker stepped out onto the landing of the second floor and shot him. He landed at our feet at the bottom of the stairs." Bloody Bill had been sitting looking at the ground as he told the story. He looked up. "I picked up the gun to shoot Baker and realized there was nothing but caps in it. Somebody rigged Daddy's gun." "It was Eli Sewell," Jim said. "Daddy stopped by and got another drink on his ride over. He told Eli what he was going to do. Maybe Eli thought he could save Daddy's life. We're certain he didn't mean to get him killed." As we sat around listening, thinking about our own families, a quiet decision was made by those of us hearing their story. Standing, Quantrill was looking at us, perhaps it was the light of the roaring fire, but there was a look on his face I'll never forget. Distorted and angry, enraged at what he was hearing. No one realized the extent of the story of his early dealings with Baker himself and he wasn't going to clarify it now. But revenge was in the air. If we learned one thing from the border wars, it was patience is required in exacting revenge.

George Todd returned from Ark. He and Quantrill then left for Hannibal, Missouri on the eastern side of the state. Arrangements to purchase 50,000 pistol caps had been made and they were going to retrieve them. They went by train leaving their horses near the city. After coming back, they rode upon Andy Blunt and Billy Bledsoe doing a little jug fishing on the Missouri near Harlem outside Kansas City. This is the best means of catching those old river cats. Put a jug with a hook and line on it out to float attaching it to a nearby limb. When the old cat takes the hook and runs with it, the jug and limb pull him back snagging him. He just swims around until you can get back and run your line. Some boys would have several jugs on a single line. When they got back to camp, the ones that knew how to cook were heroes of the day because it took more than one person for this job. One old cat was as big as a man is tall. We enjoyed a rare treat, fried catfish and hush puppies, spoonfuls of cornbread dropped into hot grease. The little bits and clumps of batter off the fried fish left in the cooled grease after cooking the fish were given to the dogs to keep them quiet, "hush puppies." No one knows who cooked them up first but Southerners don't have fried fish without hush puppies and when you can get them, sweet pickled green tomatoes. Smiling to myself, I thought about the story of hush puppies I'd been told. It was really to keep the children, the "little pups" quiet. It sure worked on these hungry men.

Capt. Osby Dillard and a few of his men from Col. Tom's Co in Ark rode into camp on their way to the war conference. Aunt Lucy Mims had given him clear directions to our house and a letter of introduction. When he got to Momma's she gave him directions to our camp. After traveling north to attend the war conference they were headed to Alton Prison to check on the conditions of Col Tom and the men who had been taken prisoner of war in Feb. They hoped to broker an exchange with information and papers from Gen Price. Os brought us up to date on the middle White River. There had been a battle about a mile northeast of the Salem square during March. Union Gen Curtis then made camp at Cypress Creek before moving his men on out to Batesville. Though really insignificant it spurred many Union families to move to safer areas. Others decided to form a Home Guard with over 150 men and boys signing up.

On May 11, 1862, ferry owner Charles "Charley" Grigsby and William "Bill" Chitwood rigged the Grigsby ferry with explosives to mimic a snag in the water. Eleven Union soldiers, including Capt. Thomas McClelland were killed when it exploded and sunk. The Grigsby Ferry remained a vital means of crossing the White River so "The Union army has very little options in crossing the White River," Genl. Samuel Curtis wrote in his report. The Union officially deemed it an accident and rebuilt Grigsby Ferry. Charles Grigsby's momma, Margaret Houston, was a cousin to brothers Genl. Sam Houston and John Paxton Houston. James Grigsby, Charley's daddy and Col Andrew Jackson Grigsby, Commander of Stonewall's Brigade under Genl. Stonewall Jackson were children of own cousins. I delighted in being able to relay word of Col Grigsby through our cousin Wirt Woodson, Genl. Stonewall Jackson's half brother.

Saturday May 17th was a rainy cold morning. Travel was slow in the mud and muck left by the slow soaking May rain. Horses were bogging down trying hard to walk, sinking clear up to their knees as wagons slipped sideways in the gray clay. War is hard and desperate; nothing of young men's imaginations had lived these conditions. Men of Lt. Col. Marion Chrisman's Co were determined to stop the Feds advance and capture of Little Rock. At Prospect Bluff on the Little Red River south of Batesville Gordon and his men headquartered. Scouts came into camp reporting movements of Union Col. George Waring and the 4th Missouri Cav. It had been raining and the lower river plains were severely flooded, crops were underwater and ruined. Foraging for food necessary to feed 10,000 men and their animals, horses and mules was exceptionally difficult and the flooding would devastate food supplies. The rising and falling water had left the clay banks slick and impossible to climb. With no bridges and few ferries the boys were at risk. An ambush was set up on the opposite banks of the river from West Point Bluffs, high enough to fire down on the foraging party from Union Col. George Warings' Cav. When the Federalists were in line beneath the cliffs, our boys fired on them. Chrisman and his men captured 30 mules and a few of their men. One of them joined up stating he was a Southerner who had been forced to join the Union or face torture after they burned his parent's home.

Lt. Col. Francis Marion Chrisman, born and raised in Macomb, Illinois about 75 north of Hannibal, MO was the second cousin of JoeC, Joseph Chrisman Porter. Marion come down river enlisting to serve the South in Missouri with JoeC. Their cousin of whom they were very close, James Monroe Chrisman from Jackson Co, joined the Union. Marion volunteered under Genl. Price to move into Ark south of Batesville protecting the area between Jacksonport and Searcy under McRae. Along with Indian Capt. William Hicks assigned under Genl. Shelby to Col. Freeman's Co they guarded the river ports. They were significantly responsible for the harassment of Union Genl. Curtis leading him to abandon plans of attacking Little Rock. Curtis set up base in Batesville. He sent out some of his German mercenary forces to go down the Little Red River reconnoitering. On May 19th, the Germans and our boys engaged at Whitney Lane, Searcy Landing. Our forces in Little Rock were under Chief James Emory Rogers of the Twelfth Texas Cav. The Chief was the grandson of James Emory Rogers, brother of Tiana Rogers, wife of Genl. Sam Houston, children of Chief John Headman Rogers. When Sam Houston left the Cherokee in 1838 headed to Texas, James went with him.

Genl. Houston vowed to stay out of the War Between the States, but with family living near Batesville, he sent the troops his cousin Margaret Grigsby requested. After his daddy Maj Samuel Houston died in 1806, John and Sam had lived off and on with their cousin John Houston, son of their Uncle Matthew, brother of their father. His daughter Margaret was Charlie Grigsby's Momma. She wrote Genl. Sam Houston requesting aide, Chief James Emory volunteered. His great aunt Mary "Arky" Rogers, a sister to his grandfather was living north of Batesville near Cedar Grove. Troops were converging on Little Rock to protect it from Union forces, Chief Emory and the Texas Rangers were a welcomed site. The newspapers reported their arrival.

Curtis ordered his men to break camp. They crossed the White River moving south. The Germans under Curtis moved out earlier foraging near Searcy were unaware of Chief Rogers and Lt. Col Marion Chrisman watching them. When the foraging detachment divided into three groups, posting one near Whitney's Lane, a few miles east on the West Point Road, Rogers attacked with 100 of his men and fifty locals under William Hicks, Richard Hooker and Chrisman. Riding into the pickets at Whitney's Lane, they cut them down killing them all. A rider had been sent north to alert Curtis turned back a few miles outside of Batesville. The irregulars and guerillas of Ark along with the Cav of the Texas Rangers clearly were a more formidable force than Curtis estimated. The success of the guerillas in Ark were considerably more effective than in Missouri, their tactics and ability to spread misinformation convinced the Union they faced greater challenges. The brush and swamps were familiar hunting grounds which they knew how to navigate in the worst of weather. Confederate Maj Genl. Thomas Hindman was determined and optimistic as he took over command in Ark. I'm certain it was with immense delight Maj Chief Emory Rogers' great aunt Mary Ark "Arky" Ugalusta Rogers (Vickery), Genl. Sam Houston's sister in law, read about the action in the Little Rock newspaper, "Maj Rogers deserves the thanks of the people of Ark for the check he gave the enemy."

Hindman sent orders to keep the Yankees occupied in direct combat destroying communication and transportation lines. Capt. Richard Hooker and his men left out headed west and north towards Augusta and Jacksonport with the sole purpose of burning bridges and destroying telegraph lines. Hindman commissioned Capt Hooker to recruit commission and mobilize units in the area. The low lands of the river valleys had been so inundated with floodwaters they were nothing more than a quagmire of flooded marshes. Lt. Col Marion Chrisman was left in charge of the area around Searcy.

Newspapers in Ark and Missouri reported the city of Osceola, MO were destroyed on May 27th. This was Jim Lane's second visit. He first sacked Osceola in Saint Clair Co on Sunday Sept 22, 1861. In addition to Osceola, he raided Butler and Parkville. One of the largest towns in western Missouri, Osceola was decimated. He told his men to shoot "everything disloyal, from a shanghai rooster to a Durham cow must be cleaned out." They found some gunpowder and lead. With that excuse they arrested nine local citizens, held their own court finding them guilty of being Southern sympathizers aiding the guerrillas. They shot and killed all nine. Lane stole 350 horses and mules, 400 cattle and 200 Negroes, household items, merchandise taken from stores, wagons, buggies and a carriage for himself.

Os Dillard, 2nd Lt., Co A of Col. Tom's command received communications of the events in Ark and was jubilant in sharing them. Momma invited a select group of neighbors to the house to hear his stories direct. It felt like we were the men of the round table, hearing the stories of the knights of the kingdom. I thought of our plays as children and envisioned the drama in my head of each event. I was taken with the stories of Genl. Houston aiding the people of the White River Valley. When Lt. Dillard decided to leave headed for the war conference, Jesse and I rode with them several miles enthralled with the stories and reports from Ark and their successes against Genl. Curtis. Jesse was particularly interested in the stories of the spies, men and women, boys and girls, who were able to walk among the enemy unsuspected.

Our forces, the guerillas and irregulars, were growing in strength from North Ark through Missouri into Southern Nebraska. Most of us felt our families would not be adequately protected during our absences and we simply could not leave them for long periods of time. The war was in everyone's front yard. In Ark, during Col. Tom's term as prisoner of war, and in the absence of Lt. Os Dillard, Capt. Bill Chitwood Co C led the First Missouri Cav engaging Feds at Kickapoo Bottoms, north of the river port town of Sylamore. On the morning of May 28, 1862, a detachment of 150 men under the command of Maj William C. Drake, Third Iowa Cav, reported to Maj William D. Bowen at Grigsby Ferry. Here they joined 150 men and two mountain howitzers and began their march. The next day, May 29, they captured picket, Rebel rock thrower Bob Porter. He disclosed the boys were camped at Kickapoo Bottoms along the White River, three miles north of Sylamore. They reached Sylamore the night of May 29. The Union walked about a half mile to the camp of our boys surrounding them. The fog was thick and the night pitch black, with no stars the Union got lost, their movements alerting our boys. They fired on the Union killing Sgt Stanton B. Millian, a battalion saddler, wounding two men; Private Joseph T. French and Capt Israel Anderson, shot in the thigh. The Union pursued our boys capturing twenty-five men, forty horses and mules and forty guns. The Union camped with their wounded assessing their insufficient supplies and rations. They decided to return to Batesville the next morning.

Our boys camped on the Perrin Farm keeping watch over the Union through the night. W.W. "Will" Perrin was riding with Col. Tom's men. The next morning our boys began firing from the east banks on the Union camped across the river as they watered their horses. The Union brought out a howitzer canon firing into the woods and fields. The Union broke camp by noon, then moved south on the river road toward Sylamore. There they secured a buggy continuing along the river road reaching Levisay Mountain where they ascended toward Riggsville. Our boys continued attacking their rear guard. No one was reported hurt but our boys wounded one Union man with a shot passing through his molasses-filled canteen. Because Col. Tom was being held by the Union and the necessity of making sure no records fell into enemy hands, few records were kept. Co records were at risk, marriages, land deeds and legal transaction. Izard Co Clerk, William Carroll Dixon, hid the records in a cave near Jeffery Slough keeping them from being destroyed.

Chapter 10

Cole Younger, now 2nd Sgt was having trouble with some of the new recruits assigned to him for training. Proving his control of his men, on June 11, 1862 Cole shot and killed Isaac Shoat for deserting. I thought of young John Wood being killed in the War of 1812. I wondered if I should tell him the Wood family story and how he, like Andrew Jackson, might be remembered. Al and Cave Wyatt walked up about that time. They served under Quantrill. I knew those boys and was glad to see familiar faces. I decided the Wood story could wait.

There could be a handful of us in any one place and within a day 100 to 500 or more. It didn't take long to get to know who was who and those that could be trusted. Bloody Bill was telling stories one night about how his Gramps, our Unc, Wild Man had trained us to which Cole took offense; saying nobody could do all of that. Now mind you Bloody Bill could be a braggart but when it came to his Gramps, there wasn't anything he was saying that wasn't true. Bloody Bill suggested we give the boys a little demonstration of our riding skills. Neither of us weighed more than a fly in a poke. Most described us as tall and lanky, "a little wormy" some Momma's would say. Our antics hanging on the side of our horses was exciting, the boys went wild.

Quantrill challenged Bloody Bill asking, "Can you shoot riding like that?" Before he drew his next breath, Bloody Bill, hanging from the far side of his horse, put a hole in his hat. The boys and Quantrill were speechless, then broke out laughing and clapping. With everyone watching wanting to be able to ride the same, shoot the same, Quantrill put us in charge of training all of the boys. I'd been through this already with Col. Shelby and here I was again, the teacher, the trainer, trying to be like Unc. But, Bloody Bill had a better idea. We took the boys we knew to be the best riders and trained them, then put them in charge of training 10 more. The same we did with those who were the best shots. Within a day or so, everyone had improved and was challenging each other's improvements. No tree, rock or bottle was safe.

Quantrill had already developed a bit of a yell, but when we screamed out our deep from the gut blood curdling yells, that too became part of our training. The yells came like a good song, deep from inside your gut, long and loud, cutting and yipping. When we'd first exercised them at home, Momma had proclaimed, "Are you trying to wake the dead?" Unc had learned it from the Indians and seems a great many of the young men of Missouri and Ark had a little Indian in them and making our yell was easier for them. Soon we heard boys from home were using it all over the place in the war. Others adopted their own form of it, each scaring the dickens out of those northern boys. Most thought it some kind of wild cat.

Aunt Lucy she knew her neighbors, friends and family and who was where serving with whom and how to get word about. She had lived at Piney Creek through the first courthouse at the Wolf House, then when it was moved in 1830 closer to her home on Piney Creek at Athens. It was there John Houston died at his desk in 1838. She knew him personally and could tell great stories about him and his constant bickering and fighting, mostly a result of his love of liquor, especially with Sheriff John Adams and his brother Mathey. They were married to sisters of Maj Jacob Wolf. It was the Adams brothers, John, Matthew and Robert who sold their sister Mary to Chief Peter Cornstalk of Searcy Co as a wife, so Robert Adams could be the first white settler there. The newspapers in Marion Co reported what a sorry sight it was when the Indians came and took her.

"Maj Jacob Wolf of Pennsylvania came here in 1818 with his folks Michael and Margaret Hedrick Wolf and his niece Sally Waters, daughter of his deceased sister Lydia and George Morgan Waters of Rhode Island. Maj Wolf served in the War of 1812 earning himself the title of Maj in the Kentucky Militia. He never said nothing of being an Indian agent until the Indians started taking up residence across the river from his settlement. He tried to get the Arkansas Gov. to intercede. He arrived with several slaves to locate a place to build an outpost. The confluence of the two rivers there provided just the location. He had equipment to build a smith shop and axes to hewn out the yellow pines to build a home. He stopped at Livingston's ordering milled boards. The Partee's and Livingston's first settled on the south side of the White River but had to move when the treaty of 1817 set aside those lands for the Cherokee. Robert Livingston and Lewis Partee set up a board mill and Livingston he established a grist mill. Wolf brought large quantities of salt, sugar and ammunition with him, the gold of the day, allowing him to trade for anything he needed. Partee poled those boards upriver to the Wolf settlement where his slaves worked the boards smoothing them so there was nary a splinter. The Indians across the river were growing in number bringing bearskins, bear oil and other pelts. The salt old man Michael Wolf purchased was in such quantities this area became known as Salt Trail with people going back and forth trading with him. I dare say, it was his daddy, the late Michael Wolf who was the real thinker of that family," Aunt Lucy told us.

"It was in 1819, around the time these lands became the Ark Territories things really started jumping up at Liberty. Maj Wolf returned from a trip with John Houston. He'd found him jurying in Little Rock and convinced him to move up here with him." He was one of the biggest men Aunt Lucy said she'd ever laid eyes on. Houston was more than happy to move up into this remote area, happy to have all the Indian women he wanted and alcohol. The things happening at Liberty were the talk of the every church goer. People often said "if only those walls or Aunt Julie, the head slave woman would talk." One of the funniest things Aunt Lucy told us was Aunt Julie a running and screaming and gathering up the children "Run, childs, she's a gonna bust," when the first steamboat arrived at the settlement. That was in the late 1830's maybe 1840", Aunt Lucy said. "Maj Wolf and his daddy got a mail route from Little Rock all the way up to Liberty settlement, that was in '22.

When talk started about the Indian reservation might be gonna end, white folks started marrying up to the Indians so they could get a toe hold in the Indian lands. Maj Wolf was no different. He married off his niece, Sallie, to George Sequoyah Gist, son of Betsy Watts, a sister of Duwali, Chief of the Ark Cherokee. John Houston married up a lot whites and Indians. When they finished work on the courthouse in 1825, seemed everybody wanted to be married there. He married Sally, close to 40 yr old and Sequoyah nigh on 70 in 1826. She had him five childs. Maj Wolf now he figured out marrying up Robert Adams baby sister, Mary, just a girl to Chief Peter Cornstalk, twicest her age, maybe more. Some say he bought her, others say he traded for her, but the truth of it was, Robert Adams and his brother's wanted that land and Mary was a small sacrifice. Their folks died and her brothers wanted to get their foot into the land around the Buffalo, so John Houston, he married them up in 1825. The reservation ended in 1828 and the Indian were ordered to move west."

Casey House built 1858

"Now Wolf's daughter Miss Malinda, she married Tandy Young Casey, one of our Col.s and of some kin to Rhoda Casey, wife of Thomas Riggs over at Riggsville. Tandy and Miss Malinda built them a beautiful home up at Rapps Barren and you remember now, she is the Aunt of

Michael Hedrick Wolf." We all smiled listening patiently engulfed in Aunt Lucy's story. I knew Col. Casey. He was serving as the Quartermaster under Genl. Shelby assigned to Col. Thomas Roe Freeman's Missouri Cav. "Old Wolfie, the daddy, that's what people called him. He and the Maj's momma both took sick in '30 and died just a few months different in '31. People can say what they want, but truth is, that's when the Jeffery's got a toe hold and was able to get the seat of government moved on down to Athens. John Houston he didn't much want to move, but Mrs. Williams and me, we done him up some good cooking and he was satisfied to move. "

In November 1861 over two dozen emergency companies organized at Athens. Men and boys converged on Pocahontas, Pitman's Ferry, Batesville and Hesstown mustering into Confederate service for a period of thirty days. The 1st Ark was a 30 day volunteer infantry under the command of Col. James Haywood McCaleb. He served as the field commander of the 25th Militia Regiment out of Lawrence Co. Aunt Lucy knew him and the boys who served under him well. Her home on Piney Creek along with the Jeffery White House was a frequent stop. The local Capt.'s were A.G. Kelsey, John W. Peter, Shelby Kennard, Thomas Simington, Joshua Wann, Israel Milligan, Daniel Yeager, James Campbell Anderson, Beverly B. Owens and L.W. Robertson. Over a 1,000 men and boys joined McCaleb; barely 100 survived the war.

Michael Hedrick Wolf, was one of the 49 survivors of Co I surrendering at Greensboro North Carolina, on April 26th, 1865 a member of the 1st Ark Consolidated Infantry Regiment with the Army of the Tennessee. He was a fine horseman which saved his life more than once. Israel Milligan son of Rev. John Milligan of Milligan's Campground south of Smithville at a place known as Strawberry for all the Irish folks' red hair who settled there, where our boys camped and rested repeatedly during the war, survived. Michel Shelby Kennard, son of Reverend George Kennard who would marry my friend Carroll Wood and Nannie Wilson, survived. Beverly Owens husband of Jane Gibson, brought two of his sons, Gid and Wally, all survived the war living out their lives in Batesville. We'd visit these men and the men of Col. Tom's command on our trips through the White River Valley after war's end.

On June 17, 1862 Col. W.O. Coleman's boys under Capt. Wiley Jones engaged with the Union under Commander Seley near Smithville. Our boys and Col. Tom's were camped at Milligan's campground several miles away closer to Strawberry when our scouts encountered a group of soldiers under Seley stealing cattle from a local farmer. We had been contending with James McKinney, a neighbor to Milligan's campground loyal to the Union. The McKinney family was being escorted by additional troops to safety at the Union camp at Smithville, 10 miles east. Another of their neighbors having seen our scouts and knowing where we were camped warned the Union. Seley immediately sent about 50 men to the McKinney farm four miles west of Smithville. Col. Jones and the boys were taking shelter in the abandoned house and were caught off guard. They had sufficient cover within the house and outbuildings returning fire as the Union pressed forward. Col. Jones volunteered himself and a dozen of the boys to stay behind fending off the attack allowing the boys to escape. They left behind some previously captured horses which were recaptured by the Union. None were killed but four seriously wounded, with a dozen or more captured, including Col. Jones. From Smithville they transported them to St. Louis. They were held for six weeks then moved to the prison camp at Alton, Illinois. Several of them were being moved to New Orleans by way of Memphis, Tennessee for exchange when Col Jones and four men managed to escape. Col Jones swam the Mississippi River with shots ringing out allowing the other four time to take cover and hide. All of them returned to Ark rejoining their regiments. Upon his return Col Jones set about organizing Baber's Regiment serving with them until war's end.

1859 Map Used by Col. Thomas Roe Freeman's Men

The same day in Mount Olive a skirmish between local Union and Confederate boys took place in the midst of town. A Union man had wandered into town, having been captured and separated from his command, he was very ill. He had been provided care, nursed back to health. Leaving his rescuers home some of our boys come upon him, killing him only a few miles from where he had been cared for by a local family. A few of the Union boys heading into Mount Olive for supplies, found his body and buried him near the hill top where he was found. Encountering our boys further up the road a skirmish, more a clubbing and fist fight took place. There were lots of injuries but no deaths. The ones involved told their story at camp indicating they were not among those involved, but the cuts and bruises told differently.

Genl. Price and his troops were called to move east of the Mississippi to Corinth. After swearing to the oath of allegiance to the Union Col. Tom was paroled on June 18, 1862. He began the journey to return to his regiment headquartered at Spring Mill on the Ark Missouri line near Mammoth Spring in Fulton Co, Ark. Capt. Bill Chitwood from the Barrens outside Batesville had been left in charge of the local guerrillas protecting the munitions effort during Col. Tom's four months of imprisonment. Sgt. Maj Will Perrin was left in charge, during Osby's leave. Col. Shelby sent Lt. Joseph Love to northwest Ark. Col. Tom's surgeon moved east toward Jacksonport where there was heavy fighting. Capt. Robert Trimble was assigned to the area inland of the White River between Calico Bluffs and Salem. Christopher Cook of some kin to John D. Cook husband of Sarah Grigsby, niece of Margaret Houston Grigsby, had taken ill with small pox and was being cared for at a cave near the Grigsby home. Along with half a dozen other soldiers they were quarantined away from the others to prevent further spreading.

In June as Col. Tom was being released, back in Ark in the early hours of June 19, 1862, Lt. Ferdinand Hansen and forty of his men crossed the White River, men were both using the ferry and riding horses through the low waters. The McClellan family, who lived upriver of the Grigsby Ferry, sometimes worked the ferry and was known to "sing the songs of whichever side was crossing." When the boys found out one of the McClellan boys was to be a guide for the Union to Riggsville. Chitwood and his men hogtied McClellan, replacing him with William "Bill" Marion Turner. After the troops crossed the river they moved along the bottomland over the ridge along the Batesville to Harrison Road. After being led as far as Hunt's Ferry on the Little Red River they turned back, crossing into the settlement of Rich Woods descending through Riggsville. They turned east at the farm of Andrew Hinkle, moving along Rocky Bayou Creek and Bickle's Cove continuing to Knights Mountain. Turner led them on a planned route returning to descend Knight's Mountain into the cove below.

Lt. Hansen was told the guerillas had gone to Fairview west of Riggsville where they were joined by Texas Rangers under Maj Emory Rogers. Sent under direct request of Genl. Sam Houston, he was under orders to assist during the capture and imprisonment of Col. Freeman. The Rangers had been seen coming through Van Buren and Searcy Co but Lt. Hansen failed to find them. They rendezvoused with the boys and were hidden in the hills above the cove on the Knight family farm. Laying in wait they watched a group of Union soldiers foraging food for the men and animals of the Fourth Iowa Cav and Eighteenth Indiana Infantry. The Federalists were going through the Knight family's corn bin, raiding the farm and livestock when the Union soldiers under Hansen descended the mountain to join them. Waiting until the two units approached each other, the boys and Rangers began their attack, wounding a number of men, including Private William Becker, whose horse was shot out from under him. Sgt. James Harvey Henry, a sharp shooter and his son 14 year old son John were in charge of the ambush under the direction of Capt Chitwood and William Hatfield. The Feds returned fire, killing Jody Culp son of Thomas Culp and Lavina Jeffery. Jody's own cousin, Daniel, son of Daniel Culp older brother of Thomas, served as the personal secretary of Genl. Sam Houston. He'd died in New Orleans. Genl. Sam paid to have his body shipped to Galveston and interned rather than sending him back home for burial. The Culp's were fellow Kentuckians.

Grave marker of Daniel Culp

Hansen arrested anyone he could, including Corp. Andrew Jackson Hight of Co B under Capt. John Peter. Andy served as a 1st Sgt. in Co C of the Missouri 10th Infantry Regiment from Wright Co, Missouri before moving down into Ark to serve with the 1st Ark. He was living near McGuire's Store in Batesville. Hansen arrested him accusing him of being a spy. Even though they spelled their name different I thought he might be part of our family of Hite's from Tennessee and Kentucky. People's names were spelled differently because many people didn't know how to read or write or how names were spelled. This led changes in family names because the census taker would list their name however they thought it sounded like it ought to be spelled. The good ones would leave a piece of paper with their name spelled out on it. People of the same family with different census takers ended up with names spelled differently. This was the way many people learned to print out their names but couldn't read or write anything more. I considered myself a lucky man because Momma and Daddy placed such value on education.

The Union reported only one man injured and reported they loaded him onto a wagon transporting him back to camp at Batesville. This same day Col. Tom released from Union captivity in Illinois was put on a train headed to Kansas City, from there he began his long trek back through Missouri to Ark. He secured a horse and was traveling south to Salem in Dent Co to see his children. I was at home when he came through Liberty, I got a little crazy, hallooing and shooting off my gun. I got myself arrested and lost the $1,000 bond Momma posted in May. Some said it meant I lost my parole too. They held me for three days before Col. Tom could negotiate my release. He left Liberty headed to the home of John and Catherine Adams Freeman. After respite and time with his children, he headed to his camp at Spring Mill where he could oversee the operations protecting the White River valley continuing his campaign to defend the munitions efforts throughout the area. More and more of us boys were finding our place in the woods and hills of the White River Valley of Ark. I loved it there, the trees were so thick little grew beneath except magnificent ferns. You could ride head low at a faster pace. I wondered what those old trees had been witness to. Some were bigger around than two or three men could reach before their hands touched.

Genl. John Sappington Marmaduke had a huge camp south of Col. Tom's at Springfield on the Ark River, 100 miles east of Fort Smith. Two southern regiments had formed on the courthouse square which led to attacks in the area by a local mountain boomer Capt. Thomas Jefferson Williams. He vowed to take Springfield and nearby Lewisburg. Some say it was his relative Bill Williams who was wrecking havoc in the White River Valley. The Williams family was half breeds, Capt. Williams' momma Rebecca Jackson, a Cherokee. They had been part of the white savages that got money from the government to move their own people from their homelands in Georgia to the reservation. It was called the trail where they cried because so many people died. Williams and two of his brothers were part of the Tennessee militia forcibly moving the Indians west. Springfield lay on the crossroads of the Old Cherokee Boundary line and was one of the main routes to Indian Territory a 100 miles west, past the boundary at Fort Smith. Springfield got its name from the great artesian spring in the field. It became the Co seat of the new Co and it was there Genl. Marmaduke set up camp. The massive spring amply supplied both man and beast. The old road ran to Batesville, Little Rock and on to Fort Smith. The Cherokee under Chief Duwali lived here with Sam Houston. Springfield known as the Georgia Settlement under Chief Duwali. In 1835, the Stell brothers built a water fed grist mill on Cypress Creek. It was here Sam Houston married Tiana Rogers, daughter of Chief John Rogers. A trading post was built and operated until the forced relocation Capt. Williams had been part of. Then the Indians moved west past Fort Smith into the new Indian Territory. After Prairie Grove, Genl. Marmaduke returned to Camp Lewisburg at Springfield.

Genl. Hindman maintained his goal of securing Missouri for the Confederacy. Missouri's Springfield was the base of supplies for the Union and a critical point for communications to St. Louis. Genl. Hindman learned of the successes of the boys in Missouri and that Quantrill was a natural at hit and run, burning bridges and tearing down communication lines. Hindman sent orders north to recruit and secure the services of the guerillas. The goal was to cause the Union to focus on Missouri minimizing their ability to send men east to fight.

In June 1862 Genl. Hindman ordered Genl. Price to send Col.s John T Hughes, Joseph "JoeC" Porter, J Vard Cockrell, John T Coffee, Horace Brand, Gideon W Thompson, Warner Lewis, JA Poindexter, Sydney Jackman, Jo Shelby and Upton Hayes to Missouri to recruit commissioning Partisan Rangers reinforcing guerilla warfare operations. Commissioned by President Jefferson Davis throughout Missouri and Northern Ark, Partisan Rangers serving the region included W.O. Coleman's Missouri Battalion, Lawther's Missouri Regiment, 10th Missouri Cav, William Clarke Quantrill's Missouri Co, Capt. Woodson's Missouri Co, 1st NE Missouri Cav, 2nd NE Missouri Cav, 10th Missouri Cav, Robert C. Wood's Missouri Cav, Tracy's Missouri Cav, Marmaduke's Missouri Co, The Macon Rangers, McDonald's Missouri Co, Ralls Co Rangers, Schnabel's Missouri Cav, Pool's Missouri Partisan Rangers, Col. William Adair, Col. Holt, Col. Thomas Roe Freeman, Capt. Christopher Cook, Col. Upton Hayes, Col. Joe Shelby, Col. Sydney Drake Jackman, Col. Jeffers, Col. J Vard Cockrell, Capt. Johnson's, Capt. William Osby Dillard, Maj Livingston's Missouri Scouts, Lt. Col. George Maddox, William Thomason "Bloody Bill" Anderson, Alf Bolin, Boone, Ephraim Bowles, Conger, Downey, Col. Elliot, Gabbert, Goode, Hadley, Joe Hart, Sam Hildebrand, Doc Himes, Hinson, John T Hughes, John T Coffee, Hutchins, Hutchinson, Jeans, Rector Johnson, Hyde Johnson, Kane, Keisengro, Kendrick, Joe Kirk, Warner Lewis, Marchbank, Marmaduke, Mathews', Capt. Nevins, Osburn,

Overson, JA Poindexter, Parcel, Maj Pool, Col. JoeC Porter, Potter, Purcell, Rafter, Reid, Rucker, Ruff, Small, Smith, Stacy, Steward, Col. Calhoun "Coon" Thornton, Woodson Thornton, Gideon West Thompson, George Todd, Turk, Vanzoot, Vaughn, Watson, West, Hinch West, Col. White, Yeates and Ike Zeigler. Although not all of the leaders in Missouri and North Ark, these I knew joined Genl. Price.

The North wasn't going to recognize the majority of the guerilla and irregular leaders or their men. They issued an order anyone fighting who was not a regularly commissioned solider forfeited his life upon capture and was nothing more than an outlaw. Although commissioned by the Confederacy, the Union wasn't recognizing Partisan Rangers. The only recognition was separation from the Union allowing authority of the Federalists to kill at will any Southerner. Although this would be the first time we were considered outlaws for many of us it would not be the last. The North was not going to treat captured irregulars and guerillas as prisoners of war. Instead, rangers were to be hung as criminals, robbers and murderers, outlaws. Without discrimination they began shooting all captives, even many who were regularly enlisted soldiers. Word of their executions spread, our boys responded with similar actions, but more importantly public opinion began to change. Boys and men who enlisted with nothing more than the clothes on their backs, joining regular service of the Confederacy were routinely shot and killed, the Union refusing to accept their papers. They claimed soldiers wearing uniforms and their papers to be forgeries. It was this treatment of men serving, both regular and irregular by the Union, their failing to abide by the rules of war that most significantly impacted Northerner's reputation, a hatred that only increased after the War Between the States. Southerners, both Union and Confederate came to despise Northerners during "reconstruction", the years after the war. Genl. Sterling Price, the former Gov. of Missouri familiar both with the lay of the land of the mountains and forest of Missouri and Ark not only understood but supported guerilla warfare, seeing the utilization of these forces for special reconnaissance and internal defense in the face of northern aggressors. It was the actions of the Feds themselves who gave the South their best recruiting tool.

The first of the river attacks began on June 22. Our boys attacked the steamboat Little Blue on the Missouri River at Sibley Landing. Mostly a push and shove event, our boys captured a large amount of military supplies. Upton Hayes joined Shelby's Brigade of the Missouri Cav with John T. Coffee. They made camp at Big Springs on Indian Creek. We called it Camp Coffee. Hayes was head of the Partisan Rangers between the Osage and Missouri Rivers, until Quantrill was assigned. Genl. Price sent Upton Hayes directly to Jackson Co to raise recruits for a cavalry regiment for the Confederate Army. Rather than join the independent fighting groups, many of the local boys joined regular Confederacy units; Tom Maupin joined Co A of the 16th Missouri Infantry. Hayes enlisted Quantrill's help in distracting the Feds while recruiting. Lt. George Todd along with a dozen of the boys went with Hayes to help recruit providing both protection and introduction. While out recruiting in June they gave specific orders to the newest, rawest and most anxious new recruits to wreck havoc on the Union. There's nothing more dangerous than a young boy bent on revenge and we had a camp full of such recruits. Homeless boys who had lost their homes, mothers and siblings, orphaned found a family with us. Their fathers often tortured, killed or in hiding, they were alone. Both Hayes and Quantrill were dreaded names in Union camps and both were delighted by it. Like most of us boys, Sydney Drake Jackman joined the regular Missouri State Guard in 1861. He led a raid on Neosho in May earning him the position of Col. placing him among Genl. Price's choices to recruit. He and Col. Tom spent a great deal of time in Ark recruiting. Col. Tom raised huge support in comparison to Jackman's lack of it.

Genls Price and Hindman ordered Francis Marion Chrisman, Richard Hooker, Christopher Cook, Joseph B. Love and Milton Barber to recruit in Ark. Col. Hooker knew the lay of the land and how to use the swampy Cyprus trees, undergrowth, and canebrakes to his advantage. The Union was not accustomed to navigating marshes and flooded roadbeds. This was life in Ark, especially the bottoms where the rivers merge. With supplies running low for both north and south, foraging was a daily duty. Big Bottom and Akron were covered by Capt. William Hicks. A picket reported Union moving about 15 miles downriver from there, 4 miles north of the Grand Glaise, a major river port town. They were headed to receive a supply of grain. Two men were sent to alert Col. Hooker of the movement. They allowed the troops of the Eighth Indiana Infantry and the Third Iowa Cav with empty wagons to pass. Using the canebrake to hide, they waited until they returned with loaded wagons. The Union was unprepared and fled abandoning half of their wagons full of grain. Sufficient grain was secured for the horses and for milling bread for our boys to feed themselves.

These tactics were being used in Missouri and Ark, but Ark had not had the tumultuous years of the Border Wars experienced by Missouri. The bloodshed and violence we grew up with had callused the most tender hearted. The Mormon Wars arose while the War of 1812 was still fresh in people's minds, then the Border Wars, a precursor to this the War Between the States. There's nothing good in war. Families lost brothers, sons, fathers and husband's. In July and Aug 1862, the sons of Germans, Jacob and Nancy Caroline Yount Sipe from the Barrens, neighbors of Bill Chitwood's family, had four sons join the Confederacy; Marcus Philo Sipe,

29, Rufus Monroe, 25, William Sidney, 21 and Jacob Pinkney 19. Rufe was the only one to survive the war. Their youngest son, Elk, joined Col. Tom remaining at home in the hills along the river. Families on both sides in western Missouri and North Ark were destroyed more by loss of life than everything together; such wounds aren't easily healed.

In Missouri on Tuesday July 8th, 1862 Union Maj Gower of the First Iowa Cav met Capt.'s William H Ankeny and William A Martin of the Seventh Missouri Cav. Capt. Martin Kehoe of the First Missouri Cav joined them attempting to lure Jackman into an ambush. They approached George Lotspeich's farm in Johnson Co but found it deserted. Col. Jackman sent ten guerillas ahead to scout the area who saw the Union gathering. Jackman and the boys engaged with the Feds killing most of them. The bush tactics Unc had taught us, the fighting style for which the guerillas were famous for was wrecking havoc with the organized style of fighting of the Union. Every day our Co was growing, men and boys coming in. These men possessed a growing hatred for everything Northern. They didn't hate the United States, nor were all of them even supporters of succession, but they would defend the idea of a person's right to self govern to their own death. I met a few who were slave owners; most only "knew a man who had a slave."

On Wed the 9th we camped on Sugar Creek near Wadesburg in Cass Co. Just before dawn we were ambushed by a hundred Feds under Maj Gower. We outmatched them two to one and more with our expert skills in warfare on horseback. Thoroughly whipping them, they limped back to headquarters with their dead and wounded thrown over their horses. It was a pitiful sight. The commander was outraged and humiliated. He called for all units in surrounding counties to rendezvous the next day at the farm of George Lotspeich not far from our Sugar Creek camp. However, how hard is it to realize part of our tactics were to immediately disperse and regroup elsewhere. When they arrived the next morning, our camp was empty. A scout spotted some of the boys near Big Creek in Johnson Co and reported back to Maj Gower. We watched as they headed towards Johnson Co galloping in the heat and humidity. Our boys and our horses were more accustomed to Missouri summers. Maj Gower joined Martin Kehoe's men around seven o'clock at the Hornsby Farm on the edge of Cass Co. Most of our boys had time to eat, including Quantrill and 20 or so of us at Hornsby's earlier in the day. We knew the importance of resting the horses' mid-day riding in the early hours of dawn and dusk. We moved back north making camp on the farm of James Sears about 5 miles west of Pleasant Hill.

The Feds camped at the Hornsby farm clearly unaware we had been there and returned north. Dawn on July 11th came on hot predicting a blistering day, the humidity engulfed us. Union Martin Kehoe and most of his men were Missourians and understood the heat and the need to move early. They quietly left Gower's camp around five o'clock in the morning against Gower's orders that all troops were moving out together. Exchanging a few shots with one of our pickets, they sent word back to Gower they were on our trail. Martin Kehoe wanted the feather in his hat when it came to Quantrill. He was determined to get to him first. When they entered the field, they saw the Sears house sitting in the midst of the field with only a few trees nearby. Several of our men ran about in the yard as if they had been taken by surprise, all part of our ambush plan. Kehoe decided to attack. Riding at the head of the column with spurs digging in and sabers drawn Kehoe lead the charge as they entered the lane leading to the house. We were prepared with men hidden on either side, scattered along the lane. We waited until Kehoe was at the gate of the house.

The first volley killed half a dozen and wounded twice that many. Kehoe was shot through the shoulder. Bill Gregg had suggested Quantrill himself be stationed close to the house, near the gate leading to the barn lot and if successful, he could open the gate for the galloping horses to enter. We fought for nearly 3 hours and as morning passed the heat became unbearable. We captured the horses of the dead. Gower didn't arrive until nearly eleven o'clock. By this time we were fighting hand to hand combat. The undergrowth had been too much for the horses. The Union sabers always amazed me, the quickness in which they severed a head from a body, sliced an arm or left a hand dangling, blood squirting as the wounded fell dying. "Cowards die many times before their deaths; The valiant never taste of death but once. Of all the wonders that I yet have heard, it seems to me most strange that men should fear; Seeing that death, a necessary end, will come when it will come"... Julius Caesar. This hand to hand combat was the stuff of Shakespeare. This was not how men should die. Some of the boys fled to nearby ravines but were unable to escape. When ammunition ran low many of the men used rocks and clubs. With thirst driving all of us, men on both sides were retreating to shade and trying to find water. The Union suffered heavy losses with more than 25 men killed and as many seriously wounded. Neither side counted the wounded that were able to continue fighting. David Butler was wounded, captured and taken as a prisoner of war along with Jerre Doores. He had been hit in the knee and died from gangrene. Ezra Moore, a regular had joined us along with his father in law David George. They had taken a herd of cattle to Texas some time earlier in the year. The Union had gone after Ezra on June 11th and the next day burned down David George's home. This caused not only them but several friends to join up with us. Ezra was killed trying to climb the bluff behind the Sear's home, shot a couple inches above the heart. He's buried in the George Cemetery in Oak Grove. William Tucker was wounded. Brothers, William and Perry Hayes were new recruits. William led the charge and had a horse shot out from under him, knocking him unconscious. George Morrow rushed out during the battle gathering guns and ammunition from the dead as some of the other boys captured horses without riders.

We headed towards the Blue River. The Liberty Tribune ran a story on the battle on July 18th, citing that 5 of our men had been found with signed loyalty oaths on their persons. They reported they found a roster of Quantrill's men. Some days later, our scouts managed to capture Union communications.

JULY 9-11,1862.--Skirmishes at Lotspeich Farm, on Sugar Creek, near Wadesburg; at Sears' House, near Pleasant Hill; and at Big Creek Bluffs, near Pleasant Hill, Mo.

No. 1. -- Report of Maj. James O. Cower, First Iowa Cav.

HEADQUARTERS CLINTON, HENRY CO, Mo., July 13, 1862.

COL.: I have the honor to report that, on Tuesday, the 8th instant, I received information that a band of guerrillas, numbering some 200 men, commanded by one Quantrill, was in camp on Sugar Creek, near Wadesburg, Cass Co, Missouri, whereupon I sent Lieut. R. M. Reynolds, of Co A, First Iowa Cav, with Lt.s Bishop, Foster, and Whisenand, and 90 enlisted men of Companies A, G, and H, First Iowa Cav, in search of them.

The detachment marched at 11 p.m., 8th instant, with orders to reach and attack Quantrill's camp, if possible, at daylight on the 9th instant. Quantrill's camp was discovered at about 6 a.m., 9th instant, and the advance guard, under Lt. Bishop, of Co A, First Iowa Cav, was very gallantly led to the attack, but, not being supported by the main column as soon as expected, retired without loss, though receiving several volleys. Lt. Reynolds, charged them with his command, but finding the ground unfavorable and their position very strong, retired with a loss of 3 men wounded, 1 fatally, and since dead. Quantrill lost 1 man killed and several wounded.

Upon the return of the detachment I immediately sent dispatches to Butler and Warrensburg for details to meet them at Lotspeich farm, Cass Co, Missouri, about 1 mile west of their camp. I marched, with 4 commissioned officers and 75 enlisted men of Companies A and G, First Iowa Cav, at 5 o'clock on the morning of the 10th instant, reaching the Lotspeich farm at 11 a.m., finding a detachment of 65 men, First Iowa Cav, from Butler, Mo., under command of Capt. William H. Aunkeny, with Lt.s Dinsmore and Mcintyre, and also a detachment of 65 enlisted men of the Seventh Missouri Cav, fresh Harrisonville, under command of Capt. Martin.

Shortly afterward my command was increased by Lt. White and 60 enlisted men of the First Missouri Cav, from Warrensburg, under command of Capt. M. Kehoe. Upon inquiry I ascertained that Quantrill and his men (estimated at 250) had left their camp on Sugar Creek about 4 p.m. on the 9th instant. At 2 p.m. 10th instant I received word from Capt. Kehoe that he had found their trail and was pursuing. After striking the trail I pressed forward with my command in a northeasterly direction, passing east of Rose Hill, Johnson Co, and thence passing up Big Creek Bottom in a northwesterly direction, overtaking Capt. Kehoe at 7 p.m. 10 instant at the farm of Mr. Hornsby, at which place Quantrill and his men had taken dinner. Having marched 50 miles during the day I went into camp, distributing my command at farm-houses for subsistence and forage, some of the details having marched without rations.

Capt. Kehoe marched without my knowledge in the morning, and in direct disregard of his orders, meeting Quantrill and his band 3 miles west of Pleasant Hill, at Sears' farm, Cass Co, Missouri, about 10 o'clock a.m. 11th instant, and was repulsed, with loss of 6 men killed and 9 wounded. His entire advance guard was killed, except Lt. White, commanding, and himself (Capt. Kehoe), wounded in the engagement. Capt. Kehoe not being able to hold his position at Sears' farm, it was impossible to ascertain Quantrill's loss, but it is reported heavy. Had it not been for this attack by Capt. Kehoe I feel confident that we would have secured Quantrill and his entire band.

On crossing the road from Pleasant Hill to Independence I sent Lt. McIntyre, of Co L, First Iowa Cav, with 50 men, through the timber, on the Independence road, with instructions to march up on the open ground on the west side of the timber. Pressing forward with the rest of my command on their trail, passing where they had encamped at night, reaching the farm of Mr. Sears (where Capt. Kehoe was repulsed) at 11 o'clock a.m. 11th instant, I found a portion of Quantrill's band, who fled down a wood road into the Big Creek timber. My advance guard, under command of Lieut. John McDermott, of Co G, First Iowa Cav, pressing them closely, and the head of column close upon them, came upon Quantrill's main force, lying in the cliffs of the ravines, about half a mile from Sears' house. Their position was very strong indeed, but the vigorous and determined attack on the part of both officers and men routed them completely and punished them severely. Under the great disadvantage of position our loss was much less than could be expected, being but 3 men killed and 10 men wounded. The loss of the enemy known in this skirmish alone was 14 killed and 15 to 20 wounded, and in the three skirmishes Quantrill's loss could not have been less than 18 killed and 25 or 30 wounded. Quantrill himself is reported wounded in the thigh. Quantrill's men were completely routed and disbanded, fleeing in small squads in all directions. Out of the 4 commissioned officers in the command with me from this post 3 were wounded, and the action of the men was highly commendable and entirely satisfactory. The details from Butler and Harrisonville, though not suffering so much on account of their position, did their duty with honor to the Government and themselves. Especial mention is due to the following officers and non-commissioned officers wounded in the last skirmish: First Lieut. David A. Kerr, adjutant, Post Clinton; First Lieut. R. M. Reynolds, Co A, First Iowa Cav; Second Lieut. E. S. Foster, Co G, First Iowa Cav; First Lieut. John McDermott, commanding advance guard and leading it with much credit to himself, not wounded; Joseph T. Foster, Sgt.-Maj, Post Clinton; Quartermaster-Sgt. H. L. Dashiel, provost-marshal. I have as yet no report of skirmish near Lotspeich farm on the 9th instant, as also none of skirmish at Sears' house on the 11th instant, but am informed that Capt. Kehoe and his men, First Missouri Cav, met them with commendable resolution. Particular mention is due to Dr. C. H. Lothrop, additional assistant surgeon First Iowa Cav, for very prompt and efficient services rendered on the ground, paying attention to and relieving the wounded in the thickest of the conflict. Not having as yet received accounts from detachments or companies of the loss or capture of property, I am unable to report upon it. Loss in the three skirmishes, 11 killed and 21 wounded.

I have the honor to be, very respectfully, your obedient servant,

JAMES O. GOWER

The roster they found had William C Quantrill Capt. at the top, W. Haller, 1st Lt, George Todd, 2nd Lt, W.H. Gregg 1st Sgt, John Jarrette 2nd Sgt, JL Tucker 3rd Sgt, Andrew Blunt 4th Sgt, FM Scott Commissary, and Richard Maddox Quartermaster. The list included Henry Akers, Hugh Anderson, John Atchison, Ves Atchison, Wiley Atchison, and H. Austin. W.A. Baker, Lee Ball, D.S. Barnett, George Barnett, James M. "Jim" Barnett, O.S. Barnett, W.C. Bell, William Bledsoe, Quartermaster John A. "Alf" Booker, James Bowling, J.A. Buckner, W. H. Burgess, Dick Burns, William Butler, William Campbell, William Chamblin, W. F. Cheatman Samuel Clifton, Synes Cockrell, Thomas Colclesure, William Henry Colclesure, Robert Davenport, DeJarnett, John Dickers, William T. Doake, Jerre Doores, Dr. W.M. Doores, Noach Estes, I. G. Freeman, William Haise, Robert Hall, Thomas Hall, Bill Haller, William "Bill" Halley, J.W. Hone, Matthew Houston, Mike, Robert Houx and William Howard, 2nd Lt John Jarrette, W.F. Judd, Capt John William Koger, B. L. Long, CA Longacre, James Lyons, Brothers, George and Dick Maddox, Ezra Moore, Boone Muir, Otho Offutt oldest and tallest of our men, Harry Ogden became Lt Gov of Louisiana, Billy Ogden, John Oliphant, H.C. Pemberton, Dave Poole, George and Mart Rider, Francis Marion "Gooly" Robinson, Fernando Scott, A.B., F.F. and John Teague, JH and William Terry, James Thompson, 3rd Sgt. James Tucker, William Tucker, Charley Williamson.

Some of the newest recruits were on the list however it was an incomplete list, both myself and Wyeth James and a 100 more could have been on it. The list was being compiled for official listing by the Confederacy of Quantrill's command. He forbade anyone from further maintaining such a list ordering me to keep it in my head until quartered with Genl. Price. I had a memory for things able to recall conversations word for word. No one knew how much I remembered but it was clear I could recall things better than most. Alf Booker, he was our quartermaster, in charge of provisions and supplies. He could be a little scary to some of the boys. He wore his hair pushed up in the back like he'd been standing over a blow hole or something, big bushy eyebrows and a full beard. His hair was trimmed short up top. He had a mean scowl but his jolly laugh told on him. He had delighted in being on the list, laughing because he thought the Union would think it complete.

Chapter 11

In the fall of 1861 Union soldiers had stolen Henry Younger's fortune, Cole's daddy. They robbed him of four thousand dollars, his carriages, wagons and 40 saddle horses at Harrisonville and carried it off to Kansas. It had only been a couple months since Bloody Bill and Jim's daddy had been laid to rest when we got news of Cole's daddy, Henry having been murdered July 20th, 1862.

Cole's oldest brother Dick died in Aug of 1860 of a ruptured appendix. When war was declared, Cole joined the Union leaving his father and mother at home in Westport. After his daddy had been robbed of his fortune by the Union, he changed sides. I reckon Cole felt responsible for the family. His daddy had been to a cattle auction in Independence and was returning home to Strother when a squad of the Fifth Missouri Militia Cav under Capt. Walley encountered him in his buggy. They killed him and took all of his belongings. Charlie Pitts and his mother Margaret Wells came upon the body of Col. Younger. Charlie stayed with the body while his momma went for help. He was taken home to be buried next to his son Dick in an unmarked grave. All southerners worried about being jailed for burying their dead, a crime if found by the Union. I never really knew why Samuel Wells called himself Charlie Pitts. Maybe it was a way of having himself two identifies in the wake of the war. Cole's mother had been forced to burn down her own home and the family walked through the snow to a nearby neighbor's house. It was the actions of the Union and Jayhawkers upon Union families that lead Cole to join Quantrill.

One of the boys brought the Kansas City Tribune to camp which reported events surrounding the death of Bloody Bill's daddy in early July:

"It will be remembered that some few weeks ago, we gave the particulars of the killing an old man named Anderson by Judge A. I. Baker. Baker had branded Anderson and his two sons Bill and Jim, as belonging to a band of horse thieves; and for this and perhaps one or two other reasons which it is not necessary to make public, Anderson sought his life and was shot by Baker in self-defense. At the same time a Mexican, one of the gang of horse thieves and desperados to which the Andersons belonged was hung by a mob. Bill Anderson was arraigned on the charge preferred by Baker, and bailed out. They swore vengeance on Baker and others, and left the country. It was supposed at the time and the awful tragedy which we are about to relate proves the supposition to have been true that they had gone to Missouri to join Quantrill.

On Thursday evening, the 3d of July, at about 8 or 9 o'clock, Bill Anderson, Jim Anderson, Lee Griffin, accompanied by Jim Reed and William Quantrill, arrived at the residence of Judge Baker on the Santa Fe road, when one of their Co proceeded to his house and reported himself as a lone traveler, and told Baker he wished to procure some whiskey. Baker went to his store, a short distance from his residence, to get the whiskey, and when in the act of going into the cellar the other four members of the gang rushed in and discharged several pistols at him, two of them taking effect in his body. Baker reeled upon the steps, drew his revolver, and fired into the crowd, hitting Jim Anderson in the thigh, but not seriously wounding him. Baker fell into the cellar in an expiring condition. A young man, Henry Segur, a brother-in-law of Baker's, was present, and was shot and thrown into the cellar with him. The cut-throats supposed this latter gentleman to be Elisha Goddard, of Americus, against whom they have a grudge for taking s prominent part in the hanging of their comrade, the Mexican, and against whom they have sworn vengeance. They then closed the door and piled boxes and barrels upon it and set them on fire. In this position the two dying men lay until the roof of the building fell in. Baker, who was in the agonies of a horrible death, reached over his hand and bade Segur farewell, saying, "I am going." Young Segur, although mortally wounded, recollected a back window in the cellar, and through this he mustered strength to escape from the horrible fate of burning to death. He lived about twenty-four hours after his escape, time to tell of what had happened. Judge Baker's head, arms and legs were literally burned to ashes. A portion of the body was saved from burning by some object which had fallen upon it during the conflagration. The devils then set fire to the remainder of his property, consisting of a large stone dwelling, several out-houses, a carriage, etc. They also stole two fine horses. In Co with Mr. Goddard and his brother, Mr. Baker visited Emporia about noon of the day on which the dreadful murder was committed, in the very carriage which was burned, and with the very horses which the Rebels stole. He was in fine spirits, and little dreamed of the terrible fate which awaited him ere he closed his eyes in slumber that night. Little did he think that the slumber which he should take that was to be the one that know no waking this side of eternity. It is a little surprising to us that, with his natural shrewdness, he should not have been more guarded. He jumped into the trap laid for him without hesitancy, and that, too, when he knew the Andersons had sworn vengeance, and had even sent him word that they were coming. His friends state, however, that he did not believe these reports, and had said that he did not believe the boys would harm him.

After they had completed their hellish work at this point, the murderers started toward Missouri on the Santa Fe road, committing degradation and stealing horses at every point which they passed. After leaving Baker's the first settler is a man called Dutch Henry, whom they robbed of clothing and money. They then went to the residence of Charley Withington and after placing all the men about the premises under arrest, they demolished a saloon, knocking the proprietor down with a pistol, and setting fire to his house. Owing to the lumber being green, the building did not burn. Jim Anderson seemed determined upon killing our friend Withington, but his life was spared through the intercession of Quantrell and Bill Anderson."

The paper had not reported the story exactly as it happened but close enough. Some of us were glad to be unknown to the news writers as our names had not appeared alongside Jim and Bloody Bill's, this time.

In March, Union Genl. Halleck had issued Genl. Order Number 2 which warned "if they join any guerrilla band they will not, if captured, be treated as ordinary prisoners of war, but will be hung as robbers and murderers." On April 21, Confederate President Jefferson Davis responded by authorizing commissions for those forming bands of partisan rangers. The Union authorities refused to recognize them. On May 29, Brigadier Genl. John Schofield responded with Genl. Order No. 18 to the Missouri State Militia which read in part: "When caught in arms, engaged in their unlawful warfare, they will be shot down upon the spot." Most of the boys and men had chosen sides by now, or fled with their families south or north depending on their persuasions. The Union was having great difficulty maintaining numbers in light of the success of the recruitment into the Partisan Rangers. In an effort to raise a sufficient number of men for community defenses, on July 22, 1862, Union Genl. Schofield with the aid of Missouri's provisional Gov. Hamilton Rowan Gamble ordered a compulsory militia enrollment, the Enrolled Missouri Militia. Schofield issued Genl. Order No. 19 requiring all able bodied loyal men to enroll in the militia and the disloyal to register stating their sympathies. Young men not only in Jackson Co but throughout the region flooded into Quantrill's camp to speak with Col. Hayes. Really, can you imagine going in and reporting you were a southerner siding with the Confederacy? Did the Union think us all idiots?

Col. JoeC Porter engaged Union Maj Caldwell near Florida in Monroe Co on the 22 day of July for over an hour and a half. Two days later Caldwell with over 100 men pursued JoeC into the dense undergrowth near Bott's farm at Santa Fe. Word was over 400 men with JoeC were fleeing when Col. Guitar of the 9th Missouri Union Cav blocked him at Brown's Spring. The following day pursuing them to Moore's Mill where JoeC and his men were severely beaten. Fighting along Auxvasse Creek, JoeC and his men ran out ammunition and fled. Col. JoeC Porter and Capt Alvin Cobb camped about 10 miles north of Fulton at Brown's Spring. When the Union got word from their scouts of the encampment they headed to it. When they arrived the camp was abandoned. JoeC with about 250 men, 65 Boone Co men of the Blackfoot Rangers under "Chief" John Bowles and another 75 under Capt Alvin Cobb were prepared with an ambush of their own. We called John Bowles "Chief" even though he wasn't a chief just as we called Maj Emory Rogers, Chief Rogers. His daddy was Lightening Bug Bowles son of the great Cherokee Chief John Watts Bowles, Arkansas' Chief Duwali.

Cole Younger and Chief Bowles were family. Cole's grandfather, Charles Younger had a bunch of wives', black, white and Indian, one was Dorcus Wilson, the granddaughter of Ooloosta Tachee, one of Chief Duwali's wives. Both Cole and Chief Bowles learned many of the same skills Unc taught us in the woods behind our farm. One of those lessons had been learned the night Bloody Bill got his nickname. Even though he was the oldest, he had taken Jesse as his partner, the least experienced of us and youngest. Rather than give in and go hungry, they done what it took to get us supper. And these men, rather than avoid battle prepared a successful ambush along the banks of the creek.

John Watts Bowles, Chief of the Ark - "Chief Duwali" 1756-1839
Son of John Fork Tongue "Little Tassel" Watts and Ghigoneli Bowles

Men of age, some of whom were so old they could barely walk were being put to service. Col. Thomas Freeman and Joseph Shelby under orders from Genl. Price were recruiting heavily and successfully throughout North Ark and Missouri. The recruits didn't want to leave home and mostly didn't fit well into discipline organized battles. They had their own jayhawker bands to contend with. Looting, murder and mayhem were happening at the hands of men on both sides. Ironically, both the Union and Confederacy called upon their guerillas to keep the peace, to stop the looting and killing of neighbors against neighbors. Although President Jefferson Davis was against guerilla warfare, he understood its purpose in particular localities, like the Ozarks. Trusting Genl. Thomas Hindman and former Missouri Gov. Sterling Price, President Davis authorized the commissioning of officers with authority to form from the ranks of the guerillas, Partisan Rangers. The Partisan Ranger Act required at least 10 men to organize by electing a Capt., 1 Sgt., and 1 Corp. and shall commence operations against the enemy without waiting for special instructions. It had been news of the Partisan Ranger Act in April that had finally swayed Momma. The success of southern recruitment had led the Union to force men into taking sides, joining up, and now, men and boys, from all walks of life made their way to Southern camps. The Union had also put into effect an order that their troops were to forage for their food and supplies during the pursuit of their enemies. This meant that more and more men who feared leaving their families alone chose to join the Partisan Rangers, guerillas and irregulars to stay closer to home for longer stents of time. The Union refused recognition of Partisan Rangers as having any legitimacy and gave license to their men to shoot and kill any sympathizer or resister.

By the first week of Aug, 1862, Quantrill and Hayes forces were consolidating when they learned Coffee, Cockrell and Shelby were moving northward to join them. Hughes and Thompson had roughly 75 recruits while Hayes and Quantrill had over 325 men with horses, trained by the best of us to ride and fight Indian style. Although the recruitment numbers were growing with ease managing these numbers of men was proving to be difficult. Col. JoeC Porter alone had upwards of 2,000 men with him. JoeC headed south to Ark with his recruits to Clem's Mill, five miles west of Kirksville where he was to join Col. Poindexter and his 1,500 recruits. They were seeking to secure training and equipment for them. They encountered the Union State Militia engaging in hard fighting for over three hours. Although they outnumbered the Union, JoeC's men, untrained and unarmed fled. They had the desire to fight but with nothing more than rakes, hoes and axes to fight with, they fled defeated.

On Aug 7th, we met at Charlie Cowherd's farm near Strother to discuss a plan of attack on Independence, Missouri. Charlie's daddy, Kirt Cowherd had been twice hung from a tree by the Union in efforts to gain information from him. He talked them into letting him down each time. Col. John T. Hughes was familiar to most of the men as he was a Maj recruiter along with Col.s Upton Hayes and JoeC Porter. Col. Hayes took Dick Yeager, Cole Younger, William Young, Virgil Miller and Boone Muir to scout Independence. Morgan Maddox had joined Quantrill at the age of 15. Hayes sent him alone into Independence as a spy. We moved camps while Morg was gone. Arch Rockwell brought him to the new camp on the 10th and stayed joining us for the fight at Independence. Col. Hayes sent Cole Younger dressed as an old woman peddling apples to scout out the town. His surveillance was vital in the plan of attack.

Recruits and returnees trickled into camp. Waiting, we told stories, got know each other. Jim Crow Chiles had been a freighter on the Santa Fe Trail. Sol Bassham was a wagon master and freighter on the Santa Fe and California trails. He told us his brother Bill Bassham returning home from the overland passage had been arrested accused of being a guerilla, specifically of being one of Quantrill's men. He was being held in the Independence jail. In 1861, Kansas Redlegs stole the family silverware, killed over 100 hogs and burned the Bassham barns and haystacks, after Missus Harriette fed them. When the Cols and boys returned from scouting, Sol talked to Bill Gregg about his brother being in jail at Independence. Plans were laid out. Col. John T. Hughes under Genl. Marmaduke would be leading the attack on the garrison in Independence. Col. Hughes ordered Quantrill to cut Union Col. James T. Buell, commander of the garrison, off from his men and picket the city after it had been taken.

John McCorkle showed up just as Cole Younger returned to camp. John was telling us, his own cousin Mollie Wigginton, also a cousin to Cole Younger, all Fristoe descendants, had been threatened with arrest by the Union. He'd sworn his allegiance to the Union and had intentions of staying out of the fight until the threats on the women, in this case his cousin Mollie, daughter of John Wigginton and Mary Ann Fristoe.

John McCorkle

George "Bud" Wigginton

Missouri Valley Special Collections, Kansas City Public Library, Kansas City, Missouri

He and George "Bud" Wigginton, Mollie's brother, were at a singing school at Big Cedar. They watched some Feds looking over the saddles on the horses in the church yard for marks of guns being carried or drawn. Arriving back at home Mollie told them Feds come to the house looking for them demanding they report for service or she would be arrested and put in prison. The thought of her in a northern prison was too much, so, John and Bud decided to join up with us. Since John was the first to show up with a long range rifle, Quantrill appointed him scout, spy and sniper. George "Bud" told how they had first gone to Dave Talley's house, who after they had provided him the correct passwords identifying themselves provided directions to Cole's camp. Upon arriving at camp, Cole examined them and what provisions, ammunitions, guns and supplies they brought. They found Jabez, John's brother, in camp and stayed on about a week before word came to meet up with the rest of us. On Sunday they went to the home of John and Mary Ann Fristoe Wigginton, daughter of Daniel Fristoe to eat. Cole was a cousin, John and Jabez McCorkle, nephews, George their son, and Tom and Dick Talley cousins, with Jim Morris and Tom Rice, neighbors. Cole was in charge of his family. He would have to report on their deaths differently, carrying the bodies home to be buried or explain why he couldn't. I understood every day why Momma held Jesse back, keeping him home as long as she could. It wasn't just for him, or her, but me knowing what having my little brother fighting would require of me.

We gathered on Aug 11 near the bridge at the Little Blue leading into Independence just before sun rise. The town and its Union occupiers were sleeping. Quantrill was ordered to lead the charge using all the men who had revolvers. Col. Hughes would go straight through the town to the camp. Cole had learned their fortifications were the court house and bank. Hayes and Thompson were to bring up the rear with about 350 men. We entered the town on Spring Branch Road. Two of the boys went ahead killing the sentry standing guard just as we came into view allowing for our dash to the square. Guns blazing, windows shattering and our deep rebel yells could have woke a dead man. A sentry across the street managed to get his Co awake, armed and half dressed. They made their way through the street to the building where Buell headquartered saving him. Col. Hughes was immediately behind us riding so fast and furious he jumped the fence surrounding the camp on the outside of town riding over and through the men still in their tents. Those fellas may not have been dressed but like us, they slept with their guns on them and struck back. John McCorkle had a long range rifle, the best for sniping. He was ordered to make those hiding behind a big rock to get their heads down. They looked like the boxed devil, their heads popping up and down and John's gun the crank. Big Barney Chambers a minister himself volunteered to go in first with about 30 men, the Feds first volley mowed down the hedges where they had taken cover killing Barney. Buell yelled from his window for his men to get to the bank building. Surrounded, they were trapped in the brick building. We had succeeded in cutting Buell off from his men. George Todd took a dozen of the boys for the jail break of Bill Bassham, Sol's brother. The soldiers guarding the jail fired at them then turned and ran. Todd sent some of the boys to the blacksmith shop to get whatever tools they could find. They came back with a large sledge hammer which succeeded in breaking the men out. Frank Harbaugh was nothing more than a farmer who was accused of having offered relief, a meal, to guerrillas. Bill Bassham suspected of being a southern spy because he carried the mail wanted arms to fight but Harbaugh, he took out on a dead run. We lay seize to the bank building for over an hour. Col. Hughes was killed in the first volley, then Col Thompson was shot in the leg and Col. Upton Hayes took over. He was shot in the foot, which left Quantrill commanding. Quantrill called for someone to burn'em out. Cole Younger and Jabez McCorkle volunteered to set the bank on fire. They gathered wood shavings from a nearby shop; one went to the rear and the other to the front. As the smoke swirled Buell offered up a white flag of surrender. Shouting from the window, Buell was insistent they be treated as prisoners of war and not handed over to Col. Quantrill.

Once a ceasefire was called, Buell and his soldiers entered the court yard surrendering to Col. Gideon Thompson. We wanted nothing more than to kill Buell and he knew it. Col. Hughes was dead and Col. Hayes foot injured so severely it had to be amputated. Andy Blunt and Dick Burns who had a good aim survived. Minister Barney Chambers, a Presbyterian was among the first ones killed. Col. Kit Chiles was killed leading the charge. Samuel Clifton, Kit Dalton and William Gaw survived. John Jarrette fought hard; few would know he had been wounded on the Harrisonville Independence Road earlier in the year. Edward Koger and John Little were killed. John's brother James took him home to bury him. They had to do it at night due to the Union law against burying guerillas. They buried him in the Lobb Cemetery. John William Koger survived. George, Morgan and Dick Maddox survived. Ed Marshall was killed. Indian Jim Martin and Tom Maupin rode with Pat O'Donnell during the raid. Tom and Bud Maxwell, Dr. Lee Miller, brother of Clell and Ed, James Morris, Jesse Morrow, John Hicks George and William Gregg all made it. Bill Haller captured a man named Smiley. Haller had shot out every load in his pistol but pretended they were loaded and commanded Smiley to surrender. Sam Hamilton and Daniel Williams were wounded. They made their way to Clark Hockensmith's who protected them. They were discovered by a Kansas Cav in Sept and were killed. Hockensmith escaped. John C. Hope survived. Jeremiah David "Dave" Hylton was wounded. He hid out for 6 months recouping then returned to fight with us. He wore his curly yellow hair long and his face shaved except for a large well trimmed mustache. For Jabez McCorkle's brother John this was his first battle. He was ordered to get a wagon for the wounded. Dave Parr, Dave Poole, John Ross, Fernando Scott and Fletch Taylor were men who fought like a horse and steam engine rolled into one. George Todd, Harrison Trow, James Tucker, Dan Vaughn, Andy Walker, Press Webb, Warren Welch, Si Whitsett, Bud Wigginton, Dick Yeager and Cole Younger fought and survived. We captured 20 wagons of supplies and ammunition. There were enough muskets, rifles, and sabers for all of the new recruits and improvements for some of the more seasoned men. Quantrill caught a horse following the battle that was high spirited and good looking; he called him “Old Charley.”

Buell’s command had 37 killed and 63 wounded, with the Majority having run away, we had 150 captives. They were all paroled and treated in accordance with the rules of war. This might not have been the case had we of known what had happened to some of JoeC Porter’s men captured just days before, all shot to death. It was agreed the Union would surrender unconditionally. Buell was paroled along with his men. It was all we could do to keep John McCorkle from using that long range rifle on him. We left there heading to camp on the farm of Morgan Walker, the same man whose farm Quantrill had ‘saved’ from the Jayhawkers in Dec 1860.

The next day at Walker’s, Mrs. Bass, J.W., Sam and Bill’s momma, presented Quantrill with a small black silk flag. Three days later on Aug 14, 1862, Quantrill decided to form his own Partisan Rangers. Col. Gideon W. Thompson was authorized to swear us in as Co E of Shelby’s 2nd Missouri Cavalry. The order was signed by Thompson with the authority from Genl. Thomas Hindman. Elections were held: Quantrill as Capt., Willie Haller was 1st Lt., George Todd 2nd Lt., William Gregg 3rd Lt., James Tucker First Duty Sgt., Cole Younger 2nd Sgt.. Quantrill and the officers were commissioned and 150 of us men became Confederate soldiers. For most of us this was not our first enlistment.

Fletch Taylor Harrison Trow

Missouri Valley Special Collections, Kansas City Public Library

The Union’s defeat at Independence was a horrific blow to the Union Army in Missouri. The reputation of the irregulars and guerillas grew and with it the living legend of Quantrill. Even if they had paroled Buell, if Quantrill could succeed in getting Buell where others failed, who was safe from him, from us, the guerilla's the new face of war fare. It was such a disaster to Buell the Union mustered him and his soldiers out in St. Louis under threats of court martial. Buell had ignored warnings refusing to believe a large Confederate force was preparing to attack Independence. His arrogance cost him his career. It became known across Missouri; Buell left his men vulnerable, spreading them out in open tent camps while he made his quarters in a large brick building in the middle of town. His guard Co was across the street occupying a building there and another next to the city jail. Buell retired for the night without informing his troops or guard of the possibility of an attack. The Capt. of the guard was like us, more alert; he didn't go to sleep without his gun by his side and ordered his men to do the same. The Capt. saved Buell. Had we had the opportunity to kill Buell during the seize we would have certainly paroled him all right.

The Union underestimated not only the recruitment efforts in North Ark and Missouri and the effectiveness of the men doing the recruiting but the courage of those recruited. After we won Independence the Federal commander, Genl. John Schofield was stunned to learn the defeat came at the hands of such untrained and undisciplined men as guerillas, especially William Clarke Quantrill. Schofield ordered Genl. Totten to deal with the growing threat, meaning get rid of Quantrill and his men. Union Maj Emory Foster under orders from Totten led his men from Lexington to Lone Jack. When they got to Lone Jack, Foster learned we had about 1500 men under Col. Coffee and Lt. Col. Tracy camped, ready to attack.

The Union had pie on their face after the loss at Independence, especially to soldiers they considered guerillas. But they were arrogant, talking of having all but eliminated Poindexter and Porter's men as our men donning Union uniforms simply walked among their camp gathering vital information on the goings on and attitudes. The Union was sure they would "wipe out the guerillas and John T. Coffee's men". They were planning to circle Lone Jack. They grossly underestimated the effectiveness us boys had destroying communication lines and roads around Lone Jack. No telegraph lines or bridges on the central routes remained. The Union could not get where they wanted when they wanted and couldn't relay the information to other commands. Maj Emory Foster and 800 men arrived. Around 11 o'clock, Foster attacked the camp of Col. Coffee. Their cannon fire provided direct knowledge of their firepower and position. After dispersing Col Coffee's men, tired from days in the saddle and marching, Foster and his men camped along the main street of Lone Jack.

Charles Thomas Duncan had been left guarding Independence following the attack. Quantrill who had difficulty taking orders from "officials" used this as an excuse not to fight at Lone Jack saying he had to go check on Charlie. He left with around 60 men headed to Independence to grab as much loot and supplies as could be carried off. While he was gone, Bill Haller was under strict orders to keep George Todd and the rest of us in camp. Col. Cockrell met with several of the other men in command and a plan of attack for the morning was agreed and set out. Our combined forces would overwhelm them. Hunter, Jackman and Tracy's men were to position themselves in a field west of town before sunrise and await confirmation of the fight to attack. Hays laid out to begin with a mounted attack from the north and a surprise flank attack. As planned when morning came the boys surrounded Foster's men, circling them like wild Indians circle a wagon train but Foster's pickets got sight of Hayes' men eliminating the element of surprise. It led to frontier fighting hand to hand combat, fought in the streets, gardens, and homes over about five hours, with significant losses on both sides. George Webb who had formed his own Co was at the head of the battle along with Dr. and Capt. Caleb Winfrey. Dr. Lee Miller and Mart Rider captured the Federal Battery. After the war, Mart he turned to preaching and became a Methodist minister. With the sun rising Jackman, Hunter and Tracy attacked. When Hayes rejoined them, they were able to force Capt. Brawner of the 7th Missouri Cav back towards the artillery. A desperate fight ensued with the cannons blasting. Union Capt. Long's men took cover behind a row of Osage orange trees pouring fire upon our boys.

James Hambright rode into camp with orders from Col. Hayes to reinforce their units. Haller refused unwilling to disobey Quantrill. I had remained in camp with Bill Haller even though I understood the plan of attack included us. When the second demand came for help, Bill Gregg and Haller nearly come to blows. Bill Gregg won, insisting Col. Hayes was higher in command and refusal to respond could end in us all being court martialed, shot before Quantrill ever returned. About 100 of us had remained in camp; the rest rode out with him to Independence. We headed toward the battle. By the time we arrived bodies were laying everywhere pouring blood, shot, stabbed and beaten with farming tools. It was awful hand to hand fighting. Cole Younger figured out the men on the front lines were running low on ammunition. He slung a basket of ammunition over his shoulder and rode into the thick of it, right up to the front line throwing ammunition to the men with one hand and holding the reins with the other. It was a scene out of Shakespeare, out of the Knights of the Round Table. Col. Hayes ordered him to get out of the way, get off his horse or he'd shoot his horse out from under him himself. "Though this be madness, yet there is method in it." The fella next to me looked right at me smiling. I hadn't realized I'd quoted Hamlet aloud. I smiled, shrugged my shoulders and returned to firing. When Cole dismounted, troops sent up a rousing cheer for his bravery, men on both sides that hadn't known him or his name did now. War stories are told by both sides and this one gets better every time it's repeated. When an event occurs, people see it from different angles so the same story is seen with different eyes and told in different ways. No one repeating it ever downplayed what Cole did that day at Lone Jack. Union and Confederates called us guerillas, even though we were regular soldiers in Shelby's Co E Second Missouri Cav, fighting under commissioned officers. Cole had a way of making each of us feel a little safer, some of the fella's wanting to be under his command, thought Cole should be elected Capt., maybe even be made Colonel.

Someone called out above the fighting "Foster's shot." Severely wounded he gave command to Capt. Brawner who ordered a retreat. Both wounded, Foster and his brother were left behind and captured. The Union spiked and hide their cannons before retreating but Col. Cockrell found them and when he left for Ark took them with him. Maj Foster was taken to a tent and placed on a cot so his wounds could be examined and treated. As he lay there, one of the boys entered the tent threatening to shoot him. Seems he'd had a run in with him earlier. Cole a hulk with a voice to match grabbed him throwing him out. Maj Foster so trusted Cole he asked him to take $700 he had on him and deliver it to his mother in Warrensburg. Cole warned Union Maj Warren Bronaugh against riding into Confederate lines, whether perceived as a threat or a warning, it saved countless lives. Some of the boys, neighbors of the Younger's thought Cole's daddy, a former Union man, might have known Foster and Bronaugh. Or, they knew of him because there was more trust there than a chance meeting.

It's difficult to say how many men were lost to each side. In two days time we buried 120 Feds and near 50 of our own men, notwithstanding the families who came for the bodies of their kin, carried home, from both sides. We walked among the fields putting horses down with a single shot. Many had served as rampart's, their bodies riddled with bullets while others lay dying. Men, boys, soldiers' and guerilla's, Northerners and Southerner's were crying, praying, moaning and begging the Lord to see their Momma's. Aunt Charlotte told me that's a true sign the sick and dying ain't gonna make it. Having lived through hers and Momma's treatments, I understood calling out to the Lord for mercy. The guns and ammunition on the field helped supplement our ranks. Many of the men had fought hand to hand combat with nothing more than hoes and rakes. Some used tree limbs as clubs. Inadequate clothing gave rise to the boys stripping the dead of their clothing before burying them. It didn't matter what side they were on. The cries of the wounded, both man and animal, are still heard in the sleep of the men who fought and survived.

Momma said when you lose a child, you belong to a club you don't want your worst enemy to belong to. You hope there would never be any new members. People look at you differently almost afraid they could catch your sorrow. She said, "War is like a brotherhood, no matter what side you fight on. Only those who have fought and stood face to face understand."

Col. Tracy, Hayes and Hunter were wounded but survived. Col. Hayes captured Lt. Copeland of Neugent's Regiment. When Quantrill got word Hayes had him he demanded he be turned over to him, along with two other prisoners from Woodsmall's camp. Whether it was his intention to allow the boys to shoot and kill Copeland or to use him in a trade for Perry Hoy was not clear, but he and Hayes nearly got into their own shoot out over it. Quantrill stated he would attack Hayes if they were not turned over to him. Just as several of the men were preparing to mount their horses a squad of men appeared with the prisoners.

When Coffee and Shelby headed south a number of the boys went with them, others stayed with Quantrill and Hayes in Jackson Co. Lt. Col. John Burris and the Kansas Cav didn't pursue Coffee or Shelby. They stayed around lagging, looting and burning houses of known sympathizers. Within two days Union arrived with men belonging to Jennison's Jayhawkers. They over ran the town pointing their guns at local citizens shouting, "Let's shoot the dam Secesh; they have no right to live." Just as Quantrill was becoming a living ghost, a legend that was everywhere doing all things good and bad, so it was for Jennison and Lane.

On Aug 18th, Washington Wells, father of Samuel Wells (Charlie Pitts) was killed in the White Oak battle in Jackson Co. He was shot while shouting out the battle cry. Just a month before Charlie and his momma found Cole Younger's daddy killed on the side of the road by Union Capt. Walley and his men.

On Aug 22, 1862, we camped near Charles Cowherd's Farm, near Strother in Jackson Co. His home was a safe place for guerillas, irregulars and Southerners trying to move south to Texas. Both Quantrill and Col. John T Hughes used it for recruiting purposes. It was nearly dark when Union Lt. Col. Burris made camp. His scouts informed him there were a "1,000 men camped with Quantrill in a dense wood about four miles upstream on the Sni a Bar on the farm on Charles Cowherd." At dawn he sent two companies to draw us out into the open fields, however, even though we might fight like a thousand men, there wasn't 1000 of us and instead of going into the field, we retreated into the woods. Burris didn't know anything about fighting in the woods. He tried to draw us out by setting fire to Charlie and Emily house, outbuildings and barn, along with their wood, grain and hay stacks in the fields. When that failed, Burris left. Under Col. Upton Hayes, about half of the "1000" men, close to 130 headed south into Ark. Capturing Union communication's we learned they greatly exaggerated their successes and losses. We reckoned they needed to increase our numbers when fighting or running, in order to justify their defeats and retreats. The rest of us remained encamped near the Cowherd's farm to ensure their safety.

William Howard brought Quantrill a copy of the Missouri Republican on Aug 28th. William later joined the regular boys and went to the eastern theatre to fight. He was killed at Nashville, Tennessee, Feb 1865. The paper reported a month earlier Perry Hoy had been executed under Burris' orders at Ft. Leavenworth. Quantrill was outraged shouting he should have killed Burris when he had the chance. Buell had got his just due and so should have Burris. Quantrill ordered everyone to saddle up. Uncertain of what he was planning, some headed home, including me. Quantrill headed into Kansas with the intention of carrying out the Brotherhood of Death in Perry's honor. He was throwing a typical fit full of drama and hysteria, screaming and shouting, "We're going to Kansas and kill ten more men for poor Perry!" The boys with him rode less than an hour towards the state line before killing 10 men. Quantrill ordered they not be touched, their bodies in full uniform left for the scavengers, rotting in the hot sun, for people to see.

Sometime afterwards an elderly man, Mister Richard Hopkins came to the Cowherd farm seeking help. He found the buildings burned and farm land scorched. Only a few of the boys were still with Quantrill by this time. Mister Hopkins wife and daughter were dead and the Union had run off all of his cattle. His son William, 20, his only means of support had been arrested. Quantrill refused to help as he had no one to trade for the boy and was uncertain about trading a soldier for a civilian, especially after what happened with Perry Hoy. Col. Fernando Scott sympathized with the old man and asked for volunteers to go with him to Independence to free the boy. Cole, Sim Whitsett, Dave Poole and Bill Haller joined him. They came upon nine Fed Cavalry men. They hid in the brush until they passed then fell in behind them. After Quantrill had looted Independence the town fell to the control of the Federalists. Traveling along Blue Springs Road the boys saw the picket station was manned by four men with a camp nearby with a dozen or more. They fell off hiding in the brush waiting until dark then positioning themselves between the pickets, reserves and outpost of men. Hearing horses approaching more than 100 Federal Cavalrymen rode past at a walk. They moved out of the brush falling into line with the column able to ride past the pickets and reserves. The boys quickly turned pointing a pistol at each of their heads capturing the pickets. Col. Scott saw the reserves were unaware the pickets had been captured and decided to attack. They rode straight into the camp approaching the Union Sgt.

opening fire. Shocked, the Union boys fled in all directions leaving behind wounded and dead. Col. Scott and the boys rode into the unguarded town demanding an exchange of the pickets for William Hopkins, five for one, the Union complied. When they returned Will to his daddy, Richard Hopkins, both vowed whenever we needed either one of them for anything, they'd be available. It was this kind of loyalty that served us well with safe houses, farms and places to rest, during and after the war.

We heard Col. Jackman's Cavalry reached the Ark camp on Aug 31. Maj Genl. Thomas Hindman dismounted and mustered them into service designated as the 7th Missouri Infantry. Us boys we were certain this wouldn't last long, the making of foot soldiers from cavalrymen. We knew things were bad when they dismounted the boys killing the worst off of the horses to feed the men.

Jesse would be having his 15th birthday, Sept 5th, 1862 and I knew Momma would want all her children home. This year we would celebrate everyone's birthday with a home coming. Momma was expecting a baby in Oct. Yep, it was time for her oldest baby child, her Mister Frank, her young Buck, to be home.

Chapter 12

I rode into the yard the day before Jesse's birthday. Momma had anticipated my coming home and invited lots of family. Uncle J.R., Momma's little brother Jesse Richard Cole and Aunt Lou were already at the farm. Aunt Lou was the daughter of Alvah Maret; he'd helped Momma and Daddy get the farm. Uncle J.R. motioned me with a nod of his head to come outside. We went around the side of the house to talk. He told me he wanted to give Jesse his rifle for his birthday. What did I think about Jesse having such a fine piece of artillery? Uncle J.R. showed me the gun as we talked. I brought him up to date on Jesse cleaning and loading guns for us, assuring him Jesse had not lost his finger tip in that manner but rather in the tobacco field. Uncle J.R. slapped his leg hee hawing at that one but we agreed, Jesse was better with guns than the tobacco knife. Uncle J.R. talked to Momma who agreed it was a fine gift, however, she insisted he talk to me about it beforehand. Uncle J.R. told me, if I had not of made it home, the gift of the gun would have had to wait. I could feel my chest swell with pride that Momma left such a final decision as this to me. Jesse was very happy with his gift and set off with several cousins to shoot at whatever caught his fancy. The men of the family cornered me asking questions about the status of activities, anxious to hear what was really happening. One of them had received word Col. Tom's mother, Rebecca Roberts was very ill. A wire had been sent informing him. Col. Tom's daddy, Reverend James Freeman died in May of last year, just after war had been declared. Life moved on, with or without war. It was good to be home, evenso, I felt the weight and pride of being a soldier and the oldest son.

Quantrill and the boys arrived at Olathe on the evening of Sept 12, 1862 finding it defended by 125 militiamen, outnumbering our boys two to one. The boys rode into town no differently than any other group of citizens, peacefully tying their horses to the rails. The militia didn't realize who they were seeing until our boys had formed a line and drawn their pistols. We always carried more than one gun, pistols and revolvers in our waistbands, belt's and saddles. They were easy to use and replenish especially compared to the single shot muskets and rifles the Union carried. Several of the boys had adopted wearing the loose fitting shirts worn by the Zouave. We had taken over 20 wagons a couple months back, one loaded with fabric and colorful materials. These had been taken to New Hope church. Mothers and sisters sewed red shirts for their sons, with extras for other rangers. These were becoming part of our attire, along with wide brimmed hats and a sash worn sufficient to conceal two or more pistols. Life is short and should be lived with gusto. The boys may have been out manned at Olathe but they certainly weren't out gunned. Quantrill ordered the militia to surrender. Then the boys went on a pillaging and looting rampage throughout the town taking what they wanted including money, jewelry, clothing, food and horses. Quantrill intended to make certain Col John Burris knew he was responsible for his own men's death. Come dawn before paroling the Union, he informed them our boys had killed 14, completing the brotherhood of death in revenge for Perry Hoy's execution. Burris was furious when the news was delivered to him.

Quantrill and the boys crossed the Blue River at Crenshaw's Bridge then burned it allowing them to rest a bit before the rear guard rode in with news Burris was closing in. They headed toward Lexington where they were able to set up camp, eat, get a little sleep, refresh supplies and clean their pistols. A clean pistol could mean the difference between life or death, not only had Unc taught us this but William Gregg told us on more than one occasion of his experiences with a snap rather than a fire. Just before dawn locals warned them of a detachment of seventy five Union Cav about two miles west near Wellington. Luckily, unfamiliar with the lay of the land they appeared to be lost.

Quantrill and fifty of the boys including Andy Blunt, Willie Haller, Cole, Dave Poole, George Shepherd, Fletch Taylor, George Todd, Tom Talley, Ki Harrison, Bill Gregg, Sim Whitsett, John Koger, Hix George and Fernando Scott moved south and west. They attacked from the rear chasing the Union over three miles. A few were allowed to escape to get word back to Burris. He immediately set out in pursuit pressing the boys hard back over the Sni. They caught up with our boys near Big Creek. On top of the ridge our boys were looking down on the Union, there was no way out except to ride right through the Union line. Riding a dozen men wide, they began a slow walk down the hillside then charged plunging down through Union ranks into the dense timbers along the creek. Breaking into groups of two or three they dispersed with most heading home or south to Ark. A group came by Momma's for a little respite talking of Olathe and the chase by Burris and his men. Cliff Turpin whose parents owned the Turpin House, a hotel in Olathe, had joined the raid. He led Quantrill and his men to homes full of loot and goods, enough to fill several wagons, most which they lost during the pursuit by Burris. The boys saw a side of Quantrill many hadn't seen. He strutted around the streets telling people he knew to call him Capt., not Bill. They destroyed the town newspaper, the Mirror, along with taking captives. After sacking the town, Quantrill shocked the boys paroling and releasing the captives. Gathering together men of the Fourth Kansas Cav Burris set out "in pursuit of Quantrill". Anger, frustration and embarrassment took over as Burris continued the chase through four counties without success. They began burning farmhouses of suspected southern sympathizers.

On the other side of the state, Col. JoeC Porter was wandering around the forest, like Moses in the wilderness feeding entirely off the land. On Friday, Sept 12, JoeC entered Palmyra with 400 men for supplies. He ordered Capt. J.W. Shattuck who had been arrested due to Andrew Allsman, to arrest Allsman. Strachan, a Union officer, sent JoeC a letter stating he either return Allsman or ten citizens of Palmyra would be executed. When word reached JoeC of the murder of the 10 citizens, he said he never received the letter and Allsman had escaped. Col. Strachan had brought 10 innocent civilians before a firing squad and shot them.

Col. Joseph "Jo" Shelby organized his forces of some 1500 Cavalrymen during the second week of Sept establishing a training camp at Camp Coffee, just south of Newtonia. Leaving home, I headed to rejoin Col. Shelby there. When I arrived the men were preparing the body of Col. Upton Hayes to be taken to Kansas City for burial at Forest Hill Cemetery. Col. Hayes was proud of the fact he was the great grandson of pioneer Daniel Boone. His parents were Boone Hayes and Lydia Scholl. His daddy was the son of Will Hayes and Susannah Boone, daughter of Daniel. The Scholl, Morgan and Boone's were all Quaker people like Pappy Fielding's family. Boone Scholl was riding with us. He and Col. Hayes were cousins of the closest kind. Boone's full name was Daniel Boone Scholl, son of Nelson Scholl and Harriett Boone, the great granddaughter of Samuel Boone, brother of Daniel Boone. Her husband Nelson was the great grandson of pioneer Daniel Boone. Their family was frontier dynasty. Boone went with the boys headed south to rejoin Col. Shelby and was there when Col. Upton Hayes received his official appointment Sept 12th at Camp Coffee. Three days later he was killed, shot in the head while attempting to drive in some Union pickets. Boone was escorting him home to his wife, Margaret Watts and children to be buried. Col. Hayes had recruited a majority of the men in camp and they were visibly upset. Realizing this Col. Shelby set them to different tasks preparing for the next battle.

I learned Col. Tom received word his momma died on Sept 18th. His brother, Reverend Richard Monroe Freeman and wife Martha Taff had moved to Dent Co and were there when she died. His wife's parents, the Lamb's lived close enough they were able to take the children. Missus Rebecca was buried in Freeman Cemetery next to her husband. Col. Tom lost his wife and both parents in a year's time. Births and deaths didn't stop just because there was a war. Life went on. I thought about Momma and Daddy, both of them losing parents and grandparents at such young ages. I suspect that was in part why Momma and Col. Tom became such friends, they understood each other. They were part of that club Momma said no one wanted to belong to.

Samuel H. Hardison, Jr gg grandson of George Washington Hardison (1824-1897)
17th Infantry Regiment of Tennessee, CSA "Regular Enlisted Soldier"

I arrived in time to join them at the Battle of Newtonia. Scouts reported columns of Union headed toward the mill at Newtonia for much needed supplies of bread. Around 7 o'clock in the morning, Sept 30th, the Union attacked. At first we fell back, then with reinforcements arriving we put the Feds on the run. Their reinforcements arrived and they counter attacked which threw us off guard for half an hour then something welled up inside of us and we pushed back, gaining the upper hand. I think the boys were letting go of their rage and sorrow at losing Col. Hayes. The Union gunners tried to block our pursuit by placing artillery in the road. Their fire gave away their location. Some of the boys chased them all the way to Sarcoxie more than 10 miles away not stopping until dark was upon them. A hundred men were walking about the dead and dying looting them, taking clothing, shoes and arms. Orders came that the regular soldiers were to retreat back to Northwest Ark and the guerilla and irregular commanders were to prepare for a war conference at Sibley, the rest were to report to their Capts for orders.

At Sibley the decision was made for the irregulars and guerillas to disband on Oct 5th with orders to head home, join the regular companies south in Ark or move into Texas for the upcoming winter. Before the war conference was fully concluded, the guard skirmished with Federalists where the Lexington, Independence and Sibley Roads meet outside Sibley. Capt. Dick Chiles ambushed Union Capt. Daniel David and the 5th Missouri Cav. Purposely misinformed Capt. David made the decision to move his troops until reinforcement could arrive. Thinking he was situating himself safely on Big Hill to await reinforcements, he rode into our ambushes. Hide and attack, hit and run, over one hundred and thirty of us with Quantrill rose up out of the brush firing on the column, wounding and killing men and horses. Capt. David's men were mostly armed with long rifles, almost impossible to shoot accurately from the back of a horse. He ordered them to dismount and with sabers drawn they chased us into the bushes scattering our men. Pat O'Donnell was shot in the hip. Reinforcements arrived for Capt. David enabling them to chase us through the next day. Dick Chiles was shot. Hit in the lungs he had to be left behind and was taken prisoner. Capt David had no means of treating him and expected him to die. The Union paroled him and abandoned him at a nearby spring. The heat took as much a toll on all the men as anything, with the hand to hand combat in the brush. After dispersing, we gathered with Quantrill on the banks of the Little Blue River. The weather was turning, leaves were falling, days were still warm but the nights could be cold. Dick was found by the spring by Judge William Stevens, a Union man, who hid him in the cellar of his home. Secretly treated by Dr. Isaac Ridge, a Southern doctor, part Indian, he survived. Then we heard William Gregg's father Jacob and his brother Frank had been arrested. I was really upset because Frank and I had become good friends. He was a solid man whom you knew you could trust your life to. I spent a great deal of time with him at the home of his sister Mary Francis "Fannie" and her husband Samuel Ralston, always happy to see little Annie.

Chapter 13

Ed Cockrum ran the local Mountain Boomer gang north on the White River from the Wolf House to Buffalo Ford in Ark. He had alerted the Union of Genl. James McBridge commander of the Seventh Division of the Missouri State Guard having headquartered at Yellville. Union Brigadier Genl. Francis Herron ordered an expedition to advance from its post at Ozark, Missouri, to Yellville, Ark. Cockrum had been charged by the Union with spying and receiving contraband along the Buffalo, White and North Fork rivers, sufficient to supply the troops in the area. He had stolen, looted and pillaged farms and had ample supply hidden in wait for the Union. They intended to surprise our men stationed at Camp Adams, at Yellville, burn or capture supplies, take prisoners and return back to Missouri. On Oct 12th, 1862 some 200 men of the Union MSM Cav reached a seriously flooded White River. One thing was certain the heavy rains had not only caused flash flooding pushing the waters out of banks along the creeks but kept the rivers flooded as water poured from the hills. The flooded river forced the Union to move west along the river toward Talbot's Ferry. Locals hollered from ridge top to ridge top spreading word of their presence. Most northerners were unaware of the difference between a holler and hollow. Hill tops that were lines of communications that could be heard from one to the other were "hollers" while the others were hollows and box canyons. They were different lays to the land. Our scouts kept a watchful eye on their movements. They made camp about 10 miles from Pierson's Ford on the 15th with plans to move on to Talbot's Barren early the next morning. Our scouts learned of the planned attack allowing Col. Shaler and 2,000 men to advance to protect Yellville forcing the Union to abandon their plans.

Thursday, Oct 17, Quantrill attacked Shawneetown, Johnson Co, Kansas. He had voiced the need to resupply both provisions and ammunition lost during Burris pursuit. Shawneetown, Kansas was like Shawneetown, Yellville, Ark, both were early Shawnee Indian settlements established before and during the forced removal of the Five Civilized Tribes by President Andrew Jackson in the 1830's. While most of us friends with the locals, called it Shawneetown, the area had been laid out as the new city of Shawnee a few years before the war began. Not unlike Olathe, the boys attacked killing and torching the town securing food, clothing, provisions and ammunition, all of which was seriously low.

On Oct 22, 1862 Boone Schull and George Todd attacked Lt. Satterlee eight miles east of Harrisonville. After the death of his friend and cousin Upton Hayes, Boone was armed with a hurt that was driving him like a dog gone mad. Quantrill ask him to go with a group to Shelby's camp in

Ark to communicate events and needs. He brought word Uncle Till's cousin, William Bullitt "Bull" Howard was arrested and jailed at Independence. He was released a month later on a $25,000 bond.

Col Jackman didn't dally long in Ark. After being dismounted it seemed there was nothing but bickering, constant reassignments and no centralized effort. As Momma says, "Too many injuns not enough chiefs." Completely fed up Col. Jackman threatened to resign the regular army on Oct 25, 1862 stating he was returning to Missouri where he knew the boys knew how to fight. The command didn't disagree with him. He was ordered to continue recruitment back in Missouri and by fall, he had more men than all of the others combined.

On Monday Oct 27, Union Col. William Dewey surprised Confederate Col. John Q. Burbidge's Brigade at Pitman's Ferry on the Current River, a Maj crossing on the South West Trail on the Missouri Ark border at Buck Skull. Ferries were of Maj importance to both sides. Pitman's Ferry was put in by white savage William Hicks around 1804. Then it was called Hick's Ferry at Indian Ford. Even Henry Rowe Schoolcraft wrote about visiting Hick's Ferry on Monday, Jan 25, 1819. "At three o'clock I reached the banks of the river at Hicks' Ferry, and was conveyed over in a ferry-flat, or scow." "It is 1,000 feet wide at the Ferry, and has an average depth of eight feet." "At Hicks's Ferry, a town is in contemplation. The site is dry, airy, and eligible, and will command many advantages for mercantile purposes." Schoolcraft according to our teacher Mister Bird was looking at the possibility of mining in the Ozarks. He wrote about his three months of travel from late 1818 to early 1819 describing the people and places he observed. The Natchitoches Trail came through and in the 1830's the old Indian trace was improved as the Military Road, under the direction of Sam Houston, in cahoots with Steve Austin, son of Moses Austin who had received a large tract of land under Spain to settle Texas. Moses had taken the first 300 settlers from Missouri and Ark to Texas. Sam's brother, John Houston, Thomas Riggs and Jehoiada Jeffery influenced the route intersecting Batesville, Ark and the Cape connecting with the Red River Valley of Texas. Steve Austin needed the road for his lead mines. Riggs and Jeffery looking to improve their economic standing had ancillary roads pass in front of and through Jeffery land and right through Riggsville. Cherokee Chief John Ruddell Benge used the road during their relocation in 1838. Friends and namesake of Abraham Ruddell who had been taken captive by the Shawnee in 1780 at Ruddell's Fort, Kentucky, Chief Benge brought his people through Batesville to see Abe and have their wagons repaired. From there they went to Athens in Izard Co near Aunt Lucy's to see John Houston. Both Sam and John had been adopted into the Cherokee by Chief John Jolly Due, uncle of Chief Benge. Chief John Jolly Due's mother was Wurteh Betsy Watts, sister of Chief John Watts Bowles, Chief Duwali of the Ark Cherokee. Both Betsy and Chief Jolly had become sick on the route. Chief Jolly had returned early under separate travel to Oklahoma, he died there in 1839. His Momma died at Iuka, Ark. She was the mother of Robert "the Bench" Benge, the most feared of eastern Cherokee. John Ruddell Benge and his brother Richard were leading the wagon train west was his son's, her grandchildren. She was also mother of George Sequoyah Gist, inventor of the Cherokee alphabet who married Maj Jacob Wolf's niece, Sallie Waters, at Wolf House. After they left Athens, the Indians rendezvoused with other members of the contingency that walked from Davidsonville, at a place between two springs, north of Calico Bluffs. There many people died, including Wurteh Betsy Watts and her nephew Thomas Watts, son of her brother John Young Tassel Watts. Thomas' younger brother Jacob Ostooli Watts and his wife, Emily Ross, daughter of Chief John Ross were also traveling with the Benge group. She delivered a son in the midst of all that death, on Jan 6th, 1839, James Monroe Watts. They traveled to the Wolf House where Maj Wolf aided many of them in settling here rather than continuing on to the reservation in Oklahoma. In the spring, the flooded creeks were full of moccasins off the dead. The creek is called Moccasin Creek.

The main routes we traveled were the old Indian roads unless in large numbers then we could travel the Military Road, Jacksonport Road. Hick's Ferry had been sold to Doctor Peyton Pitman. First he ran it then his son Eramus took over. And, like Grigsby Ferry, it was a necessary means of transport across the river for both the Union and South. Oct 27th, the Union attacked 1500 of our boys killing several and taking over 40 men prisoners. With the Union in pursuit some the boys fled along the road toward Powhaten, Pocahontas and Jackson, through Red Banks headed west to Camp Adams. For over three days others fought with the Union engaging Boone again near Bollinger's Mill before reaching Pocahontas, Ark, from there heading to Milligan's Campground, then west to Liberty and Calico to Yellville. They captured Col. Given Campbell and Col. John S. "LongBeard" Green, who wore his beard to his waist and his hair trimmed. One of the Union boys, a Private Richard Lloyd swam the Current River from the Missouri side capturing and returning the ferry back to the banks for the North. Now in possession of the ferry, Dewey and his men rested before returning to Camp Patterson on Nov 2nd.

Quantrill sent word to assemble on Nov 3rd, on the east bank of the Little Blue River near Lone Jack readying for the march to Dripping Springs, where Col. Shelby's was camped in Ark. Winter was on its way, harsh strong winds coming in from Kansas. The trees were barren. The rain had glued the fallen leaves to the ground. New recruits were coming in daily and temperaments and attitudes were edgy. Bill Haller and George Todd got into a heated disagreement threatening blows. Bill decided not to come south instead joining up with Ki Harrison. Capt. Joseph Lea stayed in Missouri with several of his boys. Shelby and Col. John T Crisp endorsed and recommended Lea to replace Jarrette, Younger and Poole. Afterwards Lea chose to go to Louisiana. He stayed there through most of the war. About half of the men decided to make the trek south with Quantrill, most others returned home for the winter and hoped for the best, including Cole Younger. After his daddy's murder, he was concerned for his Momma. She had John 11, Emma 10, Bob 9 and Henrietta 6.

Shortly after heading south the advance located a Union wagon train with 13 wagons between Harrisonville and Sedalia escorted by Union Lt. Newby and twenty-one soldiers of the 6th Missouri Cav. Quantrill ordered William Gregg and forty of us to attack. We circled them Indian style, whooping and hollering. We always managed to put the fear of God in young soldiers like this who had only read about Indian attacks. Crouching and trying to get off their shots, within minutes ten were shot in the head and another half dozen seriously wounded. Lt. Newby and half a dozen of his men were captured. They set fire to their own wagons to prevent our capture of the supplies. Rifles never matched our pistols. Bill Lawrence, one of the half dozen of Col. Freeman's men riding south with us to join Col. Shelby, managed to pull wooden crates from one of the burning wagons full of Union uniforms. He and another fella wrapped as many as they could inside blankets slinging them across their horses. Union Col. Catherwood close behind us forced us to move out. Our scout watched from a distance as Catherwood walked among the dead. We knew when he mounted up, the pursuit was on. Around nine o'clock near Rose Hill, Catherwood caught up with us. We skirmished in a horse to horse combat but it was clear everyone was exhausted, his men and ours. Quantrill let Newby and his one unharmed man led the horses with the wounded, releasing them. We moved on south toward Ark. Entering the prairie of Bates Co, near the banks of the Osage River, we spotted a Federal regiment in the distance. Exchanging fire we increased our pace. The waters of the Marais Des Cynges Creek were low. We rode down the creek bed about three miles emerging near the old Osage Indian mission at Papinsville. Riding hard to nigh on ten o'clock we stopped to rest, feed and water the horses. Less than an hour later we were on the move and by four in the morning we reached Lamar and there made camp.

Col. Warner Lewis with about 40 men heading south joined us making us over 200 men strong. Col. Lewis convinced Quantrill attacking the Union garrison in Lamar was worthwhile. He said raiding the Federal garrison would provide additional needed supplies and ammunition. A plan was set out for us to come in from the north and Lewis from the South. Lamar was held by Capt. Martin Breedon of the 8th Missouri Cav. Around ten o'clock at night we rode down the main street straight to the court house. The Union learned of our approach and were holed up in the brick courthouse. Fighting took place over two hours with several of our boys crawling up firing directly into the windows. John McCorkle and Will Haller at the old blacksmith shop adjacent to the courthouse were both knocked in the head with wood timbers when the Union fired a volley near them. Our black man, John Noland, was hollering out directions for Shelby and Marmaduke to go this way, hoping to frighten Breedon into surrendering thinking there were considerable more of us. A member of Capt. Chiles command, John had joined Quantrill after Sibley.

We finally retreated with our wounded and 6 dead tied to their horses including Jim Donahue and Peter Burton. About two miles from the courthouse at the end of a lane we dug their graves. Some of the boys set the town on fire keeping the Union at bay. It was nearly dawn when we finished. We put a rail fence around the graves marking them with crosses. After helping to burn the courthouse and bury the dead, Dick Yeager decided to stay in Missouri heading back home rather than go south.

We rode south through Indian Territory toward Fort Smith. We arrived at Marmaduke and Shelby's camp at Dripping Springs north and west of Van Buren, Ark, the place where Parley Pratt the Mormon apostle had been killed by Hector McLean, the outraged husband five years earlier in 1857. Marmaduke and Shelby were making plans to move east towards Jacksonport on the White River. Marmaduke attached us to Maj Benjamin Elliot's Co under the command of Shelby, under Maj Genl. Thomas Hindman. Col. Gideon W. Thompson had sworn everyone in on Aug 14th as Partisan Rangers, Co E of Shelby's 2nd Missouri Cav, with Quantrill. Now we were being made part of Maj Elliot's Co, Missouri Infantry dismounting. Most of the boys weren't happy with neither the dismounting nor being "regularized". After resting for nearly two weeks at Dripping Springs most decided to head back home to find other Partisan's groups while a few others rode south to Texas.

Col. Freeman joined us along with several of the men from his regiments discussing both progress and problems. I spoke to him about his Momma's death. He had reached home but not before she had succumbed. He did enjoy visiting with his in laws and seeing his children, he said. I sensed his need to change the subject as he rose to shake the hands of the half dozen of his men approaching who had safely moved south with us. We felt we were part of something bigger at Dripping Springs, part of the Confederacy. We were treated as troops, soldiers. Our mere presence of having ridden with Quantrill created a sensation among the troops and other

Partisans. We were daring and brave, fighting without direct commanders and doing well at it. They wanted to know about our warfare tactics, "guerilla fighting". Many of the officers sought out not only Quantrill but a variety of us men who had set ourselves apart in one way or another. Having heard or seen Cole Younger in action, they were dismayed to learn he had remained in Missouri. While Cole's ego would not have been inflated atal, it was different with Quantrill. We were seeing signs of his need for personal glory. Quantrill didn't keep his thoughts to himself nor within our group, he was vocal to anyone who would listen. "If I am responsible for the Majority of Federal disruptions in Western Missouri then why am I only a Capt." was his repeated refrain. Although Col. Thompson commissioned him a Col. the higher ranking authorities said elections were up to the men within that group and he had been elected Capt.. Quantrill stated he understood from Col. Thompson he was a Col. not only on his commission but due to the number of men he was able to recruit and command. Even with his temper tantrums the higher ranking commanders wanted to meet him. He dared to say, "If I alone have kept the Feds at bay in western Missouri, surely I deserve to be more than a lowly Capt. of Partisan Rangers." He recognized no authority but his own at Dripping Springs. We weren't surprised when he and Andy Blunt announced they were heading out east to Richmond. It was late Nov, Andy planned for them to move west across Ark to Memphis, then across Tennessee into North Carolina and finally north to Richmond, a ride of over 1,000 miles. Although he commissioned by Thornton, Quantrill had every intention of meeting with President Jefferson Davis seeking a Presidential appointment of greater rank. He left Bill Gregg in charge of us boys, under Col. Elliott.

It was becoming more apparent to all of us we were not suited for the discipline of the regular military. Even those of us who had served had grown accustomed to the attack and run, attack and disperse style of Indian fighting and guerilla tactics. And, we were good at it. Some of the boys were stunned to find the formations style of fighting, drop and shoot was being used. They laughed saying it made for better targets, us. We had our ways and this was not it. Perhaps because I had been raised a Baptist I understood order and position, authority more than most of them. They come in from the fields with little to no education or experience beyond a few miles around their homesteads where they were the big fish. Here they were the little fish in a rapidly moving river. They were fish out of water flopping around. Most of the boys said they would rather die riding free than in a military line. Bill Gregg convinced a number of us to stay with him riding under Elliott, including Sim Whitsett, John McCorkle and me. But half the boys left under George Todd headed home before Quantrill ever left with Andy. With Quantrill gone more headed home.

On Nov 7th, 1862 George Todd and the boys with him were camped near Gainesville when they learned Union Capt. Hiram Barstow was camped at Clark's Mill, the old town of Red Bud, renamed Vera Cruz just before the war broke out. Unbeknownst to our boys another group of Confederates were moving south toward Clark's Mill along the Hartville to Rockbridge road down Bryant Valley placing the Federalists in the middle. They engaged the Union for nearly an hour with the Federalists holding the road leading into the mill before unknown reinforcements arrived from the northeast. Together in a fight lasting over 4 hours the boys of the South kept the Union hemmed in then finally under a white flag demanded the Union surrender. The blockhouse at Clark's Mill was burned. Our boys cleaned up, refreshed themselves and their horses in the clear clean waters of Bryant and Hunter Creeks.

Our boys that remained home had joined up with other Partisan groups. Maj Genl. James Blunt was sorely distressed over their continued presence. Headquartered at Camp Bowen in Benton Co, Ark he ordered Union Col William Cloud to go as far south as Fort Smith if need be to root out the irregulars, Partisans and guerillas and eradicate them. Then he sent troops north toward Springfield. Similar orders were issued against Col. Thomas Roe Freeman in the White River Valley under Union Maj Baxter to Col Baumer. On the 9th, Col. Cloud's scouts discovered one of the Confederate tanneries with upwards of 30 vats of fresh leather destroying them and the buildings. Continuing south near Cane Hill the advance guard met a detachments of Col McDonald's troops at William Graham's house. After only a few shots being fired, the detachment fled. Moving south, they ran straight into Col McDonald's men who were trying to move a baggage train. The men lost most of their supply wagons to the Kansas unit. However, their most humiliating loss was the flag. Returning to Camp Bowen Col. Cloud used our tactics; placing the flag bearer at the head of his column with the Confederate flag flapping in the wind, he was able to dupe loyal Southerners thus taking a number of civilian's prisoner.

We had been at Dripping Springs Camp about a week when Stand Watie's men and Capt. Bud Shirley arrived reporting their skirmish with Blunts men near Yocum Creek. Genl. Hindman with forces of over 11,000 gathered ordered Genl. Marmaduke to move back north with 2,000 men. Stand Watie and Bill Gregg volunteered us as the advance guard. The Boston Mountains could be formidable and the last few days of rain had made muddy troughs out of the roads. Wet weather springs flowed from the mountains washing the road away making movement treacherous if not almost impossible. Traveling with 500 men was horrendous, I couldn't imagine the difficulty of the 1500 troops behind us navigating this terrain, indeed 10,000. Rocks and limbs were gathered and placed under the wheels of the wagons and artillery which barely allowed horse and man power to push and pull them through the muck. For all the rest we'd had at Dripping Springs we were fast becoming exhausted and our animals weren't fairing any better. Shuddering at the effort before us, I thought of the difficulties of moving canons, wagons and 10,000 men on a good day. I felt I was better prepared for this than most due to Unc and I was overcome with a sick feeling of foreboding.

One of Stand Watie's men rode back alerting us of their discovery of a Union camp at Lindsey's Prairie in Benton Co. We moved northwest through the edge of Indian Territory effectively skirting the camp. On Nov 25^{th,} a few miles south of Buzzard's Roost a young boy rode up on a donkey informing us of Union in the area. He pointed up the road to a perfect spot for an ambush. Not wanting to alert the enemy of the larger forces moving behind us Bill Gregg ordered us not to engage any more than necessary. We were to fall into place for an ambush but fire no shots, allow the troops to ride through unless sighted. The boy told us he was a neighbor of the Hayhurst's, a Union family and had to be very careful. Should he be stopped, he said, patting the sack of grain hanging about his donkey, his ruse was he was headed to the mill to have the grain ground.

We moved rapidly into place. Gregg sent three boys back south as decoys to lure the troops to our ambush so that we might not be the ones caught in their ambush. Within half an hour, over 100 men on horseback galloped through swiftly chasing after the three completely passing us by. One of their men in the rear guard happened to spot one of our boys in the brush and fired. He was quickly shot down as was another who saw what was happening. Our boys were dead shots with their pistols and in the wake of the galloping horses, the rest of the Federalists continued the chase unaware they had lost two of their men. They were dragged into the brush; their bodies hidden. We headed south with their two horses.

When everyone gathered, Stand Watie, Bill Gregg and the other officers decided to send a dozen men in pairs of two alerting Marmaduke of Blunt's position and growing forces. We moved into camp about 15 miles south of Cane Hill within a few miles of Blunt's camp. Our spies and pickets were on high alert; even so, three days later on the 28th, just before dawn, the Federalists fired cannons into our sleeping camp. Some thought it thunder and lightening or another torrential Ozark rain instead shocked out of sleep we found ourselves heavily outnumbered. We fled into the Boston Mountains running pulling ourselves together, some stopping on bended knee to return fire, others gathering the horses.

Even though we were now officially part of the Confederacy assigned to Elliott's Battalion and Quantrill was no where around, those of us who had ridden with him maintained the moniker, "Quantrill's boys" or

Quantrill's Raiders. Marmaduke began a retreat ordering Shelby's Cav using us, Quantrill's Raiders to hold the Feds back while the rest of the men and wagons headed for the mountains. Riding in the rear guard with Shelby, we were cut off. Dick Turpin was with Shelby when Shelby's horse was shot out from under him. A new horse was secured and three times more Shelby had his horse killed out from under him. Dick told the story real good, slipping, sliding in the mud, Jo Shelby trying to get on his feet. Every step a struggle. It became everyone's story as if they had been there, each one impressing their own importance and involvement. Finally, we made it over the mountain descending into Cole Creek Valley. The Feds stayed on our rear guard, firing on us.

Detailed on watch, John McCorkle reported seeing the enemy coming up the creek reporting such to Gregg and Col. Elliott.

"Returning to my post, I saw that they were advancing very rapidly and immediately returned to Elliott and Gregg and told them if we stayed there a few minutes longer we would be cut off and would have to cut a hole through the enemy to get out. Col. Elliott, as soon as he saw our perilous position, ordered a retreat, and, as we crossed the creek, about fifty yards ahead of them, the enemy poured a heavy volley of grape, canister and minnie balls at us, and nothing but the poor shooting of the Yankees saved us all from being killed, but only two of Elliott's men were slightly wounded. We kept us a constant firing as we went up the mountains. During this running fight, one of our Co, Dick Turpin, became separated from us, and, riding up to where Genl. Shelby was, the Genl. asked him what command he belonged to. He replied 'Quantrill's.' Shelby replied, 'I thought those boys always stayed in their places.' To which Turpin replied, 'I can go any place you can: come on.' The Genl. started to follow, when his horse was killed under him. Turpin turned in his saddle and saw Shelby getting up and said, 'Genl., what in the hell are you stopping there for? Why don't you come on?' Going up the mountain, Genl. Shelby had three horses killed under him. After getting over the mountain, we started down Cove Creek, the baggage train being ahead of us. The Feds closed up and made a saber charge on our rear guard. Capt. Gregg then told me to go down the creek and find a place to form, as he wanted to check that charge. I started and took Dave Poole with me and, just past the spur of the mountain, I found a place about large enough for forty men to form on. Leaving Poole there, I rode back and notified Gregg. The boys came on down on the double quick, about half of them forming and the remainder forming in the rear. About that time, Capt. John Jarrett, who had formerly been with Quantrill, but who was then in command of a Co of Cav under Shelby, came up and asked me what we were going to do. I told him we were going to check that charge and to get in the rear. Before we had time really to re-form, the Feds came to within about thirty yards of us, and Capt. Gregg gave the command to charge. We rushed forward, yelling and shooting and, at the first volley, we unhorsed thirty-seven of them, among them being a Maj Hubbard. The Feds immediately turned and went back up the mountain at a more rapid pace than they had come down, we following them about a quarter of a mile, wounding and killing a good many more. When one of the men came up to where Capt. Hubbard was lying wounded, he dismounted and took his belt, revolver and sword and a fine, new overcoat that Hubbard was wearing and told him he was going to kill him. Just then Genl. Shelby came along and asked what he was going to do with that man, and being told he was going to kill him, Shelby very sternly, said, 'No, you are not. Return that man his belt, sword, revolver, and overcoat,' which was very promptly done. In about an hour from this time, the Feds came down with a flag of truce and took up their dead and wounded."

Hindman ordered Jo Shelby to lead the advance using our men under Lt. Bill Gregg. Our march back north started in the early morning hours of Dec 3, 1862, the day after Union Genl. Herron set out from Springfield heading south. Learning of Hindman's plans, Blunt sent runners to Springfield, Missouri requesting divisions to move south to reinforce his Co. Herron decided the risk was worth it but they would have to cover 130 miles from Springfield to reach Blunt, a difficult journey in any weather. His men were allowed to carry nothing other than gear necessary for battle, no knapsacks. They marched 24 hours a day with little to no rest, in a cold rain with nothing to eat. I reckon if Confederate Genl. Stonewall Jackson could move his men in such a manner in the Virginia's, then so could they and did.

The rain chilled us to the bone. It was a cold rain falling in torrents like an old cow letting loose on a glade rock, wet splattered every inch of us. We were drenched. I had a good coat Momma and Aunt Charlotte had greased down so it shed water. I could see men shivering and hear teeth chattering. Watching the sky turn darker I knew from Momma and Aunt Charlotte more bad weather was on the horizon. I smiled looking around for a weather forecaster cow I could tell Doc about but none was in sight. At nearly four o'clock Col. Shelby ordered a halt for the day. The wind had picked up and we could feel the temperature plummeting. Freezing rain was attaching to the trees, coating the rocks, everything around us and us. We were grateful when it turned to snow. Shelby knew we hadn't covered as much ground as needed, but he also knew with exhaustion and cold it could be far worse. We made camp for the night and thankfully some of us boys were able to get fires going. No one was ashamed to huddle tight next to the man beside him, some gathered under wagons, trees and among the horses. We had insufficient cover for this weather.

The light of the sky just before dawn put a magic spell over the land. I'd often arose in the early hours before dawn heading out to run a jug line, hunt for squirrels or sit in my favorite spot watching for a white tailed deer. I never failed to see the beauty of the land about me during those hours. Except when I'd take Jesse with me, he was not graceful. He would lumber about typically frightening off the animals, so I didn't like taking him. Until Unc made it clear to me, I was the big brother, the man of the house and not only was he my little brother, it was my duty. What if something happened to either one of you? I could hear him telling me how Momma needed us both, especially if one or the other passed on for some reason. I laughed under my breath recalling the first time Jesse had been given the task of wringing a chicken's neck. He had grabbed an old fat hen by the feet. She had strong wings and flapped and fluttered attempting to get loose pecking at him, finally he managed to grab her by the neck. He swung her around but she was fat hen and heavy, he hurt her but hadn't killed her. Thinking she was dead he'd held her out in front of him. With an unexpected twist she managed to get free, dropping to the ground she ran around with her head tilted over to the side, not dead and not really alive but willing feet. We chased her down catching her. I'd finished her off, then required him to chop her head off. We hung her from the tree to bleed her. It would be Momma, Aunt Charlotte or Susie who would be tasked with plucking her feathers, gutting and cooking her. I smiled thinking about Jesse and home, trying to teach him to be a man, to do the right thing. I wondered if Daddy would be proud of me.

Few were stirring and for a moment, the fat little robins and red birds perched on the branches painted their own portrait of God and all was good with the world. I talked to God as I did every morning. The light of the sun dancing off the trees sent a chill through all of us realizing just how much ice had fallen, frozen hard beneath the snow. Heading north it was bitter cold, the wind felt like a knife cutting right into you. I thought of Momma and Aunt Charlotte with their persimmon seeds. The breaking tree branches heavy with ice sounded like gunshots, spooking everyone, man and animal alike. We moved along the western border of Ark. to Cane Hill about 10 miles north and west of Van Buren and 18 miles south and west of Fayetteville. Nearing Cane Hill southwest of Prairie Grove, word spread like wildfire through the ranks, "Hindman's expressing doubts of his plan." Removed as the Commander of the Trans Mississippi District and placed over Ark, he had convinced his replacement to support this plan and now 'he' doubted it. This shook us worse than the cold. He diverted us from his initial plan of moving to Cane Hill, instead moving along Cove Creek ahead of him. I could see the fear in silent faces. Heads bowed against the cold, I believe there was not one among us who wasn't praying.

Stand Watie's Indian brigade rode up with 22 men they had captured from Blunts scouting party. Col. Shelby and Gregg interrogated and paroled them. They hoped they would report guerillas' were advancing on them rather than the huge force of men under Hindman. By nightfall Dec 5, we were within eight miles of Cane Hill. We set up camp near the home of John Morrow on Cove Creek Road there waiting on the remainder of the troops. Our scouts were reporting detachments from Union regiments both infantry and Cav steadily arriving to reinforce Blunt. If Herron were on his way, he could be here the next day. At midnight on Dec 6, Hindman called his commanders to meet with him at a farmhouse. He set out his plan of attack to move north striking any incoming armies and then back to Cane Hill to finish off Blunt. We were to leave the camp fires burning creating the illusion we were in camp. Any attack would come in the morning hours and continuous skirmishes with Blunt's front line through the night would maintain the illusion. Everyone was nervous. Those trying to sleep held their guns tight like a shepherd with his staff on guard against the wolf.

Around 4 o'clock on the morning of Sunday Dec 7th, Col. Shelby ordered Maj David Shanks to start for Fayetteville with Bill Gregg and Dave Poole leading us. Shelby would follow with a second force. Dressed in our stolen Federal blue uniforms, we went around Blunt's army undetected and raced down the Fayetteville road. Shortly after reaching the road, we encountered a convoy of twenty-one commissary wagons headed for Blunt's lines. They were taken off guard by our Union uniforms. That's all we needed, they were stunned when we attacked, panic over taking them as they turned and ran. We stayed hot on their tails. Col. Shelby coming up behind us took possession of the wagons.

A detachment of Union Cav under Maj James Hubbard heard the shots and headed towards the source of the gunfire. They came upon Col. Shelby and the wagons surrounding him and a dozen of our men ordering them to surrender. Bill Gregg, George Poole, Bill Chitwood, Walter Canard, Bill Lawrence, Dick Partee and myself were the first men to come into sight of what happened. Gregg let out a howl Unc would be proud of. We knew instantly what it meant. The men in front of me started firing circling the Union like Indians circling a wagon train just as they had surrounded our men and wagons. Hubbard's men were dumbfounded. What were these men in Union uniforms doing? I rushed in reaching down grabbing Col. Shelby's hand pulling him up behind me on my horse, just as Bill Gregg, Poole, Chitwood, Sim Whitsett and others rushed in grabbing more of our men. When we reached high ground we could see Shelby's men left behind at the wagons hadn't wasted any time. Taking advantage of the confusion, some knocked Union soldiers from their horses taking them in order to flee while others ran. All but one escaped unharmed. Bill Chitwood under the command of Col. Tom had become skilled in attending to the medical care of the wounded on the battlefield. Chitwood with Walter Canard by his side assisting checked Shelby over. The men under Col. Emmett McDonald went after the fleeing Union troops surrounding them in the counter attack shouting like wild Indians, bringing a smile to all of us guerillas. Yes, I'd say, Unc would be proud. I knew he was somewhere smiling.

On the other front their panic turned to fear and fear to fighting. Union troops charged through the corn and wheat fields of Archibald Borden taking our cannons. They continued advancing but we opened fire with small arms and with remaining small cannons surrounding the Union on three sides forcing them and their cannons into the valley. This may have been the first real successful guerilla attack in Ark but it was short lived. Thrilled we chased them into the valley where we were met with the most horrendous kind of blasts from their cannon fire. They had cannon balls packed with sawdust and scraps of metal that when fired were more like a giant shotgun blast. Men were left on the ground all around us forcing us back into the woods for cover. They continued their attack returning us back up the hill toward the Borden family apple orchard. The Federalists fell back into a fence line in the valley where they stopped another group using Colt revolving rifles. Reinforcement arrived for both sides. Brigadier Genl. Mosby Parsons in command of the Confederate Missouri Infantry attacked across the William Morton hayfield around four o'clock in the afternoon. Advancing the men met with what some say was as many as 50 cannons firing. While Herron continued battling, Blunt remained at Cane Hill waiting for our attack. He had not realized we had slipped away and firing into an empty encampment as Hindman anticipated. Col. James Monroe's skirmishes along Blunt's front line worked. Once he realized what happened Blunt marched his men to Herron's aide. Union Genl. Parsons launched his attack driving our forces back into the edge of the woods along the ridge. Every man was thankful when darkness fell. The fighting stopped, guns and canons were quiet. We talked quietly of their cannon while tending to the horrific wounds it left. Arms and legs looked like Momma's pounded meat, tenderized, stripped. Sides of men's faces were gone exposing bone and teeth. Not only was it deadly, to care for the wounded required tedious work to remove the imbedded metal and dirt. James Duncan was one of our boys killed at Cove Creek. I'd liked him. He wore his hair clean cropped like my own. He wore a mustache and had been trying to talk me into growing one. My hair was fine; I was afraid it would be thin and wispy. We'd talked of things not of the war. War was a day at work and night in camp we were among friends.

Word we were retreating spread quickly and quietly through the ranks. We had no choice but to withdraw under the cover of darkness back south. We walked past the Federal soldiers sleeping on the battlefield in freezing weather with nothing more than what they had on their backs. If anyone saw us, they stayed quiet. To silence our cannon wheels we wrapped blankets around them. Hindman sent out a white flag seeking a 12 hour truce to retrieve the bodies of the wounded and bury the dead. Union Genl. Blunt agreed and both sides quietly started removing their dead and dying from the field. I was glad not to be part of the burial regiment. This truce gave the rest of us a good 12 hour head start out of the mountains. Many stayed behind to gather the dead and wounded and by dawn women riding in on horseback were tending to the wounded on both sides. The horrors of the battle became more horrific when the women found most of the dead had few if any wounds at all, having died from exhaustion and exposure during the night. The women told how the northern boys had crawled into the haystacks seeking shelter from the cold, especially the wounded where they fell asleep. When the shelling started, the haystacks caught fire roasting the men alive. As men from both sides were retrieving their wounded and dead, a horde of wild Ark hogs of all sizes attracted by the smell of the burnt flesh came into the field and began pulling the dead bodies from the haystacks. They ripped and tore the bodies dragging heads, arms and legs about the field. There were so many bearing huge tusks with razor backs the men had to abandon their duty watching out for the hogs.

Our retreat during the night allowed the Union to claim victory. We were certain there would continue to be great difficulties in North Ark where most of the munitions were being made for the South. By the time we reached Van Buren, Ark on Dec 10th footsore and ragged, we were without a solid leader. Those not before aware that Hindman had been removed from his high ranking position did now. Talking on the march back we learned one of the Ark regiments had refused to go fight and Marmaduke under Hindman's orders sent the Cav with sabers drawn forcing them to march into battle. Most of the fellows from these parts were instructed to go home, get some rest, see family, help in whatever way they could and then return to rejoin the effort. This was the way it was especially with no military issued supplies. Most existed on what could be killed or what we brought with us. Those of us that could hunt and fish did so. I taught more than a few how to spear a fish using a limb. Those boys use to gigging fish were better than I was. It was a tricky business if you thought the enemy was nearby. I was thankful for all Unc had shown us boys. Grateful for Bloody Bill and Jesse teaching us how to fish a rabbit out of a hole. I dare say, I no longer minded eating a baby rabbit. Most of the men for whom this was home remained in North Ark throughout the winter with plans to join back up when commands neared their homes.

Chapter 14

At the request of Colonel Shelby, I accompanied him to Springfield. Enroute we got word a month earlier the boys that stayed with Cole in Missouri found four of Jennison's men near Cole's winter camp. The Jayhawkers tried to escape but they killed all but one. When attacked Tom Talley was in the dugout. He ran out, one boot on and one boot off. He tried to shoot with his pistol but it was wet from the snow and didn't fire. Al Cunningham and George Clayton had joined Cole Younger and George Todd. Al and George remained in Kansas City area for the winter while John McCorkle, John Jarrette and Koger headed to the Sni Hills looking for winter shelter so they missed out on the fray. Job McCorkle was with Joshua McCorkle, Cole Younger and Tom Talley when they killed the Jayhawkers. These boys were first cousins. Tom's momma Mary Ann Fristoe was a sister to their momma's. The Talley brothers all had full heads of hair, thick wavy, chestnut brown. Tom wore his mustache tightly trimmed.

Col. Shelby was alarmed at the news of Maj Genl. Ulysses Grant having issued an extermination order against the Jews. Genl. Order Number 11 was issued on Dec 17 and went into immediate effect. All Jews and their families were to be expulsed from Holly Springs and Oxford, Mississippi and Paducah, Kentucky. Should they not leave they would be shot. Grant apparently felt the Jews were in cahoots with us Southerners managing a black market trade for cotton. Most Southern cotton was being funneled into New Orleans then sent to the highest bidders, mostly countries willing to come into the war zone to get it. The North wanted control of Southern cotton and "no Southerner was going to get in the way, much less a Jew," Grant had said.

Shelby and Marmaduke began planning an expedition into Missouri hopefully keeping Blunt busy and out of mischief in Ark. Genl. Hindman ordered Genl. Marmaduke to take Shelby and Porter's Missouri brigades, cut Blunt's main lines of communication around Springfield, Missouri, and hold it until Blunt was forced to let go of his grip on the Ark River. Hindman was hoping these efforts would prevent Blunt from attacking Little Rock. While Quantrill was still east at Richmond lobbying for a commission, the boys that had not returned home remained with Col. Shelby, only a few with families already in Texas had gone south. Meanwhile, Genl. "Granny" Holmes as he was referred to by us boys due to his slow moving manner, was placed in command of the Trans Mississippi to succeed Maj Tom Hindman.

We now realized Hindman's command of Northwest Ark had been a demotion. He ordered Genl. Marmaduke and his 4th Division to fall back to the Springfield Camp at Lewisburg between Fort Smith and Little Rock. From there Hindman ordered Genl. Marmaduke to move north. On the last day of the year 1862, we broke camp at Springfield, 50 miles northwest of Little Rock. It was a clear and sunny morning; a cold wind was biting the air. Us Missourians led by Col. Shelby was followed by Col. James Monroe's Ark boys with Col. Emmett McDonald's Missouri Brigade. Most of us under Bill Gregg, Quantrill's Raiders, were part of Elliott's command attached to McDonald. Genl. "Granny" Holmes ordered Col JoeC Porter and his men to come from Pocahontas, Ark into Missouri to reinforce Marmaduke. Col Porter was to form the right column for Marmaduke. Including Col Porter's Missouri Cav and Col Emmet MacDonald's Regiment, Missouri Cav, Col James Monroe's men and our boys, we were over 2,500 strong headed from Springfield, Ark to Springfield, Missouri. It was ironic, so I think in order to keep positions straight and confusion down, in official communications they began referring to Springfield, Ark simply as Lewisburg.

Our regiment was called to the front by Col. Shelby. We were to ride advance guard of the 2,000 men moving from Lewisburg ahead of Hindman, scouting and reporting back both the conditions of travel and any sightings of Federalists. Most of the boys were not prepared for this march especially under these conditions. It was worse than the march to Cane Hill. The blizzard of Dec had passed leaving in its wake a cold wind chaffing and freezing the faces and hands of many of the men. Both Unc and Doc had taught us boys how to protect our faces from the cold with rags covering everything but just a slit for our eyes. I saw boys and men alike putting on all the clothes they carried to keep warm. I helped many tie extra shirts over their heads protecting their faces.

I grew up in the fields working with Uncle Till and Doc as a field hand and later as an overseer. Knowing the weather is an important part of successful crop yields. Momma and Aunt Charlotte would busy themselves when necessary lighting the fires in the fields to protect the young tobacco plants from a late frost. The day might be warm and sunny but they knew the night could kill. I don't know how they knew anymore than I did now, but I felt it as we marched out. Even more bad weather was on the horizon. The roads were wet and muddy making movement slow, snow was more than a two feet deep in the shade and deeper in the drifts. We headed north across rolling hills from Camp Lewisburg marching north towards Burrowsville in Searcy Co. Our second day out a cold rain fell. The sun stayed behind the clouds and temperatures never rose above freezing. By late afternoon, it was freezing on the trees, sleet hitting us as we marched face downward. My skin hurt. I thought of Doc as I scanned the horizon. I saw no sign of a cow but it made me smile to myself remembering the day.

I'm certain most of the farmers had their cattle well hidden, from us and the Union. Men were starving, we had no cook wagons and almost no one had their own cooking gear. Even those that did couldn't feed 2,000 men. The sunlight coming through the ice covered limbs was blinding. We'd just went through this on the march to Cane Hill but even so, when the weight of the ice breaking the tree limbs popped like gun fire, we flinched, afraid.

In the foothills of the Boston Mountains at a place called Witt Springs, Jan 2, 1863 two scouts, one a local fella, William Andrew Jackson "Jack" Marshall came upon a force of 60 Jayhawkers, called Mountain Boomers under a man called Chris Denton. Fierce fighting ensued. Our scout's guerilla style yelling and shooting alerted Lt. Col. Charles Gilley's Cav regiment. Followed by Elliott they quickly scattered the men killing their leader, Denton, as well as 20 others in the skirmish, 20 more were wounded and captured. Col. Shelby and Elliott made the decision to parole the wounded men swearing them not to take up arms again. They were released to go home and told to take their dead with them. Now, I didn't want to see anyone die, this was a horrible war, but I knew just as they knew, these men, boys, fathers, sons, they would return to fight and some of them before the day's end. Us Raiders, guerrillas, were not taking well to this game of catch and release. I knew of no situation where the hunter releases his prey, especially if you stood a chance that prey would come back as the hunter. But, we had little say. "Men at some time are masters of their fates: The fault, dear Brutus, is not in our stars, but in ourselves, that we are underlings." We moved through Burrowsville then east through Yellville to Camp Adams. Nearing Yellville, Col. Monroe received an order to withdraw from the expedition to attack Feds along Van Buren Creek.

Jack Marshall was married to Miss Martha Ann Hemphill, both the Marshall's and Hemphill's were early settlers of the area. Jack and Missus Martha had a daughter Aprilla "Rilly", 3, and a baby child, Seppie not yet 2. Like Given Horn, they knew the area and the sympathies of families, critical to the movements of the troops and our ability to forage. Jack told stories about his daddy, Joel Marshall having fought in the War of 1812. He received a military land grant and their family moved west into the new territories. The Fristoe's were descendants of Judge Marshall of the Virginia's, so I inquired as to their relationship. Jack told me his grandparents, John Marshall and Rebecca Montgomery had come from Ireland but were of kin to the Houston's. He didn't know the Houston's but would like to make their acquaintance. We visited about the Grigsby Ferry and Missus Margaret Houston, cousin of Genl. Sam Houston and brother John. I was pleased with myself to be able to impart family information that would gain him acceptance with Missus Margaret who might know the relationship between his family and theirs. The smile on my face couldn't adequately express the deep feelings I had inside when Jack told me he thought I would make a good teacher. Life challenged me daily on my calling as a preacher but I still believed I could be a good teacher. We learned the group returning had attacked the Mountain Boomers skirmishing near the Buffalo River. Joined by an advance of Genl. Marmaduke's men, they had killed, wounded and captured most of the enemy. Those captured were executed. I had inquired of Given Horn why the Buffalo River was so named. He told us a story about the herds of buffalo roaming there and the wallows on the hilltops. They were plenty in number when Chief Lewis arrived with the Shawnee in 1815. He reckoned Chief Lewis probably named the river. The nearby Red River was named for a massacre that occurred before the sale of the French territories in 1803, when the Spanish and Osage Indians were attacked by a French Canadian named Valliere and some Shawnee who were coming in to check on his mining efforts and land claims. The river had run red with blood. Nearby Tomahawk Creek had been named for another massacre where the Osage had been attacked, tomahawked to death by Cherokee kinsmen of Chief Duwali.

We continued northwest from Yellville through Omaha entering Missouri at Taney Co on Jan 5th moving north headed to Ozark south of Springfield. Col. Shelby ordered Elliot to take Bill Gregg and us men as scouts, detour around the fort at Ozark cutting off its garrison. The Federalists learned of our approach and retreated to Springfield. Although we lost the element of surprise, the fleeing Union left provisions that were sorely needed, dried meat, bread and a little whiskey.

Unc made certain all of us boys knew how to survive on nothing with no more than a knife. He taught us to cook corn dodgers using the fat removed from any animal we killed. The fat cooked down to liquid mixed with a little water and ground corn meal was fried on a dutch oven lid or skillet if you had them, if not, on hot rocks or the side of your knife. I knew the boys arriving in camp with a little sow belly and corn meal knew how to survive. As night fell sitting next to a newcomer, newer than me now considered an old timer, no more a green horn, I realized I was staring. The sowbelly he was eating still had the rough hair of the hog on it. I started a little when he reached out his hand offering me a piece. Grateful I thanked him. He built up the fire while I located some large flat limestone table rocks perfect for making some corn dodgers. His sowbelly would provide a bit of fat increasing the taste and adding a little fat into our diet. He introduced himself as John Imboden. We stoked up the fire heating the rocks. I showed him how to cook down the sowbelly for the fat, breaking the now puffed up skin, chitlins, into bits to add to the meal mixture. We sat around the fire cooking and eating, joined by several more boys, we found ourselves laughing at our disadvantages. One of the boys thought the hair of the hog stiff enough to pick his teeth, made us all laugh. For a moment we were friends on a camp out, ne'r say a bad one. I believe the Union's retreat from the garrison at Ozark saved a thousand Southern lives. We secured the remaining supplies before setting fire to the fort. Another detachment under Col McDonald overran a small outpost, Fort Lawrence, yielding additional vital food provisions. Most of us felt reprieved by the Union if not by the grace of God. "The men of Israel took captive from their fellow Israelites who were from Judah two hundred thousand wives, sons and daughters. They also took a great deal of plunder, which they carried back to Samaria." 2 Chronicles 28:8 Times hadn't changed.

We talked about the Union boys dying from exhaustion and starvation, freezing to death in their sleep and the wild razorback hogs. Col MacDonald's men returned having gathered over 400 arms and ammunition, 150 horses and 20 prisoners. The troops around us immediately improved in spirit when he ordered the arms distributed to the among us. All of the detachments were having similar successes which was literally feeding and arming us both real and of heart. Little did we realize we would be eating the meat of those horses before the month was over.

Neither Genl. Marmaduke nor his scouts had heard from Col. JoeC Porter but had learned Springfield was weakly garrisoned. The Genl. made the decision to attack on Jan 7th without waiting on Col. Porter to arrive. The attack began around 10 o'clock in the morning on Jan 8th. The Feds had two or more militiamen stationed at every house along the road. We donned our Union uniforms and in groups of six went into the homes dragging people from their warm beds ahead of Col. Shelby's advance. We captured large numbers of much needed wagons, horses, slaves and clothing. Springfield was under armed due to Genl. Blunt having most of the soldiers with him near Prairie Grove.

A few miles outside of Springfield in a timbered area, Genl. Marmaduke was preparing to attack. They pushed Union troops who stood as patrols to the center of the city. More than 100 of us under Bill Gregg reconnoitered the city assessing their defenses and position. The center of the city to which the patrols retreated was a large earthwork fortress flanked by rifle pits and deep trenches for infantry. The former female academy, a large brick building on the south side of the city, was being used as a military prison. Marmaduke formed a formidable line of defense in an open field two miles south of the main part of the city. One of their commanders with a large body of men escorting him boldly rode out to view our ranks. They rode along the front until Col. Elliot ordered a group of 40 of our men after them. Before he could escape, our boys wounded him. Those of us riding with Shelby charged the Union in front of the stockade killing or wounding most of them. Shelby was a sight to see, his hat in his hand held high yelling "Charge", his long hair streaming. He had picked up our wild yell. A number of our boys decided they weren't going to cut their hair after seeing the sight he was. Reaching the first of the rifle pits, we drove the Union back towards a large cemetery where they had a cannon. Twenty of us broke off from Shelby rushing the men preparing to arm the cannon. Capturing it, we lassoed it dragging it to the rear turning it on the Union. The Federalists began falling back managing to set fire to the building containing their supplies and ammunition. They continued their barrage, as did our men. The Union began pouring out of the earthworks and trenches engaging with us in hand to hand, house to house fighting. We had not taken them completely by surprise. They were able to defend themselves and the city against our assaults. By mid afternoon, it was clear this was a stalemate but fighting continued until night fell. The sound of bugles from both sides finally signaled a cease fire. Even though we had done well against the Union, taking supplies and over 200 prisoners, Genl. Marmaduke ordered a full retreat. We had not taken Springfield, but we had accomplished the goal of harassing the Union and breaking down their supply lines. We began withdrawing around midnight by regiments. The least weary of the Cav ordered to make up the rear guard continued to skirmish until daybreak thus giving over a better chance of retreat to the first men out. When dawn came and the Union discovered the full retreat, they came after us. Genl. Marmaduke stayed with us in the rear and had to make a full run for it. Once again "Quantrill's men" riding under Col Elliott halted the Federal's charge. First in, last out, the troops saw in us, a kind of fighting their fathers and grandfathers spoke of, men who had fought in the War of 1812, Mexican War of '48 and the War for Independence. They looked at us as leaders, brave and daring, knights of old, soldiers of the realm. I missed Momma and our plays, innocent days long gone.

We headed down the Rolla road toward Marshfield. Marmaduke ordered everything in our path destroyed. There wasn't much remaining. The Union had already been through. The snow and cold freezing rain saved a number of fields and homes from complete destruction. Our boys intercepted a much needed wagon train of supplies headed to Blunt in Ark. We learned JoeC Porter still hadn't arrived and scouts had been sent to look for him. Our columns split with Col. Shelby's men burning forts, bridges, culverts and communication lines. We joined back up near Marshfield with Col. McDonald. Genl. Marmaduke and his commanders made the decision to attack the 1,000 man garrison at Hartville, 30 miles east. The scouts caught up with JoeC Porter, his command and Col.s Colton Greene and J. Q. A. Burbridge, 900 strong enroute to join us. JoeC left Pocahontas on Jan 2nd marching to the North West corner of Fulton Co where he planned to go via West Plains. He learned a large force of Union was camped there so he headed further west via the Gainesville Cotter Road, Rockbridge, Red Bird and Hartville, a very sparsely populated area with difficult terrain. Having recruited a Majority of the boys, Col. JoeC Porter had a solid reputation among us. We didn't have the worry Marmaduke had.

The California Gold Rush of the late 1840's lured men from all parts of the country, including brothers Joseph "JoeC" and James "Jim" Porter along with my daddy, Reverend Robert Sallee James. Within a month of arriving in the California mining camps, Daddy died. JoeC and his brother returned to Missouri where they farmed before the outbreak of the war. JoeC and his brother married sisters' Mary Ann and Carolina Marshall, great grand daughters of Chief Justice John Marshall of Virginia. They remained close friends of our family as well as Bill Wilson, fellow Missourian and lone guerilla, who also had been lured west to the gold mines. With the onset of the war, JoeC and Jim Porter enrolled under Col. Martin Green's Missouri State Guard. These men were of the stuff that made this land.

JoeC had been ordered to move south into Ark to recruit for the Confederacy. Proving difficult, Genl. Sterling Price ordered him to return home to Missouri, along with Gideon Thompson, Joseph Shelby, Upton Hayes, and Calhoun Thornton to raise recruits. They were to establish supply drops, weapon caches, and a network of pro Southern supporters and informants, safe houses. Many of the men, guerillas, and irregulars, even the recruiters were not recognized as legal combatants and faced execution if captured. As unsuccessful as he had been in Ark, he proved successful in Missouri. JoeC Porter was a good recruiter quickly earning the trust of the families of the young men. He recruited not only young boys and men into service but gained the allegiance of the families and neighbors securing safe havens on farms. He understood the need of the families to have their men close but he made certain everyone knew the risks they faced if found out.

It was JoeC's attack on Memphis, Missouri that perhaps most significantly soiled his reputation. He and his men raided the Federal armory securing a hundred muskets with cartridge boxes, ammunition and uniforms. They rounded up all adult males taking them to the court house. They had the captives swear not to tell about the raid for at least 48 hours or they would come back and hunt them down, unmercifully killing each of them. JoeC's men destroyed all the indictments held at the court house, from horse theft to guerillas and freed all prisoners. Northerners took this as lawlessness on the part of known criminals, guerillas. However, Southerners viewed it as an act akin to Robin Hood knowing many of the men were in prison on trumped up charges. "Small things make base men proud" - Shakespeare.

In Memphis, Capt. Tom Stacy and his men captured Dr. William Aylward, a prominent Union man confining him to a house and the next day reported he escaped. His body was found and by all appearances he had been hung or strangled to death. A local Union man inquiring after Dr. Aylward reported Col. Porter told him, "He is where he will never disturb anybody else." This was taken as proof JoeC approved of Aykward's death. Following Memphis, his men dispersed and with fewer than 100 men remaining of the 2000 recruits JoeC made his way to Ark at the end of Dec. At Pocahontas, he met other Missourians under Col. Colton Green and J.Q.A. Burbridge. Acting as commander of the combined forces, they headed to join Genl. Marmaduke on his attack on Springfield. However through miscommunication JoeC and his men did not move out timely then had to change their route. Our scouts located them successfully uniting them with Marmaduke east of Marshfield. JoeC and Col. Tom knew the southern central and eastern part of Missouri, having camped at a number of the well secluded springs in the rolling mountains and with family residing in the area. They were leading us back to Ark headed toward Batesville; there the train would take us to Little Rock. Bill Lawrence and I talked about hunting and fishing along the way, anything to make life seem a little more normal. We talked of fishing and fish fries, yapping dogs and laughing children. Bill Lawrence was Daddy's age. I liked talking to him, a man, a father, more than the boys that made up most of the ranks, regular and irregular. He told me about his life. He had married young full of hope and with his wife, Elizabeth King, had a house full of children. His oldest, James Daniel was 14, George 12, John Martin 10, Tom 7, Joe 4 and Isaac Newton 2. His wife died leaving him with a houseful of boys, not a girl one. He needed a wife and they needed a momma. He married Elizabeth Alzira Clark. He called her "Zee or Zir" but in the howling wind, I wasn't certain. I didn't want to interrupt his story. They married just before war was declared. He'd left her at home with a houseful of boys who all thought they were men but he was certain she could handle them. He was anxious for us to make it back into Ark hoping to get home before the worst of winter hit. I liked this man. I told him about Doc's cow weather gauge. He made me feel safe talking to him. Even more, I missed Daddy. I didn't remember what Daddy's voice sounded like, but I thought it might be like Bill Lawrence's, strong and unwavering, yet gentle and kind when he spoke of his family. I wondered if I should voice, today is my 20th birthday. The 8th Missouri joined us, William Howard Crouch had been listening the best he could in the howling wind to Bill Lawrence's stories. When we halted, he came closer talking to Bill, he and his wife Mary Ann Bookout were from Fulton Co not far from Col. Tom's camp at Mammoth Springs.

When we reached Hartville on Jan 11, 1863, we found three regiments of infantry, three Cav and six pieces of artillery defending the town. The infantry was concealed by deep ditches behind a huge ten rail fence. The Cav was on both flanks protected by heavy timber and the artillery battery was on a high hill in the rear. Jo Shelby dismounted our entire brigade marching us boldly to attack in front. JoeC Porter's brigade advanced by the road charging the left flank once Shelby commenced attack. The artillery men covered Shelby's advance marching up the rail fence row grabbing the rails; the Union opened fire enveloping Shelby's and our men in a barrage of gunfire felling all but four Capts, dead or dying. Shelby and Marmaduke charged the fence forcing the Federalists to retreat dragging their artillery with them lest it be captured. I swear no man lost more horses than Jo Shelby. He had two shot from under him at Hartville and he himself took a bullet to the head. To his dying day he carried the Cav badge on his hat that saved his life. The bullet left a huge indent ricocheting off. Marmaduke was unhurt. His horse fell and his overcoat was riddled with bullet holes but his pride and his life remained intact. JoeC led his brigade at a full charge up the hill. His horse was shot dead plunging JoeC into the frozen ground; he was shot in the hand and leg.

After four hours of fighting, we won the battle, but suffered a severe loss of officers killed and mortally wounded. Among the captured was William Howard Crouch. When Marmaduke made his report, Col. Joseph C. "JoeC" Porter was among the men listed as wounded. We gathered the dead and wounded, no one was exempt from the detail, still it was nigh on two o'clock in the morning before we were able to resume moving south. Genl. Marmaduke sent Gregg back with orders to remain in Missouri recruiting. Gregg turned his command over to Lt. Fernando Scott and was back in Jackson Co by Jan 19, 1863. He sent John Ross to Jackson Co along with John William Koger to recruit. George Todd ordered Joe Hart to go to St. Joseph for pistol caps. He was captured while leaving town but managed to escape again. The rest of us remained with Genl. Price and Shelby. We arrived at the Big North Fork of the White River there setting up camp. Marmaduke paroled and released the prisoners.

One of the scouts came back reporting having seen a small herd of deer and a turkey. Shelby ordered us, Quantrill's men, to go see what we could kill. There were only a few of us with turkey hunting skills, so while the most of them went off to see about that herd of deer, two of the fella's with long range rifles went with me to see if we could find that turkey. Gobblers are unpredictable. You can give a low tree yelp and maybe he'll fly down, maybe he'll land close by, maybe it will be a few hundred yards away. We tied the horses near the water and set out walking, not talking. Hunting turkey requires patience to outwit those wise old birds. We found ourselves a good listening spot and hunkered down. Dick Partee certainly possessed deer ears because he heard the crackle of the leaves before we ever heard the first gobble. Hunched down close enough to nudge me with his elbow, he nodded his head pointing just as the old bird let out a big gobble. Bill Lawrence smiled nodding. All of us experienced hunters, we stayed quiet watching. Smiling to ourselves and dreaming of cooked turkey we watched the big gobbler strut and scratch. Since Dick spied the bird we agreed with a nod of our heads he should take first shot. Raising our guns our eyes widened when into the midst of the little clearing came two more gobblers and some hens. We saw some small turkeys but no chicks. We portioned off the group, 1, 2, and 3 for maximum kill then unloaded our guns. One gobbler got away, the rest we killed. We gathered them up; only one had to have its neck wrung. Tossing them over our shoulders we headed back to the horses discussing how it was someone else's job to do the plucking. We laughed talking about the hunt. I told them about Jesse and the chicken. For a moment we were just men out hunting.

Back at camp, some of the women were busily making squirrel stew. The coals in the fire were perfect for spitting these birds. While we played one against the other to whom the duty of plucking would fall, we were grateful when the women took them from us. We knew they'd save the big tails of the gobbler's and none of the soft down would go to waste. It would be saved for any number of uses. The women plucked all the birds saving the feathers in less time than us boys would have managed one. The deer hunter's returned with two good white tails. All of this was insufficient to feed the number of mouths we had, but somehow, the skilled hands of the women and commissary fed every man among us.

Us Southern boys were astounded by the barbarity and waste of the Union. They would kill farm animals they couldn't take with them; clearly without the skills or knowledge of how to prepare them in order to feed themselves for days, especially in cold weather when meat travels better. No flies to blow it. We heard the tales of local Missourians fighting with the Union trying to intervene, herding the cattle, sheep and pigs but were made fun of for their efforts. I am certain at night when those boys were roasting a squirrel or rabbit to eat and those northern soldiers smelled them cooking, they took a new attitude. Hunger will do that. We passed farms where every building was burned except the slave houses. Women and children, white and black, nannies and little farmhands huddled together expressionless watching us move past. They showed nothing on their faces. They were neither curious nor afraid. What more did they have to lose? In starvation they answered the call of our redeemer.

On the night of Jan 18, 1863, a heavy snowstorm lasting ten hours hit covering everything in two or more feet of snow. The ground was still frozen with snow and ice holding tight in the shadows making this new snow worse. We struggled on towards Batesville. Momma, Doc and Unc had always made certain we knew how to care for our hands and feet. We knew how to take care of our shoes. The boys around me were walking in leathers that could no longer be called shoes. We struggled as we moved south toward Batesville. Genl. Shelby, he was a true leader. Bill Wilson and I remained with him assigned as part of the burial detail. The cold and frostbite were so severe men had to have fingers, toes and feet amputated along the way. They were going into shock, dying. We would see to their burial if their homes were too distant or send a rider to have their families come for them when we could. But most were buried in twos and threes in a single grave covered in rocks along the way. We couldn't carry them in the wagons with us as most were full of men whose lives might yet be saved. The scouts, commanders and burial detail worked in close communication with the doctors. Graves marked each place we stopped. We buried amputated hands, feet, arms and legs in single graves and sometimes if their amputee did not survive, their limb was buried with them. The first time I came upon a field tent hospital where amputations were taking place, I was sickened at the sight of a massive pile of limbs stacked outside. Now as we traveled, men were removing limbs in worse conditions. Although no longer did my face reveal the horror I felt inside, young men rushing to the bushes remained common. We were lucky to have two doctors with us. In most cases, there was one doctor to 5,000 men or more. Doc had had a long talk with Col.s Shelby and Hayes when they had been recruiting. He told them they would lose more men through infections and disease than through actual combat. Doc had been witness to the ravages of disease when large numbers of people were forced to live together in a "hospital" which he called a poor house. Most of the men with us were from rural areas, without close neighbors and contact limited to their family. When anyone ventured through sick in some cases Doc said almost entire villages, communities could succumb due to the illness, scarlet fever, measles, mumps and malaria. He was adamant every command have a doctor to treat the sick and injured. If unable to do so, they needed to have some means of getting the men to a safe place to recuperate away from the others or entire commands could be wiped out. Doc helped recruit other doctor's in the area willing to provide services to us when needed, cash on hand, but sometimes it was a chicken or quilt or other means of payment, often nothing at all. Col. Shelby comes from a rich family. His family had access to the best care of the day and had witnessed firsthand how lack of medical care could devastate as Doc said, not just entire families, but entire villages. He understood completely and as a result, we had two doctors with us and a slew of men who knew how to assist, country doctoring.

Crossing the Ark border it became necessary to discuss with Col. JoeC, amputation of his hand. Mangled it was severely infected. I overheard the doctor talking to him and Col. Shelby about the possibility of gangrene. I thought about what Doc told Col. Shelby. I knew from other instances that if it were spring or summer there would be flies and they would lay eggs which would become maggots. These maggots could eat the decaying and rotting skin of the infected area and would in some cases help but this was winter. No, this was worse than winter, this was the worst winter I'd seen in my short life. I wondered if it was this kind of winter preventing Daddy from getting home to Momma the winter I was born.

We made the long trek through deep snow, ill dressed and under nourished, out of ammunition passing through areas that suffered the ravages of war as much as we had ourselves. Destroyed homes, barns and crops left almost nothing for man or animal. Bill Wilson was a friend of JoeC's. He had been with us when JoeC was wounded and understanding the gravity of JoeC's condition remained working the death detail as they had started calling those of us still strong enough and willing to bury the dead. He volunteered to ride alone to Salem to get JoeC's wife and children escorting them to Batesville. It's difficult to express what I saw of these men. They were starving. I had a little smoked turkey meat which I'd chewed on for days, as if it was a cud of tobacco in my mouth. The men were so hungry those that smelled it thought perhaps it was their imaginations. When we passed farms, although we were under strict orders not to loot, steal or otherwise endanger or encumber citizens, if there was the possibility of any food, it was taken from the fields, barns and hands of the people who offered it to us and sometimes those that didn't. There were a number of us guerillas who were use to this kind of fend for yourself traveling, foraging, even in the worst of weather, but we were thousands riding and marching, not a couple hundred. Horses were dying on the roads of fatigue, exhaustion and hunger. We stopped long enough just inside Ark with plenty of water to slaughter and cook them. The snow and mud was deep. I couldn't put my horse George in danger, so I couldn't take on a second rider, but I could walk and sometimes, I did. Several of us riders took off our shoes giving them over to the barefooted men, over 500 of them had no shoes at all. We could walk and let their feet thaw wrapped in blankets, shirts and extra clothing as they rode. Everyone was trying to save themselves and everyone else. The Feds slash and burn policy had driven people away from their homes. Half burned abandoned crops and buildings dotted the way and now, graves. It was my job to keep up with who died, when and where we buried them. Families could be notified and chose if they wanted to re-intern them in their home cemeteries. Either way, they knew where they were buried and that words had been said over them.

Entering Ark many of the troops, soldiers, men and boys with us that felt they could make it home, were not only authorized to leave but encouraged to do so. They left in pairs and groups of three or four, some headed home with friends they'd made. At night when we made camp, the groans and screams of the men were horrific. Being on the grave detail and the suffering I seen sat heavy in my heart. Just before we got to Batesville we learned the train that was to take us to Camp Lewisburg was stuck in the deep snow in the mountains and unable to move forward to Batesville nor go back if it was able to get there.

Genl. Marmaduke noted in his report on Jan 25th from Batesville, Joseph C. Porter among the wounded in contrast to the listing of officers killed. JoeC survived the march arriving in Batesville very ill, his body racked with infection, chills and temperature weakening him. He was taken to Catalpa Hall, home of William Byers. Word of the train stuck in snow banks unable to retrieve us had an eerie effect, some of the boys seemed grateful and others were ready to point their guns at themselves if they had ammunition. We made camp. Miss Nannie Wilson, step daughter of William Byers and her friends began immediately attending to the men, seeking and providing clothing, food and medical care. Cleaning the bodies of the wounded with hot water was instrumental in their improvement both medically and spiritually, not to mention the effect of a woman's caring touch. Many of them had not only been injured with minie balls but adding to it, had dirt and grit in their wounds making their infections worse. Simply cleaning and bandaging them, providing a hot bowl of anything to eat, was enough for most to survive.

I had never seen such a sight of welcome. We moved through Batesville crossing the White River, under Shelby setting up camp on the farm of Col. Franklin Desha. Genl. Marmaduke moved further east toward Jacksonport setting up camp near Moorefield, closer to Big Bottom across the river from Oil Trough, a place on the river named due to the sale of bear oil. Headquarters was at the Cox house in Batesville. Having met a great many of Col. Freeman's men, some still with us, we rode through the area to the homes of people asking them to take in the sick and injured troops. Families spread the word faster than we could ride, sending riders to Batesville picking up men on horseback, with mules and wagons taking them to their homes. The people fed and nursed the men. I was one of the lucky ones as were most of the men who had been fighting guerilla warfare. We had been taught to survive differently than these men. Most of them were the sons of men who moved into this country as youngsters with their parents or were the grandchildren of pioneering settlers. Although life was hard for them, they had homes and roots; they didn't travel far and were protective of their own. On the other hand, our families had moved into the war zone created by the Mormons, expanded by the Border Wars culminating in the War Between the States, we'd been taught from a young age about survival. Whatever our heritage, we were thankful for the good people of Batesville with whom us Missourians would fall in love.

The Majority of the men were on the neighboring farm of William Byers. I was in Elliott's camp with Jo Shelby on the farm of Franklin Desha and wife Elizabeth Searcy. Miss Lizzie as everyone called her was the niece of one of Batesville's most prestigious residents, the late Richard Searcy, the first judge in the Ark Territory. Her father, James was his older brother. Searcy Co bordered Independence and was named for her uncle. They offered us refuge and care. Franklin Desha was a prominent attorney in Batesville himself. I did not realize how close I was to any family other than Aunt Lucy up near Athens and Calico Bluffs. Sitting by the fire warming myself, Col Elliott approached with a man he introduced as Daniel James. He shook my hand grinning then pulled me into him with a big bear hug, like my Daddy's. For a moment, I was without words. I was that little boy riding with Daddy the day before he left for California. It was clear Daniel James was having a similar reaction as tears clouded his eyes. "My father's Alvah James," he said. Daddy's father a man called by God himself was John Martin James and Alvah William James if I remembered right was his brother. This man whose arms felt so much like my Daddy's, was Daddy's own cousin, sons of brothers. Daddy's Momma was Mary Poor. Aunt Lucy Mims lived up river at Athens, Daddy's great aunt. Grandma Mary Poor's daddy Robert Poor and Aunt Lucy Poor Mims were brother and sister. And now here I was with another of Daddy's cousins, a man who looked, sounded and felt like Daddy. What fear I'd felt vanished. I was among friends and family.

Chapter 15

Daniel James lived about eight miles southwest of Batesville at the base of Jamestown Mountain near Jamestown Creek. A land speculator he began settling this area in the 1840's, the same time my daddy was learning to be a preacher in Kentucky. Along with his land speculation, Daniel James donated the land for the local Methodist church, leading to the area becoming known as "James' Town." He invited me to join them at their home. This was more than acceptable to Col. Shelby and Elliott. If any of us had family to go home to, "go home", was the order. During my stay, Mister Daniel told me about cousin Reverend Burwell Lee, one of the founders of the Ebenezer Methodist Church east of Batesville at Moorefield near where Genl. Marmaduke was camped.

Daniel James and Mary Pickett

After their parents, William and Mary Hines James, were buried in Virginia, their children moved west. My grandparents, their oldest son, Rev. John Martin James and wife Mary Poor moved into Kentucky and are buried there. Drury Hines James and wife Anne Jordan settled in Crittenden Co, Ark. Alvah "Alvie" William James and wife Rebecca Hodges settled in Tennessee, their oldest son Daniel who stood before me moved to Ark, living several places before settling in Independence Co establishing "James' Town." Their parents lost some children early and Mary did not want to move away. Their sister Mary James married Gambol Kimball

Powers settling in Craighead Co. He told me of another cousin, also a bit of land speculator, Elisha K James, and wife Katherine Frost who moved to the Ark Territories acquiring land in St. Francis, Lee and Desha Counties in the 1830's, before moving to Independence Co.

The state lines changing as new states were formed from larger states and territories. Lands west of the Mississippi River were opening up to anyone willing and brave enough to move into Indian Territory. The 'new nation' was in a state of flux and our families, the James, Poor, Mims, we were pioneers, men and women willing to move into new lands to establish them and people of faith, desiring to spread the word of God. All of the brothers fought in the War of 1812, and likely it was then, many of those moving into Missouri and Ark first laid eyes on the lands they later claimed. Daddy was a young missionary moving into Missouri to fight the rising cult of the Mormons while his kinsmen Burwell Lee, Daniel and Elisha James moved to Ark. Daddy was as instrumental in establishing the Baptist churches in Missouri as Burwell Lee was in spreading the Methodist faith in Ark. These were pioneering men of faith and entrepreneurs.

Daniel James felt he could safely get a letter home to Momma informing her of our difficult trek and safe arrival. "Shelby's men are camped on Byer's farm, spread out all along Greenbrier Bottoms across Desha's farm. Frank arrived here sick from the cold. He gave his good boots to a married man with children, completely wearing the soles of his remaining boots through to his feet. He complains of pain in his left foot. There's some fear his toes may have frozen. We shall attempt to get him to Aunt Lucy's where he will be at home and cared for. It may be his will to remain here with his regiment until this plays out," he wrote Momma along with news of other family in the area. I asked him to add "Buck wishes you Happy Birthday." The camps extended for several miles along Greenbrier Bottoms, fields along the river and ridge. William Byer's stepdaughter, Nannie Wilson, was the "belle of the camp" so much so they started calling it "Camp Nannie Wilson."

Col. JoeC Porter was at Catalpa Hall. Bill Wilson arrived with JoeC's wife and children whom the Byers graciously accepted into their spacious home. It had been turned into a hospital with cots and pallets on the floors. I dare say should I of been one of those men there, I would have feigned illness to stay a little longer. The only home I'd known of this beauty and size was the Hudspeth's, both of which I marveled. With a slight improvement in the weather, I left Batesville, headed west up the White River towards Athens. I had traveled a short distance when I came upon the home of Samuel and Elizabeth Porter Blair, sister of Bob Porter, the rock thrower. Nearby I met with several men of Col. Tom's Co headed toward Batesville. I told them of our march from Missouri. I continued on my way accompanied by a couple of men heading home. In a short distance, we came upon a picket of men on a monstrous bluff overlooking the other side of the river. They explained it was called Penter's Bluff. The Penter family lived there one said while another argued it was the way the Indians said panther. They still roamed this area and at night screamed from the top of the bluff. You could see a long distance down river towards Batesville as well as upriver. One of them pointed out Grigsby Ferry to the east in the distance and Coker to the west. I smiled remembering the story of the ferry's demise and rebuilding. Just as one of the boys was about to go into the story himself, he stopped short. "Listen," he said. All of us fell quiet. We couldn't see anyone but we could hear someone talking on the river bank below. When we did spy them they were so far away they looked like ants busying themselves as they rode along, a group of 3 men. We could hear every word they said. I recognized Lt. Dillard's voice and yelled out, "Osby, Frank James here." We could see them looking around with uncertainty hearing something, fearful it might be the Union. Again, I called out and the boys with me chimed in. This time they heard us and started waving. They entered the low waters of the frigid river crossing near where Lafferty Creek flowed into the river. We headed to meet them.

I rode the rest of the way to Athens with Osby and his friends. Osby told me the big river bottom I had been looking down on was first settled by John Lafferty and his wife Sarah Lindsay. They applied for the first land patent here in 1810 but were denied because he couldn't prove having lived there for the required 10 years. Indians couldn't testify and since they were the first whites, well, who could speak for them. He went off to fight in the War of 1812, was wounded and died back at home in 1816. His wife Sarah continued to live on the south side of the river in what became the Indian Reservation. They had an established trading post there thus meeting the requirements. Henry Rowe Schoolcraft had even stopped "at the widow Lafferty's on the south banks of the river," in 1819. The rest of her family moved across the river to the Barrens. The creek became named for them after their move. Lafferty's son in law, Charles Kelly became the first Sheriff of Independence Co.

Sarah Elizabeth Lindsay was the daughter of John Tolson Lindsay and Mary Masterson, granddaughter of Anthony Lindsay and Alice Page of England who immigrated here. John Anthony Lindsay, founder of Powhaten, Ark was their grandson, son of Jesse Cole Lindsay and Priscilla Ficklin. Gramma Sallie was a sister to Jesse Cole Lindsay children of Anthony Lindsay III and Alice Cole. Great grandfather Anthony III and Sarah Lindsay Lafferty were own cousins children of brothers, Anthony Jr and John, children of Anthony Lindsay and Alice Page. I was beginning to understand Momma's reasoning about family.

Henderson and Benix Creswell are the grandsons of John Lafferty and Sarah Lindsay, and like Momma, the great great grandchildren of

Anthony Lindsay and Alice Page. Momma, Hen and Ben Creswell were second cousins, along with Samuel Harvey, father of Frank Creswell, all serving under Col. Tom. Osby explained the Creswell family moved to Ark with the Lafferty's and their sons and daughters were married to each other. They were wealthy folks and the Creswell boys fighting with us, were of the Lafferty family and mine. I wondered what my life would have been like had Gramma Sallie and Gramps Bob of chosen to move to Ark instead of Missouri. They had a town named after them, Creswell. Aunt Lucy lived on Creswell Road near White House Landing a mile from Osby and his wife Avarilla near White House, named for the monstrously large beautiful home of her parents James Jeffery and Melinda Benbrook. Missus Melinda's nephew, Charles Elbert Benbrook, son of her brother Elbert and wife Sarah Langston was riding with us, a Sgt. of Col. Tom's command Co A. Osby 1st Lt. was charged with protecting the White River Valley from Calico Creek Landing to Sylamore. After visiting with Os's family and Great Aunt Lucy, I returned to Batesville, finding Col. JoeC Porter doing poorly.

As Jan turned to Feb J.D. Hailey, of Freeman's Co rejoined the men at Batesville. He had been captured and paroled on Jan 25th at Van Buren, Ark near Fort Smith. He trudged through the snow walking the distance from Wiley's Cove near Burrowsville to Batesville. He managed a ride from Van Buren to the Cove. James Neal was captured in Texas Co, Missouri on Feb 9. I had just returned from Aunt Lucy's when on Feb. 4th, the Union attacked from the north of the city. One of the scouts found Genl. Marmaduke at the Cox House headquarters alerting him of the advance. Rallying around 800 men we moved north along the river. The Union faced a similar trek south as we had. The snow and ice remained difficult to traverse and continued to fall. There had been no reprieve in the weather. Union Col Waring sent a detachment of men to seize and destroy the ferries preventing our men from crossing confining us to the south banks. By 10 o'clock that night the Feds occupied Batesville. Waring set up his headquarters at the home of Abram and Mary Burton Weaver on Main Street, a sister to Nannie's momma, wife of William Byers. Some of the Union rested while others pillaged and looted the town. Col. Waring didn't realize the strength of the troops camped on the south side of the river and east of town. He ordered his men to stand guard maintaining huge bon fires to keeping them both warm and allowing them to see along the river's edge for sign of any imminent attack. They returned north early the next morning. Emily Weaver, a spy for the south, Abram and Mary's daughter and a cousin to Nannie Wilson, spent most of the approaching day delighting commanders and officers as well as troops with stories of how the Union stayed in their home but fled by day break. Shelby crossed the river with over 3,000 men. Some 20 miles from Batesville, Union Col.

Waring chose to parole and release his prisoners. They would need everything they had to safely return to Missouri. Our scouts returned with the prisoners, reporting the Union attacked the community of Three Brothers in Fulton Co mostly foraging.

Daniel James told me about Burwell Lee and I wanted to make acquaintances again. I'd had the opportunity as a small boy to meet him and Elijah James in Missouri. They came with their families for a week long revival Daddy held. That perhaps might have been the same revival Momma said more people were brought to know the Lord by Daddy's preaching than any other time known in those parts. Riding out east of Batesville, I followed the creek leading north to his home. Daniel was a Southern man but he told me cousin Elijah's family had chosen the side of the north. Cousin Martha Goodwin James was the widow of Willie James, son of Elijah James and Katherine Frost. Lt. William "Willie" Elijah James died at Benton's Barrack's in St. Louis. He and Martha had a dozen children. They buried their first born then had Caroline in 1839. Caroline married Lewis Robert Turner. He too joined the north. Three months earlier, in Nov 1862, her daddy died. Elijah James enlisted as a private in Co C 1st Battalion, Ark Infantry on June 10, 1862 in Lawrence Co. At 44 years old, he was one of the older men and was elected 1st Lt of his Co on the same day. Hearing the news of her daddy's death, Caroline went to see her Momma and while there, the rains flooded the creeks and river. To get back home she had to cross the swollen creek. Neighbors closer to Burwell Lee's home found her floating. They buried her, keeping the apron she was wearing for her Momma. When news of her death reached her mother, Martha believed her daughter was routed by Confederate sympathizers who suspected Caroline was a spy. Caroline knew the area well and drown in an area where she would have known better than to cross and would only have done so fearing for her life. Daughter Sarah married Rodney Morgan. Martha received word during this time their 19 year old son Thomas Jefferson wounded, captured and placed on a Confederate prison ship on the Mississippi River had died. The family believes he became ill and died as a result of starvation and mistreatment. The reality is few people were surviving the prisoner of war camps, Union or Confederate nor the prison ships. The conditions were horrible, diseases rampant, lack of food and especially clean water made it worse. Most of the dead were placed on barges set afire and put to drift down open waters of the great Mississippi.

Young Mary Elizabeth was sweet on Billy Hodge; Belle was 15, then Pete, Elijah Jr, George, Buck, Ben and the youngest Amos only 2, were all still at home and mostly babies. Even if they were Northerner's they were family and Daddy, although he had planted us firmly on the side of the South, would turn over in his grave if I didn't help out. When cousin

Burwell and I arrived we found Sarah, their 20 year old daughter taking care of the house. Martha was doing all she could, neighbors were helping but losing a husband, son and daughter that close together was more than most anyone could take. I'd seen that same sorrow in Momma's eyes. I remembered her tears, crying that day in Daddy's chair. It was clear Sarah was a strong woman and taking care of her momma by taking care of her siblings was at the top of her list. The winter was harsh. I returned to Marmaduke's camp, securing some of the boys to help me get them better prepared by cutting wood and getting in what we could of fresh kill. Energy filled their home as everyone had a job to do preparing the wild hog we'd killed to be salted down. The ladies prepared a meal of fried pork, creamed potatoes, gravy and cat's head biscuits for us before we headed back to camp. Before departing, a prayer for our safety, the safety of us all was said; Mrs. Martha beseeched Our Lord for an end to this war.

In the meantime, Daniel James home at Jamestown just off the Military Road had become a strategic point and his home the Confederate headquarters south of the river at Batesville. It served as a meeting place for many of the commanders and leading men. Daniel James passed on word to Lewisburg of the condition of the troops, many had serious frost bite with amputation the only answer. We were delighted to learn the Feds had orders to strengthen their garrisons at the expense of their armies at the front. Our efforts had not been in vain. Both Union Genl. Blunt and Herron were about to leave Ark, the idea of increased guerilla attacks, men striking on horseback and dispersing at a moment's notice had proven effective. The Union had slashed and burned leaving little subsistence in the area. Now, the threat of raiders hastened their retreat. Little did they know the poor circumstances under which we were surviving.

The girls came to the camps offering assistance repairing and cleaning clothing. Nannie Wilson was like a teacher in a tornado, instructing everyone where to go and what to do. The camps were her camps, especially ours; she was lovely, excellent at being in charge. The women, many war widows, found worthy husbands among our men. A majority of the troops and our boys spent the winter in Batesville. Snowed in, they constructed barracks to help keep out the cold harsh weather. They had a social life offered up by the fiddle playing men such as Bill Wilson and Tom Webb and the opportunity to dance with the lovely Southern Belle's of Batesville.

Col. Porter's family arrived prior to his death. He had not yet slipped into that sleep which precedes death. They were able to talk to him, as was Reverend Kinnard. Shelby sent word to his cousin, Col Marion Chrisman but he failed to arrive in time. Going in and out of consciousness, JoeC talked about their cousin James "Jim" Monroe Chrisman, as children they played together, hunted and fished as close as brothers. When the War Between the States came, Jim joined the Union. The young men had come to blows about it and JoeC wanted a letter written to him. They were the great grand children of Isaac Chrisman, children of own cousins. Family history held that Isaac Chrisman had been murdered by Cherokee Indians at Rye Creek in Indian Territory on the Virginia boundary. His sons chose to move west. As JoeC talked about his cousin and their family, I heard stories I had heard my Uncle George Burns Hite tell. Married to Daddy's sister Nancy Gardner James, Uncle George told how his great grandfather Jost Hite had been one of the first of their family here in the new country emigrating from Germany. Jost made friends with George Washington when George was just a boy working with the surveyors. They stayed in Jost's home. I listened to the history of their family and knew this Jost was related to my cousins, all ex pats from Kentucky, they had come from Virginia and before that Germany. I thought about Daddy's family and the James name. Did it come from King James as some of our family repeated? Were we born of peasants who come from England under King James? Or, was it as Aunt Lucy said, we were from the British Isles of Wales.

I listened carefully hoping I would be able to share this information with my cousins. Jost Johann Hite come from Germany but had received assistance from England in 1710 as a Palatine, the English word for people from Germany. In 1709 the Golden Book proclaimed the English Carolina's with its promises of riches in the new lands. The book promised free passage to anyone willing to move to the new lands and free land from the Queen of England, both were false. Jost found himself an indentured slave in the new world along with the Chitwood's, Preslar's and many more young men. Perhaps the James brothers who first came here were among them. Maybe 20 years old, Jost worked and managed to repay the debts and became a massive land owner. I wondered about the Chrisman side of the family. His parents had clearly been proud enough of the Chrisman name. I thought again about my name and wondered for whom Daddy had named me, Momma had been uncertain when I'd inquired. I volunteered to take JoeC's letter home to Missouri to his cousin.

Most of the tissue in JoeC's injured leg was now blue and green, almost black, signs of severe gangrene. His hand, mangled and useless, had been amputated. The long trek south took its toll and infection had over taken him. He died at the home of William Byers on Feb 18th, 1863 surrounded by his wife and children, family and friends, including Jo Shelby and Bill Wilson. Joined by some of the local men we set about to dig his grave. The ground was frozen and in order to thaw it we had to build a fire to melt the earth. Then dig out the ground and ashes, working from one end to the other repeating the process until we had a sufficient grave in which to bury Col. Joseph C. Porter. Fearing retributions and acting against declared Union law forbidding burial, JoeC was laid to rest within hours of his death. Words were spoken over him at Catalpa Hall. The women orchestrated his placement into a wooden casket. We carried him to the wagon taking him to Oaklawn Cemetery. We buried JoeC in the dark of night. His son, Joe Jr joined us. He had turned 15 on Feb 9th, just nine days before his father's death. All of us were stoic watching him watch us dig his father's grave. When it came time to place the casket in the ground, Joe Jr stepped forward. He marked his father's grave with a wooden slate on which he had scratched "Father."

Returning back to camp, I spoke to Col. Shelby about going home. He seemed beaten down explaining I'd be assigned to Col. Thompson and after the winter was over, he, Col. Thompson would find me back in Missouri. Pressing him further he said it was confirmed, President Lincoln had in fact issued a proclamation freeing the slaves in the states of rebellion. The Northern States were not identified, therefore their slaves were not freed. It was a proclamation and not a law, as congress had no part in it. Commanders were debating if Kentucky, Maryland, Delaware and Missouri were included. Tennessee and the Gulf of Louisiana were Union occupied and it was expected those were included, but the border states were unclear. Marmaduke had suggested response was to include all southern states. He'd known of the proclamation since Hartville but under the dire weather and conditions were moving south had chosen not to speak of it to the men. Citizens of Batesville had heard and begun discussing it. He saw it as a further split among people. Most Southerners were fighting because of the aggression from the North, but this new proclamation would further split loyalties. "Lincoln has effectively changed the reason for this war," Col. Shelby said. "How do you fight a war when you don't know why you are fighting?" Having more pressing things to worry about, like the health of his men, Colonel Shelby extended his hand to me. I couldn't leave like this.

I told Col Shelby about the story of the Hite's. We sat talking about his great great grandfather Christopher Gist, the first of the surveyors of the colonies. He thought it might have been George Washington who aided him and perhaps he too had been at the home of Jost Hite. He knew with certainty his family had been friends with the Washington's, perhaps that was how their relationship began. I longed to know more about my own family. I hoped Aunt Lucy might be able to tell me more. Col Shelby understood the need to know and the need I had to take this letter to JoeC's cousin. I had diverted his thoughts from the horrors we faced at least for a time. The next morning preparing to head north, Henry and Bud Pence found me. They too were making good use of the slight break in weather to head home. Their Daddy's house had been burned due to Henry having joined up with Quantrill. The Union put a rope around his neck and pulled him up into a tree, hanging but not killing him, they did this 3 or 4 times, then broke a gunstock and fiddle over his head because he refused to talk. They moved to Liberty in hopes that 15 year old Donnie wouldn't join up. Will Corum, Garrett Groomer, Henry, Bud and me were headed home. The next time I saw Bill Wilson, he had a new name, JoeC.

We rode up river crossing near the Grigsby Ferry to look at a cave we'd been told about. It was a large cave with plenty of room. Local folks had taken measures to hide the entrance hiding food inside. We didn't bother anything, just looked around a bit and moved on. It was near John Mims. Riding north along the river I pointed out Penter's Bluff and told the boys about having been atop it and able to hear every word spoken below.

The Grigsby House situated on the campus of Lyon College, Batesville, Ark

We were admiring the rampart wall along the field into Cook Holler. Operating as a picket near their family home, John Cook spoke with us briefly directing us first to the home of fellow southerner Zachariah Ford, his wife Sarah Hollandworth Ford told us she had received word he had been taken prisoner. She had Albert, George and Nannie and was heavy with child. Her momma, Missus Lydia Fuson Hollandsworth was staying with her helping. We chopped some wood with the oldest boy before leaving headed to Armistead Younger's home. He gave us travel provisions and a little whiskey. He had not heard of Zachariah Ford's capture. They would see to Missus Sarah. We rode up through Cagen and Col. Black's farm, briefly visiting with the Canard's before stopping at Matt and Hattie Chitwood's house, parents of Bill. Missus Hattie made us supper and offered a place to sleep for the night. We woke to wonderful smells of

Missus Hattie's cooking. After a solid breakfast, she gave us a poke of food, biscuits with fried potatoes and salt pork. Bill came in before we left and decided to join us as far as Athens, reconnoitering. He knew the best route up through Rocky Bayou, Herpel, Round Bottom and Sylamore. Bill wanted to introduce me to the Flannery family at Forest Home.

Isaac Flannery settled the area in the 1830's shortly after the Indians agreed to vacate the reservation. Called Old Man Flannery he established a mail route and the family maintained a fine livery and stable. His place was south of White House Crossing where the river was narrow and shallow, leading up to the big white house of James Jeffery and Melinda Benbrooks, parents of Os Dillard's wife, Mrs. Avarilla. Old Man Flannery's daughter Naomya had married one of Thomas Riggs' sons. These people were critical to maintaining our troops and protecting us. Along the way Chitwood told us about the massacre at Huntsville, word was John Allison "Capt. Bud" Shirley led the raid. His daddy ran a tavern, hotel and saloon at Carthage, Missouri friendly to Southerners. Both Cole Younger and Quantrill knew Mister John well. Bud served a year in regular service before forming his own group of irregulars, mostly spying and foraging.

A month prior on Jan 10, 1863, my 20th birthday, I thought to myself, nine men were taken from a guardhouse and led to a field on the farm of Samuel P. Vaughn in Northwest Ark. They were shot by Union soldiers on the bank of the creek. Some said the massacre was in response to the Nov ambush and raid of Capt. Bud Shirley on a group of Federalists near Huntsville. The real story seemed to be resting on Isaac Murphy who was the lone delegate to vote "No" on whether Ark should secede from the Union. After Pea Ridge, his life had been threatened, forcing him and some other prominent folks to flee the area. By the fall, his daughter's, anxious to visit him, made the trip to Pea Ridge. With plans being made for the Battle of Prairie Grove they were sent back to Huntsville accompanied by Union Col. Alfred Bishop escorted by 25 soldiers ordered to protect them. While resting the escort was attacked by Capt. Bud Shirley with only 7 of the 25 Union surviving. It was reported Murphy's daughters were being harassed by locals. In response, the Union in the early dawn hours of Jan 10th, under the command of Lt. Col. Elias Briggs Baldwin executed local men, Chesley H. Boatright, a blacksmith, former Co treasurer; William Martin Berry, a prominent member of Masonic Lodge and son-in-law of Isaac Murphy; Hugh Samuel Berry, son of William Berry and Capt. in the Confederate army, home on leave; John William Moody, nephew-in-law to Chesley H. Boatright and a Deputy U.S. Marshal; Confederate Army Capt. Askin Hughes; John Hughes; Watson P. Stevens, a cousin of the Berrys; Robert Coleman Young, a Baptist minister and Bill Parks. Parks survived and told the story. Enraged, everyone was swearing to get even.

Chitwood showed us where Revolutionary Bill Wood first settled on the south side of the river after removing himself and his son from the War of 1812; Andrew Jackson shot and killed his youngest son John. Revolutionary Bill decided to move to Shawneetown in Marion Co there living among the Indians who hated Andrew Jackson as much as he did. Jackson having been a part of the Battle of Tippecanoe and the destruction of Chief Lewis villages at Lewistown, Ohio was a hated man long before he became President and forced the removal of the Indians west from their homelands in Georgia.

Ike and his uncle Silas Flannery
Emory Cantey Collection

Immediately recognizing Chitwood, Mister Isaac Flannery was happy to have Co. After introductions I told him of my friend, Ike Flannery who had gone south to Texas. When I said his momma's name, Missus Sallie Shepherd, Mister Flannery's eyes lit up. Ike was his namesake, grandson of his own cousin, Zion Flannery, sons of brothers, Mike and Jim Flannery, sons of John Flannery and Phoebe Boggs. Excited with news of family, I told him after Ike's daddy John died, Missus Sallie married Ike Wells. He grabbed me, hugging me, happy to see someone that felt like family to him. I knew these kinds of hugs, daddy, Uncle Till and the men I rode with. Smiling, happy inside, I told him about Missus Sallie taking the family to Texas further bringing him up to date on as much as I could. He told me he and John had been very close. Zion married Lucinda, daughter of Levi Shepherd. Miss Sallie, she was the daughter of Zion's brother John, sons of James Pendleton Shepherd and Rachel Gault. Miss Sallie and Miss Lucinda were own cousins and Miss Sallie had married Miss Lucinda's son, John William Flannery, Ike's daddy. Zion and Lucinda's son James Silas joined Quantrill along with Ike. Having heard of Quantrill, Mister Flannery was eager for "true news".

Mister Flannery ask if I knew George Wells, John and Levi's sister Elizabeth Shepherd's son. I told him I did relating to him the events of his death Aug 18th. I told him Missus Margaret and her children hadn't gone to Texas with the rest of the women. He shook his head laughing, "Charlie. Is Sammy still calling himself Charlie Pitts?" I smiled thinking of Samuel Wells, Missus Margaret's son a year younger than me, calling himself Charlie, shaking my head yes. Mr. Flannery told us the story of Sammy being born over in Indian Territory and an old Indian woman helping to birth him. It was a hard labor and the old Indian woman said he was as hard as a pit. He almost didn't make it. He was bound up and didn't want to breathe. She worked him over, rubbing him until he gasped for breath. When he was first named, as a baby, they called him Little Narly Pit, his Indian name from the old woman who'd birthed him. He reckoned Sammy liked the name and as a young boy started calling himself Charlie Pitts. Having never heard the story, Bud and I burst out laughing. I told him I reckoned he'd given himself the moniker due to the war, which Mister Flannery found equal humor in. I couldn't wait to tell Momma. Mister Flannery insisted we call him Ike, but true to our southern upbringings, he was Mister Ike and he indeed had a fine stable.

When we got to Aunt Lucy's we related our travels to her, then, we got a lesson in family history. She was married to Daddy's grandpa's brother John Robert "J.R." Mims one of six kids born to Shadrack and Elizabeth Woodson Mims, along with Drury, Mary, Sally, Linah, Martha and Susannah. "By the time, J.R. was 13, his parents were dead, and he and his siblings spread out among relatives. The Great War of Revolt was raging in Virginia. In 1788, J.R., now 23, married Mary Lucille Poor, your Aunt Lucy," she said, patting herself on the bosom. They had William in 1788 followed by Mildred in 1789. Both children succumbed to the fever in 1793. I ask about the James family and she told us there were two, maybe three brothers that immigrated to the new world from England before the great revolt against the mother country. One of the brothers had two sons, John and William who married sisters, Irish girls, Nancy and Mary Hines, that's about all she knew. Aunt Lucy knew nothing of our history in England. She doubted we were of any nobility, she said, "more likely our ancestors were men who served under the King of England, King James perhaps, who came to defend the colonies. Maybe they were James' or maybe they took the name James but not from King James, his name was James Stuart, son of Mary Queen of Scots and Lord Henry Stuart." I told her about the story of the Hite's. She listened and agreed I should take the letter to JoeC's cousin, James Monroe Chrisman in Strother. She then told us more about her own life experiences and our family.

Children lose their parents every day. As a society, we're raised to expect to lose them, but as parents, we're stunned when we lose our children. It changes us and life, as we know it. We wondered aloud if Aunt Lucy cried begging her husband not to leave her as he headed for the Mississippi River at Paducah, on to Mexico and Arizona? Was she so distraught at the death of 5 year old William and 4 year old Mildred, just days apart that she screamed at him, told him to get out of her sight? I'd seen things happen in Momma when Daddy died and her baby with Mr. Ben. There is nothing normal and nothing wrong with any reaction to such sorrow. J.R. left. Aunt Lucy went to her mother Judith Gardener Poor's, Daddy's great grandmother. Having buried her husband and 3 children of her own, mother and daughter offered each other comfort and strength. Aunt Lucy continued her story. "Somewhere along his travels, J.R. joined up with a band of Indians. Living and traveling with them, he attacked and raided with abandon earning the name "White Renegade." In 1796, they attacked and killed a group of miners out west and took their gold. Heading back east the men began quarrelling and bickering. Jealousies erupted among them and one thing lead to another, ending with only 5 of the original Apaches and J.R. Mims left standing."

He and the Apaches crossed the White River to the area of Piney Creek where Aunt Lucy lives. "It was here he buried the gold in a cave. His name had become so well known on the frontier by the time they reached the newly established Ark Post, he was using the alias Sam Jones. Then, he comes home to Virginia bringing them Apaches." He and Aunt Lucy reunited and in 1799 little Lucy was born, then Drury in 1802 and John Wilson in 1808. Daddy's Momma, Mary Poor was named for Aunt Lucy. "Talk of an impending war with Great Britain loomed, threats that England was going to retake the new America's. We moved to Hickman Co, Kentucky, on the Mississippi River, south of Paducah, where he and the Apaches enlisted as scouts and spies in the coming war."

Their son David was born in Clinton, Hickman Co, in 1814. Many families utilized the military warrants for land grants settling in the Missouri Territories. They were among those. Rivers were the highways and Uncle J.R. already had his own bank in the hills of the Ozarks. They settled in the area of Piney Creek in Izard Co across the White River from the Cherokee Indian Reservation. A formidable frontiersman, Uncle J.R. and his Indian friends would venture off from time to time, gone for months, a year at a time in some cases, leaving Aunt Lucy alone with her children. She became good friends with the Jeffery's, William's, Trimble's and other families settling the area. The Trimble's, Partee's and

Livingston's had to move from the south west side of the river in 1817 when their lands became part of the new reservation. These were the frontier days; Ark didn't become a territory until 1819, that's when John Paxton Houston, brother of Sam Houston became the clerk under Maj Wolf. Aunt Lucy lived comfortably and moved freely back and forth across the river into the Indian Reservation. She was the greatest of friends with Jane Mason Jeffery, mother of Jehoiada the first settler in 1816 at Mt. Olive on the east banks. Missus Jane and Aunt Lucy made no bones about tending to anyone needing doctoring, especially Missus Jane who by all accounts answered to no one but the good Lord. I smiled to myself, understanding that kind of doctoring having lived through Momma and Aunt Charlotte's concoctions. Aunt Lucy testified to the fortitude and incredulity of Missus Jane, who had died in 1853. She was the grandmother of Missus Avarilla. Aunt Lucy was present when Avarilla was born, watched her grow up, marry and have babies of her own. Missus Melinda, her momma, loved everything French and accordingly wanted to name her first born daughter a French name, she chose Avarilla Therese Jeffery. The women looked her over, discussing if she was an Avarilla or a Therese – "pronounced Thayer ese", Aunt Lucy said. Aunt Mandy, her nursemaid, started calling her Rillie and before long, that's what everyone called her. I thought about Jesse and Aunt Charlotte and Alex calling him "Dingus," short for Dingle and shorter still for Dingle berry, that little piece of shit.

Aunt Lucy understood her husband didn't want to talk about all of his dealings which supported them but on occasion he found need for "continued use of the name Sam Jones", she said. Having been married almost 40 years, suffering the agonizing death of her first two children and her husband, Aunt Lucy is a frontier woman. This is her home. In 1826, its clear Uncle J.R. suffered a stroke before passing. "J.R was sittin' at the table havin' jest finished up eatin' when he fell out on the floor. When I finally got him comin' around he weren't able to talk clear and his hands seemed no more a part of him. He weren't able to get'em to do what he wanted. He couldn't even feed himself, weren't no way he could draw a map, splain to us where he'd hid the gold as he weren't able to relieve himself without my help. He passed on before the month was out." They buried him on the hillside next to their home. Their son Samuel, born 1817, continued to live alongside Aunt Lucy, searching for the gold and in 1860 just before the war broke out, he married Elizabeth Jones. Sam enlisted in May 1861 as I had in Missouri. I wondered if Aunt Lucy was imparting this story to us hoping we might continue the search for Uncle J.R.'s hidden gold and the lost cave. I ask about any earthquakes, flooding and such that might have closed off an opening and unfortunately there had been many she told us. I knew Jesse would get a kick out of this and would bug

Momma about coming to visit so he could search it out for himself. Aunt Lucy's son John married daddy's sister, Mary. She is our great grand aunt and our own cousin Zerelda Mims' grandmother.

We'd stopped by cousin John Mims at Hesstown above Ennis cave but hadn't found anyone home. 1850 had been a brutal time in our nation, yellow fever, small pox and other diseases wiped out not only entire families but entire areas, rich and poor, death touched all. Dr. Davis Mims lost his young wife Elizabeth Cresap to yellow fever leaving him to raise their six sons, Byron Otho 13, John Harrison Marcellus 10, Linah 7, Robert Marcellus 5, Russell 4 and Davis 2. Dr. Davis Mims was a cousin, like me, to Samuel Mims. They lived near the banks of the great waters of the Mississippi plagued with mosquitoes. It was an easy choice to leave their home in Clinton, Kentucky, moving with the Davis and Mims family to the White River Valley. This was a chance to start again. They moved in late part of 1848 settling at the upper end of the river bottoms not far from Armistead and Rebecca Younger's place.

Dr. Davis Mims sons were industrious, working as farm hands and laborers on the Davis and Ivey farms, as store clerks and ferrymen. By the time he was 10, young Robert Marcellus was working as a gopher for local ferryman, running messages, leading animals on and off the ferry, whatever was needed he would "go for." He was well liked by the Grigsby, Hess, Wall, Coker, Price and Penter families living nearby. The Grigsby's owned and operated the ferry from Hesstown to the river bottoms below the Barrens leading to Batesville. When the war broke out in 1861, these young men and their father were Southerners to the core. Byron, John, Linah and Robert were among the first to enlist May 1861 at Little Rock. The youngest boys, Russell and Davis were sent to family in Kentucky.

Avarilla Jeffery Dillard

Lt. William Osby Dillard

While at Aunt Lucy's we got to meet Samuel's wife Elizabeth called Eliza and her baby boy, Thomas. Osby Dillard and his wife Avarilla rode over to Aunt Lucy's along with their daughter Mary and son James. Missus Avarilla was with child "due in late spring," she said. We stayed on for the night visiting leaving come morning with well fed horses and a satchel of provisions. Missus Avarilla inquired after Momma and sent us some special candied fruit she made. Laughing, she reminded us we'd best make it back to Missouri with that fruit, "It's for your Momma, you hear."

Riding north along the river toward Calico Creek Landing we talked about "Uncle J.R.'s gold." A fairly large settlement was growing at the landing which lay north of Athens and Creswell. You could see down the river from atop the mighty bluff. Colors ran from blue to yellow glistening in the morning sun, "there's gold in them hill", I thought, "maybe even in these rocks." From there we continued west to Yellville. Along the way, we talked about home, in Missouri and Kentucky wondering if life would ever be the same. We saw things no man should ever see, especially young men. We were grateful for what Unc taught us. Riding along our talk turned to fishing and life after war. This might be life in Kentucky and here in Ark but for us Missourians life had always held war. We'd become good at what we did in the wake of it, the art of disappearing into the woods as guerilla's under Freeman, Todd, Quantrill and Bloody Bill. We were experts at it, some thought us heroes, others villains. I'm certain it was the same on the Union side. They were doing what they must in order to survive. Our talk grew silent. My thought's turned to pretty little Annie. I would be making the most of any opportunity with Frank Gregg to visit his sister Mary, hoping Annie might be there. I knew Frank understood the girl had a bit of a 'soldier's crush' on me but I had been able to hide my enthusiasm at seeing her, so far. She was just a girl, but that wouldn't always be so. I had seen Mattie, Momma's half sister, go from the little girl I played with into a beautiful young woman, seemed like over night. And, who knows when this war will be over. Even with the snow and ice hanging on, the sun was shining and the day was reasonable for traveling. When it disappeared behind the hills we were all pulling our coats a little tighter. We were lucky enough to find refuge from the cold in some abandoned shacks and barns before nightfall.

Heading out before daybreak we moved at a faster pace knowing we were nearing Missouri soil. We skirted areas we suspected Union encampments might be. Once back in Clay Co, Garrett Groomer, Bud and Donnie headed directly home to their parents, Adam and Anna Pence. Garrett married their sister Sarah Francis, expected he would find at her there. Will Corum rode with me a ways before heading off in the direction of home. When I rode into the yard Momma was waiting on the porch.

Someone alerted her of my approach and she was anxiously waiting to lay eyes on her first born. After all the hugs and hello's pats on the back and cheek pinching, Momma sat me down to a full plate of potatoes and roasted pork with cornbread and fresh honey butter. While I ate Momma and Doc filled me in on the news. My sister Susie tended to Sallie and John Thomas so we could talk. I found myself watching her. I'd missed her a great deal. I wanted to tell her about Annie Ralston, I knew they could be great friends even though Susie was nearly three years older and changing from a girl to a young woman herself. There were plenty of boys around but Susie didn't get much opportunity to visit with girls so I'd suggested to Frank Gregg he plant the idea of Annie and Susie getting to know each other. Momma snapped her fingers in front of my face, "you listenin'"? I smiled my mouth full of food nodding yes.

She was full of news. When we headed south to Dripping Springs in Dec, Cole stayed in Missouri. Him and some of the boys got in a skirmish in Dec near New Santa Fe, Kansas, with George Todd leading the charge. Jack McDowell of John Jarrette's men was wounded, his horse killed out from under him. He called out to Cole for help. Cole managed to pull him up behind him on his horse. With his feat of handing out ammunition to the men on the front lines, news of Cole was something most Momma's, including mine, liked to talk about. She liked brave daring men likening them to men of old, King Arthur and Knights of the Round Table. Sometimes, without seeming to realize it, she'd rise from her seat and begin acting out the scene just as we done in our plays from behind the piece of cloth she'd hung as a curtain so long ago. I knew Momma differently than the others, I knew her playfulness and her smiles, before Daddy died.

Momma waited until I'd had time to catch my breath before she told me the biggest news. The district commander ordered Capt. Walley the man responsible for killing Cole's daddy, court martialed. On Dec 25th, 1862 Cole and the boys ambushed and killed all the witnesses on their way to the trial. "Just a week or so earlier," Momma said, "Union soldiers burned out his momma and the rest of the family turning them out into the cold winter. His younger Jim wanted to join Quantrill right then and there, but only 14, Cole was afraid for him and their Momma. He knowed he needed Jim with her, so the decision was for him to remain her."

Cole's family always called him "Bud," like my Momma called me Mister Frank and Buck. You could always tell when people met you by what they called you. And you could always tell when Momma was mad, "Alexander Franklin James." "Jesse Woodson James." "Susan Lavinia James." You got the full name treatment. And you hoped she didn't have a young tender switch in her hand when she said it. Any one older than yourself you might happen to be on a more personal level with, their first name was always preceded with Miss or Mister and married women Missus.

"With Cole's momma being turned out into the cold once again, it was all he could take," Momma continued. "Cole and George Clayton, his brother in law you know, rode into Kansas City dressed as Union Cav along with Ab Cunningham, Fletch Taylor, Zach Traber and George Todd. Enough men to kill the six Union soldiers who murdered his daddy. Traber held the horses. After the killing, they went to Reuben Harris' house, Cole's uncle." Momma did that, she always qualified who was who when telling a story and best you never ask her who someone was because you got a history lesson with it, including who they were married to, what illnesses they had and where they might have lived and moved and so on. "He was married to Cole's momma's sister, Laura Fristoe, you know," Momma said making sure I was still paying attention by having to acknowledge what she was saying. "I know, Momma." "Afterwards, everyone was afraid some of the Union boys might make it their own calling to kill Cole so Jeremiah David "Hel" Helton started riding with him acting as his body guard. He's pretty much by his side acting as eyes in the back of his head. Everyone knew it was Cole who'd killed Walley." Hel not only carried a gun, he carried a short handled axe with him and could throw it like a tomahawk. Unc would have liked him a lot. Aunt Charlotte retrieved my plate asking if I'd had enough to eat.

Doc had been sitting quietly letting Momma get her news spilled out took the opportunity to talk. The Union was attempting to bring Jennison, Lane and Montgomery under control but not unlike accusations placed upon Quantrill, Bloody Bill, Todd and Fletch, these men did as they pleased. And, no matter the crime, it was blamed on them whether they were around or not. Earlier on Feb 3rd, Sam Hildebrand may have crossed the boys leading them into a massacre at Mingo Swamp. Nobody was saying much except a whole lot of boys were killed and some said it was because he betrayed them. Doc said David George, a man of 65, was killed near El Dorado Springs. We used his home as a meeting place, his son John Hicks George was one of our Corp.s. His younger brother Gabe had been killed a year earlier at Independence, John and their brother Hiram both wounded. The Union hung Mister George several times swinging him from a tree torturing him before burning the family's fine home on the Sni A Bar.

Boone Schull went over to Bull Howard's, a cousin of Uncle Till's, to eat. He had been followed by a scout of Union Capt. Johnson. His men surrounded the place. Boone escaped but Johnson and his men pursued him. Near the Hopkins house on the Little Blue, George Todd, Cole Younger and Boone ambushed Johnson putting him on the run. Our talk became less specific, less about war anyway and more about home.

Chapter 16

Quantrill returned to Batesville from Richmond to find most of the boys had returned home or joined other Partisan Ranger groups, some even signed up for regular enlistment. Only a few had been with Col. Shelby all winter. Although Quantrill got his commission he no longer had a command. He sulked and complained to anyone and everyone, speaking directly to Col Shelby and Gen Marmaduke he voiced his concerns over what he called his defecting troops. Both of them tried to convince him to join with the regular troops. Marmaduke told him he was certain to achieve Brigadier Genl.. Quantrill talked to the boys who had remained at Camp Nannie Wilson. They hadn't been able to abide by the way the regular soldiers were treated and fought. They felt as we all did, having no voice, no control we were nothing more than raw meat for the kill. Ike Flannery's momma and her family had moved south, so when Quantrill approached the few remaining in Batesville, they convinced Quantrill to head south to Texas for the rest of the winter. Every one was tired of the cold.

By early April, Quantrill and the boys returned to Missouri making camp in Jackson Co. Soon after Quantrill made camp, widower Betsy Harris Crawford, brought her sons to see Quantrill. Betsy was an own cousin of Tom Harris and Cole Younger, John McCorkle and Tom Talley's momma's. Mrs. Betsy told Quantrill, "First they come burning houses and farms. Anyone they wanted to burn out, they did. Just say you were enemy was enough. Some of Penick's men came on Jan 29th there was fourteen inches of snow on the ground and the temperature read 10 degrees below zero. And took John Saunders and my husband Jeptha prisoners. John was taken to Federal commander John Burns house in Independence. They shot him then come back and burned down the house. You know from Tommy that my husband never took up arms against either side. We got nine children. Our youngest, Vol is only seven. Daddy," as she called her husband, "left the house early to go to the mill to get a sack of corn ground and was to be back before noon. We were without anything to eat and the kids kept asking about him. Noon came, and two, and three o'clock, then I saw a Co of soldiers coming. They rode ride up to the door and there he was in their midst, tied up. They told him to get down. I could see along with the children what was happening but we were afraid to go outside. When he got down, he was told to step aside. He stepped away from the horse and he was shot right there where he stood. One of them yelled for us to come out of the house if we wanted to live. Another screamed, "We're burning it down, whether you come out or not." The children and I huddled in the yard. They wouldn't let me go to my husband. I asked them for something to eat for my children. They sneered at us and set the beds on fire. The straw went up fast. I tried to get into the house but they held me back. They stayed until there was nothing we could have done to save the house or anything in it. We walked to a neighbor's who took us in. We really have no place and people have been kind enough to help but I want you to take my sons." She pushed Marshall, a boy of about 17, Marion 15 and 13 your old Riley to where they were standing in front of Quantrill. The oldest son William a man of about 22, holding a gun in his hand walked up next to his brothers. "Make soldiers of them. They're all I have left."

The Union killed Samuel Kimberlin bout the same way. It was happening every day to someone we knew. Now, Mrs. Betsy wanted Quantrill to take her boys into his band, including the youngest Riley, barely 13. William, Marshall and Marion stayed with Quantrill then decided to join the Missouri State Guards under Genl. Price. Riley being too young to enlist with the regular army remained with Quantrill. There was no home to return to but even so it would have meant death once word was out his brothers joined Genl. Price.

The boys were slowly trickling into camp as word of Quantrill's return reached them. Stories were being told of the winter months. Cole's winter camp about eight miles south of Independence had been attacked on Feb 10th and his momma burned out. The boys had two houses dug into the hillside barely able to be seen even when you were right on them. Cole had saved John McDowell three months earlier at New Santa Fe, Kansas after his horse was killed out from under him and John had been wounded. It was John who led Col. Penick to the camp. Cole trusted him even against the caution of some of the boys. On the 10th, John told them he needed to go see his sick wife. He rode straightway to Independence to Col Penick. Surrendering, Penick paroled him. McDowell not only revealed the location of the camp, he led Penick and his men to the camp collecting part of a $1,000 reward. During the attack Penick and his men killed Ike Basham and Dr. Tom Hale. Sgt. Otho "Oth" Hinton was trying to get his boots on and Cole fought off Penick's men while he pulled them on managing to escape. Oth was a skinny fella with a long face. He wore a mustache. When he stared at you, you knew he meant business. Oth, William Hulse, Nathan and William Kerr were all there. James Morris was hit, wounded bad but managed to get away. John McCorkle was severely wounded. George, Tom and Wallace Talley were at the camp when it was attacked and Penick's men killed George and Wallace. Tom escaped taking John McCorkle with him. Most of them escaped on foot without shoes, coats, hats or little else, in over a foot of snow. They headed to grandma Mary Sullivan Fristoe's house. The boys stood in the snow on the edge of the timbers watching as the Feds forced her to set her house on fire. A strong and righteous woman she didn't scream or cry, but she did condemn them to burn in Hades suggesting she'd certainly meet them there if God deemed her wrong. Lest on that was the polite way the boys told it in Co of women. They had been able to reach John and Josie Moore's house where they were taken care of, given clothes, food and medical attention.

They set up a new camp. As word got out, the attack and burning of his momma and Grandma's house worked less against our boys and more as a recruiting tool for us. People were beginning to realize the war wasn't letting up. On March 8th, on his fifteenth birthday, a young red faced boy, John Frank "Bud" Dalton showed up at Cole's camp wanting to join. Born in North Ark, the son of Lewis Dalton and Elizabeth McKenzie. His momma died in 1850; Bud and his older brother William went to live with their great grandma Susannah Sebastian Dalton, then she died. They had been passed around from family member to family member from Missouri to Kansas, Ark, and Oklahoma. His big brother Will came with him but only to make sure he got there. He was headed north to family in Illinois. Their daddy David Lewis Dalton married a new wife in Feb and the boys wanted nothing to do with her. Cole and Jim grilled him about who he was being their sister Addie was married to James Lewis Dalton. After considerable discussion even a trip to Addie and Lewis' house, they figured out they weren't of any "American" kin. Perhaps they were descendants of Dalton's from the old country in Ireland but it was too far back to know. Even so, they took him under their wing welcoming him into their home. He was a boy without a family something they understood all too well.

While Cole, Bud and Will were gone, Dr. John W. Benson captured Dec 19th at Blackwater Creek rode into camp. He had been sent to Gratiot Street Prison, in St. Louis. Once there he found himself treating men who were dying of starvation and disease at the hands of the Union with little he could do. He swore to the oath and was released. He high tailed it back taking the train from St. Louis to Kansas City. He joined us both carrying a gun and treating men among us sick or injured. He had news from other prisoners brought in, the Union was focused on wearing down Confederate resistance especially among the irregulars, guerillas and partisan rangers in the north part of Ark. and Missouri. Since food supplies were in shortage everywhere they had developed a plan of starving Southerners in the Ozarks out by capturing hogsheads of sugar, flour, bacon, quinine and salt. Originally a secondary goal it was now as important as destroying the salt peter works and any munitions they might locate.

Genl. Price ordered a number of the commanding officers familiar with the area to return to North West and north central Ark specifically along the White and Buffalo River's to protect the salt peter caves and munitions efforts there with the added task of protecting our supply trains and capturing or destroying those of the Union. Capt. Horace Holley Brand captured at Wilson's Creek, along with Col.s Sydney Drake Jackman and Coon Thornton were to lead the efforts at the convergence of the White and Buffalo, south to Batesville along the Military Road. Born in 1833 in Kentucky, Capt. Brand moved with his family to Missouri along with many other families during the revivalist movement and Mormon expulsion. He married Rebecca Wilson and had two daughters. On March 13th, 1863 shortly after leaving camp on the Freeman farm near Big Flats, Capt. Brand accompanied by brothers Riley and Ed Gillihan Co A of Col. Tom's command were attacked by Mountain Boomers. They were riding toward Big Springs to check on the munitions efforts located nearby when Capt. Brand rode into a rope strung on the path knocking him from his horse. Shots rang out. Taking cover Riley and Ed returned fire. A short skirmish between the brothers and half a dozen Mountain Boomers ensued. Two of the Mountain Boomers grabbed Capt. Brand and began hitting him about the head and back with the butts of their guns. One of them proclaiming he was too vile to waste a bullet on. Capt. Brand had only recently come into Ark with Col.s Jackman and Thornton. Riley and Ed doubted the men even knew who they were attacking except that he was a Southern Col. The younger of the two brothers Ed wanted to try to rescue him, but Riley, 20 years older, married and with children, prevented him from intervening. The Mountain Boomers appeared to be singling Capt. Brand out forgetting there had been three of them riding together. Ed and Riley watched as the men kicked, punched and gun butted his body until his clothes were soaked in blood. One of the men grabbed his head pulling it up from the ground between his knees and with a quick slice of his knife scalped Capt. Brand. Blood gurgled from his mouth and with horror and fear gripping them Riley and Ed were unable to move, neither one having witnessed such brutality. One of the younger men in the attack grabbed Brand's arm, with a knife in hand and one quick movement severed a hand. The rest joined in dismembering him. Riley got his senses about him and began pulling his younger brother away from the scene. Their horses had been frightened off but were standing not too far in the distance at the edge of a cedar glade. They quickly made their way to them, mounted and rode off. They later heard the men had fed the hacked body parts and remains of Capt. Horace H. Brand to wild hogs. They heard it was family of Tom Morrison's who attacked, believing it was Capt. Brand who was responsible for killing Tom.

Capt. Franklin Wright, a fellow Missourian serving under Col. Tom had been with us at Dripping Springs. Learning of the death of Capt. Brand he returned to North West Ark from Hartsville bent on revenge. He was in a skirmish with the Union at Frog Bayou. The Union took Capt. Wright and 100 men by surprise. The Union captured the camp, tents, arms and provisions as a wounded Capt. Wright and his men fled. He made his way back to his momma, Mary Taylor Wright, a widower, his daddy, Moses died in the fall of 1860. He never talked about how his daddy died. Most of us figured it was at the hands of Jayhawkers. He became a doctor due to all he'd seen and endured in the war. And all his life, he hated Northerners.

He'd had every intention of carrying out the Brotherhood of Death on behalf of Capt. Brand, instead he and his men had to flee to save their lives.

Henry Hockensmith and John Ross, Quantrill's main confidante, helped capture the steamboat "Sam Gaty" as it was docking at a wood yard on March 30th, below Sibley. Several of the boys boarded the boat finding Negro Federal soldiers along with some of Col. Penick's and McFaren's men. Penick had ordered his men to kill not capture bushwhackers. Our boys killed his men. William Reynolds and some of the boys attacked the steamboat Waverly. Efforts to cease river traffic was a priority. John Ross was a hulk of a man with a square jaw covered by a beard under his chin and no mustache. He parted his hair low on one side which made some of the boys think he was hiding a balding spot. He was slick in the way he maneuvered. An old man among us, he did whatever Quantrill wanted him to do and always knew where Quantrill was when the rest of us were left wondering. The man carried a top hat with him in camp. I never understood how that hat survived from one circumstance to another. It was the kind you just wanted to knock off his head, maybe because it made us think of President Lincoln.

Joe Hart our escape artist had been arrested and was scheduled for court martial at Olathe, Kansas. The day before he was to be executed he was taken to Kansas City where he again escaped. We never knew until he showed up if he was alive or dead, or if the capture and escape were more tales of the boys. He did have small hands and could win any bet placing him in cuffs. He never failed to wiggle his way out of them and the boys couldn't wiggle out of paying him.

I talked to Momma about going to Strother to deliver the letter to James Monroe Chrisman or his family on behalf of Col. JoeC Porter. She was reluctant but since the founder of Strother, William Howard was a kinsmen of Uncle Till's, she agreed. I was to use that card she said if need be. He had named the town for his wife, Maria Strother. Momma knew her from Samuel's Deport and knew they were Confederates. She instructed me to go to the Howard's home seeking information on the Chrisman's rather than go directly to there. As founders of the town directions to their home was an easy find. Once there I learned they left months earlier moving back to Kentucky to wait out the end of the war. Riding toward the river headed to Uncle John and Aunt Mary's house my horse lost a shoe. I stopped at the local livery and there talking to the farrier learned the location of the Chrisman home. He eyed me wondering which side of this war I might be for, but never ask. I made my way to the Chrisman home. Before I could knock on the door a beautiful little girl opened it, her mother standing behind her. I could see the terror in the mother's eyes, fearful I'd brought news of her husband's injury or worse his death. I quickly spoke introducing myself as a friend of his cousin Joseph Chrisman "JoeC" Porter. Her terror vanished but I could still see concern. I'm certain she knew JoeC was Confederate. I reached into my coat pocket pulling the letter out. I told her I had been with JoeC when he was wounded, when he passed and had aided in his burial. He had dictated this letter for her husband, who he considered his closest friend. With tears in her eyes she said, "This war is a horrible thing. Please come in." She did not open the letter but inquired of me about his injury and death. She found some solace in the fact his wife and children made it to his bedside before he died. She told me her husband had been at Cane Hill, the Battle of Prairie Grove and at Helena in Ark. She hoped her husband had not been at the battle at Hartville. She felt it would haunt him if he had. He'd been at home during the worst of the winter but moved out again with the troops. She would see to it he received the letter. She never told me her name, simply introducing herself as "Mrs. Chrisman", her little girl, "Amelia". I knew Col. JoeC had called her Dosha. Meeting them gave me a different understanding of the war, how people, family, once so close could be pulled apart. As I rode away, I too hoped her husband had not been at Hartville where JoeC was wounded.

In April, Quantrill received orders to renew efforts distracting and harassing the Union forces in Missouri and now, Kansas. He had little difficulty burning the houses of known Union. It was becoming more difficult for me, having met Mrs. Chrisman and her little daughter and cousin Elijah's widow in Ark. I could see what this war was doing to people. It was clear, no one, Union or Southerner felt safe. We continued to destroy the mail routes, telegraph and railroads. River travel had all but stopped. The only way mail and other communications were getting through was by lone rider. Whenever we captured enemy we tried to frighten information from them, especially pickets and scouts, we were told to feed them misinformation releasing them unharmed.

In Lafayette Co at James Hicklin's farm, William Fell, Phil Gatewood, Lex and Jason James and William Yowell were in a skirmish. James was the son of James Lanier Hicklin and Catherine Searce. The boys hid in Hicklin's watermelon patch watching as James Sullivan, a local man spying for the North led a column of Federalists into our camps and hiding places. William Fell saw them first. Sullivan and several of the Federalists were killed in the attack. Seems as though where we killed one of the enemy, two more popped up. Col. Tom's men weren't fairing much better. On April 14th, 1863, James "Jim" Henson was captured by Genl. McNeil's forces in Butler Co, Missouri. It was not uncommon for us to go home when we could, but it was dangerous to do so alone. Jim Henson was sent to Myrtle Street prison in St. Louis but we heard he was transferred to Gratiot Street before being sent to City Point, Virginia, for exchange.

Things were heating up in the east and I was grateful to be able to remain home. David Boone was captured in Texas Co, Missouri on April 20th. He died of typhus malaria in Alton prison in Dec. John Lewis Partee in Col Tom's Co B from Izard Co, Ark was riding with Capt. Joe Hart in Shannon Co when he was captured. He was sent to Gratiot Street prison. Those boys were great turkey killers and I hoped to hunt with them down at their place near the White River. Lewis said the turkeys weren't as boney as the ones from Missouri suggesting they had plenty of wild berries and nuts on which to fatten up. Lewis as we called him survived, he and his wife moved to Eureka Springs, Ark after the war. Along with Jesse, I'd visit Lewis in Eureka Springs with its hot mineral baths and Dick who returned to Partee Spring with its fresh clean water near Aunt Lucy's and Mister Flannery's.

We had a couple boys with us with Black Dutch in them, Germans. Most of the folks with German ancestors come to this country as mercenaries during one of the wars mostly the Great War of Revolt. It made me think about the Hite's. Jost Hite might have been enslaved, a debtor to the Crown but he was no mercenary. They were guns for hire and the new United States used them to their advantage. Billy Hickman knew of a group of them near Perch's Prairie. The boys robbed all of the Union clad men and killed one man they knew for certain was German. The Germans who identified themselves as Black Dutch were really part Indian and German and didn't fight with the mercenaries. The German word for being German was Deutsch pronounced like dough itch. The Indians couldn't pronounce it and maybe some white folks too, so they said Dutch and since they were no longer fair skinned after marrying with the Indians, they became known as Black Dutch. It helped us identify who was who. Bill Stone attacked a German settlement in Lafayette Co. He was injured when a German threw a pitchfork at him, hitting him smack in the face. Blood shooting out from the holes the pitchfork left in his cheek, barely missing his eye, Stone took aim with his pistol killing the German. Stone was later captured and taken to St Joseph prison to be shot. He escaped and made it to back Todd's headquarters. He always had a slight indentation in his cheek from where that pitchfork pierced his face. Word arrived Joseph Fickle and Joe Henning had been killed by Lt. Col. King and his men about 15 miles south west of Lexington.

Col. Tom's troops were made up of Ark and Missouri boys and although they were assigned to protect the White River Valley, like us, they fought across Missouri and Ark. Our boys officially under Col Elliott under the command of Capt William Gregg were ordered by Col Shelby south into the White River Valley to aid Col. Tom. It was a decision made early, no one would travel alone. The idea was if one should be captured the other one could make it to either their home or back to camp to advise family and

Col Shelby. We had been ordered into Ark to rid the area of the Mountain Boomers. The brutal murder of Capt Brand had set off both regular and irregulars wanting revenge, some of the boys from the area were attempting to learn the identities of the murderers from Riley and Ed's descriptions. Both said they would never forget the faces of the men, nor would they ever be willing to step foot back into Searcy Co.

We gathered at Ozark, Missouri south of Springfield under Col. James Monroe. With his Cav, Stand Watie's Cherokees and regiments from Freeman and Quantrill, we totaled 500 men. I looked for some of the boys that had gone home back in the winter. There were a few, but seems most had remained closer to home. When we left Ozark with Genl. Cabell, our goal was to attack the Federalists at Fayetteville and drive them out. We were to rendezvous with men from the Middle and Upper White returning with them to Sylamore, from there bands of men were directed by Genl. Cabel to find and kill Mtn Boomers. After the men had been removed to Springfield they set up an outpost using the Tebbett's home as headquarters. Col Sissell was to meet with us south of Fayetteville increasing our numbers to 1000. On the 17th, Sissell and his men were attacked by Union troops. Taking them by surprise in the early morning hours, they chased them from their camp capturing over 20 horses, 25 stands of arms and camping supplies, tents, blankets and provisions including saddles.

At dawn on the morning of April 18th, Cabell's scouts engaged with Union pickets. The gunfire alerted the Union troops at the outpost who attacked from the east and south. Col Monroe ordered us to advance on the left flank. Fighting became hand to hand. To both Col. Tom's and our men, irregulars and guerillas, we didn't fight this way. We knew how to use our horses and rarely lost one. The attack and disperse tactics we used were more effective than the 1,000 men here today. Even though we were firing upon fewer numbers, it was certain we would not break their lines. When Col Monroe ordered his Cav to charge, we did not join him. We knew an ambush was waiting. It's what we would have done and it was exactly what the Union did. Col Monroe led his men into a cross fire from the Union. By mid morning we were withdrawing, without sufficient ammunition and leadership. We lost 50 men killed and wounded about the same as the Union. We're certain Genl. Cabell was delighted to learn the Federalists withdrew vacating Fayetteville within days. Col Tom's men returned back southeast to the Middle White River with half our men accompnaying them continuing the hunt for Capt Brand's murderers. The other half of "Quantrill's men" headed back north; simply headed home, no discussion. Call it discipline, call it too many chiefs, this was no way to win a war. We knew where we were effective and this was not it. I sent word with Will

Wyatt and Jim Friend, some of the Ark boys to tell the rest of the boys certain Partisan Rangers were asking after them.

We rode hard north out of Ark until we reached the area south of Neosho. We camped and refreshed our horses at the Ellis Farm. Neosho had been designated the capitol for Missouri when Jeff City fell to the Union. Col. Tom talked a lot about Neosho. He loved the place. We moved west through Baxter Springs, Kansas skirting the state line heading north along the old Shawnee Trail. We stuck close to Dry Wood Creek, camping along the banks. Reaching Raytown, I thought about the drills and exercises when we'd first enlisted. Now nearly two years had passed and I'd had more than I could take of regular service. I was feeling home now, familiar paths, creeks, streams and roads our family traveled. With the drought and destruction of war, the landscape was changed. I found myself past the markers that were once a clear path between places. The winter had been hard on Missouri, its people and animals. I made it home in time to help get the tobacco crops out. Jesse hung on every word as Momma and I talked. When he paused too long, Aunt Charlotte scolded him, "Misser Jesse, git yursef back workin". I knew it would not be long before he'd defy Momma joining up, as a regular or with us irregulars. He was dreaming of being a Partisan Ranger. I didn't know which was safer but it was becoming clear, home was not safe. I worried about Momma and Doc if he joined up. Suzie was just 14, Sallie 5, and John Thomas, a baby child of two. Worse, Momma was pregnant. Should Jesse join up, even with Uncle Till close by, there wouldn't be anyone but Doc to care for them.

Col. Sydney Drake Jackman returned from Ark continuing recruiting in Howard Co with great success. The Union considered him a serious threat. Fearing for their safety, Genl. Price had a unit of 25 Union soldiers to escort his wife and children to St. Louis where they were put on a ship headed for Natchez, Mississippi. From there they were sent to Shreveport, Louisiana where they were able to settle. When Jackman arrived home and found his family gone, he was very upset. No one got word to him of the danger they were in nor their relocation for safety reasons, he'd discovered their fate through neighbors. I can't imagine his horror and rage, fear. I didn't want to let my thoughts settle on what it would do to me if I came home to an empty place. The town of Franklin became New Franklin. It was the home of early trader William Becknell who founded the Santa Fe Trail. Old Franklin was destroyed in 1828 when the Missouri River flooded. The old town was replaced by New Franklin but most people just called it Franklin. It was at Franklin near Pleasant Hill, Capt Samuel Steinmetz attacked Jackman but the boys were able to defeat his men. Lou Railey was killed during the attack. Maj Reives Leonard of Guitar's Regiment heard of Steinmetz's defeat and tried to break up

Jackman's recruiting camp in Howard Co. This was how we were fighting, strike, be chased, hit them, be hit, strike back, a game of cat and mouse.

Three miles west of Pleasant Hill, in Cass Co, Cole attacked Lt Jefferson and 32 Cav troops. Joe Lee was to cut Jefferson off from Pleasant Hill. William and Perry Hayes, John and Noah Webster, Sterling and Irish David Kennedy, James and Edward Marshall, Henry McAninch and Edward Hinks rode with Lee. Instead of forming a battle line and letting Cole trap the Federal soldiers, Lee and his men charged Jefferson and his men head on before Cole was in place. Cole was too late to block the remaining Federal troops but with his quick thinking and slick maneuvering only four Federalists escaped. This would be another story Momma would love to tell. Ed Hinks and Jefferson were killed. Wins were still not really wins, on either side. John Webster was a grandfather to us boys. He was an elder, kind with a listening ear. He had the look of an Amish man about him and displayed every bit of reverence for our Lord. Sometimes after we had had a particularly hard day, he would counsel with those who needed him. This was one of those days, many sat in prayer with him.

Lt John Drury Pulliam from Howard Co was riding with Jackman. On April 23rd in a pre dawn raid Pulliam helped Jackman kidnap Gen Thomas J Bartholow from his mother's home on the outskirts Glasgow. Bartholow's mother passed away and he was staying at her home. The garrison in town held 150 men and most of the roads were guarded but Bartholow was at home unguarded. Jackman, Confederate Genl. John B. Clark Jr., Maj John Rucker of Rocheport, Drury Pulliam, Polk Witt, E.P. De Hart, Ben Shipp and four more of the boys pulled off the raid and kidnapping. They were a hoot telling the story. They woke the Genl. by simply knocking on his door. He came to the door fighting mad demanding to know what was so important as to wake him. Rucker was at the door claiming to have an important message. Cautious Bartholow stepped back, peered through the window but could only see the messenger. Pistol in hand, he opened the door. Bartholow stepped outside where Rucker was, the men flat against the wall surrounded him sticking pistols in his sides and back. He gave up without fighting. They held him at gunpoint as they slipped through town to their horses. By dawn they made it to the Blackfoot Hills on the Co line. During the day, he and Jackman talked. Bartholow refused to take an oath or accept a parole. Jackman's real goal was to get Bartholow to rescind his decision regarding the treatment of guerillas and irregulars. They argued back and forth, as gentlemen, soldier's of war negotiating, finally, Bartholow agreed. Back in Glasgow, Capt. John Tillman commander of Co B of the 46th Enrolled Missouri Militia known to be an evil man by both sides, swore he'd kill every known Southern sympathizer in the town if the Genl. wasn't immediately returned.

He took six civilians hostage, posted sentries on the roads leading into town and set out with a column of men to search for him. Genl. Bartholow was back at his headquarters as if nothing at all had happened by the time Tillman returned. He had to let the people go and should have suffered humiliation but instead was enraged.

News arrived daily via one command, scout or man returning from respite. Patrick Nagle was killed in Dade, Cedar Co, Missouri while taking correspondence from Quantrill to Gov. Reynolds exiled in Ark. Benjamin Frank and Moses Maples of Col. Tom's command riding with Col. Jackman were captured near Emminence in Shannon Co. Ben on April 29 and Moses, the next day. Then D.J. Cantwell was captured on the 29th near Rolla. They sent Ben and Moses to Rolla, from there to Gratiot Street and D.J. to Myrtle Street, in St. Louis. I never understood why one would be sent for exchange and the other one released. Perhaps like my little brother Jesse, one would have a 'smart mouth.' D.J. was released July 18 after he swore to The Oath while Ben and Moses were sent to City Point, Virginia for parole and exchange. Momma said it had to do with how well the Union thought they could survive. Jesse thought it had more to do with the officers and who had captured who and if they had more position than the others in what got said and done. I figured it was both of those coupled with the 'smart mouth'. It was a game of chess and they needed the ones who could survive in order to play their games.

Chapter 17

Just above the bootheel of Missouri near Bloomfield in Stoddard Co, Genl. Marmaduke struck at Union Brigadier Genl. John McNeil. When McNeil retreated, Marmaduke followed striking again near the Cape on April 25th. By the time Marmaduke assessed their numbers, McNeil had fortified his troops. He ended with only a few men killed and seriously wounded while Marmaduke lost over 300 men, dead and dying. Among the dead was John Gabbert, son of William Gabbert and Rebecca Wade. John always wore a suit. He looked like he was ready for church any day of the week, or politicin'. He wore his hair cut short and his bread trimmed out nice but no mustache. He was a dapper fellow with manners. A month later, on May 25th, Feds attacked John's home where several of the boys were camped. His wife Lenora Mayfield helped bury the dead guerillas killed. Less than five months later, after receiving word that his son had been killed, William Gabbert was killed Oct 16, 1863 in Benton Co, Ark.

John Gabbert

Lenora Mayfield Gabbert
Emory Cantey Photo Collection

Vying for his own full command and catching the eye of Col.s Shelby and Jackman, May 3, Bloody Bill raided Kansas,. Realizing the strength of his skills, elections were held and he was elected Lt. Col. He came by the farm; Jesse begged Momma to go with him. Bloody Bill vouched for him, talking to Momma of Unc's training, going back to his courage and willingness all those years ago to do what was needed. But, Momma was stoic in her commitment. Jesse was not joining.

Capt. Dick Yeager and a group of the boys stopped a stage in Black Jack, Douglas Co, Kansas, near Lawrence, carrying 9 people including the drivers. It had been here in 1856 John Brown attacked the camp of Henry

C. Pate. The battle at Black Jack most people believed led to the division starting the War Between the States. Dick had the boys take the passengers guns, watches and money. Mrs. Kelly of Missouri the only woman passenger was treated politely and not robbed. We laughed heartily. Mrs. Laura was Cole Younger's oldest sister Laura Helen, wife of William Kelly. Her trunk was never even opened. One of the passengers Col Jones of New Mexico had been a former neighbor of Dick Yeager's and was robbed. The boys took the stage horses. The male passengers had to borrow money from Mrs. Laura Younger Kelly to pay for their meals and lodging until they reached Santa Fe. We all had a hoot and holler about that one.

Capt. Dick Yeager
Missouri Valley Special Collection, Kansas City Public Library

Returning to camp Joe Hart was captured near the Big Blue by Penick's men. Someone suggested we wager on his captures and escapes. No one could really say how many times he had been captured before but he was becoming an expert at escaping. Knowing his ability to escape, having captured and lost him before, Penick had his men tie Joe to his horse. As they were moving along George Todd and his men attacked Penick. Joe was shouting, "It's me boys. It's me." Because he was tied to the horse, Todd knew he was a prisoner of war but didn't recognize him right off hand. We knew the Union was trying to infiltrate bands using this ploy. Tying one of their own up to a horse, getting into a minor skirmish and letting him be captured in order to return information to the Union. George was taking no chances, he had his gun pointed right at Joe who was talking fast showing his hands when Bill Gregg come up and started laughing. "Joe Hart, I'll be damned if you ain't got yourself captured again and George here was just a second away from killing you dead." Bill saved his life. George Todd wasn't going to take any prisoners of war, not even presumed Southern ones. Joe had learned the Union captured John McDonald in Shannon Co on the 7th. But like Joe he was good at escaping. Mc didn't disappoint. He escaped from the Gratiot Street Prison on June 20th. A private in Co B of Col. Tom's command he returned to Ark.

Capt. Moses McCoy was captured recruiting for the Confederacy on May 15th. They jailed him and were waiting on orders for transfer or execution. Moses was married to Lurena Adler, a Boone descendant, which carried a lot of weight in Missouri, with both southerners and northerners, they were frontier dynasty. The Union was arresting more and more women, knowing us boys, husbands, brothers, sons, Southern men would come to their rescue. We rode into Missouri City on May 19th to release the wife of one of our boys. Missouri City lay just 6 miles from Liberty and was an old town. Established around 1820 as Atchison, it had originally been a fur trading post for Brother Antoine and Bernard Lafford during the time this part of the country belonged to France. Right next to it at the mouth of Rose's Branch, a man by the name of Shrewbury Williams operated a ferry, a booming little place called Richfield. The ner do well's established a bar across from the landing and a stock Co calling it, Saint Bernard. In Dec 1857, Atchison was renamed to Missouri City, then in 1859, just before war broke out, St. Bernard, Richfield and Atchison become incorporated as part of Missouri City. But, to us locals each place remained separate. We took our hemp to Saint Bernard for shipping. There were a number of good hiding places and easy routes along the river there. When we arrived at Richfield being most familiar with the place, I led the advance. With ease we released the women being held. Some of the men found a keg of whiskey and on empty stomachs were fast becoming drunk.

I myself had a hankering for a smoke. I went over to the mercantile to get some cigars. It was clear the storekeep would have shot us dead if he'd of known who we were. I got my cigars and did him the favor. The boys were bragging shooting off their pistols which got us arrested and thrown in jail. There we found ourselves with Moses. Col. Fernando Scott heard what had happened and knew the real target was Capt. Moses McCoy's wife Lurena Adler "Lou" McCoy. They had seen us talking to her and figured we had to be with her. They hadn't placed us with the killing of the storekeeper nor did they realize we were Partisan Rangers, yet.

Joe Hart set up an ambush for Caption Sessions, head of the Union garrison at Richfield, who had Lurena arrested. He run on to a local boy,

Peter Mahoney who told Joe he would have to report him and the boys. This was exactly what Joe wanted in order to led the Feds into an ambush. It was a mile or two ride into town where Union Capt. Sessions was at. He listened to Mahoney and took the bait. Lt. Col. Scott, James Barnard, Joe Hart, John Jackson, James Little and others hid near a bridge in a thicket ready to pursue any of Sessions men escaping. Sessions and Graffenstein along with three privates approached the bridge. Sessions had been at Shiloh and who knows what he had done to get assigned to chasing us Missouri bushwhackers, but here he was at the bridge. Hidden on both sides of the road, the boys opened fire killing Sessions and wounding Private Rapp and Lt Graffenstein. Col. Scott and several of the boys charged after the two who were doing their best to get back to town. Rapp was bleeding heavily. The boys took his valuables, gun and uniform. Even though Sessions was dead the boys poured more shots into him. Lt. Graffenstein tried to surrender and was shot in the head. Private Rapp must have realized the seriousness of it and pretended to be dead escaping more harm. He was found by some town folks who got him to Richfield for medical treatment. Col. Scott secured our release and Lurena's, but hers was to be short lived. Rapp survived, was found and turned over to us. This time, three shots were fired into him and he fell, dead for sure this time. I really don't know what kind of stuff he was made of, perhaps a cat with nine lives because he survived. We learned both Moses and I had been identified by local boys now Unionists to Capt. Joseph Schmitz. If they didn't know we were Partisan Rangers before they did now.

Momma told us the Union was blind in their goal to hunt down and kill Lt. Col. Fernando Scott, so much so they were leaving their posts under manned. Taking advantage of that news we left out headed toward Plattsburg in the northern part of Clay Co. The town was armed by less than thirty men and a few women under the directions of Lt. Birch. We captured him and pushed him at gunpoint to the steps of the courthouse. There Col Scott was able to broker a deal in which everyone laid down their arms. The women cooked for us, laughing and joking in a way no one would have believed an hour earlier we had guns pointed at each other. This was the atmosphere of the war. During dinner, someone said they had taken a woman prisoner to St. Joseph, charged with giving aid and comfort to the enemy. They described her fighting and screaming obscenities yelling if she had no children, she too would join the guerillas. When they told she had had on her person red shirts and coats for guerillas, we realized it was Lurena. She had those made for Joe Hart and Louis Van Diver. Lurena was unaware her younger sister Lydia Ann had sworn an affidavit Lurena had them made by tailor James Moffitt. Lurena maintained she would do what the good Lord told her to do, no man would be turned away hungry if she had food in which to share. Both Lurena and her sister, swore to and signed Oaths of Allegiance to the Union.

I headed home, several of the boys in tow. Jesse and Momma routinely scouted the area, watching the comings and goings of folks and associating with who. When we got to the farm, they were just coming in from one of their scouting trips. They informed us of a number of areas where the Union was weak. Several of us camped in the woods north of the farm, past Aunt Charlotte's new house. Talk was of the prisoners of war from the various commands. Dick Douglas a local boy serving as a 1st Lt under Col. Tom was captured on May 22. He had been sent to Springfield for transfer. We talked about the possibility of raids on the garrisons but an election would be needed and there weren't enough of for a full vote.

May 25th, 1863, we met Jim Griffith on the road near Mount Gilead Church. The boys riding ahead were taking his house and saddle, when I approached I made them return them to him. I don't think I believed him when he said he would have to turn us in. But indeed, he went into town and swore out a statement. That same day, Union soldiers arrived at the farm. Jesse was working in the tobacco fields along with several hands when he heard the troops coming. Momma and Doc confronted the troops denying they had any knowledge of where we were hiding. One of the little hands was making his way unseen into the woods to alert us.

Two boys I had grown up sitting next to in church, hunted and fished, learned together from Unc, enlisted and rode with were among the Union, Alvis Dagley and Brantley Bond. My sister Susie would later confirm it was them who put the noose around Docs neck hoisting him up to be repeatedly hung from the big oak until he almost stopped breathing for good. Repeating this until he had no choice but to die and leave my mother alone with the babies or tell where we were. Susie and Momma were held at gunpoint in the house. We did not blame him for exposing us in the woods. Momma was pregnant and his dying just wouldn't do. We had been playing cards resting and making plans when we were alerted. Escaping, we fired off some shots as the Union came upon us.

Momma and Susie pushed their way out of the house as the soldiers dashed about uncertain if they were to join the pursuit or hold the women. Doc was arrested and loaded into a wagon. Jesse stayed hidden behind the barn, uncertain if he should hide or run. Two soldiers saw him and chased him down in the tobacco field. Dragging him to the house, one of the men grabbed Doc's razor strap, lashing him with it. They shouted obscenities at Jesse, laughing about Stonewall Jackson having met his death. Momma was screaming as Doc was hauled off, Susie held back by Aunt Charlotte when Uncle Will drove up. He later told us, Momma was giving the men a severe tongue lashing as the men rode off with Doc.

Confederate Maj Thomas Jonathan Jackson earned the name "Stonewall" at the Battle of Bull Run. Brigadier Genl. Barnard Elliott Bee challenged his own weary and disheartened men shouting "There is Jackson, standing like a stone wall." Stonewall and Daddy's cousin William Wirt Woodson were half brothers, sons of the same mother Julia Beckwith Neale; Stonewall's daddy Jonathan Jackson died and his momma married Blake Woodson, then after having Wirt, she died. Stonewall and his sister Laura were sent to live with his Uncle Cummins. Wirt lived with the Woodson's. Wirt moved to Marshall, Saline Co, Missouri and when war broke out joined Robert C. Wood's Partisan Rangers. He was in Ark fighting when Stonewall was killed. Although we were certain the Union meant only to taunt Jesse with the loss of such a great Confederate leader and knew nothing of our family relationship, it sent rage through Jesse's veins. Their words failed to impress the desired weakness instead rage swelled inside of Jesse Woodson James.

At Chancellorville, Stonewall Jackson had marched into the midst of the Union capturing many of them without having to fire a single shot. When they charged shouting out their rebel yell, the Union fled. Stonewall had pursued until darkness started to fall. Returning to camp they were fired upon by the 18th North Carolina Infantry who thought they were Union. Stonewall was hit three times, twice in the left arm and once in the right hand. He lost several of his men, staff and horses in the confusion. Dr. Hunter McGuire had to amputate his left arm. He was believed to be improving and his complaints of chest pain were thought to be from the rough handling necessary in getting him out of the line of fire and to the field hospital. He had taken pneumonia but even on his death bed remained strong in faith, saying "It is the Lord's Day; my wish is fulfilled. I have always desired to die on Sunday." He passed from this earth on May 10, 1863 from pneumonia. Genl. Robert E. Lee sent a message to the family through the Chaplain: "Genl. Jackson lost his left arm but I my right." The entire Confederacy had taken his death hard, especially however mistakenly and regretfully having come at the hands of his own men.

When Uncle Will started loading up the children to take them home with him, Jesse refused. He was taking a stand. He was leaving headed out to find us. We had scattered, as was our pattern of defense, leading the chasing troops in various directions. It would not be until later we knew who had been injured, shot, captured or killed. Momma found Doc the next day in the Liberty jail. It was clear the multiple hanging had done something to him, his speech was slow and he looked at you like he wasn't certain of his words or even who you were but then, it would come to him. His neck and throat were so severely damaged he never fully regained his normal speech. He sounded like he was sick, losing his voice, raspy.

During a skirmish on May 27, 1863 between Harrisonville and Pleasant Hill, Al Cunningham was killed. James Vaughn was captured and hung on May 29th at Fort Union in Kansas City. Confederate Col. Parker avenged his death by hanging 4 Union men. I was concerned that the war was escalating and this was what Jesse was entering into. The Union took no sympathy for the women, even those clearly expecting as Mrs. Lurena was. I feared this was too much for Jesse. I was grateful when Bloody Bill took charge of him. They fed off each other, one would do something the other would challenge back. A disaster in the making, as Momma would say if she had known but I felt him safer with Bloody Bill than at large with me. In May and June alone, Jim Lane was responsible for the killing of hundreds of people in Missouri and the efforts of the special troops like us, independent irregulars fighting guerrilla warfare was the only way to answer him. Like the Bible said, "An eye for an eye."

On June 1, at Rocheport, Lt John Drury Pulliam under Col. Sydney Drake Jackman, and one of Todd's men, John Vance were captured. Union Genl. Thomas Ewing became determined to harass and torment the families of all guerillas as a means of demonstrating no one was out of his reach. He set out to have wives, mothers and sisters arrested. The Union returned to the farm arresting Momma, Susie and again, Doc. They were jailed first at Liberty then taken to Plattsburg and on to Saint Joseph separately. Neither Momma nor Doc knew what was happening to each other. Susie come down with malaria. Afraid for her, Momma swore to the oath of loyalty to the Union on June 5th. It would take a letter signed by three friends and neighbors, fellow Kentuckian Art Courtney whose brother James married Lou Pence, a sister to Donnie and Bud, Alvah Maret who helped Daddy get the farm and whose daughter Lou was married to Uncle J.R. and Unionist Edward Madison Samuel, Doc's cousin, great grandsons of brothers as well as D.J. Larkin to gain Doc's release. Doc swore to the oath on June 24th.

Shortly after having arrested Momma, Susie and Doc, three of Jeptha Crawford's' daughters, married women, were arrested by the 11th Kansas Jayhawker Regiment while buying flour for their family in Kansas City. Their daddy Jeptha Crawford killed in Jan by Feds in front of his wife and children. Their Momma, Betsy Harris brought four of her sons to join Quantrill. The crimes of these women were aiding guerillas, even if it was their husbands, brothers, sons and fathers. Laura and Susan married brothers Stewart and William Whitsett. William passed in 1855 and Susan remarried Thomas Vandiver. Armenia was the widow of Charles Selvey killed a year before. These women had children in their homes. Laura had Lee born 1853, Isaac 56 and Cynthia 58. Susan was the mother of Armenia Vandiver born 1855, Jeptha 57, Susan 58 and Thomas 59. Armenia the widow of Charles had Jeptha born 1855, Lewis 56 and William born 58.

The Crawford girl's momma, Betsy Harris, was a sister to Reuben Harris, husband of Laura Fristoe, sister of Cole Younger's momma Bersheba Fristoe; Cole and the women were first cousins. Betsy's niece, Nancy "Nannie" Harris was arrested the day after her daughters. Nancy's husband Jabez McCorkle had died two days before on June 2 from an accidental gunshot wound. During May, June and July the Union arrested over 100 Confederate women cramming them into the second floor of an old hotel and tavern in Lawrence, Kansas. We were beginning to understand the depth of the atrocities the Union had perpetrated upon the women and the lengths to which the women had gone to keep these acts from us, knowing our reactions. Their experiences of having been physically violated, their homes burned and the inhumanness of not being able to bury their dead had bonded these women of war who cared for each other and us. When it came to a vote, we knew what we had to do.

Two weeks earlier, May 20th, Cole rode over to visit his grandma Fristoe hitching his horse to a tree in the orchard he'd headed to the house. One of their Negro women came and told him the Feds were looking for him. He had to abandon his horse in order to escape. When he got back to camp, Quantrill had ordered John and Jabez McCorkle, Tom Harris, Jesse and me to gather up all the other boys who had camps nearby or had gone home. John and the men under him were camped only a few miles from Jabez's camp. John was up on a rock ledge overlooking the valley to see if he could see any fires from other camps. He was doing a little yodeling which was one of our ways to holler from one ridge to another to alert the boys or locate other camps when Jabez and his men rode up. Some folks think southerner mountain folk just can't spell the word hollow.

Jabez's men waited below talking with John's men while Jabez climbed the hill to talk to John. Somehow, while climbing or standing the rock under his foot gave way. Stumbling he dropped his Springfield rifle. It discharged striking Jabez in the right leg just below the knee moving upward shattering his knee joint. The boys rushed up the hillside to get him down. They wrapped him in a blanket and moved him under the bluff ledge making him as comfortable as possible. His wife, Nannie Harris McCorkle and sister Laura Harris come to his aid. They cared for his wounds, dressing and cleaning them daily, still infection set in. He died 13 days later on June 2, 1863. Laura Fristoe Harris joined her daughters Nancy and Laura preparing Jabez for burial. That's when their brother Tom Harris and I rode up with Col Fernando Scott. We helped get his body to his mother in law Laura Fristoe Harris' house. Then we all hid in the nearby woods while the coffin was being made. As the women watched over the dead, Feds came to the house searching it. Seeing Jabez' dead body, they left. The next day we buried him in the graveyard near the house. Nancy returned home after burying her husband, the Feds showed up arresting her for having buried a guerilla, her husband.

George Todd, Bill Gregg, Dave Poole, John Jarrette and Bloody Bill cut a path across western Missouri making sure everyone knew we meant business and the Union arresting women was not going unnoticed. June started in Rocheport on the 1st, and Doniphan, Waverly and on to Camp Cole on the 8th. Jasper Co June 10th, 16th, Westport 17th and near Wellington, the 18th Blue River and Rocheport. Sibley was destroyed on the 23rd with conflict in Papinsville and Carthage 27th and 28th thus ended June, a difficult month. Near Blue Mills, my horse George got caught in some quicksand. I was able to jump free but my horse didn't make it. James Combs gave me another one. He called him "Little George." I asked him why and he told me the horse reminded him of George Todd. He was steady, true, a fighter and had all the qualities of a true friend. Losing an animal of that quality was difficult financially and emotionally. Not every horse can stand the sounds of battle. I had to agree Little George was as true as George Todd and served me well. My other horse, a sound Missouri Fox Trotter, was named George, now I had Little George.

Quantrill had been leaving us for several days at a time without giving indication of where he was going. He was always moody and most of us just figured that was it. A couple of the fellows went with him and never said a word. When they came back, they announced Quantrill had married Sarah Rebecca Katherine "Kate" King by preacher Hiram Bowman from Oak Grove, near the Blue Spring camp. Kate was the daughter of Robert King and Malinda Stringer. She had a houseful of brothers and sisters, Nancy was the oldest, Jasper, Martha Jane, brother Francis, then Kate, the youngest girl and baby brother Samuel born in 1852. Kate, born in 1848 had just turned 15. Quantrill and Kate met when Quantrill approached her father about safe quarters. Not long after having made several visits to the King home, Kate had gone with Quantrill to Howard Co. Whether her Momma and Daddy wanted her to go or not remains of question. Fletch Taylor had been with them and said Kate's daddy let her go willingly but some of us questioned if he had paid him off or threatened him. Quantrill's legend in these hills as a hero was dowry enough, or so Fletch said. Fletch loaned Kate his horse so she and Quantrill could ride to the preacher about 6 miles from her family's home to get married.

We were all a little more than concerned about having women with us but a young girl and that girl being attached to Quantrill himself. She would spend time in various homes near where we would be camped and back at her parent's home. Quantrill was never very far from her and that was an even greater concern as Feds pursued us. Should they learn of the marriage, not only would Mrs. Kate be at risk but so would her momma, daddy, brothers and sisters, and equally all of us. We were fighting because we believed in what we were fighting for. Knowing who you could trust and who you couldn't was critical to our survival and success. Quantrill began talking crazy after meeting with Kate's daddy and some of his friends, members of some organization wanting to turn Texas into a new country where slavery was allowed. Knights of the Golden Circle came up in talk on more and more occasions. If only, if only, if, if, if, were the mainstays of his conversations. All centering on a notion of the south rising again if defeated and a growing idea of assassinating President Lincoln.

Tuesday, June 16th we fought Capt. Thatcher near Kansas City between New Santa Fe and Westport. We originally planned to capture Kansas City but met Thatcher's men along the way. Todd led the attack. But as the Feds were retreating a larger Co fell in behind them offering the opportunity of counter attack. After the event, Dick Yeager, Dick Berry, Oth Hinton and James Little were ordered to guard the bodies of the men killed in the battle until burial. Among the men lost were Lt. Col. Fernando Scott, Boone Scholl and Al Wyatt. Oth Hinton, Fletch Taylor, John Jarrette, John Ross, Jesse and I took the body of Fernando Scott home. He was buried in the Smith Cemetery at Raytown in Blue Township, Jackson Co. Al Wyatt was buried in Grandview Cemetery. Boone was taken to Mrs. Younger's home. The family got him ready for burial. He too was buried at the Smith cemetery in Raytown. This wasn't the first or last time I'd see to it that boys, men, irregular and regular soldiers were laid to rest whether with their families or not. It always kinda sickened me to leave them to the elements, rotting for the animals to scavenge. It brought to mind the wagon train and the Mountain Meadows Massacre.

On the trip back from Boone Scholl's grave, we came across some Federal soldiers escaping into a nearby barn. John Ross, Fletch, and I set it on fire. Some of the soldiers ran out and we shot them. The others burned to death in the barn. The stench of death hung on our clothes as we rode. I reckon we thought it might make us feel better but it didn't. My mind was on the boys who burned to death in the haystacks, eaten by wild hogs. I began to question what we were becoming. Boys, young men fighting on both sides, seeing and doing things that would inhabit our hearts and minds the rest of our lives.

We had safe refuge, a meal and bed any time it was needed at the hotel tavern of Judge John Shirley in Carthage. Both Quantrill and Cole visited there on several occasions, getting a meal and information from both Judge Shirley and his son. John Allison "Bud" Shirley was a year older than me. He enlisted with the Eighth Missouri Volunteer Cav in 1862. After the Huntsville Massacre in Ark, many of the men went on to join other units or simply returned home. Earning the rank of Capt., Bud had a few men he trusted ride with him but he was most known for providing scout and spy services to the guerilla bands and Partisan Rangers. He and another scout were at the home of a Confederate sympathizer on June 20th at Sarcoxie when Union troops surrounded the house. Bud was shot and killed trying to escape. His momma, Eliza Hatfield Shirley and sister Myra Belle went the 15 miles from their home by wagon to get his body. Belle's momma was of the famous feuding mountaineer clan the Hatfield's and McCoy's. I never knew if Moses was part of the McCoy's. Never really thought to ask him. The Shirley tavern was a rough and rowdy place where men that mattered met and a few outlaws. The Shirley livery stable, tavern and hotel was used by horse thieves as a trading station. Belle learned to ride like an old cowhand and cuss like a man. Belle and her momma swore revenge against the Union Army after Bud was killed. Belle became a Confederate spy riding with Quantrill's raiders and others, picking up where Bud left off. Belle and Cole Younger developed a fondness for each other. In Sept 1864, the family lost all of their holdings when the Union raided and burned Carthage. Judge Shirley left taking the family to Texas.

George Scholl, Boone's brother was hard to console. They had both joined up with Bloody Bill. George had seen his brother die. It's hard enough to watch a man die but your brother? The feeling of being able to do nothing, helpless to change the outcome challenged each of us, awake and sleeping. They were the great great grandson's of the great pioneer and frontiersman, Daniel Boone. Joseph Scholl married Lavina Boone, pioneer Daniel Boone's daughter. Their families had been friends for a very long time. The School's and Boone's fought together in the Great Revolt. The Mims, Woodson and Poor's had married brothers and sisters, cousins, leading to multiple relationships through those marriages. George and Boone's mother, Harriet Wright Boone was a third cousin of their father Nelson Scholl. Harriet was a descendant of one of pioneer Daniel Boone's brothers. George decided to go to Texas with Dave Pool, Archie Clement and Jim Anderson. He surrendered at home at Lexington at war's end.

After being released as a prisoner of war, Doc Sanders found the boys in camp near Wellington. On June 29th, Cole, Doc, Joe Lee, Joe Hall, Ben Parker and Dick Kinney rode into town. They found some Unionists robbing a store. In the skirmish that followed the Union killed Capt. Ben Parker. Jim Smith of Co H of Col. Tom's command was on his way back to Ark when he was captured in Fulton Co, Ark on July 1. Same day, Tom Moore rode with Frank Gregg and Warren Welch to the home of A.W. and Mary Hutchins house in Lafayette Co for a meal. They were attacked and Tom Moore was killed by McFerrin's soldiers.

Genl. Robert E. Lee's invasion of the North ended in defeat at the Battle of Gettysburg. Union Genl. Ulysses Grant captured our Confederate stronghold, Vicksburg, Mississippi across the river from Helena, Ark. Although the tide of overall war seemed to be turning against the Confederacy, we continued fighting. Every day there was a new grave to dig, body to get home and mother whose heart was forever broken. Ben Roach and John "Lewis" Partee from Ark had been paroled in St. Louis after swearing to The Oath on June 2. They decided they wanted to be part of Quantrill's campaigns and made it to Liberty to Momma's rather than heading back to Ark. For now, Genl. Price was encouraging the boys from North Ark to go home. It was under siege. Lewis and Ben chose to ride with us through the fall.

On July 4th, 1863, 87 years after the onset of the War for Independence from Great Britain, we were at war with our brothers at home, another War Between the States, certainly not the first. It was weighing heavy on our hearts and minds. Our teacher Mr. Bird had told us about the War for Independence, people believe it was just the British against the Colonists, but that wasn't true. The British called it the Great Revolt, but it was a War Between the States. People did the same things they were doing now. The Tories, people who chose to remain allied with Great Britain were burned out, women raped and mistreated, husbands shot and children taken as forced slaves. Families fled into Canada in order to save their own lives. The British awarded those loyal to the crown with 200 acres in Canada. After the war was over and the colonists established control over the new lands, it was 1789 before George Washington became the first President. We celebrate the 4th of July 1776 without much thought to the decade of fighting, betrayals and war people endured. Within a decade Gov Wilkinson of the new Missouri Territories and Vice President Aaron Burr were trying to establish a new country west of the Mississippi River. In part, it was a country loyal to Great Britain and a country where Gov Wilkinson could be supreme ruler, President. It was the 1804 Wilkinson Agreement signed by many of the people who allied with the British in the Great War of Revolt who chose to settle in the mountains of Missouri and Ark. Many of these people married into the Indian tribes who were also being forced out during this time. After the destruction of his villages at the onset of the War of 1812 Chief John Lewis and his wife Mary Succopanous moved from Lewistown (Ohio) with 4,000 Shawnee to the White River Valley of the Ozarks. First called Shawneetown, it is now Yellville, Ark. Given Horn riding with us was from that area. Wars are never one sided and there are never any real winners. People think of the Great War of Revolt and think everyone on this soil was for separation from England, but no different than now, people were taking sides against their neighbors and families and it wasn't so long ago that there were people alive who had lived through those wars. It was fresh.

We had story tellers among us, all of them I wish Unc had known. I had been trying to tell the history of the Indians moving to Yellville and several of the boys had added in their whoops and hollers as I went along. They would get into challenges and while one would tell the main story another would add in sounds, clack clack of the wagon wheels, horses whinny, rooster's crowing, but my story wasn't holding their interest. Maybe it was the heat of the day, maybe it was me.

Capt. Andrew Jackson Campbell, Joe Hart, Henry Cowherd, Tom Crews, William Gaw and Sgt. Louis Vandiver were given units and ordered to raid Clay, Clinton, Caldwell, and Livingston Counties. Henry Cowherd was one of the grandfather's of our boys, a man whom we all listened to. He had the look of a commander, tight lipped and staunch. Lou Vandiver had a baby face but was every bit a hulk of a man. He grew a little crop of hair on the bottom of his chin. He had curly blonde hair worn at his collar and piercing blue eyes, like my brother Jesse. He was among the ones who went to have their images made into photographs before we headed to Lawrence. The Vandiver's lived near Camden in the lower south east corner of the Co. Tom and Bill Crews were old men in our ranks, both over 40 years old. A Union Cav surprised them while they were asleep at Moses Curtis farm near Spring Hill twelve miles north of Chillicothe on July 13th. The Capt., Vandiver, Cowherd, Crews and Gaw escaped but Joe Hart, the escape artist, just 22 years old was killed. He'd been captured and escaped more times than we could count. He had small wrists and could wiggle out of the cuffs and bonds when tied. Andy Campbell was wounded, captured and taken to prison in St. Joseph. When he returned home he told that Joe had written his parents a letter just hours before he was killed that was found on him along with his commission from Col. Parker of Jackson Co, a black silk flag, a field glass, memorandum book and letters from his lady friend, Miss Virginia Kennison of St. Joseph. The Union made Andy and another captive dig Joe's grave. They ordered them to throw his body into the grave which they did but only because they were holding guns on them. Andy who had been with Joe when he was writing the letter requested of Union Lt. David Gibbs over the command that the letter to his parents be mailed. An unruly dislikable man with little regard for human dignity even in death Gibbs refused to do so. However, Andy had a very good memory and believed that Joe's parents, Felix and Becky Hart had fled to Canada. He took it upon himself to get the news to them. He did get word to them of Joe's death and the existence of the letter but he never knew if the actual letter which Joe wrote ever reached them.

Near Chillicothe, Livingston Co, Missouri July 13, 1863

Dear Parents, Being in this country with a body of Partisan Rangers on a raid, I have concluded to drop a few lines to you, letting you know my health, which is fine, and also of my operations and of my brother George. I saw some boys and have some now under me, just up from the army, who saw George about the 20th of May and after the battle of Cape Girardeau. He was well and in excellent spirits. John is dead. He was wounded at Springfield, Jan 8, 1863 and died soon after. Don't weep over him. He fell like a hero and Marmaduke and McDonald say that he never flinched amid the show of balls which fell so thickly around him, but led the charge on the enemy with the coolness and gallantry of a veteran. Cols. Sweet and Parsons say that he was the shining star of the 15th Texas Cav. At Pea Ridge, his comrades say that he was always in advance, uncovered and exposed, yet unmoved and immovable. Genl. Henry McCulloch, brother of Ben McCulloch says that he and Stillwell Shirley led the charge at Parakeet Bluffs on Curtis entire Cav, routing them and killing 230, when their Maj failed to lead them. I, with you, will always mourn his untimely death, yet he could not have died in a better cause. He was a second Lt.. George is now a first Lt..

I captured a lot of Andrew militia and killed several. The boys under my command caught Harrison Burns, George Henry Ward, someone else, I don't know who yet, and killed them. They refused to give up their arms, which were navy revolvers, and tried to shoot while in the house, when they were killed in the presence of the women. I could not help it. It was their own fault; they should have surrendered. We got four fine navy revolvers from them. They helped to murder George Breckinridge and old Sam Mason and shot Mrs. Mason in the arm.

You did not get out any too soon. I am going to cross the whole Quantrill regiment, and kill off Andrew Co, every last devil and they know it. You bet, they fly when they hear of me up here. They say I am a damned sight worse than Quantrill and that, my men would sooner die than live. I captured $30,000 in greenbacks on my last raid from the Federal paymaster at Plattsburg. I think our boys killed Bill Ogle.

My headquarters are in Jackson Co. Write to me and tell me how you are getting along, and where you are at. I may do something for you. Don't come back. Tell me what post to direct to. Answer this immediately. Enclose in it a small envelope and direct to Joseph Lawrence, then enclose in a large envelope and direct to James Butts, Liberty, Clay Co, Mo., and don't sign your full name. Better just sign Emma. How had I better send you money, by letter, express or special messenger? I will send you some sometime this summer. Tell me where my cousins are at and who is in the army. Give my love to all.

I was wounded in the head not long ago, but am well now. We, twelve of us, charged 71 Feds. with our navy revolvers a few days ago in Jackson, killing 40 some odd, capturing 50 breech loading rifles, 54 or 55 navy revolvers and about 60 horses, with their equipage and lost only 3 killed, none wounded or taken prisoners.

I remain your son,

Joe

Capt. Commanding 1st Batt., 1st Regt. Frontier Line Brigade of Partisan Rangers, C.S.A.

Cousin Sallie:- I have directed this to you because I do not know where pa or ma are at. Please send it to them and oblige. I wrote you last spring but never received any reply. Yours, Joe

On July 14, 1863 Ed Hinks was sent out to get word to the boys to gather at the farm of Edmund Cowherd in Jackson Co. Francis Cowherd father of Edmund and Charles owned a very large farm there. Due to the varied terrain and vastness of their land holdings both Edmund's farm and his daddy's were a favorite meeting place. From there we headed to David George's farm. David had been killed in late Feb. His wife Betsy was managing with her young children but needed help. We understood the necessity of stopping by when we could. She had a young boy Frank Smith, 17, who was helping her. He wanted to join up with us and finally when Quantrill, Poole and Blunt arrived he was allowed to join. McGrew met them there with specific orders from Genl. Price.

Five days later on the 19th, Tom Campbell and Henry Cowherd were captured and taken to St. Joseph with orders to be shot. They managed to escape along with William Stone. They found a mule which turned out to be blind, but it got them to Todd's headquarters. Did we have a laugh when they rode in. They said they must be the best of the men because they could not only ride a blind mule but get where they wanted on him. Laughing was becoming a rarity among the boys. So many families had been banished, burned out, women raped and husbands, fathers, brothers and sons killed. In some cases, there were conditions worse than dying; men with arms, legs, hands blown off, half of their faces missing, survived, unable to work or contribute to their family's well fare. Many more were continually relying on the pain killing properties of laudanum. There was good news from time to time, someone's birthday, a healthy birth of a child, someone marrying. At the end of July, Synes Cockrell, a brother of Col. Francis Marion Cockrell got married. A joyous occasion that for a little time all seemed normal, except for the pickets posted.

SAINT LOUIS, Mo., July 30, 1863.

Brigadier-Genl. EWING, Kansas City:

Genl. Brown reports a concentration of rebels in Saline Co, under Jackman and Quantrill. Genl. Brown wishes you to send a force from Lexington to co-operate with Maj Kelly, at Marshall. Please do so, if practicable.

By order of Maj-Genl. Schofield:

C. W. MARSH,
Assistant Adjutant- Genl..

Daddy told me about one of the best known frontiersmen, along with Daniel Boone, was Davy Crockett. In 1835, he said, "In my part of the country, when you meet an Irishman, you find a first-rate gentleman; but these are worse than savages; they are too mean to swab hell's kitchen." He was referring to the Five Points where the poorest of the poor of the Irish lived in New York. Now newspapers across the nation were reporting three days of rioting there, a thousand people were reported killed in Hell's Kitchen and Five Points. July 13th to the 16th people rioted protesting the draft provision allowing a man of privilege, with money to pay to get out of service. Wealthy people could pay $300 fulfilling their term of service while the less fortunate had to send not only a son, husband, father, brother, but all who were of legal age to fight were required to enlist with the Northern United States Military. Thank you, President Lincoln, a new way to enslave people, poor white people. Justice in this land treats a man much better if he is rich and guilty over poor and innocent. The Northerners were rich men on the backs of Southern farmers and their slaves. They owned them by extension and did not want to allow the South to sell their cotton to the highest market. If it wasn't coming north, then "there'll be war."

The hot humid Missouri summer was upon us and the creeks were calling. We tied a solid rope high in an old sycamore tree where we could swing out dropping into the cool deep waters. We were boys, children at play, laughing and horsing around, except for the pickets who stood guard guns ready. I headed home as often as I could always taking some of the boys with me, typically it was boys from Ark who were the farthest from home. Rutch Smith married to Miss Jane Walker and his brother in law Green Walker accompanied Frank Gregg to his sister's Mary Francis and Sam Ralston's home a few miles from our farm. A half dozen boys from Evening Shade, Ark from Co D of Col. Tom's command came home with me. We all needed to be where mothers were only satisfied when they knew we had had too much to eat. Momma and Aunt Charlotte would see to it we were all feed and pampered just a little. We hit upon a man by the name of David Mitchell who was riding alone just outside of Liberty. He had a pass allowing him to travel into the prairies of Kansas. That was enough for us. We took his traveling money, pocket knife, rifle and pass. The boys said we needed to leave him with his saddle so we let him go his way telling him to give our regards to Maj Green. The next day on Aug 7th, the incident was reported in the Liberty Tribune. I can hear Momma now, telling us he'd deserved killing and look what our sheepishness had gotten us. She asked some of the boys what exactly was the name of their town as some called it one thing and some another.

They all looked at each other then Perry West nudged Will James, "You tell'em, you're a James." William Henry James had already tried to figure out if his folks and Daddy's were related. We figured somewhere back there, in the old country but we couldn't go far enough back to find the common ancestor. Will volunteered shaking his head at Perry, "the name comes from a big old pine tree that stands on the edge of town. It's been there as long as anyone can remember. It was over 50 years ago people started calling it Evening Shade due to the huge shadow that old tree put across the place come evening." "I reckon we all have places with names like that," Momma said.

We arrived home to find Jesse overseeing a successful tobacco harvest. He had done real good. We walked in the fields just brother to brother. He was becoming a man, solid and hardworking. I told him "Not only am I proud of you, Daddy would be proud." His job of cleaning and loading the pistols and preparing ammunition had been greatly expanded while I was away from home. Bill Gregg had convinced Jesse to dress up like a girl to spy on Federal soldiers in a brothel. He enticed the Madame of the house to allow him to have a party with some of the soldiers. Jesse reassured her he would come back with three more girls and show them all a good time. I reckon our childhood plays had paid off. Twelve soldiers came in expecting to party with girls and instead were taken off guard and killed. Although Jesse himself was not involved in the killing, which Bill Gregg assured me of, this was not the first nor the last time Jesse would be a successful spy. He was a pretty boy appearing younger than he was, few suspected him of riding as a Partisan Ranger. He'd found us back in May wanting desperately to join up, but Momma had only agreed he could go if he would come back to run the farm. After Doc had been hanged more work fell to Momma and Aunt Charlotte, she needed Jesse at home. Respecting Momma's wishes had been hard on him, but he had returned home as promised. But, she was also loosening her hold on him.

Chapter 18

We learned James Morris, wounded in the summer and taken to Georgetown in Johnson Co to recover had been discovered and killed on Aug 11, 1863. I'd been home a few days, when Henry McAninch, William and Perry Hayes, Noah and John Webster showed up headed to Johnson Co. I joined them near Howard's Mill, we were surrounded by Union soldiers. Holed up in a house, the Unionists were coming down on us hard. We knew someone was disclosing our locations but we didn't know who, yet. Kansas jayhawkers were burning down homes forcing people out by the hundreds. William Hayes barely escaped. He caught sight of two Federal soldiers on their way toward the house shooting and killing them both. One of them had a list with the names of people whose houses were to be burned the next day. Brothers William and Frank Beard were killed and Perry Hayes shot through the heart. Henry McAninch was shot through both the arm and leg but managed to mount a horse and escape. When Bloody Bill read the list, he set out a command to notify the people whose homes were on it. Unionists were burning homes, destroying property, violating the women and imprisoning them. Mothers, sisters and wives were arrested on spying for the South, feeding or clothing the guerillas.

Back in June, they arrested and imprisoned three of Jeptha Crawford's married daughters, Laura, Susan and Armenia jailing them in an old hotel in Lawrence, Kansas. Their young children were being cared for by parents and neighbors. Armenia was a widow woman. Her husband Charles Selvey had been killed a year before. If they hadn't been guilty of anything more than taking care of their family when arrested, their momma Betsy Harris made sure they had a reason afterwards when she brought her sons to join Quantrill. Riley was the youngest, 14 maybe 15 years old. Although they were not direct cousins of Cole Younger's, their momma, Betsy Harris was a sister to Reuben Harris, husband of Laura Fristoe, Cole's aunt, his Momma Bersheba's sister. They were family and their daughter Nannie Harris, was an own cousin to the Crawford girls and Cole. Nannie buried her husband Jabez McCorkle on June 2. The Unionists come to her house, saw him dead then come back after she buried him arresting her for having done so. Such evil is their natural inclination; hell is clearly in more than one place.

Jim and Bloody Bill Anderson's sisters, Mollie 16, Josephine 15 and Mattie 13, daughters of William Anderson and Martha Jane Thomason, were arrested south of Westport near the state line returning from buying supplies. The girls were put on horses riding in front of the Union soldiers who had their guns stuck in their sides. When Bloody Bill and Jim tried to rescue them, the Union soldiers said if any of them or their horses were wounded, the girls would be shot. There was nothing more that could be done. Outraged, Bloody Bill spent the summer trying to figure out a way to rescue the nearly 100 women held prisoner in Lawrence, Kansas. Men whose wives, daughters, mother's and or sister's had been arrested were coming asking for help, if not from Quantrill from any of us who they knew might know him or ride with him. Momma and Doc were growing fearful for her and Susie.

Cole Younger and John Jarrette were upset and planning to do something with or without the rest of us. Bloody Bill was in total agreement knowing it would take all of us, this was nothing no one man could do alone. Cole's sister Josie, married to John Jarrette was among those arrested, as well as his sister's, 15 year old Sally and Caroline "Duck" married to George Clayton with two young babies. It was all they could talk about. First, they had killed his daddy, Henry Younger the year before and Jeptha Crawford just six months later and now this. John McCorkle's outrage over his sister in law, Nannie Harris, widow of his brother Jabez arrested for burying her husband remained on everyone's tongue and in their minds. Taking a grieving wife away from her young children, what kind of person did that? The Union wanted to excite and inflame us. Any one of us could be killed and we knew whenever possible we would be taken home for burial. It was the women in our family who was paying for aiding and burying us. John's sister, Charity McCorkle Kerr, wife of Nathan Kerr was arrested for aiding and abetting. Their cousin, Tom Harris, Nannie's brother was beside himself unable to help his sister. He got word she was ill and said to be chained to the bed in the old hotel where they were held prisoner. I was all the more grateful Momma had signed the oath getting her and Susie released. They were safe back at home with Doc and Jesse there with them. He'd disagreed at first, arguing with Momma, not wanting to remain at home but Bloody Bill insisted. He made him understand his duty as a son and brother. He stationed Jesse "at home."

Lucinda "Lou" Munday, wife of guerilla Joseph Gray, and her sisters Susan and Mattie had been arrested for providing food to their brother James Munday, a regular CSA soldier under Genl. Price. William Grindstaff's sister Mollie was among the women arrested, daughter of Samuel and Mary Smith Grindstaff. Union Genl. Thomas Ewing, commander of the Army of Missouri, was responsible for their arrest and imprisonment. He authorized the Union and the likes of Lane and Jennison's commands to arrest any female suspected of aiding and abetting us and they were more than happy to follow orders. The women were being held on the second floor of a ramshackle building, a former hotel used as a tavern and store on the first level. It now houses "service women", prostitutes in the basement for Union soldiers whose barracks were in the adjoining building. The soldiers were guarding the women in the makeshift prison. The hazardous conditions of the building had been reported to Genl. Ewing who had it inspected and deemed safe. However due to its condition, occupants of the building began moving out.

On the morning of Aug 14th, 1863 the unimaginable happened. Any one that knows Kansas winds know how quickly a gentle breeze can become deadly. A sudden gust of Kansas wind hit the building and it collapsed. Rumors immediately spread. The most horrific was the Federalists having undermined the building with the intent of maiming or killing the imprisoned women. The truth was later revealed the Union soldiers and prostitutes had cut away portions of the supporting timbers making for a much easier access entry way between the soldiers barracks and the basement where the 'ladies' were. Although there was no ill intent the act contributed greatly to the collapse.

I was at home when word came that a building in Kansas City housing Confederate women had collapsed with several killed and maimed. "Not "the" building," Momma said. Within the hour, Bloody Bill and Jim rode into the yard confirming the worst. Bloody Bill and Jim were crying, enraged, stomping the ground. Their 15 year old sister Josie was among the dead. Martha Jane "Mollie", 16, was hurt. Mattie, 13, was shackled to a ball and chain inside the building and suffered multiple injuries including both legs broken. In the safety of the farm, Bill was adamant we attack Lawrence, the stronghold of the abolitionists. Long before the War Between the States erupted, we had been living with the Border Wars, Kansas was home to Jamison, Jennison and John Brown, now this.

It didn't take any planning, just the news of the collapse of the building, the injuries and deaths of Southern women. Men, boys, supporters from across the state and Ark, even Kentucky and Tennessee rode to join us. Attacking Lawrence and the men who lived there, those who had been attacking and killing, raiding and destroying our farms and families was something we all wanted to respond to with a vengeance. When Genl. Order No. 10 had been issued forbidding anyone giving aid or comfort to guerillas, which mostly meant our mothers and sisters, women who were relatives. We knew we were the real targets. With more arrests the women were moved to a larger building at 1425 Grand in Lawrence. Although any time news can be downplayed or exaggerated it was known at least 100 women and girls were imprisoned when the building collapsed.

No one could attest if the wounded were getting medical treatment. Were these men who had been wounded on the battlefield they would be treated and likely paroled, let go home. Then word arrived in addition to Josie being killed in the collapse, Susan Crawford Vandiver, her sister Armenia Crawford Selvey and Charity McCorkle Kerr were crushed to death in the collapse. Charity was found in the rubble confined to a bed with a chain. Everyone knew she had had no chance to escape as the building fell. I thought of how happy everyone had been just a couple years earlier when she and Nathan married.

We learned our neighbor, Anderson Cowgill knowing they were making plans to bury Jabez McCorkle, Charity's brother and Nannie's husband, reported the girls "Were rebels and were feeding the bushwhackers." He had offered us food and now we knew why. Mollie Grindstaff sister of William Grindstaff had several bones broken and her back was hurt. Maj Granville Page's wife, Venita Colcord had been there but thankfully her release had been secured the day before. The women held on the second floor building in Lawrence with access only through an outside stairwell had no chance of escape. Over 50 survivors with only minor injuries were placed in the Union Hotel under guard. Of the remaining 50, half died and the other half were severely injured, crippled and maimed. Cole Younger's 20 year old sister, Caroline, fondly called Duck by her family, wife of George Clayton and mother of two year old Ola and baby Justus was among the horrifically injured, scarred and disfigured. She would be dead within a few years.

Charity McCorkle Kerr
Emory Cantey Collection

Nannie Harris McCorkle
and Charity (r)

Caroline Younger
"Duck" Clayton

Before the building collapsed, the Union was planning on deporting them, moving them out of state to prisons either in the north or camps on the White and St. Francis rivers of Ark. This enraged George Todd who threatened to burn down the entire city if the girls weren't freed. And, to Bloody Bill and Jim who unsuccessfully tried to rescue their sisters, they were inconsolable in their rage. We had been talking of a raid on Lawrence and the deaths of these young women was too much. There was no quenching every man's desire to get even. News people gathered to watch bodies being removed and the cries of the surviving women, injured and maimed was macabre theatre. When it was confirmed, Genl. Thomas Ewing knew the conditions of the building, he ignorantly put out stories the women prisoners were digging a tunnel which caused the collapse. Many people believed it, not realizing they were housed on the second floor with no access to the ground.

Quantrill and all the boys went wild as news filtered in. There's nothing as dangerous as a nineteen year old boy with vengeance in his heart. Those of us at home or in small camps, joined Quantrill, knowing there would be a price to pay. We had been planning an attack on the home of Lane for some time with the help of other Partisan Rangers, but when this news came, everyone was ready and the target was no longer just Lane. We held elections filling vacancies created; William Gregg was elected 3rd Lt., Bill Haller 2nd Lt. and Fletch Taylor 1st Lt. under Todd. Nearly 300 of us arrived at the rendezvous at Capt. James Perdee's Farm at Blackwater in Johnson Co on Aug 18th, to discuss and vote on Lawrence. A number of the boys decided to get their pictures made while the commanders were forming a plan of attack including Sgt. Lou Vandiver. I thought of the Mountain Meadows Massacre and how just 5 years earlier how outraged I'd been. Right or wrong, I was beginning to understand "Vengeance is mine saith the Lord." No less than we felt; the Lord was with us, the Mormons believed him with them. We knew attacking Lawrence was exacting God's revenge.

Capt. Cole rode in from Martin Jones Farm, eight miles from Kansas City. William Cunningham came in from the Little Blue along with Capt. Estes and Capt. Boaz Roberts with the regular CSA. He joined us for both the planning and attack on Lawrence. This was not simply our group; we were joined by other southern supporters, bushwhackers, guerilla and Partisan Ranger bands as well as boys and men with no affiliation to any group nor in service. These numbers would allow us to approach from several directions with several independent columns converging with well timed precision; the last group to join us was Col. John D. Holt bringing our numbers to 450. It was nigh 50 miles to Lawrence and with this number of men, ready to attack, we'd make the ride in 2 days arriving just before dawn. George and Fletch rode out ahead and were already in Lawrence before we left Missouri. George Maddox disguised as a farmer and Fletch Taylor as a horse trader were watching the town, gauging responses and gathering information. Fletch stayed at the Eldridge House. A dozen men were sent to secure food sufficient for the ride. Marion Potter's grandpa, Benjamin Potter sold us cured meat, ready to eat as we rode. John Lobb, a black man in our Co, went right into Lawrence, unsuspected, looking around. John Calloo, another of our spies, lived in Lawrence. He moved his family out the night before the raid riding back with us the following day. Recognized, he was captured, confessed his guilt and was hung by the citizens of Lawrence.

During the ride there, men had time to talk, to remember, Jim Lane having sacked and burned one of Missouri's largest towns to the ground. They weren't whispering, they were shouting, "Remember Osceola." Cole ask to be responsible for finding and killing Lane. Some of them even thought we should wait, time the attack for May 27th, 1864, two years to the day Lane had destroyed Osceola. Momentum was building. There was no timing anything like this. Time would have allowed grief to subside and reason to set in. Over the last three months, Lane and his men were responsible for more deaths in Missouri on unarmed citizens than the entire population of Lawrence, Kansas. When the vote was in, women and children would be spared, unless armed. The vote had been close on killing everyone, men, women and all children. Just two weeks before, Kansas officers, Union men killed over 200 people in Missouri and in three months jailed innocent women and girls. Even so, we knew, we understood, we would be remembered differently. Is this how the Mormons felt about Missourians? My mind and my heart were troubled.

Some of the men had ridden over 24 hours to join us lashed themselves to their saddles to prevent falling should sleep overtake them. When we reached the Kansas line, we grouped and rode in columns of four crossing into Johnson Co, then south to Aubry, Kansas. The Union Capt. there brought out two companies. He didn't attack nor did he alert anyone. When the sun set on the 20th we stopped for about an hour to rest and graze the horses before heading on to Spring Hill. The moon was setting when we reached Gardner to the northwest around ten o'clock. With no light we were in need of guides. We stopped at farms along the way. To reach Lawrence moving through the night, we woke 10 men. Expecting each guide could and would alert the enemy, each of the 10 men was killed. The last man was Joseph Stone. His father George Stone had fought in the War of 1812 with the Virginia Militia under Capt. Fitzhugh. His son's George, Joseph, Latrite and Robert secured 160 acres in Kansas on their deceased father's military land grant, some 40 acres each. Around two o'clock in the morning, an advance was sent out, a dozen men each to secure two guides. They went to the farm of Joseph Stone and a Capt. Jackson Jennings. When Stone opened the door he was dragged out to the front porch. When they returned with him, George Todd recognized him as the man responsible for his own arrest at the onset of the war. He immediately wanted to put Stone to death. Just then the others rode up with a young boy, about 15, Jacob Rote. They had seen him and another boy running across a field and rather go to the door of Capt. Jennings, the boys pursued and caught this one. The one escaping, Rote said, was Joseph Stone's son. Knowing Stone's son could be alerting neighbors or sentries, Quantrill gave George Todd a nod. He rode up beside Stone knocking him down to the ground with his foot. Before Stone could get to his feet, Todd straddled him. He beat Stone to death with the butt of his gun.

Lawrence lay to the north and west of the Stone farm. The boy would be our guide. He was a yakker. He talked and talked and those riding near him could be seen shaking their heads, exchanging places with other riders to get away from him. The men were tired and anxious and this boy was getting on their last nerve. We were moving along the banks of the Wakarusa when one of the boys riding next to him told him; "Don't you know who you are riding with?" He responded he didn't care as long as he was treated well. Cocky, he said he might even join up with us. "We are under Genl. Marmaduke and Quantrill is in the lead." He clearly knew who Quantrill and Marmaduke were as he grew quieter but not silent. Quantrill having heard his remark about being treated well moved in next to him. After learning that he did in fact know the way to Lawrence, Quantrill told him his safety was his own duty. Quantrill having lived in and taught school in Lawrence was getting closer to familiar land. He offered the boy his life in exchange for holding horses while we were in Lawrence to which Rote agreed. We arrived on the hill overlooking the town just before dawn.

Quantrill knew the layout of Lawrence, the residences, stores and banks. Quantrill made sure everyone knew where they were going. We entered Lawrence Aug 21st at five o'clock just before sunrise coming from the southeast corner. Quantrill's last order to each squadron was to "Kill every man big enough to carry a gun." The people lay sleeping in their beds as we entered in squads of forty five. The first Kansan killed was Reverend Snyder milking in his yard. Quantrill, Gregg and their squadron took over the Eldridge Hotel establishing it as a temporary headquarters. The 14th Cav on New Hampshire Street was taken over and 17 new soldiers killed. Our familiar rebel yells jolted Jim Lane from his sleep. He managed to flee in his nightshirt into a nearby cornfield making his escape on a farm mule. His house was ransacked and burned. Many of the men continued shouting "Remember Osceola," "Wipe them off the face of the earth." The men looting the saloon got drunk, tied Union flags to their horse tails and rode up and down the streets shooting off their guns. A great many folks unwilling to leave their homes, were burned to death trying to protect their belongings and their person, others were chased through the streets like animals and still others forcibly removed from their beds only to be shot. Nigh on 200 men and boys old, enough to use a gun were killed.

Exaggerations have said we had a thousand men, others 400. The reality was around 450 riders descended on Lawrence in a fury lasting close to 4 hours. We had every intention of burning the town to the ground and killing everyone and anyone that got in the way, men, women and yes, children if they were armed. Not babies, but armed children, the hurt and anger of the injustices out of Kansas had, with the collapse of the building, once again rose to the surface, on every heart and mind of every rider there. These people were the culprits of over a decade of atrocities in the name of freedom, the kind of people that can justify their actions in the name of righteousness. No less righteous than the Mormons believed themselves nor each of us. Every man prayed to the Lord for safety and it was granted. When it came down to it, it was men and boys who were killed, not women and children. About 200 people were killed, half the town burned, stores and banks looted and pillaged. Not a single woman was violated or injured. There was no stopping the mad revenge once it took hold. It was never meant to be a battle, it was meant to be just what it was, an execution of enemies. This was war. These people were boastful and arrogant. Two weeks before one newspaper challenged Quantrill; "Lawrence has ready for any emergency over five hundred fighting men…." They did have such, but the soldiers stationed in Lawrence had returned to Fort Leavenworth.

The folks of Lawrence may have been asleep and thus unarmed, but they were anything but innocent. They were willing to and had committed atrocities. Bloody Bill and Jim, along with Todd, went a little crazy. Pain of losing loved ones will do that. I have never met a man that didn't want to kill the man who hurt his daughter, sister, wife or mother. Bloody Bill did just that. Stories among the men were rampant and likely true that he killed a man while his wife pleaded for his life, another holding a baby in his arms and yet these were nothing compared to what I saw. Men who were assured their safety then gunned down, others bound and burned to death inside their own buildings. I'd heard the stories about Lane and been in some battles and skirmishes. I had heard the groins and screams of the injured, wounded and dying. But this was new to me and sickening. Until Lawrence, I had not fully realized the atrocities the families of our boys had to endue at the hands of Lane, Jennison and Montgomery, with full authority of the Union nor had I fully understood the South's reasoning for succession. Our surprise attack was a swift and furious assault and departure. There was no opportunity to mount a defense. Some of the boys who'd lost their land, farms and family to jayhawkers wanted nothing more than to burn their banks destroying all the notes they held. Others wanted to torture and kill every inhabitant. The folks of Lawrence stood for what Lane, Montgomery and Jennison had done to our families and friends. They blazoned the trail of death, we simply followed.

There were 23 unmustered Union among the people at Lawrence including a young Bob Martin, maybe 14. He was in Union uniform carrying a musket with cartridges, no one knew he was only 14 and even if they had it wouldn't of mattered. He and the other new recruits were armed even if they didn't have time to get to them. Although 14 is young and Momma wouldn't let Jesse join in, most of the boys were just that, boys, 15 to 20, on both sides. Riley Crawford, born in 1847, was the youngest among us. Two of his sisters, Susan Crawford Vandiver and Armenia Crawford Selby, died in the building collapsed. We couldn't have stopped him even if he we had tried. I thought about the story of 11 year old John Watts Jr who found and killed the men who murdered his maternal grandfather, Scotsman, John Knight Bowles, then in the tradition of Indian custom, had taken his grandfathers' name becoming John Watts Bowles, Chief Duwali of the Ark Cherokee. Prior to Lawrence we arranged when the signal to leave was given, we were to depart in all directions in order to avoid pursuit and detection. We scattered and before the 22nd was upon us most had ridden the 40 miles crossing back into Missouri.

Riley Crawford

Jake Rote stayed with the horses at the hotel headquarters, watching as events unfolded in Lawrence. Heading out, Quantrill handed him the reins of a horse, told him to mount up and go home. He rode out with the boys headed toward Capt.'s Creek. We heard one of the boys, Larkin Skaggs, wanting to do just a little more looting lagged behind and got himself killed. It was reported one Negro woman was killed but even the locals considered her death an accident. Maj George Collamore, Mayor of Lawrence had been warned we might attack. He had collected guns arming people. We initially were told people scoffed at him, but in reality, our scouts found most of the people armed. When we attacked it had been one week since the building collapsed. Part of the plan, Todd and Fletch returned to help carry the dead to the Methodist Church which served as the morgue. They secured a wagon and retrieved the bodies of Josie Anderson, Charity McCorkle Kerr, Armenia Crawford Selvey and Susan Crawford Vandiver. No one was guarding the dead, but the injured, maimed and crippled remained under guard and couldn't be rescued. Cole Younger saved both the Methodist Church and the Hotel, places the women would need after we'd left. Todd and Fletch were unaccosted as they traveled back east, two men and a single wagon. The Union didn't realize they had the bodies of dead women in the wagon taking them home for burial. They were quietly buried in the Smith cemetery at Raytown where so recently we had laid Col. Fernando Scott and Boone Scholl to rest.

We had prayed for God's safety and been blessed. Suffering in his grief, John McCorkle said a prayer beseeching God had "any innocent person died, please admit them to Heaven and forgive us as it was not our intent nor in our hearts for the innocent to suffer or die." While Quantrill destroyed a city, Union troops destroyed states. To the winner goes the right to tell history their way. In the summer of 1866, the Gov. of Kansas demanded the Gov. of Missouri turn over several men who took part in Lawrence and the destruction of other Kansas towns. The lawyers decided nothing could be done legally as these were crimes of war. Missouri in turn couldn't do anything about the burning of Osceola, Palmyra, destruction of cities and other raids by Kansan's on homes, farms and towns.

The boys who rode into Lawrence left as men. Capt. Alex Adams, Bloody Bill and George Barnett who had seen his brother killed, home burned and mother left destitute, said he could fight to the death. Bill Basham, Dr. John W. Benson and one armed Ike Berry. Caleb Berry who operated a large farm distillery on Whetstone Creek in north east Callaway Co, James and Dick Berry and John "Jack" Bishop. Lt. Josiah L. Bledsoe was shot in the groin on retreat. The George brothers confiscated a carriage to carry him. He was taken to Lafayette Co and while recuperating was discovered and killed in early Sept. Andy Blunt, Ben Broomfield, John Brown son of abolitionist John Brown, John L Brown regular CSA, Dick Burns, Doc Campbell, a scout, Carlyle, Joshua Carney, Jim Crow Chiles and Billy Chiles' whose wife was arrested by the Union for aiding the guerillas but had not yet been taken to Lawrence. Archie Clements born 1 Jan 1846 only 17 was with us at Lawrence. Samuel Clifton, Cap Cole, Sid Creek, Henry Clay Crenshaw, William Cunningham, Bud and Kit Dalton. One of Dalton's men, Jim Lunn carried the black flag. Mont Daly, John W. Dickers, Warren Thomas "Dock" Doake, William Isom Westerfield

Douglas, David Edwards, Capt. Estes, Ike Flannery, Wesley Benton Gann alias Capt A.D. Jones CSA, William Gaw, Hi George; Hi and John Hicks George obtained a carriage to aid a severely wounded JL Bledsoe. They were in Anderson's party. Dock Doake was a good man. A man who would give you the shirt off his back. He wore mutton chops, mustache and trimmed out hair.

Wood Hite Baxter Mitchell William Hulse

Missouri Valley Special Collections, Kansas City Public Library, Kansas City, Missouri

Andy McGuire Frank Shepherd Tom Maupin

Missouri Valley Special Collections, Kansas City Public Library, Kansas City, Missouri

Bill Gower, Lt. William Greenwood, William Gregg, Isaac Hall and Abe Haller rode. Tom Hamilton was wounded. Jeremiah David Helton and William Hickman were among the boys. Charles Higbee stole the largest amount of loot. He was put in charge of $75,000 that was taken at Lawrence. Brothers, John, Thomas, Tuck and Woot Hill rode together. My kinsmen, Bob James, James Hines, John Jack "Jim" Hines and Ezra Jones (married to Daddy's cousin Linnie James) rode in. Ezra was captured, taken to Little Rock where he died Nov 10th, 1863.

Oth Hinton, brothers Tuck and Wood Hite, my 1st cousins, Henry Hockensmith rode in with Col. John Holt regular CSA. Holt was originally a Union man until Jennison stole his merchandise and burned his property. Genl. Price detailed him to go to Lawrence, Kansas with us. He met us south of the Blue near Chapel Hill. Holt had 104 men which made up about a third of the command. During the Lawrence Massacre, he made his headquarters at the house of H.S. Clarke and saved Clarke's life. Joe Holt, Richard Hotie, William Hulse, John Jackson and three of the Jaynes brothers were there. Cole Younger rescued John Jarrette after his horse was shot out from under him. Payne Jones, John Keagan, James B. Kelly, Nathan Kerr, John Keagan and Dick Kinney rode. Capt. John William Koger had a regiment of men under him. Capt. Joseph Lea and his brother Frank rode together. Joseph was wounded. He was elected first Lt. after Lawrence.

Emory Cantey Collection

Second Lt. James Little and Peyton Long retreated with Anderson's group, chased from Kansas to Missouri. George Maddox was wounded in the retreat. He was later captured but escaped. Joe, Morgan, Dick and William Maddox started out together. Then William got deathly ill near Olathe. He stopped at a farm where the folks took him in so he didn't make it on to Lawrence, when the people found out who he was they turned him in and he was taken prisoner. People wanted to lynch him for his participation in Lawrence, but he hadn't been there. At his trial he was released. His wife was ready with two horses in the alley behind the courthouse ready to flee. When the verdict was announced and William was released they did just that fearing he'd be hung by a lynch mob.

Tom and John Maupin, Dr. Lee Miller and Baxter Mitchell joined us just for the attack on Lawrence. Jesse Morrow retreated with Gregg. Wade Morton, John McCorkle and Andy McGuire left with Anderson's group. The Irish boys, William McGuire, Lee McMurtry, George, Henry, Bill, Tom and William Nolan were with us. George was captured later on and sent to Leavenworth and from there to Alton prison. After the war when he registered to vote, he listed himself as one of "Quantrill's horse thieves" and was denied the right to vote. Pat O'Donnell who was best friends with George Maddox. He was riding with Tom Maupin when Maupin entered a house and found six men hiding. Maupin ordered the men out and Pat shot each one as they stepped through the door. The dead men were left in a pile on the porch. Allen Parmer was with Gregg's group; he killed 23 men. Otho and Sam Offutt were at Lawrence. Mike Parr, Lafe and Hence Parvin, Jack Perry, Marion and Levi Potts; Marion Potts, 16, was murdered shortly after Lawrence. His saddlebags were full of loot. His parents had begged him to leave their house near Blue Springs for fear of his being found and killed. Shortly after leaving his horse returned home with empty saddlebags, a neighbor boy "Litchfield" was seen carrying a shovel. The family believed he killed Marion. They were both 16 and friends. Marion would have told him of the loot. Marion Prewitt, 2nd Lt. Lon Railey, Capt. Boaz Roberts, John Ross, Frank and George Shepherd, John Simms and Larkin Milton Skaggs rode. Lark was the only one of the boys killed at Lawrence. He was a hard shell Baptist preacher. He had quit his church over the issue of slavery. His brother Willis held his arm when DP Hougland voted for Abe Lincoln and Lark wanted to kill him. Lawrence was Lark's first battle. He rode to the City House where he got drunk becoming belligerent protesting he hadn't gotten a fair share of booty. He was shot and dragged through the streets, not yet dead, they threw stones at him. Finally a Delaware Indian took his scalp and threw him into a burning building.

Riding next to Frank Smith, 16 old Jack Swartz carried the black flag. Fletch Taylor led a group of the boys. Blue Thompson, retreating, was shot and killed in Franklin Co, Kansas. During the raid, eating breakfast at the Bullene home George Todd promised it wouldn't be destroyed. Bill Toler and Harrison Trow rode. Louis Vandiver lost his wife and sister in law when building collapsed. Fearing his own rage and possible demise he was among the boys who got their photograph taken before riding to Lawrence. He was so bent on retribution he didn't care if he lived or died. Dan Vaughn, Andy Walker, George Webb and his men. Press Webb who spied for Quantrill; Black Tom Webb stole $3,000 and put the money on a mule that was later killed. He left Lawrence riding behind Cole Younger. Noah Webster was wounded by Federal soldiers chasing him. Warren Welch, Si Whitsett, Andy Weir, Jim Wilkerson, Silas Woodruff, William Woodward, Al Wyatt, Dick Yeager, and Jim Younger were among us. These are the men I know riding with us and who had the right to vote on the decision to attack. Boys by age, men by experience.

They couldn't openly say so, but Genl. Price and all of our Col.s in Ark and Missouri applauded Lawrence. It dramatically impacted how people saw Partisan Rangers everywhere after that. Quantrill had been commissioned as a Col. but now no one wanted to recognize him. His papers from President Jefferson Davis provided to Genl. Marmaduke at Batesville were lost, forever. Frank Smith left with about 25 men to join Shelby. Within day's there was more disorganization among our ranks than organization. Heading home, I planned to join Col. Tom in Ark if not Col. Shelby himself.

On Aug 25th, 4 days after Lawrence, Jim Lane persuaded Genl. Thomas Ewing brother in law of William Tecumseh Sherman to issue order Number 11 effectively banishing people in the four counties nearest the Kansas border; Jackson, Cass, Bates and Vernon, the same counties that suffered the most during the Border Wars. Union and Southerners, people were ordered to leave their homes by Sept 9th. The order included everyone, northern or southern, you had to move if you were in the designated area. Thankfully, our farm was just outside this area and not immediately impacted by the order nor was most of our boys. Jennison who had made indiscriminate raids throughout the Border Wars was charged with eradicating the country of Confederates; he had a renewed license to kill, authorization that his atrocities were not only acceptable but preferable. A mass exodus of people, some say 20,000 people were forced from their homes leaving the area deserted. When they had finished the removal, Bates Co where the old Osage Mission had been at Papinsville, had no one left, not a single family. This became nothing more than a killing field for the jayhawkers and Union who came through plundering and stealing anything left behind, using the excuse they were afraid the guerrilla groups would find ample food. What they didn't realize is, those loyal to the south had hidden resources near their homes and left signs known to us where to find them. Finished with stealing and plundering, the Union and burned everything left, homes, barns and crops. Animals shot and killed. The occasional brick or stone chimney standing in the aftermath became "Jennison Monuments." Jennison was as horrific and successful in his effort as Quantrill at Lawrence. And, no matter how many rode with them, the acts perpetrated were the work of sick minds. Jennison and Quantrill were blamed or given credit depending on which side you stood looking.

The following week the boys dispersed, headed home, joined other bands and moved to join regular troops. On Aug 26, 1863, one of the boys, Thaddeus Duncan was captured and executed in Clinton, Missouri. He wrote a letter to his family and his momma stating he hoped to see them in heaven. Perry Hayes was shot through the heart and died near Howard's Mill. Capt. John Jarrette fed up with things after Lawrence began recruiting for his own command. On Aug 28, Andy, William and Samuel Hayes joined Jarrette.

With the injury and deaths in the building collapse and our subsequent raid on Lawrence, things in Missouri were difficult in Sept with conflicts at Quincy 4th, Hutton Valley, and Carthage 6th, the 7th Bear Skin Lake, into Texas Co on the 12th, near Houston, and the 13th near Salem. Jackson Co the 15th near Enterprise, Horse Creek Sept 17th and Homersville the 20th, LaFayette Co 22nd to 25th, Red Bone Church 25th, Cassville 26th and Newtonia 27th, with hundreds more where a half a dozen men would engage another half dozen. Samuel Ridings had been captured. Three days later his travel companion James Butcher was caught in West Plains, Howell Co trying to make his way to Freeman's camp. Sam he took the amnesty oath a year later and was released. Jim Butcher, he got pneumonia after being transferred to Camp Morton, Indiana. He died there Feb 15th, 1865. It was our jobs to keep these boys information to ourselves until we could get word to their commands, in this case, Col. Tom or to their families. Col. Tom wrote letters to the families of their captures. We would not get word of what had happened to them until after the war was over but he followed up on every man that rode with him.

The men who stayed in and around western Missouri were shot on sight if recognized, men around campfires or traveling in groups of two or more were considered suspect and shot, some completely innocent. The Union used Lawrence as an excuse for continued atrocities against the people of Missouri, both Southern and Northern. We just quit talking about Lawrence. Abe Haller, he was wounded retreating from Lawrence. He hid in the brush near the Texas Prairie where the Feds found him. They so mutilated his body he was almost not recognizable. They scalped him and cut his ears off. Andy Blunt discovered Abe's body and retaliation was like kind, even carrying their scalps on their bridles and belts. Still we did not talk about Lawrence. Quantrill moved from camp to camp but he didn't leave Missouri right away. On Sept 3rd, he and some of the boys who stayed behind with him attacked three steamboats the Mars, Marcella, and Fannie Ogden in Jackson Co. Riding under John Jarrette, Cole Younger, Dick Kinney and Jesse attacked a picket near Wellington, Lafayette Co. After the collapse of the building, Jesse pleaded with Momma to go but she refused. He dare not cross her. After Lawrence, I returned home. Momma allowed Jesse to leave with some of the boys in order to get it out of his system, she said. He had clear instructions to get back home in one piece before Sept 5th, his sixteenth birthday.

Capt. William McIlvaine had been killed at Baker's Creek, Mississippi on May 16th. It had taken nearly 3 months for word to reach home. When Penick's men got word of locals wounded, captured or killed, Union and Confederate they used that information in their efforts to root out sympathizers. Sometimes they would lie straight to a momma's face, telling her boy had been killed in service to the Union or the South, which ever served them in getting the other men in the family. People hid out in caves and made burrows, shelters in the sides of the hills, especially young men who were charged with staying home to protect the family home, their mother, and siblings. Calvin Gayler in Taney Co hid out in a cave with his daughter and wife bringing him food. Southerner's he lost son's Allen, Archie, Joe and Meredith in the war. People remember him today as the Old Soldier of Taney Caney and his hideout as Old Soldier's Cave.

Genl. Marmaduke ordered his "Missouri Col.s" to send at least a dozen of their men to northwest Ark to aide in protecting the munitions efforts, on Sept 1st a Union force under the command of Genl. James Blunt attacked Genl. Bill Cabell near Devil's Backbone in Yell Co. After Lawrence, many of the boys needing to be somewhere else, in different companies, had answered the call and gone to Ark. On Sept 4th near Mayesville in Benton Co, Ark. the boys learned of a movement from the north and sent two scouts out. They were able bodied and allowed themselves to be captured in order to both deliver misinformation and ferret out the plans of the Union. They quickly learned the movement were members of the First Ark Cav out of Cassville, Missouri. They were recovering from a serious drunken state with all of its after effects enabling our boys to escape. They attacked on the morning of the 5th managing to capture one man killing his horse. The Union fell back and set up pickets. Then our force of about 350 men moved on them, they fled into Hog Eye. Col. John Gardner finally surrendered and Capt. William "Jim Ed" Brown proceeded to process twenty two Union prisoners. Gardner managed to destroy his dispatches from Genl. McNeil before the surrender. They had several wounded and only one killed. They were paroled the next day. One of our boys knew the Sizemore family from whom they secured a wagon for the Union to take their wounded and dead back to Cassville.

On Sept 6th, Col. Clark and his men killed seventy five year old Benjamin Potter. He sold us meat in preparation for the ride to Lawrence. Mister Ben was preparing to move as set out by Order No. 11. His grandson, Marion, found the boys the next day and joined Bill Gregg's command. His father and uncle's John, Melchert and Steven fought at Lone Jack. His neighbor John Ryder killed his uncle Steven under mysterious circumstances a year earlier in 62. Melchert drowned in a river in Ark riding with Price's army. In 1865, Marion surprised a regiment of Unionists near Waverly eating breakfast. He was wounded shot in the leg. He and another man escaped and hid in an old farm house where Marion fell unconscious from the wound. They were found and the fella with him was shot. Marion unable to walk was put atop of a casket, carried to a cemetery and shot. Each of us entered the war as boys, innocent even if we understood that good men can do bad things. When a boy is put in charge of burying boys, it changes you. You never see the world in the same way again, no matter what you believe the war to be about. Whether on the death detail, as we became known as, or the rescue or recovery squads, we saw our own reflections in the face of the boys we buried. You don't want to become callus to death. But, survival meant it had to happen. I'd rather have been shot dead than carried on my own casket to the grave to be shot.

On the 9th Col. Cloud with 200 Federalists making their way to the Ark River Valley encountered Col. Ras Stirman. Genl. Holmes had ordered Shelby to do something about CSA deserter and Mountain Boomer leader Anderson Gordon. He chose Bill Gregg and several of the boys to aid him. The Union was trying to secure the route in northwest Ark in order to be able to move forces from there to Little Rock and on to Helena. John Ecket secured a local woman as a spy to lead them to Gordon's camp. Although they had not located Gorden himself, Col. Shelby and Gregg were returning from having destroyed Gordon's camp when they encountered Col. Rasmin fleeing the Union. He had lost cattle and supplies in the attack and was crossing the river. Believing Gordon had family in nearby Lewisburg, Shelby ordered Gregg to send men to locate him there. After several days, they returned reporting they had failed to find him but learned he was now leading a Cav regiment with the Union.

We learned that week the home of Reuben Harris and Laura Fristoe Harris, parents of Tom Harris and Nannie Harris McCorkle, widow of Jabez, 10 miles south of Independence, was burned for sheltering guerillas.

Col. Shelby who had already been proposing a raid into Missouri became even more determined. At Washington, the southern capitol for Ark, Genl. Marmaduke agreed to back the plan even though he stated clearly he didn't see much chance of success in the endeavor. It would at least provide a serious diversion to the Union slowing them and would serve as a rally of support for the people of Missouri and Ark who were becoming overwhelmingly discouraged. On the 22nd of Sept, Col. Shelby and over 500 troops moved north, along the way joined by other troops including many of Quantrill's and Col. Tom's men. On the 27th Capt. Tuck Thorpe joined him. They pulled along twelve ammunition wagons and two pieces of artillery. Capt. Thorpe advised Col. Shelby of an encampment of the Union First Ark Federal Infantry near Haguewood Prairie. It was believed this was a newly commissioned group of irregulars under the command of Mountain Boomer Capt. William Parker. They set up their camp on the Old Military Road at Haguewood Praire in clear site, allowing most of the men to visit their families in the surrounding area. Our boys attacked the Union with Col. Shelby bringing up the rear flank. Fighting for over two hours, the Federalists retreated into heavy timber in the rugged terrain. Local boys who heard the skirmish returned with family members and local Union supporters, swelling their numbers. They retreated and crossed the Ark River at Roseville before making camp that night.

Chapter 19

Jesse made it home for his 16th birthday, Sept 5th, 1863. He was full of vinegar and stories. I could tell this worried Momma. She thought we should go down to Ark for awhile, visit family. All the work that could be done was done on the farm so it seemed a good idea. She was still weeks away from giving birth and Doc would be going with us. He wasn't sound enough to be left home alone but he was in some ways as good as he ever was. There was no arguing with Momma once her mind was made up no matter how much her decision was lacking in judgment. We went by way of family, spending the nights making our way south. We ran onto Col. Tom who ask that I ride again with him and his regiment. He was heading south to the White River. Momma, Doc, Jesse, Susie, Sarah and John Thomas rode behind the troops in their wagon. I felt much safer traveling with Col. Tom than a family in a wagon alone. I gave Col. Tom the names of his troops and their status we had been made aware of.

16 year old Jesse James 20 year old Frank James

Missouri Valley Special Collections, Kansas City Public Library

Momma wanted to visit her own cousin, John Anthony Lindsay at Powhatan, not far from Milligan's Campground outside Strawberry, south of Smithville. Col. Tom obliged her changing direction from West Plains and Warms Springs to move south toward Powhatan. Momma and John had not seen each other since they were children but to them, time had not passed as they hugged and smiled, introducing each other to their families. John made certain Col. Tom and the men were tended to, inviting him to join us for supper. John was the son of Gramma Sallie's brother Jesse Cole

Lindsay, he and Momma were own cousins, children of siblings, grand children of Anthony Lindsay and Alice Cole. Henderson Creswell, riding with Col. Tom was Momma's second cousin. Full of her own news, I had forgotten to tell her of all the family I'd discovered when I'd returned home. She knew she had family, lots of family, here in Ark but when women marry, sometimes it becomes difficult to know who is who. Giving children their mother's last name as a middle name was a way to know but Momma had lost contact with some extended family. She was delighted for the time to be with her cousin John. She told him she was taking her family to see members of their daddy's family, particularly grand aunt, Mary Lucille Poor Mims living at Athens. Momma hoped Aunt Lucy would be able to tell us more about Daddy's side of the family. Momma tried her best to keep Daddy alive for us. It worked for me, but I'm not sure Jesse and Susie understood. They barely remembered Daddy and ask few questions. Doc had been part of their lives for so long, he was their daddy. He was "Pa." Momma lived with Grand Uncle James Lindsay when Gramma Sallie and Gramps Bob moved to Missouri. He died when Momma was in school. Cousin John told Momma he'd heard from Aunt Mary Keene Lindsay, his widow. She was doing well and remained in Stamping Ground, near Owenton. Momma told us if we ever went home to Kentucky she hoped we would make time to visit our kin.

William "Bill" Alexander Arnold

William Napoleon "Babe" Hudspeth

Missouri Valley Special Collections, Kansas City Public Library

Col. Tom stayed on with us, then we moved to Milligan's Campground where we camped again waiting on several of the local men to return from their families. Uz Skidmore's brother's Zach and W.B. William Blair were fighting in other local partisan groups. Married, Uz had headed to see his pregnant wife, Melia Clark and their baby son. Elkanah "Elk" Sipe, 14, joined Col. Tom's Partisan Rangers. His older brothers, Marcus, Rufe, William and Jacob were all regularly enlisted with the Confederacy. Uz would rejoin us in Batesville. I was happy to see Bill Lawrence and Dick Partee again, the Arnold's, Bill Chitwood, Os Dillard and many other familiar faces. It was like an old homecoming, talking as we rode, catching up on families, hunting, fishing, anything but this war. Rather than continue south to Batesville, we moved west some fifty miles to Athens. Col. Shelby along with Genl. Marmaduke was attacking across Missouri. They ordered Col Tom to rendezvous with the Col.s operating in the lower White and St. Francis Rivers, meeting at Batesville for a war conference. He would get there, he said. He was clearly concerned for Momma. She was very pregnant making travel for her difficult, but she said nothing would stop her. There were a few women with Col. Tom's command making it a little easier for her. She had women to talk to. After I had made it safely home through the snow and ice of the winter, I had been full of stories of our family both Mims and James' who lived in Ark. Col. Tom took us straight to Great Grand Aunt Lucy's, on Piney Creek. Aunt Lucy was very much alive and very much "old." Some of the boys thought she was a 100 year old looking at her. She had known Izard Co's first clerk, John Paxton Houston, doing a little cooking for him and some of the early settlers and could call them by name. And, she was living here when the Indians came through forced from their land in the east. Although I'd had the chance to visit, Momma had not seen her since the great revival with Daddy.

1858 Home of Andrew Creswell Harris & Lucretia Jeffery

Aunt Lucy, concerned for Momma, sent one of her hands over to the White House for Missus Avarilla, who was herself with child. Aunt

Lucy wanted them to visit and if Momma needed anything Missus Avarilla was a Jeffery which around here, Aunt Lucy assured Momma, "meant everything." Visitors were a welcome site, troops and all. An impromptu party was brought together with pies and cakes, friends and family arriving all day and well into the night as word got out family was here and Col. Tom. We came through Creswell named for the kin, Ben, Henderson and Frank, and they had a island in the river named for them. They were having their own sort of family event. Andrew Creswell Harris of Co H, was married to Lucretia Jeffery. They lived across the river a little south a little of White House Crossing at Forest Home near Mister Flannery's place. Missus Lucretia and Avarilla were own cousins, daughters of brothers. Missus Lucretia's daddy, Jehoiada was the first family to settle the area of Mount Olive in 1816. We had three William Arnold's with us, Will Alexander son of Tho, Willie Joe son of Elisha and Will Otho son of Ephraim and Mary Byler Arnold.

Mary's brothers John and Joe Byler were riding with us. They too lit out on their own but gave us directions to their respective homes. These boys would remain friends throughout our lives. We would be there when Will Otho married the year after the war was over to Miss Charity. Ambrose Culp, his momma was one of those Jeffery's. Elbert Benbrook and his son Charlie headed home, across the river near Old Man Flannery's. Babe Hudspeth had family nearby. Bruce, Bob and Jim Campbell, brothers, sons of James and Jane McDaniel Campbell lit out for home. James Riley Kelley headed towards Buckhorn, he wanted to see his wife and new baby boy William. A few of the boys went on to Riggsville, John Ambrose Killian, Co E, along with Willie T. Kendrick had left earlier headed to his Momma's, a widow woman, Elizabeth Gregory Kendrick at Wild Cherry. Baltis Hinkle went home to his wife, Missus Mariah McEntire and their children. I looked at the brothers, sons, fathers, uncles, families that were risking everything and I knew my time as a soldier without my brother was over. Momma allowing him to join in the steamboat attacks had only whetted his appetite for more. Much to Momma's dismay, those few times operating as a spy and serving as an extra gun hadn't deterred him at all. I knew, the time was at hand he was to join us.

Jesse was anxious to be doing more than visiting family. He'd had a taste of guerilla warfare and now he was no longer the hanger on, he was telling his own tales. He and Jeff, Andy and Ben Cooper went to a nearby Indian shelter exploring. When they got back, they had gone to the cemetery where John Paxton Houston brother of Genl. Sam Houston of Texas was buried. Jesse was full of stories how John Paxton Houston had faked his death to get away from his wife and debtors, came to Ark and held office here, hiding out only to be discovered by his younger brother Genl.

Sam Houston. They had duked it out. The boys were full of local stories and for a night, Jesse seemed to forget the war.

Bill Chitwood joined us. He talked about a girl, Sarah Fulks who he wanted to make his wife. She was related to the Grigsby and Houston's. Jesse began pestering anyone that lived here on the best route through Indian Territory to Texas. He was thinking he could join up with Quantrill there. Momma pregnant and beat down from traveling was relenting. With several of the boys agreeing to ride along, she finally agreed, "Go on Dingus," (you little shit.) I smiled to myself, knowing what she meant. Aunt Charlotte was visibly upset but said nothing as she helped Momma and Aunt Lucy prepare some food for him. I heard her chastise him, "You go on Dingus, don't you git yournself kilt. Your Momma couldn't stand that." I knew Aunt Charlotte was worried Jesse wasn't cured up enough. He'd always been a little on the sickly side and his two Momma's, they neither one wanted to let him too far out of sight. Bill Wilson, Bill Chitwood, Osby Dillard, John Burton Canard son of our friend A.W. "Wimps" and several others volunteered to go along. It was Col. Tom who settled matters announcing his men were going on to Batesville to meet up with other Col.s for a war conference and after that, any man could make a decision if they could better serve the Confederacy by heading south to Texas with a boy or remain with him. For a while, that settled the matter. Momma looked thankful for Col. Tom's strong presence. He was a big man towering over most of us, we felt like boys. Momma rested a day or so, then rather than go on to Batesville, Doc took Momma, Susie, Sallie and John Thomas returned home. Col. Tom sent two of his men from Missouri to accompany them.

Chapter 20

When folks found out I was riding with Quantrill's Partisan Rangers, they were constantly asking questions, especially about Lawrence. Having suffered at the hands of jayhawkers themselves, no one disagreed with what happened. Everyone knew someone killed, tortured or everything they owned stolen or burned in front of them. I saw no judgment in the eyes of the people I met. That understanding made a lasting impression on me. I saw people who took care of each other, friends were family and family meant everything. There was a code in these hills I hadn't seen before. People freely talked about their rich Scottish, Irish and British ancestry but when it came to being Indian most would only say, "the Indians left after the reservation ended." Their dark skins and deep eyes told the truth but it was not to be said aloud.

I rode with Col. Tom east to Batesville making camp at the springs north of town on Oct 4th, 1863. He was expecting other Cols as well as reports from a number of local men who patrolled the White River both below and above Batesville. Orders were to continue maintaining the munitions efforts, safeguarding rivers above Jacksonport, focusing on capturing supply wagons and wrecking havoc. We were setting up camp north of Batesville when Capt. Carroll Wood of Shelby's regiments assigned to Batesville rode into camp with a couple scouts. Troops routinely foraged for food while keeping an eye out for the enemy. We jumped for joy at seeing each other, confirmation we had survived. Seeing someone from home with memories other than war, he said it was the sign he needed. "Sign for what," Jesse asked stepping from behind. Carroll was shocked, demanding to know that we were not using boys like this in our regiment. Although most of the men who made up our group were in fact between 15 to 20, Jesse was not among them. Momma allowed Jesse to remain with me in Ark giving over final say to Col. Tom.

After recovering from his shock at finding me among the men, Carroll pointed out he had met this young woman, Nannie Wilson and promised to marry her. "She's the prettiest girl in the whole of the state of Ark," he said. I had to agree, having met her back in the winter months myself. His men made camp on the farm of Col. Desha on the south west side of the White River utilizing the barracks we'd erected. When he returned after being released as a Union prisoner of war back in the winter, he'd made his way to Batesville. Col. Shelby's camp on Col. Desha's farm was frequented by the Batesville belles' who had entertained themselves by visiting the soldiers, bringing food, making repairs to their clothing and much more. Nannie placed herself in charge of aiding the soldiers, earning it the name, "Camp Nannie Wilson." Carroll was in ill health recovering from his time in the prison camp. He was treated and cared for by the lovely Miss Nannie Wilson. Constantly by his side she made arrangements for him to be taken to their home, Catalpa Hall on the north side of Batesville. Several of the more serious cases of illness and wounds were taken in by families throughout the area much better suited to their care and recovery than tent life. Now, since he had someone from home who could and would stand up for him, this was it. This was the time. Again, Jesse with the "Time for what?" "He is green isn't he," Col. Tom announced. He had come upon where we were standing without any of us noticing. Col. Tom was delighted with Carroll's news. "It should be grand," he said. "As grand as any wedding should be, forget that we are at war."

Carroll a 2nd Lt. in the Missouri State Guards was arrested in Jan 1862 charged with recruiting within Union lines. He was held over at Gratiot Street Prison at St. Louis then transferred to Alton, Illinois Military Prison and on to Camp Chase, Ohio. For nearly a year he starved, nearly froze in the winter months and almost died from illness. He signed his parole in Dec 1862 to avoid the winter months but was held until March 17, 1863. He made his way to Batesville there recovering at the hands of the beautiful Nannie Wilson. Three months later, he was captured again in Fayette, paroled and released the same day. After we left Liberty, Genl. Price appointed Carroll as Lt. and Adjunct D.C. to Col. Shelby's command. He was running with Ki Harrison and John Moore's guerilla band under Col. Shelby's directions. We figured out we had been at the same places more than once but with upwards of 2,000 to 10,000 men, we'd not crossed paths until now.

Carroll explained after he'd been released from Camp Chase, he'd made his way back to Ark looking for Col. Shelby. Sick and worn down, Nannie had cared for him. Fairing a little better than most he had managed to capture her heart. Carroll knew Nannie's own cousin, Emily Weaver, daughters of sisters, was serving as a spy for the Confederacy and he'd solicited her help in the matter. I'd met both girls back in the winter. I easily understood how Carroll could fall in love with Nannie. After her father John Rhea Wilson died in 1845, her mother, Emily Scott Burton, moved from Pennsylvania to Batesville with her sister Mary, Emily's mother, to be closer to family members. Widowed, Emily Wilson met and married William Byers. Born in 1810, William, an early founder of Batesville built Catalpa Hall. He was 12 years older than Emily. It was there Col. JoeC Porter had faded into unconsciousness and died. Emily's daddy, Abram Weaver was a staunch Unionist and had joined the army in Pennsylvania. Her three older brothers, Abram, Burton, and Robert joined the Confederacy. Their first few years in Batesville were unremarkable. When war was declared Emily and Nannie initiated and organized the girls of Batesville providing care to the sick and wounded, reading to them and writing letters home for them especially in the winter of 62-63.

Carroll told us young Emily had been captured. She was making her way to Memphis to see her daddy who had mustered out of the army and relocated to Memphis as the family had planned prior to the onset of the war. The rivers were swollen requiring an overland route to St. Louis then taking a river boat south to Memphis. Her cousin Charles Burr, war widow Eleanor Ann Keithly King from Batesville and former CSA soldier Lee Tilley who was working for Emily's uncle Edwin Burr, were traveling with her. On June 5th, they arrived at St. Louis. Charles Burr went to school, Tilley had some business to attend to so Emily, Mrs. King and new friend Laura Linglow went to stay with King's father in law in Rolla, Missouri. There Mrs. King was arrested by the Union. Emily and Laura Linglow returned to St. Louis. On June 20th, Emily was arrested on unknown charges by two men and a squad of Union soldiers and taken to the Female Military Prison in St. Louis. Her uncle, Edwin Burr went to Memphis to see Emily's father who had just received a letter from Emily explaining her situation. Her Uncle hired attorney H.F. Fairfield on July 25th. On Aug 2, she was charged with being a spy after her cellmate; Mary Ann Pittman testified she disclosed details to her. Emily was sentenced to hang. On Aug 15th, her Uncle Edwin Burr was arrested. With intervention from his Union friends, he was able to secure his release. It was not until Sept that her daddy made his way to St. Louis, by then Emily's case was falling apart. They had nothing more than Pittman's word. Cole Younger's own cousin Missouri Woods, daughter of his daddy's sister Elizabeth Younger and Thomas Woods, was arrested and placed in the cell with Emily. Together the women planned and succeeded in escaping from the prison using a skeleton key. Emily's daddy and uncle were arrested on Sept 25th because of their escape. Burr was again able secure his own release but not Emily's daddy who remained jailed. Emily arrived back from St. Louis and was in much need of a party. The wedding would provide just such diversion. Col Tom listened intently to Carroll's story. Himself a lawyer, Col Tom told Carroll that it was likely the Union would release Emily's daddy but not until something was done about her case. He would make inquires toward getting her case dropped. Missouri Woods returned home to Clay Co. These girls were brave southern women unfailing in their acts.

While the local women readied for Carroll and Nannie's wedding, us boys and men swapped stories. Hampton "Hamp" Lynch Boone Watts, the great grandson of Daniel Boone bugged everyone about who might be of kin to him when he learned there were a number of Watts living here. He was the baby of the Co, only fifteen maybe sixteen. He had no facial hair and looked every bit a girl as Jesse. He was a pretty boy. I inquired about "the reservation" I kept hearing about. I was surprised to learn these lands had been an Indian reservation and the first slaves here were those brought by Chief John Watts Bowles. This got Hamp's attention as the men started telling us about the local Cherokee history. Chief Watts was known locally as Chief Duwali, the Osage word for "Bowl," he was Chief of the Ark Cherokee until he was killed in Texas in 1839. This Chief fascinated me. He was the young boy of 11 who killed his grandfather's murderers. Quantrill would have been very interested in these half breed Indians who lived in this part of the country. Their tactics of warfare were not unlike his, a fact not lost on Jesse. One of the local boys told of James Monroe Watts, born during the forced removal of the Cherokee through Ark had been captured, paroled and forced to join the 1st Ark Cav in Feb near Fayetteville. There were lots of Chief Duwali's family and his grand children here in Ark and those men were as ruthless as any of the guerillas they were hearing about in Missouri and as good at riding horses. With no on here able to tell Hamp if his Watts were of kin to Chief Duwali's Watts, we talked about our horses, Missouri Fox Trotters from the days of the Missouri Territories and what fine horses they are. Col. Tom introduced us to Richmond Pinkney Williamson from upriver at Wild Haws Landing, he'd shook our hands saying, "call me Pink". He and his father in law Sam Moser maintained a beautiful race track on the river's edge. Pink's wife, Catherine "Missus Kitty" had been married to John F. Bowman and had two sons, Samuel Alexander and John F. Jr. Pink and Missus Kitty had Tom, Kitty, Oma and J.W. called Dub. I learned many people who lived here had Indian in them. They stood to lose their land if they claimed their Indian heritage, so they married whites, took white names and simply quit talking about being Indian. Several of the boys, especially Jake Freeman, knew their horses, which turned all of our attention to him. He was married to Amanda Dixon, part of Sam and Will's family. Jake was of distant kin to Col. Tom and their cousin John Calhoun Freeman at Big Flats. Horse racing was something a lot of us enjoyed. The group of us talking horses made plans to race at Pink and Sam's track. Indeed talk was nothing of war, life was normal for a night.

Along with many other slave holding families along the border of Kansas and Missouri, Carroll Wood's family, like ours never knew life without conflict, without attacks that ended in homes burned, crops decimated and lives lost. Although the War Between the States would officially end in 1865, for us the conflict didn't end, no more than it began with gunfire at Ft. Sumter. There would be no delay on this happy occasion. Capt. Carroll H. Wood married Nancy Mary Wilson, seven years his junior, in fact, my age, that night 2 miles north and east of Batesville at Catalpa Hall. About 50 of us attended the wedding. Reverend George W.

Kinnard, a man of the Baptist faith performed the wedding. His son was riding with Col. Tom. Of course, the marriage was forbidden by the Union and considered illegal. Southerners loyal to the Confederacy were not allowed to marry nor were preachers not signing an oath of allegiance allowed to marry anyone. None of us were dancers but the girls were intent on making this night one to remember. Carroll and Nannie made Batesville their home. They were'nt able to officially record their marriage until 1866, three years later. Carroll told me it was a bit difficult since Rev. Kinnard died in 1864, just a year following the wedding. Thankfully, Nannie's step daddy William Byers was able to get it recorded for them. Jesse and I visited Carroll and Nannie throughout the years, alone and with friends.

William "Bill" Martin Lawrence

Allen Hazard Parmer

Missouri Valley Special Collections, Kansas City Public Library, Kansas City, Missouri

Nannie entered the great hall to a lone violin, played by Bill Wilson, turned fiddle when it was time to dance. Black Tom Webb played the fiddle left handed and those two boys were joined by more musicians gathered in one place than I'd ever laid eyes on. Black Tom was shy but looked like a dandy, small but dapper. He had a sharp looking hat, clean face and short hair. I'm not sure he even had to shave. He was probably grateful to play because it gave him an excuse not to have to talk to the girls. Black Tom's brother Press had advised Genl. Price in a number of engagements and was enjoying talking with the older men in the crowd. Tom and Press rode with us at Lawrence. Tom's horse was shot out from under him. He'd rode out behind Cole Younger. They were the sons of Asa and Mary Bridges Webb, neighbors in Jackson Co. Conrad "Coon or Mad Dog" Becker danced with every girl there. He was clean shaven except for a little tuft of a mustache with short brown hair. Allen Parmer was too shy to dance with anyone except the older women. Everybody that joined us at the White House and Aunt Lucy's was here in full force plus half the town of Batesville; the half not Union. There were extended family of Blair's, Porter's, Chitwood's, Arnold's, Grigsby's, John Bailey, Corp. Black, John and Joey Byler, Billy Hinkle and his sister Martha, Sam Bigham, John Huddleston, John Kelley, Burr Lafferty, Scrap Young, Gill Landers, John McEntire, Bob and John Richardson, Jesse Riggs, Josh, John, David and Joe Shelton, Tim Thompson, Hart Walker and Bill Cooper. Most of the men from Col Tom's Co were from these parts: Ambrose Culp, William Freeman, Wat Grimmett, Charles and Bert Benbrook, and Bill Lawrence who brought his wife who was very pregnant.

Scrap Young was the son of fellow Kentuckian Lewis George Young and Sarah Cooper. Joseph B. Gibson "Scrap" Young, earned his nickname as a young boy always more than willing to get into a scrap with someone. A Sgt. under Col. Shelby he'd come with us to Ark instead of going home to his Daddy's place in Warren Co, Missouri. His Momma died before the war broke out. He was sick from the long trek into Batesville. One of the local doctors, Dr. John Smith came from Moorefield to tend to us. He brought his daughter Delia with him. Scrap was head over heels making time with Miss Delia. Scrap, a handsome fella, wore a full beard and trimmed hair. Friends and family arrived hoping for news of loved ones and when the wedding took place, there was food, friends, family and fun. A day when life appeared normal, as childhood friends met for the marriage of the other, when I was simply the best man.

I wished Momma had stayed. Daddy's cousin Burwell Lee came to visit the day after the wedding. A minister in Batesville himself, Rev. Burwell Lee was raised Baptist, but at the age of 16 converted to Methodist. By July 2, 1831, he moved to Batesville rather than Missouri answering the call from Christian organizations to plant churches throughout the lands west of the Mississippi, especially north Ark and Missouri. In 1835, he presided over the organization of the Methodist Society during the first year of the new Ark Conference and was appointed presiding elder. He served as pastor of Batesville Methodist Church before retiring. In 1849, Burr was one of the founders of Ebenezer Methodist Church near Moorefield. In later years this church was renamed "Lee's Chapel" in his honor. Over his 43 years of service, he performed hundreds of marriages in the area, served as Co Treasurer of Independence Co and was a member of the Batesville City Council. He continued to minister and perform "illegal" marriages throughout the War Between the States and Reconstruction. William Burwell Lee was born in 1806, in Davidson Co, Tennessee to Charles Braxton Lee and Elizabeth Hatcher, the paternal grandson of Stephen Lee and Ann Poor. My daddy, Robert Sallee James was born on the Big Whipperwill Creek, in Logan Co, Kentucky in 1818, the son of Reverend John Martin James and Mary "Polly" Poor. In 1845, Zerelda Mims, named for my momma, was born in Woodford, Logan Co, Kentucky to Reverend John Mims and Mary James, Daddy's sister, the paternal grand daughter of John Robert "J.R." Mims and Mary "Lucy" Poor of Athens, the maternal granddaughter of Reverend John Martin James and Mary "Polly" Poor; Burr, Daddy and Zee were third cousins, Poor descendants. Not to mention Zee was doubly related to Daddy, his niece, being the daughter of his sister. I found in Ark an extension of our families in Missouri, Poor, James, Mims and Lee. This place on the White River, between Batesville and Calico Bluffs would become a safe haven for us, a place where friends were family and family ties were thicker than blood. This was home and Col. Tom's men were protecting it. I felt safe here among friends and family.

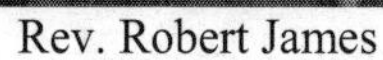

Rev. Robert James Rev. Burwell Lee Zerelda Mims

Home in Missouri, Capts Tom Garrett and John Hicks George made decisions to leave Quantrill joining Shelby. On Oct 1st, Quantrill called the rest of the boys together in Johnson Co to begin the ride to Texas. Over 400 guerillas met up at Capt. Perdee's place. There they were formed into 4 companies, Bill Gregg, 24 year old, George Todd 25, Bill Anderson 23 and Dave Poole 25. Bill Gregg would be riding south with Quantrill, leading a Co of 100 but he too had already decided come spring he too was joining Col. Shelby. I left the group the first of Sept returning home and when Jesse arrived as a family we had headed south to Ark. The wedding lasted well into the hours of morning. Carroll got to stay behind a few days while the rest of us under Col. Tom headed northwest. After the war conference, Col. Tom had not only agreed Jesse and a number of the boys could head south to Texas but used them as couriers to the Camp Lewisburg at Springfield and on to Fort Smith.

While we recovered from a night of partying after Carroll's wedding in Batesville, Ark, at Baxter Springs, Kansas, Oct 6th, Quantrill and the boys began the trek south. They discovered a newly built Yankee fort directly in their path. Quantrill split the boys into two groups with Bill Gregg and Dave Poole leading one group and Quantrill leading the rest attacking from the opposite side. Bill and Dave caught the soldiers at the fort by surprise. They killed a few but most were able to make it safely inside the fort, from there launching a counter attack. As Quantrill and George Todd went around the fort they spied a Federal column of wagons escorted by 100 Cav. The soldiers were an escort for Genl. James Blunt, one of our least favorite Unionists, enroute from western Kansas to take command of Fort Smith, Ark. The Union captured it a few weeks back and Blunt was assigned as the new commander. The soldiers escorting Blunt thought the boys dressed in their Union blues were a greeting party from the fort at Baxter Springs. Unable to hear the fighting taking place on the other side of the ridge, Blunt ordered the soldiers to form in ceremonial ranks.

It didn't take long though to recognize the men facing him were guerillas, not Union soldiers. Outnumbered 2 to 1, Blunt's panicked troops broke rank and fled. Genl. Blunt's military band was in one wagon. Mrs. Chester Thomas was traveling with Blunt's Co to join her husband, a military contractor who had become ill. She and Blunt were able to mount horses and gallop away. Fleeing Blunt held the reins of her horse. The boys let them go because of the woman. Attempting to flee the musicians in the band wagon turned too sharply breaking loose a wheel stranding them. Bill Greenwood and Bill Gregg ordered them killed. John William Koger was wounded and William Lotspeich killed. Frank Fry pulled Bill Roder up behind him after his horse was shot out from under him; they were both shot and killed. John Franklin Fry was the son of John Fry and Mary Humble, Kentucky expats. Everyone envied the beautiful buckskin coat his momma had made him. He wore what we called mutton chops, shaving only his chin. Bill Roder was one of the Black Dutch boys.

Our boys piled the bodies of the Union on top of the band wagon and set it on fire. John McCorkle, Otho Offutt, John Ross, George Shepherd, Fletch Taylor, George Todd and Dick Yeager took out pursuing the fleeing soldiers. Of the 100 Union escorts, the boys killed 85 wounding the rest who witnessing the boys in action, I'm certain wished they were dead. Peyton Long captured Adjunct Genl. H.Z. Curtis, son of Maj Genl. Samuel Curtis, a deeply hated man among us. He had issued the order Federal soldiers were to take no prisoners from among the irregulars, Partisans and guerrillas. Highest on Curtis' list were Quantrill's men, us. Peyton asked him if he would obey the order if he had captured guerillas instead of being captured himself. When he said "yes," a single shot to the head by Peyton killed him. We knew this would make things worse when Union Maj Genl. Samuel Curtis learned of his fate at the hands of "Quantrill's men." He hated us and we felt of like mind towards him.

Quantrill was jubilant, shouting his own self worth, Lawrence now Baxter Springs. More important he had come closer to capturing Genl. Blunt than both Genl. Marmaduke and Shelby. Blunt was a hated man among the ranks, responsible in large part for Union successes at Prairie Grove, Van Buren and Cane Hill. He was the biggest thorn in our side in Northwest Ark and the Union was adding insult to injury having made him commander at Fort Smith. Riley Crawford, who lost his father Jeptha in Jan and his sisters, Susan and Mina in Aug, killed in the building collapse at Lawrence got drunk on captured whiskey. He pulled a saber off one of the Union and was jumping on the dead bodies. Standing on one putting the saber in the middle of his back he shouted, "Get up, you Yankee son of a bitch." Riley stumbled backwards nearly falling to the ground when the soldier jumped up. Everyone was wide eyed but without hesitation Riley rammed his saber deep, killing him dead. Not only had the boys found whiskey in the canteens of the dead soldiers they captured Blunt's ceremonial flag, his new uniform with new boots and cavalry sword. Rarely did Quantrill drink, but his own self worth had gone to his head and he joined the boys. Heading on to Texas the boys told Riley he should have his picture taken with the sword and sent home to his Momma. Willie Bledsoe shot in the right leg and left shoulder was losing consciousness. They put him in one of the wagons. John William Koger was put in the wagon with him. Willie died but the boys didn't want to bury him in Kansas so they kept moving. The warm Oct weather was having its effects and John began complaining about the smell. They stopped in a field near Fort Scott on the Fort Gibson Road and buried Willie. He was an old man for this group of boys, at thirty three and married to Mabel Melton. They had a houseful of kids, older than most of the boys. I worried about the married men among us. What would happen to their families?

Fearing John couldn't make it the entire route to Texas, they took him to a house near Big Creek in Cass Co to be looked after. While there Union soldiers came but the woman of the house managed to convince them John was her sick husband in bed with pneumonia. The doctor with the soldiers offered to examine him but she convinced him their own doctor was enroute and he was better off not disturbed. John had his four loaded pistols in the bed with him and it's certain the doctor would have been killed and likely a few others before they captured or killed him. Riley musta talked all the way to Texas about how that Yankee tried to fool everyone playing dead but he'd caught and killed him. Further along the way they camped near Genl. Stand Watie's men who had learned Doc

Benson who had been captured in Sept had been court martialed on Oct 6th. Doc Benson was a good man. He had sandy brown hair, he wore pushed to the back. He had a beard under his chin, the rest of his face shaved. He wore a dress coat of the kind every gentleman desired. At the graveyard Doc was forced to sit on his own coffin, shot before a firing squad, riddled with bullets. They would do this to Mormon John D Lee when he was tried and convicted of leading the Mormon Mountain Meadows Massacre.

Crossing into Cherokee Nation west of Fayetteville, Ark, the boys were near Cabin Creek when Capt. Emmett Goss leading 30 Kansas Jayhawkers and Federal Cherokee charged them; the same Emmett Goss former neighbor of Marcus Gill's. Our boys survived, no one killed but several hurt. They killed all but three of Goss' men. Later years it was said Jesse killed Capt Goss but he didn't ride with them through Kansas nor Indian Territory. He'd gone with us to Ark and did not catch up with Quantrill and the boys until after crossing into Texas at Colbert's Ferry. The advance guard had already set up camp at Mineral Springs about fifteen miles north west of Sherman, Texas. Jesse and the boys arrived in time to clean up for the ride to McCulloch's headquarters at Bonham. Genl. Kirby Smith advised Genl. McCulloch once they arrived to use the boys to capture deserters and bring in recruits.

A week later Quantrill wrote an official report to Genl. Sterling Price. He was vague about Baxter Springs and Lawrence exaggerating the other small skirmishes and successes against the Union. Along with the report the courier was to present Genl. Blunt's flag, official paper's and saber. When Genl. Price received the communications, he was eager to read Quantrill's report expecting details of Lawrence. There were none. He didn't know what to make of all that was being said about the raid. Genl. Kirby Smith ordered Genl. Maxey to bring the majority of the guerrillas, irregulars and Partisan's into Louisiana. John Jarrette was under the orders of Genl. Smith to stop contraband trade and clear out cotton thieves, speculators and spies along the Louisiana border on the Mississippi River. The town of Floyd, Louisiana was about 600 miles from Liberty. It was south of Ark on the Mississippi River due north and west of Jackson, Mississippi about 100 miles into Louisiana. An easy place to apprehend scoundrels from either side attempting to move their contraband, the boys headquartered there. Cole Younger, Dave Poole, William Greenwood and Joseph Lea were each put in charge of groups to guard the Mississippi under Genl. Kirby Smith's orders.

The guerrillas under Capt. Joseph Lea's leadership fought at Wilson's point, Tester's Ferry on Bayou Macon, Goodrich's Landing, Omega, Tensas Parrish, Horse Shoe on the Mississippi River and the Lum place on Will Bayou in Madison Parrish. Cole Younger and William

Greenwood captured a cotton train near Tester's Ferry, Bayou Macon, Louisiana. Greenwood was in charge of taking the money, $180,000, cotton wagons and mules back to Bastrop. Greenwood commanded a squad of 10-25 men patrolling the Mississippi River. About five miles from Goodrich's Ferry on the Mississippi River, he and Thomas Little were wounded. Mac MacBurgess was with Jarrette at Goodrich's Ferry when they captured 27 wagons and killed and wounded several Federal soldiers in the battle.

Capt. Joseph Callaway Lea
Missouri Valley Special Collections, Kansas City Public Library

Capt. Joseph Callaway Lea was the son of Dr. Pleasant John Graves Lea and Lucinda Frances Callaway. In Dec 1861, Joe and his brother Frank were gathering corn from the field when they were arrested by Jennison's Jayhawkers, by then official militia of the Union. They had already made several arrests and had captives with them. Realizing they were going to be killed, Joe and Frank managed to escape and were still within hearing distance when the Jayhawkers killed the rest of their captives, all young boys. They knew it would not be safe to return home so they enlisted in the Sixth Missouri Cav. They got word to their daddy. Their momma had died in 1857. The Lea's were among the earliest settlers of Jackson Co. Dr. Lea had been postmaster of Big Cedar in 1855. Like Doc, he was an educated medical man, not a country doctor trained under other local doctors or during wartime. Before a year passed, Aug 1862, Jennison's, Lane's or Montgomery's Jayhawkers returned. They rode into the yard and when their daddy went out to see what they wanted, he was shot and killed. They looted the house, burned it and the barn, taking the carriage and horses. After the war, I went to the official dedication when Strother was renamed for Dr. Lea. Someone failed to make their letters perfect or thought it was Lee instead of Lea, so Strother became officially Lee's Summit.

Col. Shelby was wrecking havoc in Missouri. Jesse Muse a private in Co K with Col. Tom had been captured on Oct 2, in Oregon Co. While we were in Batesville preparing for Carroll and Nannie's wedding, on Oct 4th, Col. Shelby attacked Neosho, Missouri with 1100 men. They shelled the courthouse forcing Union Capt. Charles McAfee and his 200 men to surrender. Some of his men captured communications on the 11th:

Report of Capt. Charles B. McAfee, Sixth Missouri State Militia Cav (Union), to Col. J. Edwards, Commanding Southwestern District of Missouri, Springfield
SPRINGFIELD, Mo., Oct 10, 1863.

COL.: I have the honor to report that, in obedience to Special Orders, No. 197, from Headquarters Southwestern District of Missouri, dated Oct 2, 1863, I moved from Newtonia at 8 a. m., Oct 4; arrived at Neosho at 11 o'clock, on my way to join Maj [A. A.] King in the field. Not learning anything of the whereabouts of Maj King, I immediately started in a southwest direction, on the Buffalo road, in search of him, and when I had marched about 2 miles from Neosho, I met Coffee's band of guerrillas, about 300 strong. They formed line, but immediately fell back, and started through the woods in direction of Neosho. I sent messengers back by the road to apprise the guard (left with stores and baggage at that place) of their approach, and moved my column by small circuit back to Neosho, and entered the town on one side at the same time that the rebels entered it on the other. We opened a brisk fire upon them, driving them back. They recovered in a few moments, and again moved upon the town, and at the same time I discovered three or four different bodies of rebel Cav approaching from different directions. I saw that it was impossible to cut our way through their lines. We therefore immediately occupied the brick court-house and again drove them out of the town. We remained in the court-house about one and a half hours, and fought them, and until they had shot four cannon balls through it. At this time a white flag appeared, the object of which was to demand an immediate and unconditional surrender, which I refused, but offered to surrender provided we were treated as prisoners of war, the men to retain their clothing, money, &c., the Enrolled Missouri Militia to receive the same treatment, and the Union citizens to be unmolested, to which Genl. Shelby at first objected, refusing to treat Enrolled Missouri Militia as prisoners of war. I replied that we would all share the same fate, and would not surrender unless all would be treated as prisoners of war. Genl. Shelby replied that he would accept my conditions, provided I would agree to have my whole command paroled on the ground. I positively refused to agree to the paroling of my command in this way. Genl. Shelby refused to parley any further, and said he would shell the town in four minutes if we did not agree to the above conditions. I therefore surrendered my command, consisting of 123 men and 5 officers of Third Battalion Sixth Missouri State Militia Cav, and 34 men and 1 officer of Capt. Stall's detachment of Sixth

Missouri State Militia Cav, a few Enrolled Missouri Militia and citizens, making in all about 180 men; were paroled by companies, the officers in writing. The men's names were taken by Shelby, and they were sworn not to take up arms against the Confederate States of America until duly exchanged. No written parole was given .

We lost our entire train and baggage, which had been moved to Neosho on that morning. The loss on our side was 2 killed and 2 wounded, and 2 Enrolled Missouri Militia (one a Lt.) killed by Coffee's men after they had been paroled. The rebels had 5 killed and 9 wounded that I have learned of. I believe their loss was greater. Our men fought bravely, and we could not have been taken if the enemy had had no artillery.

Genl. Shelby was in command of the rebel forces, which I estimated at 1,500; they claimed to be 2,200 strong. They had three pieces of artillery, one of them a good gun, the other two indifferent. I understood that one of the indifferent ones got bursted or otherwise damaged at Neosho.

I have the honor to be, very respectfully, your obedient servant,
C. B. McAFEE,
Capt. Third Battalion, Sixth Mo. State Militia Cav.

Union and Confederates were engaging across Missouri. Brigadier Genl. John McNeil left St. Louis, Missouri on Oct 9th entering Ark commanding portions of the Eighteenth Iowa Infantry, the Sixth and Eighth Missouri State Militia Cavalries and the First Ark Cav that James Monroe Watts, nephew of Chief Duwali and grandson of Chief John Ross had been forced to join. Sending communications under ruses, Peyton Long killed one of their couriers disguised as a mule driver. The courier had two human ears in his dispatches. Peyton killed and scalped him, but not before he cut off the couriers ears. "There's daggers in men's smiles," Macbeth.

Tuesday, Oct 13th, 1863, Shelby engaged with Union near Marshall, Missouri east of Kansas City. With over 600 troops he continued moving south and west crossing into Ark on Oct 20th. Both men and animals were fatigued, movement slow. Riding with over 50 men, we joined Shelby in north Ark. On Oct 24th, we camped at Buffalo Mountain, near Jasper, what no man can call anything less than God's Country. We were joined by Capt. John Cecil and his Partisans. He was Sheriff of Newton Co when war broke out. It was here late in the day when McNeil and his forces found us. They unexpectedly attacked bombarding our encampment. We not only loved the beauty of this place, we understood the rugged terrain and knew how to use it to our advantage. Quickly moving across the mountains, south 50 miles to Clarksville, crossing the Ark River on the 27th we continued southward to Washington, Ark' Southern Capitol arriving on Nov 3rd. We lost many men including William C. Berry, Co I of Col. Tom's command captured Oct 18th near Sedalia about 30 miles south of the Missouri River in Pettis Co. He was sent to Alton, Illinois Military Prison. William White was captured along with Lewis Williams. William was sent to Gratiot Street, then to Rock Island Illinois, in Jan. He died there March 21, 1864. Carroll told how they only had the clothes on their backs, no real shelter and most of the men, simply froze to death in the cold harsh winters. Lewis after being sent to St. Louis was transferred to Camp Chase, Ohio in Oct, by Nov he was sent to New Orleans for exchange. On the 18th, William Wilson was captured in Lawrence Co, Ark. He too went to Alton, Illinois. I learned from Carroll he was exchanged in Feb 1865 but refused to take The Oath and was held until war's end.

As word of Lawrence seeped out, more and more of the troops, soldiers, regulars and irregulars were becoming curious about Quantrill wanting to meet him. I wasn't surprised when several of the boys in camp with us decided to head south. Following Nannie and Carroll's wedding a month earlier on Oct 5th, the boys headed south from Batesville thankfully taking the lead in getting my little brother, Jesse to Texas for the winter camp. With death all around us, a bit of happy news arrived. The boys traveling with Jesse crossed Indian Territory safely entering Texas at Colbert's Ferry on the Red River. Momma safely gave birth to our little sister Oct 18, 1863. Proud of our efforts to protect the people of the area, proud of our service, she named her Fannie Quantrill Samuel.

By late Oct, Quantrill and 400 of our boys including my sixteen year old brother Jesse were camped near Bonham, Fannin Co, Texas. Quantrill reported to Genl. Henry McCulloch on Oct 26th. To the commanders and regular soldiers, the boys were uncouth, unmannered and without discipline, hardly men in any sense of the word. Yet, there was a hardness about them that allowed each of them no embarrassment when stared upon. The boys returned gaze's were more glaring and menacing, hardened by the guerilla warfare tactics of which we were famous. They were either liked or not liked at first meeting. The regular troops practiced drills and had military duties. Our boys did as they pleased, having a little fun which was seen as wrecking havoc by the regulars. Fighting soldier style, you lined up in a massive row, shooting at a distance for as long as you could watching as the fella next to you was wounded or killed, too much time to get scared and think. Then, the regulars walked straight head on into the enemy line fighting hand to hand. I'd never understand this kind of fighting. Our horses were critical to our ability to hit and run as many times as was needed to win or retreat.

Peyton Long and Ben Broomfield killed an Indian named Colbert. The Colbert's were of famous Indian blood going all the way back to Alabama and Mississippi when Frenchmen owned all of these lands. William Colbert married Ishtanarhay, one of Chief Doublehead's daughter's, rather like the English royalty, she was Indian royalty, grand daughter of white man Christian Priber and Ooloosta Hop Rainmaker, grand daughter of Water Beaver Moytoy, Emperor of the Cherokee. Like the sons and daughters of kings and queens marry the sons and daughters of kings and queens uniting countries, the Colbert's united France with these Cherokee. Any Colbert Indians were that family and although Bloody Bill condemned the killing and stood by Peyton and Ben that wasn't enough. An Indian runner reported the death to the commander at Boggy Depot. The Lt. surrounded Bloody Bill and the boys, including Jesse. Bloody Bill refused to give up Peyton and Ben. The Lt. ordered his men to fire on Bloody Bill. I reckon they didn't realize who they were dealing with because any one of us would have done the same, Bloody Bill turned and fired back, his aim true, killing the Lt.. Outraged, Genl. McCulloch demanded Bloody Bill, Peyton and Ben all be court martialed.

Ben Broomfield Peyton Long
Missouri Valley Special Collections, Kansas City Public Library, Kansas City, Missouri

Quantrill got in his face stating either I am or I am not a Col. and therein my men are soldiers, Partisan Rangers. Genl. Shelby arrived in camp using his persuasion to save their lives. I'm certain there was some fancy talking going on and I have no idea how they dealt with the Indian issue because like our boys, they believed in blood for blood. I thought of Chief Duwali finding and killing the men who murdered his grandfather in 1769. A hundred years is not a long time, I knew people almost that old and just as the Indian removal barely 20 years ago was fresh on people's minds and in their hearts, this war regardless of outcome will be fought for generations to come. Atrocities are not easily let go of and this war was clearly an atrocity of the horrendous kind.

Genl. Ben McCulloch received a wire informing him on Nov 18th, Quantrill and 33 of the men were indicted in the Douglas District Court in Kansas, accused of murdering George Burt on Aug 21, 1863 during the raid on Lawrence. He had not gotten a straight answer out of Quantrill or any of the boys about Lawrence and now, he knew had to get the boys out of camp away from the regular soldiers. From his headquarters at Bonham, Texas, Genl. McCulloch ordered the rest of them go home to Missouri or aide in cleaning up the deserters and independent groups. The locals didn't know the difference between a bushwhacker or jayhawkers nor did they care. They wanted the killing, looting and pillaging to stop. Quantrill agreed the boys were bored and knew hunting down deserters would be a challenge for them. Not having laid out rules of war or conduct, McCulloch was horrified when he learned a hundred of our boys encountering a band near McKinney, Texas, captured 43 'banditos', hog tied then hung them on the lawn of the courthouse. Another thirty or more were killed in a well executed ambush. It didn't matter how successful the tactics were, McCulloch didn't want to have any part of it, no more than our boys wanted any part of regular soldiering.

Back in Missouri, on Nov 25, Sam Hildebrand plundered Farmington. Brigadier Genl. Clinton Fisk offered a reward of 80 acres land for anyone who could bring him in, dead or alive. Hildebrand was as notorious in eastern Missouri as Quantrill was in western Missouri. Who was worse? Time will have to decide for itself but for McCulloch, it was Quantrill, face to face with him and without means to exert influence much less control over him. Bored most of the 400 boys with Quantrill continued to remain in Texas creating a new kind of hell for McCulloch. The boys found the flat lands of Texas perfect for horse racing. They took bets on whose horse would win and some of the boys bet on how each of the winners and losers would respond. Mixed with Mexican agave juice these boys were like a preacher's boy away at school, mischief was at hand. McCulloch was so concerned about the real and potential risk they posed he assigned regularly enlisted troops to protect the locals from their antics, fun could and did turn deadly at a moment's notice. The men whose wives accompanied them to Texas, including Quantrill having brought his new bride Kate, were involved with scouting out possible ranches and hacienda's to which they might move if returning to Missouri proved impossible. Jesse noted there was growing discord and rivalries amongst the boys. Without a leader, without a man, these boys were getting out of hand. Even a child could recognize when a fresh peach tree limb would no longer do.

On Christmas Day, Bloody Bill, Jesse, Archie Clements, Peyton and a dozen others rode their horses into a hotel, straightaway into the lobby. They demanded to have their photographs taken, probably from the same fella that took Riley Crawford's. Bloody Bill wanted a photograph to send home to his momma in time for his 27th birthday, Feb 2nd. Not liking what he saw, Archie took the lead kicking over the man's equipment smashing it upon the floor. Quantrill unable to control the boys flew into a fit of rage upon Bloody Bill when news of it reached him. Bloody Bill and the boys come up with enough money to pay for the damages.

I remember as children Momma checking Bloody Bill and Jim over, along with the rest of us, like a cow, examining our teeth. She didn't hold to none of us smoking or drinking. She said our teeth was the tell all on us, how we were fairing and what we didn't want to tell. Uncle John, Daddy's brother was a dentist, maybe he'd told her to check us. Wherever she learned it, she always checked our teeth, grabbed us by the jaws with her hand putting her pointer finger and thumb just so you couldn't close your mouth until she was done examining us. She felt strongly we should commit no actions we couldn't stand before the Lord or the members of New Hope Church and attest to. For all that Bloody Bill's reputation said about him, it didn't. He was thoughtful, courteous, liked to read and was mild mannered. He wore his black hair long and had a broad forehead. He looked like a pirate, gray eyes, dark red and black beard, nice white teeth and was over 6 ft tall. He had his momma make his shirt to look fanciful, like the cavaliers of a king's court or the Zouave soldiers. The women fashioned us shirts in the red cloth we'd captured from the Union. Bloody Bill enjoyed telling the story of having crossed the plains with his daddy and a mule team. He said if he cared for his life he would have lost it long ago, but since he wanted to lose it, he couldn't throw it away. We taught the boys to ride and shoot. We carried at least 6 loaded guns in our belts at any given time. As word came out of Texas, I was worried about Bloody Bill, alcohol had never been his friend. He and Quantrill nearly drew their guns on each other when Quantrill ordered Lige Morgan, drunk and belligerent, arrested. He sent Bill Gaw to arrest him. Lige went for his gun and Gaw killed him. Bloody Bill was furious. Lige was one of his boys and they knowed he was too drunk to kill anybody.

It was clear from Jesse's letter home to Momma, Quantrill's hold on the boys was almost gone. Having received a commission from Genl. Price, Bloody Bill was the first to leave Quantrill taking 65 men with him toward the Mississippi River. Samuel Hayes, brother of Upton Hayes chose to become Genl. Marmaduke's body guard. Others were talking of joining regular soldiering, some headed out to curtail the cotton thieves on the Mississippi, Cole and Lea had already left, camped at Floyd. Jesse was torn, not certain if he should ride with Bloody Bill or remain with Quantrill. In the end, he chose to ride with Bloody Bill since it was he who promised

Momma he'd take care of him. Jesse and Bloody Bill weren't afraid of much, but they didn't want to get on Momma's bad side.

At Sherman, Texas, about twenty miles west of Bonham, Jim Chiles, John Ross, Fletch Taylor and Andy Walker robbed and murdered Col. Alexander and Maj Butts. Quantrill wanted them court martialed and shot. Jesse said no one could believe the way Quantrill was acting, especially since John Ross was among the boys involved. He was Quantrill's unofficial Aide de Camp, confidante, courier, liaison, call him what you will, wasn't no body new getting to Quantrill without John Ross knowin' it. He had joined up under George Todd but quickly brown nosed Quantrill. Any time he left camp, you could be certain John knew where he was going and sometimes only John knew. Fletch claimed they were acting under Quantrill's orders. Which since John Ross was with them, likely was truth. Todd and Anderson saved them. Although George Todd came to their defense, he and John Jarrette left afterwards joining Shelby's regular service headed to Louisiana.

A week or so earlier drunk, Todd defied Quantrill. He shot at Todd and missed, then Quantrill ordered those standing near him to shoot him but they refused. John Barker was the only one who stood with Quantrill. Both men shot at and missed him. Todd shot at Barker and cut his coat. The other boys put a stop to it and everyone ended up laughing. Jesse said it was "tense" for a few minutes. Every day there was some new disaster in the making. Fletch Taylor had enough and left. Upset over the growing problems among the men Bill Gregg who had already decided to join Col. Shelby took it as his cue and left as well. Quantrill offered him a 90 day leave of absence granted by McCulloch. He reported to Genl. Kirby Smith and was assigned as Capt. in Co I of Shank's Regiment, Shelby's Brigade in Louisiana. Theodore Cassell and Simeon Davis joined Shelby's men under Gregg in Co I. Jesse had rode into a mess but was happy to be part of it all.

Our teacher, Mister Bird Price Smith taught us a game that stayed with me. He would tell one person a word, whispering it in their ear real fast. No repeats. They would write it down on the tablet and turn it over so no one could see. Then, that person would whisper the word in the next person's ear real fast. This continued around the room until it came to the last person. That person would then write down what word they heard whispered to them. Then, the first and last person would hold up their chalk tablets showing the class the words. They were never the same, but sometimes it didn't make sense how they could change so dramatically. Mister Bird even altered the game a few times and had each person write down the word they heard after they had passed it on just to make sure someone wasn't jimmy riggin' the game on purpose. The same was true with the boys in Texas, there were truths and exaggerations and where one ended and the other began remains unknown. One thing for certain, their tales got bigger and bolder every time they told'em.

Col. Stand Watie, a grandson of Giyosti Tachee, sister of Ooloosta, Cole Younger's' step grandmother, even came to talk to the boys. Cole later told us it was then he decided it was time to move on, with or without Bloody Bill or Quantrill. He'd had about all he could take. That day Col. Isaac Stand Watie and Cole met away from the Texas camp, both Southerners under orders from Brigadier Genl. Henry McColloch they knew there could be unnecessary deaths. Col Stand Watie and his Cherokee soldiers were with us when Col Shelby was surrounded at Prairie Grove. No one knew what to do with Quantrill who was happy where he was but knew he was losing control of his men. Col Stand Watie made the decision to head back north into Indian Territory. He advised Cole our boys needed to part ways. Several of the boys volunteered for service on the Mississippi and left out headed to New Orleans under Genl. Kirby Smith. It was then Cole Younger, along with Dave Poole accepted orders from Genl. Smith to stop the contraband trade, clear out the cotton thieves, speculators and spies along the Louisiana border fighting under Joseph Lea, headquartered at Floyd in Carroll Parrish. It was in Louisiana where they became friends with Capt. Frank Brand of Miles Legions, the guerillas of the bayous. Capt. Brand returned to Missouri with them.

Bill Gregg and Cole Younger were sent to report to Genl. Marmaduke in Warren, Ark on direct order of Shelby. There Cole was assigned a recruiting trip to New Mexico. His recruiting failed but he fought Apaches and was sent further west to California. With his fill of Quantrill, he stayed west until the end of the war. Other's trickled out leaving camp returning to Missouri. Elk Sipe, riding with us under Col. Tom learned his brothers Marcus and Rufe, had been hospitalized in Louisiana, Aug or Sept. Allowed to go home from their units they were captured and forced to enlist in the Union or be killed. They joined Union commander Elisha Baxter's 4th Ark Infantry.

North in Ark, the drought of 1863 was having harsh effects. With no rain the rivers were low, just barely running, crops and gardens failed. The weather fell to 10 below zero and stayed there. The river froze over so thick at Batesville loaded wagons could cross over it. The Mississippi river had chunks of ice the size of small boats floating in its waters. By Dec the Union was at it again, capturing Richard Henry Powell on the 2nd at Batesville. He was sent to Gratiot Street, and then transferred to Johnson's Island in April. He was paroled after taking the oath but not released, instead they sent him to New Orleans for exchange in Jan 1865.

Dec 10th, a number of the boys under Col. Tom got into a skirmish east of Wideman, Ark on the farm of Ben and Polly Daniel Croom. In

1861, their son Thomas joined Col. McCarver, CSA. He'd been captured in May of '63 fighting in Mississippi. Released he returned to Ark to fight under Capt. Wiley Jones. They reported no causalities on either side at Croom's Farm. But news across north Ark and Southern Missouri was the Union forces were capturing as many men as possible, even rounding up people on their farms charged with being sympathizers. They were afraid to round up the women after Lawrence. Lt. Lewis Todd was captured in Dunklin Co on Dec 30th. After several transfers he took the oath, was paroled at Johnson Island then sent to New Orleans for exchange Jan 1865. Oth Hinton, wounded and captured near Lexington, was tried, found guilty and sentenced to hang. Andy Blunt tried to rescue him but failed. The Lexington Union reported on Feb 27, 1864 Oth had been executed.

Most people didn't know there were women, in fact, entire families traveling along with the regular soldiers. They made clothes, fixed meals and took care of not only their husbands, sons or fathers but several of the other men. They didn't think too much of the "service women" nor did our boys. These were women who traveled with the regular enlisted troops providing "services" for them. Some women became the doctors and nurses for us. There were mothers and sisters from Clay Co along with us and other parts. Momma traveling with us to Batesville wasn't such an oddity nor the fact she was heavy with child. She'd made the trip from Kentucky to Missouri when expecting me. The families of most of the troops traversed the country when they first moved west of the Mississippi; few were native to Missouri and Ark. Even so, the boys were nervous with Quantrill's new bride, young Kate with them in Texas. She was a huge distraction for him, one that was easily seen by all the boys. I wondered how Carroll would do now that he was a married man.

In 1841 William Thomas Wood married Marie Harriet Payne; Carroll was their first born child. They made their home in Lafayette Co neighbor to Clay where fellow Kentuckian my daddy and his new wife, my momma made their home. I was born Jan 10th, 1843 their first born child. Daddy received his diploma from Georgetown College in Kentucky and was preparing to begin ministering in a new church in Missouri. That church would be New Hope Church in Liberty, home of the Mormon's "New Zion". There along with the Wood family large numbers of other expat's from Kentucky were not only members but officials in the church. It was at New Hope in 1856 the decision to split from the abolitionist north was made, a side Daddy placed us on. This split was an early decision to support the South should the talk of War Between the States become a reality. Baptists split due to the war, forming the Southern Baptists in slave states. With the Border Wars between Kansas and Missouri raging, we never knew life without conflict. Missus Harriet's youngest brother, Jacob "John" Payne enlisted with Carroll.

Us boys were church family, friends who went fishing, rode horses and attended school together. Schools were held in churches and family homes. Families got together and hired someone who could teach their children to read, write and do arithmetic, all ages, from 5 to 20 attended. In the wealthier families, they learned science and geography. It was into a wealthier status of life Carroll Wood and I was born and lived. Our daddy's were fundamentally farmers, growing hemp from which rope was made supporting the Southern cotton industry. The hemp made our families solid land owners and wealthy people for the day.

I had somewhat of a famous memory, able to retain places, dates, names, birthdays and ranks more than most. We couldn't keep records so I heard it all, good and bad. I not only collected letters from men but wrote them for the boys who wanted to make sure if they didn't make it word was gotten to their families. I remembered their kin. I delivered more than I cared to, and in doing so, made friendships with people who lost loved ones. Southern people who felt simply because I delivered the news to them, I was a good man, a man worth protecting. It was these acts which endeared me to people across Missouri and North Ark. "When sorrows come, they come not as single spies, but in battalions," Hamlet. I met people who were family, kin from Tennessee and Kentucky who had made their way west of the Mississippi. The diasporas of people I was kin by blood or experience was everywhere around me. When they shared their stories and lives with me, with each one I became friends and family. I always thought it was from my daddy I inherited my memory, a gift from God. With death all around us, I no longer knew if it was a gift or curse.

With so many members of our family in Ark I found myself as much at home there as in Missouri, except for Momma of course. Home is where your Momma is. Sarah Powers, Daddy's own cousin, daughter of his daddy's sister, Mary James and Gambol Kimbrell Powers, lived north of Batesville. Sarah married a man named John Ross. He died a few years later when he was only 22. She then married James Seaton. He died in 1858 at 32 years old. Like Momma, Sarah buried two husband and babies. Her life was hard but had not hardened her. Even the smallest of kindness endeared us boys to her. She had George born in 1854, John 1855 and Louisa 1857. George was the oldest at 8 when I first met them. The Powers lived near Newburg in Izard Co. Whenever we found ourselves near her home, we camped there and making certain as many of the labor chores we could do were done. In mid Dec, Capt. Worthington was leading a Co of men scouting the area near cousin Sarah Powers Seaton's place. She reported to Col. Tom many of the men were Mountain Boomers who lived across the White River in Searcy Co, a days ride by over the ridge. Although the Unionists had not captured, wounded or killed any of our boys they were keeping them scattered and on the run. Sarah reported a local man; Bill Williams with a command of 20 or so men looting, plundering and taking advantage of women, especially those without a man in the house. He and his men would claim to be against or for whatever side the family stood for, saying and doing what was needed to gain the upper hand. At least everyone knew Ed Cockrum was a Unionist hoodlum.

Coon Thornton told us about a new game he'd read about a called baseball, where a hard stick of wood, called a bat was used to strike a ball. He'd explained how the game was played and that Native Americans played a similar game. He said the person getting to go first was the person with the upper hand on the bat. They would put a hand on the bottom, each placing their hand over the others until the last hand on the bat at the handle was the upper hand. People were using the saying to describe how a person would get the upper hand in order to take advantage, as Bill Williams was doing. Col. Tom was gravely concerned with the increasing numbers of these kinds of men roaming from Newton to Independence Co. He ordered Capt. C.G. Marshall's command to move north along the river toward Camp Adams at Yellville for the purpose of locating and eliminating such. Riding with a 100 under his command joined by another 100 of local men and boys gathered by Given Horn they attacked Capt. Worthington riding with only 75 men. They attacked then scattered guerrilla style leading them into the brush. The night was cold and many men who had come with Given returned to local farms where they could sleep in the barns while Worthington and his men camped on the south side of Yellville. On the morning of the 24th when Worthington broke camp, 100 men were armed and watching preparing to attack as the Unionists headed toward the Buffalo River. Their movement was slow, hacking out their path hauling a canon. The boys skirted them as they moved to the river. The Union set up camp at Richland Creek. Scouts were sent to Col. Tom to mount a Maj attack before the Union could fully break camp. Lt Col. Joseph B. Love, under Col. Tom, brought his men from Van Buren Co. Capt. James Love, commanding about 50 men, joined Capt. Marshall and Col Tom at Big Flats. There they were joined by Maj Gunning with 150 men. They descended on the Union encampment. Joined on both sides by local men, the fighting was brutal hand to hand combat. Many men had only pitchforks and hatchets, no guns or horses. They fought against neighbors. Col Tom agreed these were the worst of battles. A neighbor would attack his neighbor then try to help him, save him from the wounds he inflicted upon him, childhood friend's and neighbors at war. Men who had likely sat in church together before this war began. Col Tom went forward with a flag of truce requesting suspension of fighting until morning. Worthington, a true Union man allowed only for an hour and a half, no respect for his men nor ours, no respect for the relationships among the boys who were dead or dying. Nor was he interested in exchanging prisoners.

Given volunteered to move south and west toward Horn Mountain. From there he could overlook the area the Union would have to move through. Capturing their canon was critical to a successful attack. With over 200 men, we charged the Union. Their cannon was too much, killing and wounding many. Horn made it back with the boys to Col. Tom's camp, about two miles up the Buffalo from where the attack occurred. While discussing plans for a morning attack on Dec 26th, they were attacked from the south by Worthington. Few were killed on either side with only a half dozen wounded. We learned Hen Cole of Capt James Love's band had been wounded and taken to a cave near his uncle's home. Larken Hendrix of the First Ark, was also wounded, they were both residents of Searcy Co. Their fates did not reach us. Cousins, Frank and Joe Wright and Capt. Giles Wright in Capt. Love's local command were chased by Unionists. They shot Capt. Wright's horse out from under him on Bear Creek, north of Burrowsville. When the boys found his body it was full of bullet holes. The Union then went to the home of Lt. John Minton "Mack" Hensley under Capt. Love's command taking him prisoner. Sent to Gratiot Street Prison in St. Louis, Hensley died there. William Thornton "Thor" Hensley joined us after his capture. Two were captured from Col Tom's command Co A; Ed Beeson died in Little Rock Military Prison a year later of diarrhea and Jim Nesbitt from Round Bottom on the White River, son of James and Zillie Peacock Nesbitt was sent to Gratiot Street, then Alton Illinois prison. He died Jan 8th, 1865. A larger number captured from Co C were sent to Springfield, from there transferred north or to Little Rock: Stephen Fore, William Proper, Archie Hogue, James Friend and E.B. Reeson all survived. Bill Davis, Co C sent to Little Rock died there Nov 7th 1864 inflammation of the liver. Bill Hurst and Bill Patton were sent to Camp Douglas, Illinois. Hurst died Feb 25th, 1865 and Patton died Dec 19th, 1864.

Col. Tom's voice was strong; he was in command in every sense of the word. He met with the boys explaining the successes achieved were making them all known. Neighbors knew who was fighting on each side and what had been witnessed at Richland Creek was something no one every needed witness again. He encouraged local men to go home and do nothing more in the War Between the States, simply protect their families. Should they choose to return, they should do so only after making sure their wives, mothers, sisters and children were safe. One of the Arnold boys upon return reported 30 women at the Bigham House prepared to do battle. Their root cellars would provide hiding under the house for children. A nearby Indian shelter was being used for hiding valueables. Col. Tom made the decision we should move south toward Batesville, two camps would be set up, one near Blue Springs, north of Batesville and the other at the Bigham House. The ride across the ridge between the two was well known to locals who led the way. Few went home and didn't return to fight.

William Thornton "Thor" Hensley born 1838

Jan 1864 was a cold and bitter month. I turned 21 years old, Jan 10th, 1864 camped with Col. Tom at Mammoth Spring, on the Ark side. The drought and grasshoppers had ravaged the fields. Little Rock was held by the Union. Although we had not scalped or beheaded anyone until after the Union, us boys, Bloody Bill and I, we knew how and weren't nearly as sickened by it as the others. Peyton Long had been among the first of our boys to scalp a man. Word was circulating Bloody Bill was not only scalping but decapitating prisoners. The Union acted horrified even though they were doing it long before we were. They responded by capturing as many of us they could. I've often wondered if they kept boys together to break one hoping it would break the others seeing their friends suffering. It's easier to hear the screams of someone you don't know or haven't served with than it is a friend. The boys in Ark were as highly pursued as the boys in Missouri; the Union desperate to put an end to the bush warfare. Returning to camp, on Jan 15, 1864, Capt Henry VanFleet was captured near his home in Izard Co and E.A. Williams near his home in Independence Co. Two of the boys who had been out scouting returned reporting that Elijah Miser of Co E had been captured on the 21st near his home at Riggsville. Miser was sent to Little Rock, transferred to Rock Island, Illinois where he died Aug 14, 1864.

The Confederacy was under siege from its own citizens as local men across Missouri and Ark dressed in stolen uniforms of both the North and the South plundering and looting, taking pretty much what they wanted. These were not men of war who donned the enemy uniform as a ruse in battle they were bandits who killed people, burned homes and plundered, they were not soldiers. These were not irregulars or Partisan's, these were hoodlums and gangs, vigilantes using the war to their advantage. While some blamed it on actual troops depending on their loyalties, the fact remains there are always those who will take advantage of any situation to their own advantage. Bloody Bill likened it to the Border Wars and how the Kansas Jayhawkers stole themselves rich. Bill Williams, a local man from Izard Co, cousin Sarah Powers warned us about, was just such a man. He was causing problems for everyone and no one seemed willing to turn him in despite his actions. Both the Union under Col. Robert Livingston and the Confederates under Col. Tom were charged with trying to bring some sense of safety to the area of the middle White River Valley, west of Batesville. Enemies had a common enemy preying on innocent people, especially the women and children left behind. During their efforts to root out Bill Williams the Union was also charged with continued orders to find and kill every man riding with Col. Freeman. Union Col. Livingston captured and threatened a local man by the name of Bob Porter, the rebel rock thrower, who gave away our encampment. We moved in the night from the Bigham place to Cooper Valley near Lunenburg.

Union orders received: "Sat, Jan 23, 1864, Batesville, Ark Hdq 1st Nebraska Cav to Lt. Col William Baumer. You will proceed immediately and attack every Rebel encampment you find. Move via Hookrum, Lunenburg, Sylamore. Shoot every Rebel soldier you find in Federal uniform and destroy all armed Bushwhackers. On North Fork of Sylamore you will find and destroy a powder mill operating there. Should the town of Sylamore be occupied and fire upon you, burn them out. The object of this expedition is to destroy Freeman."

"At 9:00 a.m. Jan 23, 1864, 1st Nebraska Cav and 6th Missouri State Cav 297 men strong and 5 guides moved north." "The first night, they camped at Hookrum, next day traveled through Franklin making camp at Lunenburg. The third morning two companies split off. One engaged at Cooper Valley."

It was there in Cooper Valley Bill Wilson swept into camp announcing Union troops coming down Rose Trail along Wild Haws Road toward us. A second detachment of Union troops moved down to Mt Olive, under Frank McBride. Union Capt. Baxter operating under orders to take no prisoners, burn any home or town that offered resistance, did just that. The Union burned the Mt Olive, Baxter's advance killed unarmed Isaac Jeffery a cousin of Ambrose Culp's. Isaac had gotten a furlough mid Jan to come home for a few days. He had come home to make sure the late field corn was gotten in, husked and stored. On the way home he encountered some men, hoodlums, beating another man, all of whom he knew. After aiding the man to fend off the attackers, they told him, "We'll get you Jeffery." When folks gathered for Isaac's services, the full story was told. Isaac rose early hiding the horses, livestock and other immediate valuables, a daily requirement due to the war. Then he and his little baby child Caroline, only 2 year old rode into town to take care of a few things. There he bought her a little tea pitcher. Riding in front of her daddy in the saddle, she clutched the pitcher with her little hands. She couldn't have been happier. When they arrived back at the house, she went with her daddy to the corn shed to husk corn. As Isaac pulled the husks from the corn Caroline played by her daddy's side. Then they heard horses coming at a gallop. Isaac told her to run to the house. It was Frank McBride, USA 1st Ark Infantry and neighbor Isaac had seen beating the man now reconnoitering as advance for the Union. Their feud was older than the war. Isaac had told Frank about a piece of property he wanted to purchase near Lunenburg in 1860. Frank beat Isaac out of the property getting to the recorder's office. Isaac had let it go but Frank knew he'd done wrong and spread lies about Isaac. Frank was leading the charge of group of four armed men in their Union uniforms. Caroline froze in place screaming with the horror only a small frightened child can muster as she watched her father running then being dragged across the field toward Pelham Creek. Lewis and Dick Partee neighbors and friends from across the river at Partee Spring were on their way to Isaac's to help him finish up the corn harvest when they heard the gunshots. Running toward the sound they saw the men holding him, beating his bullet riddled body. The three friends were to head together to Col. Tom's camp but realizing Isaac was dead or dying and there was nothing they could, they fled. They split up heading in different directions. McBride's men captured Lewis.

Caroline's mother Hulda ran to her side along with the family slave Aunt Mandy. Then they heard the guns. Running across the field, they found Isaac near a tree where he had been shot at close range, then beaten with the stock of a gun. They loaded him into a push cart and got him to his father Elijah's house where they laid him out on the back porch. The blood flowed as he laid there, the last of his life draining from him, blood soaking into the porch.

Services for Isaac were held at the Mount Olive Presbyterian Church, the same one he'd attended as a child and been married in.

"Born Dec 20, 1840 in Mt Olive, Ark, he was shot to death Jan 25, 1864 at the age of 23 years, 1 month and 5 days by Union soldiers near Pelham Creek near his home in Izard Co. He leaves behind a young wife Mary Muhuldah Kemp and 2 year old daughter Caroline. Isaac was the oldest son of Elijah Jeffery and the late Massie Caroline Robertson, step son of Nancy Jane Clark."

Thus, were the words spoken as neighbors talked of the tragedy of Elijah having lost first his wife and now his oldest son. Six months later, Elijah would lose his other son with Caroline, Jehoiada Miles Quincy Jeffery, fondly called Suska, also a soldier in the Confederate Army killed in Atlanta, Georgia.

Like her husband, Isaac's wife Hulda, the oldest daughter of Maj John Jacob Kemp, of the Izard Co Militia, lost her mother, Elizabeth Young when she was four years old. Cynthia Ann Reeves, her step mother, was the only mother she knew. She and Isaac shared much in their lives, so much sorrow no words were needed between them. Hudla was heavy with child when she buried her husband. She vowed her child, boy or girl, would be named Isaac. She went to her father, Maj Kemp's home in Riggsville where she and her young daughter Caroline, called Carrie, would be safe. On April 25th, 1864, she was blessed with a daughter whom she named Isaac Jane Jeffery. Caroline would be 8 and Isaac Jane 6 before she would marry again. Her second husband was Newton Jasper Gowens of Hanover.

Isaac's killers left a ring on his hand, not his wedding band, but his Masonic ring. The family knew only that his murderers, Union or otherwise, somehow had some respect for his having been a Mason, perhaps themselves Mason's. Isaac had gone fishing in the White River the day before his death. The family kept his cork and line wound just as it was when he walked in from the river, catch in one hand, placing it up against the wall of the house. Following the war of 1812, with military land grant in hand, Jehoiada Jeffery, Isaac's grandfather, was the first to settle Mount Olive in Sept 1816. This war less than 50 year later would claim the lives of four of his grand children and a host of nephews and cousins.

Ambrose Jeffery, son of Miles and Sarah Williams Jeffery was home on leave, furloughed due to a wound received at the battle of Murfreesboro, Tenn. He was captured and sent to Rock Island prison camp. Frank McBride's advance took 10 prisoners including John Lewis Partee, who had been captured April 20, 1863 in Shannon Co, and paroled at St. Louis, June 2nd. Lewis was captured a second time heading to Isaac's. After burning the town the Union crossed the river. From there they moved on the old road under the bluff to Sylamore burning the town, killing 4 and wounding one. The two story home of Judge Henry Hill Harris and wife Lucy Dillard Harris built in 1848 was commandeered as a base, saving it from being burnt. Scouts were sent to find Col. Tom. Some of our boys trailed the remaining Union troops as they moved to Riggsville, where they joined the 11th Missouri Cav, Union.

When Bill Wilson rode into camp at Cooper Valley announcing the nearby Union troops, we had very little time, to put together an attack. We were almost immediately being driven back to the north side of Cooper's Valley. Lt. Col. Christopher Cook ordered us to prepare for a second attack, but the Union withheld, which allowed us time to withdraw. Shots were exchanged and we knew several Union men were wounded with at least one killed. Only a couple of our boys had been hit but nothing preventing them from riding. Billy Hinkle, who had been at Carroll's wedding lived nearby. He joined us the night before as we moved from Samuel Bigham's to Cooper Valley. He was bleeding heavily having taken a direct hit in the stomach. Bill Chitwood and Bill Arnold stuffed a shirt into his gut, got him onto a horse and took him home. I took solace he was at home with his sister when he died. It would be hard to break this news to Momma. His momma, Sarah Ann Cole was an own cousin of Momma's, Sarah, called Little Sallie in the family was the daughter of Uncle Jesse Cole, a brother to Momma's daddy James Cole. Sarah had been named for Momma's momma, Sarah "Sallie" Ann Lindsay, namesake of Sarah Lindsay Lafferty. When the War Between the States broke out Willie, as he was known to his family, Billy to friends and fellow soldiers sought to join Col. Thomas Roe Freeman's Missouri Cav. Col. Tom had been in Ark recruiting along with Upton Hayes and Sydney Drake Jackman when he first met Billy. He'd told him he was too young instructing him to stay at home with his family aiding them who were in dire need of him and the soldiers who needed a safe place. While camped near Cooper Valley on the farm of Elisha Arnold, Billy found us, joining Co F giving his life the next day. Elisha was a brother to Tho Arnold, uncle of Bill Arnold.

Col. Tom's Cav men all had some degree of wealth each required to have their own horses. Although enlisted men, they operated like irregulars, employing the Native American style of fighting maintaining no base camp. They were operating from local homes and farms of the loyalists often families of the men serving just as us irregulars, guerillas, Partisans did in Missouri. This style of fighting was comfortable to me. It was everything Uncle Wild Man Bill Thomason had prepared us for. Many of the men had been at home the night before the engagement at Rocky Bayou Creek that cost young William Asa Hinkle his life. Willie himself had spent the night at home with his father Jesse Hinkle and his step mother Mary Coburn before joining us at the Arnold's the night before the attack. Willie's best buddy was his sister Martha. Her and her friend, Eliza, wife of cousin Samuel Mims, dressed Willie for burial and began digging the grave. The Unionists chased us across Devils Backbone down the ridge toward Mt Olive. In the face of danger, Bill Chitwood rode back to his father James Chitwood's home near the Barrens. Together they rode back to the Hinkle home. When they got there, Billy was dead and his aunt Arena Beckham Hinkle, widow of his uncle John Downing Hinkle, his sister Martha and her friend, Eliza Mims had partially dug the grave and gathered a small pile of rocks to cover it with. Bill and his Daddy finished digging the grave burying a young man whose death occurred on the banks of the creek where he went swimming with his friends, sisters and brothers, in the beauty of Cooper Valley. Unlike so many others, he died and was buried at home by family.

When Bill Arnold, son of "Tho" and Mary Ann Lackey Arnold, rejoined us near Sylamore he told us the Union were burying Union soldier William Anderson, a local man from Chalybeate Springs in the field where the battle took place. When the War Between the States was declared done and over both families moved the bodies of these young men. Young Billy was buried at the cemetery at Lunenburg and William Anderson was moved to a family cemetery in Cleburne Co.

Having joined ranks at Riggsville, Uion scouts learned Col. Thomas Roe Freeman was camped on Middle Sylamore at Rorie's Mill. Union soldiers were dispatched. Next morning, Jan 27th, Monks and the 11th Missouri Cav went in first. From Sylamore the Union moved up the South Sylamore Creek to the mill of Absalom Rorie where scouts had informed them of munitions being made and the men of Col Tom having gathered. Had they of gone up the North Fork of the creek they would have located the main source of the munitions effort at Gunner Pool.

After arriving here in the Ozarks, Absalom and his wife Sarah Meador set about building a huge two story saw mill followed by one of the first and most prosperous grist mills. These gave upper Middle Sylamore Creek its name of Mill Creek. Timber, logs and lumber were floated down the creek to White River where they were loaded onto steamships headed to Memphis and New Orleans. A small community was starting to grow including Aaron Stevens and his family, Jonas Brewer and his wife Margaret who had built a massive two story sawed lumber mill supplying people with cut boards for homes. Roasting Ear Creek did not exist until several years after the war, when following a huge storm a new creek was pushed forth out of the mountain flowing through the Steven's and Brewer's cornfields taking the "Roastin' Ears" with it. After the flood, the new creek, Roasting Ear Creek remained. The Rorie's, Brewer's and Steven's were able to hide food and other valuables in Indian Cave located west of the mill. Fresh water flowed from beneath the huge lime stone bluff where their mill sat. Absalom's business and family were thriving, as talk of war became reality. It was the Rorie family who built most of the wagons for the Baker Fauncher wagon train, slaughtered by the Mormons at

Mountain Meadows, Utah, on Sept 11, 1857. His skilled hands had carved the roses in the wagon later claimed by their leader Brigham Young.

In 1860, Ark required each Co to maintain a militia; John Jacob Kemp of Riggsville, father of Hulda, Isaac's widow was appointed Col. of the Izard Co Militia. He maintained a huge expanse of land with just over 6,000 residents with Mount Olive the Co seat. May 6, 1861, Ark seceded. The Confederate Congress urged Ark to make provisions for the manufacture of arms and munitions, including saltpeter for the cause of the South. In June 1861, the Military Board of Ark ordered the Co judge, sheriff, and clerk of each Co to serve as a commission to procure supplies for Ark soldiers; Henry Hill Harris, 34, Judge, Walter Jacob Cagle, 31 from Riggsville, Sheriff, William Carroll Dixon 29, Mt Olive, Clerk served for Izard Co. Samuel Warner Dixon, a brother to Will Dixon, would ride with us serving under Col. Tom, Co F.

In July 1861 Absalom and Sarah's 21 year old son, Absalom Josiah "Jody" Rorie joined the Confederacy as a Private in the Ark Infantry. The next month on Aug 21, the steamboat New Moon arrived at Sylamore with cargo of 30 huge kettles, a steam engine and a hammer mill to produce gunpowder for the Confederacy. They were brought up the North Fork of Sylamore Creek to an area being called Gunner Pool due to the munitions being made there. White oak baskets carried on the backs of oxen were led into Saltpeter Cave and loaded with bat guano. The guano was placed in the huge kettles by the creek and boiled. This left the saltpeter at the bottom. Charcoal made mostly from cottonwood was ground in the hammer mill powered by the steam engine. Sulphur was added to produce a more accurate shot. The Confederate Gov sent infantries to work and guard the powder works situated on the land of Isaac Teague. As steamships loaded and unloaded cargo and supplies for all of North Ark to aid the munitions effort the river port town of Sylamore became a critical location in the War Between the States. The road from Sylamore led through the mountains crossing the Buffalo at Spencer Point, north to Yellville and to Missouri. Ammunition efforts were located in caves throughout the hills. In the spring of 1862, Union Genl. Curtis invasion of Izard Co began with skirmishes at Calico and Mt Olive, with 20,000 plus soldiers spread out from Pocahontas to Yellville searching for the Confederate powder mills. He issued an order "If you can't bring it with us, burn it."

On May 29, 1862, Genl. Curtis sent 300 men under Maj Drake and Maj Bowen of the 3rd Iowa Calvary with two mountain howitzers to Sylamore. They were after Rebel's camped in Kickapoo Bottoms, one of the former Indian villages. The Union, firing the mountain howitzers at them from the east side of the river, ran about 45 men out of a cane break, killing one and wounding two others. A mountain howitzer is a mini-cannon easily packed by one mule with cannon balls about three inches in diameter. Curtis' invasion was a war against the population as a whole. In order to save official records, Co clerk, William Dixon, hid them in a cave at the north end of Jeffery's Slough.

The burning and pillaging of homes and churches was intended to produce beggary of the local population, no different than was occurring in Missouri. Grist mills and agricultural equipment, private salt works and other manufacturing were destroyed. The cartel of prisoner exchange suspended. No preaching allowed unless the preacher had taken the Oath to the Union. No traveling permitted without a pass. No marrying was allowed and parents were forbidden to name their children after Southern Genls. Military Gov.s were appointed. The atrocities of Yankee Rule enacted in Izard Co surpassed what was known in other parts of the Confederacy in Ark largely due to the well hidden munitions efforts. The folks of the White River Valley understood what we lived in western Missouri. And just as in Missouri, Genl. Samuel Curtis was a hated man.

Having served almost two years in the Confederacy, Jody Rorie deserted in 1863. Captured on July 9, 1863, at Port Hudson, Louisiana, he was paroled four days later. A skilled wagon maker, he was allowed to return home to build wagons for the Confederacy. He had been back on the Middle Sylamore only a few months with his wife and four children when on the morning of Jan 27th, 1864, Monk and his men having come up South Sylamore Creek stormed the area looking for the powder works, "Col. Freeman and his Rebels."

Our scouts alerted us allowing our departure from Rorie's Mill before dawn going back northeast toward Livingston Creek. The Union burned both the saw mill and grist mill killing three men. Col. Tom remained with our rear guard left behind as a distraction and was chased a number of miles through Big Flat. Outnumbered, eight men surrendered and summarily were shot and killed. Capt. Franks, a brother in law to one of Absalom Rorie's daughter's, was among the casualties. Sgt. John M. Bailey was captured. He was sent to Gratiot Street with intentions to use in exchange, however he contracted measles and died May 31, 1864. E.N. Herron was captured and sent to Little Rock and on to Gratiot Street prison. Col. Livingston's monthly report states, "Of this scout to Sylamore 1 Union wounded." Although the river was frozen sufficiently solid for loaded wagons to cross, Col. Livingston says the "1 wounded man was put in a dugout boat with 3 men to bring him to Batesville." We know differently unless of course they slid him along the frozen river waters in the boat. And, the east side of the river has at least 20 graves of Union dead. Col. Tom received two shots to his leg was seriously wounded and losing blood. He was taken to his cousin John Calhoun Freeman's home near Big Flat.

Angry Col. Tom escaped, they burned the prosperous mills to the ground. In an effort to determine the location of Col. Tom and the nearby caves producing powder works they tortured Absalom and his sons, Andrew and Hezekiah. They tied their arms to separate horses. The horses pulled against Absalom and Hezekiah's arms, each exacting pressure pulling the men's arms from their sockets, dismembering them as they were ripped from their bodies. Andrew tied to a tree screamed for help. He watched as his daddy and older brother were ripped apart and shot. Jody did what he had to do, using both his Confederate desertion and his ability as a skilled wagon maker, he maneuver a barter with the Union for his own life, the release of his young brother Andrew and the lives of the rest of his family. Then under the watchful eyes of Union guard, Jody and young Andrew moved the remaining family to Big Flat, buried their brother and father and then, on Feb 1, 1864 only three days after the burning of Rorie's Mills, they joined the Union Army. Hezekiah Columbus Rorie and his sixty six year old father Absalom had been horrifically tortured and killed in front of their families. Eighteen year old brother Andrew had been physically and mentally tortured then forced to join the Union. He later died at the Union camp at Lewisburg.

Hezekiah left his widow, Louisa Ticer Rorie behind with seven children. People tell stories of men who fought for one side and then the other, of brothers fighting brothers, without telling the whole story. The people here fought to protect their homes and families making untold sacrifices. Most people did not own slaves and were not fighting for or against slavery. This was exactly what was becoming horrific to all of us, the atrocities committed in the name of war, neighbor against neighbor, brother against brother. It was changing all of us, good people doing horrible things to each other.

After they failed to catch us, the Union rode south back towards Riggsville. They came upon Cooper's Mill burning it to the ground killing John William Cypert, a private under Col. Tom along with his brother William Thomas Cypert. John had gone home a year earlier to care for the mill and his family following the torture and murder of his wife, Nancy. Born in 1794, at the end of the Great War of Revolt, in Wayne Co, Tennessee on the eastern side of Memphis, near Collierville, Nancy was the daughter of James Anderson and Mary Farmer. Her father died in 1811 during the early skirmishes preceding the war of 1812. Following his death, at the age of 17, she married John William Cypert from North Carolina, the son of Francis Cypert and Abigail Johnson. Her brother James married John's cousin Mary Cypert. The Cypert's had moved from North Carolina to western Tennessee. The intermarrying of the Cypert's, Cooper's, Woody's, Partee's and Anderson's united these Southern families binding them as the issue of southern commerce and slavery heated up and a decision to move west to Ark was made.

Situated on the river ways in Tennessee, the roads of the day, they were hoping to escape the worst of the War Between the States through moving to the mountains of Ark. Their son Newton, one of 10 children, married Nancy Cooper, daughter of Samuel Cooper and Elizabeth Ross in the 1840's. Most of the extended families, young and old alike would chose to move. John William Cypert homesteaded land in Searcy Co before the war near Big Springs. In the mid 1850's, John and Nancy built their barn first, housing animals in the bottom, living in the top portion until they could build a home. It was here where dreams of a better and safer life, away from the horrors of the Tennessee River ways where Nancy Anderson Cypert and her husband John Cypert were tortured then burned to death.

At the onset of the War Between the States, Nancy was killed at Cooper's Mill in 1862 by men wearing the uniform of Union Soldiers. Some say it was Bill Williams, others say it was Bill Dark's men. Still others, say it was regularly enlisted Union Cav as both their uniforms and saddlers were Union. No one seemed to know for certain but saddles usually bore the truth. She was a half sister to William Anderson, father of Bloody Bill and Jim. The men who killed her may have been soldiers but they could have been vigilantes, more likely, Jayhawkers, Mountain Boomers or Unionists. Food was very scarce in this southern community at that time. Vigilantes put on gray uniforms in the Confederate territory and blue uniforms while in Union territory, a tactic employed by both the Union and Confederacy gave them legitimacy. When Nancy saw the men coming, she told the children to run and hide in the shed. The children saw them torture her by pulling out her finger nails with bullet molds. They did this to make her tell where her money was hidden and get information. After they had tortured and killed her, they robbed the house of all the food and everything they could use. Then they burned down the house with Nancy Anderson Cypert inside. The barn empty of stock or food had not been set ablaze. Although the children did not say, it was believed the men did atrocities to Nancy during her torture. Now, two years later, her husband John William Cypert would meet a similar fate at the hands of Union, men under Union commander Monks. After torturing and killing Absalom Rorie and his son Hezekiah, they moved along Big Springs Rd to Cooper's Mill. There finding John at the mill, they locked him inside, setting the mill on fire burning him alive. Following these horrific deeds, Gen Sterling Price, former Gov of Missouri officially assigned a number of the Missouri Col.s to operate with the sole purpose of securing the Middle White River.

The War Between the States in the White River Valley was a vicious game of cat and mouse, led primarily by Col. Tom. He had learned the blacksmith trade but spent his spare time reading law. Admitted to the bar in St. Louis, he was practicing law when the War Between the States erupted. He helped organize the Missouri State Guards which included brothers Jim and "Bloody" Bill Anderson and me. Col. Tom was first given the rank of Lt. in Gen James McBridges 7th Div Cav. Rising in rank he was promoted to Capt. and then just days later to Col. given the primary duty of protecting the munitions efforts located throughout the Southern Missouri and North Ark Ozarks. He was captured three times during the war.

Col Tom's cousin, John Calhoun Freeman of Big Flats, above the White and Buffalo Rivers, served in the Confederate 14th Infantry Reg. Both John and Col. Tom fought at Elk Horn Tavern. When Col Tom returned after having been captured at Pea Ridge, his men were officially organized as Freeman's Regiment, Missouri Cav, Ark Partisan Rangers. They patrolled the area along White River Valley with his primary camp at Mammoth Spring, Ark near the Spring River Mill. At any given time upwards of 500 men would be in camp. Typical enlistment ranged from 30 to 90 days under the militia rule principal of "you fight and go home and work until there's another fight" which means he might have as few as 200 men with him at a time but could easily rally up to 1500. With our headquarters near the Spring River unlike other leaders, both Union and Confederate, we had plenty of game and fresh water, along with forage and grain. However, record keeping was a different matter, scarcely none were kept for fear of their capture leading to knowledge of the clandestine guerilla war efforts.

Escaping at Rorie's Mill, Col Tom, seriously wounded, shot twice in the leg, was secretly guarded and cared for in the Freeman home at Big Flats. A handful of local men always knew where he was using various homes, barns and caves to hide in throughout the region including Calico Bluffs and Sylamore. The Union found and destroyed a number of powder works in the Ozarks, but the salt peter caves of the Middle White River remained undiscovered. Gunner Pool on the North Sylamore was one of the largest and most important of those. Col Tom served as a liaison between the Ark Col.s and Genls commanding the area. It was from among his command and men recommended by him secret missions were set out into other states. These were assignments we didn't talk about. Several of us were sent up to Canada to secure boats for the Confederacy; other men were running guns out of the Islands south of Texas. We operated secretly and without direct command, answering directly to the Genls who knew we could get the job done.

Chapter 21

Miles Legion, a unit of the Confederate Army in Louisiana operated under Col. Miles, called swamp guerillas due to their ability to maneuver and use the swamps to their advantages just as we did the hills and river valleys of Ark and Missouri. In April and May 1863, two thousand Legion soldiers including cavalrymen were assigned to help stop a raid on Baton Rouge. Although the battle was almost over by the time Col Miles arrived, he launched an attack but was forced to retreat. By July, most of Miles Legion had deserted, been killed, wounded or taken as prisoners of war. Among those taken prisoners was Capt Frederick "Frank" Brand commander of Col Miles. He was held along with other officers under Union Genl. Banks for exchange. The end of Miles Legion came in the fall of 1863 just as "Quantrill's" boys arrived in Texas. The disgruntlements and his inability to maintain control had led to a majority of his Capt.'s and Lt.s joining the regular Confederacy in Texas and Louisiana. It was there, Capt Brand fell in riding with the boys returning to Missouri just in time to be assigned to the White River Valley of Ark rooting out Northern sympathizers and protecting the munitions efforts.

The Union operating under take no prisoners, captured and killed a number of local men. The Union was charged with finding and destroying Quantrill's men in Missouri and Freeman's men in Ark, both of which I found myself with. We heard the Union was bringing in two thousand men camping across the hills in Burrowsville with the sole purpose of putting an end to Col. Tom and his men. We moved in several directions after escaping them at Rorie's Mill. Capt. Brand and I headed south with four or five of the boys following. There were a number of Mountain Boomers, Union guerilla's, operating in the area which we had to contend with, one of the most successful had been organized by Chris Denton, a convicted horse thief. He had been killed in an earlier battle but his men continued operating, no less than we were "Quantrill's" men with or without him. We knew Tom Morrison had a little store on the creek so we headed there to see if we could secure supplies. When we rode into the fields headed toward his place we saw smoke looming in the distance. When we arrived, the attackers had already fled. Since none of us were in uniform of any kind, there was a presumption we were there to help. Upon further inspection, Capt. Brand found the body of the older woman's husband. It was then she broke down crying, telling us this was her husband, Tom Morrison. She had been afraid at first we might be part of the attackers returning so she and Sarah, a girl of 14, covered his body hiding it when they saw us coming. It was clear he had been shot twice facing his attackers, one bullet exiting his back. Mrs. Morrison said he was in the yard, talking with the men when they first came up. He recognized the men who shot him. They were inside and pretended not to hear what was being said until the shots rang out or she thinks they would have killed them as well. It was a local man's band that killed her husband, Bill Dark, she thought. We had run across not only that name, but details of how he had been let out of prison to aide Col. Kemp ordered to root out Union sympathizers, but pretty much, wore the uniform of whatever he wanted to do, taking whatever he wanted through whatever means.

We agreed to head in the direction the attackers had left, thanking her. Bill Wilson said he would ride with them to Camp Lewisburg joining us there. We headed south camping in a protected valley deep in the mountains on the Little Red River. It was too swollen from rains to cross at night. It was there we were attacked by the still roaming band of Denton's Mountain Boomers. Perhaps they thought we were men belonging to the band of Bill Dark. They didn't ask questions, simply started firing upon us. Unarmed, Capt. Brand was outside the light of the camp fire relieving himself when the attack started. We all managed to get away except him. Denton's men shot him dead right there with his pants down. We crossed the swollen creek managing to climb the rain soaked rugged terrain.

Reaching a secure spot, looking back, standing near our fire, the illuminated men could be seen examining Capt. Brand for papers and currency. Uncertain of their actions we could tell they were loading his body onto one of the horses. We headed west before turning back moving north toward the Freeman's home place at Big Flats. The river valley maintained a clearer distinction between Union and Confederates, possibly due to Batesville. I didn't much want to be in these hills preferring the people and land along the White River. Here, the people couldn't be trusted, as to who was with you and who wasn't. When Col. Tom learned of the event he sent two scouts back to the valley ordering them to find out what had happened to Col. Brand's body.

A few days later, Bob Johnson arrived in camp telling how the following day after attacking us, Jan 28th, 1864, John Hoffmann from Rapps Barren, John Robison from Riggsville and him were at an old ladies house who was killing hogs when Bill Dark rode up into the yard with a group of his men. Fearing a battle and seriously undermanned, they fled into the cornfield. Johnson left his pistol laying on top of the wood pile. Bill Dark started chasing a young boy around the house. He grabbed up Johnson's gun, turned and fired at Bill Dark, hitting him right between the eyes killing him. No, I dare say, I've got no interest in going back into those hills. I'll take the river ruffians any day. Some say that boy, Jim Berry told it was Col. Shelby himself who give him the pistol.

Bill Dark like so many other hired mercenaries left a legacy in the hills of the Ozarks. Few remember he had a wife, sister and mother. His sister Mary Dark married Baker Cypert, the nephew of John and Nancy Anderson Cypert. Bill was said to be a looker, tall, dark skin, reddish auburn hair, dark eyes. Rachel Adeline "Addie" George fell for him but it was a hard life. After he was killed she lived in the home of Confederate Will Aiken caring for him over near Batesville. She was pregnant with their child, Willie when Bill was killed. Baker Cypert related how they understood him to have lived and died.

"In 1861, Bill Dark was an invalid in prison. Don't reckon he was an invalid really. He couldn't rectify his behavior with the Lord kind of invalid. In 1857, he'd kilt himself a man by the name of Hardy Foster and was in jail for it. He was working as an apprentice, learning to be a printer in Little Rock when he killed that man. Some say it was over his momma. They were living with James Hutchins who was a clerk in a government office there in Little Rock. They were residing at the City Hotel. Bill was 22 when he kilt that man but I reckon that Hutchins man had a good job and the right kinds of friends, Obie Greer who was Secretary of State and the Sheriff, Ben Danby, who lived at the City Hotel. Some have said Dillie, his momma, was a prostitute but that's not so Baker had assured the boys. Jim Hutchins hired Bill the best legal team he could, had 4 attorneys Absalom Fowler, Henry Rector, he's the one that come got him out of prison as Gov. of Ark, John Trigg and Joseph Stillwell. They got Judge Clendenin in Little Rock to okay changing over to have the hearing in Benton cause they thought there was so much talk of it he wouldn't get a fair trial there in Little Rock. It was nearly a year later in Oct 1858 Bill was found guilty of second-degree murder and give five years in the state pen. It seems he was in the insane part of the prison, that kind of invalid. Didn't matter much none when the war broke out his attorney, Henry Rector, got him paroled. But of course, there was a hitch; he had to join up with the Confederate Army. They put him in the Pulaski Rangers, Co F of the First Ark Mounted Rifleman. He did his year I reckon then hooked up with Col. John T. Coffee out of Missouri who was recruiting in Ark. He was a guerilla leader under Coffee. Genl. Hindman used the guerilla bands, Freeman, Quantrill, Jackman, Love, Coffee and lots of others. They were all throughout these hills. He described them as being some of the roughest, ragged rascals he'd ever seen. He ordered them to slash and burn anything that might fall into enemy hands, the spoils of war was theirs. Over the rest of the year and the next, they wrecked these hills, what the Union didn't destroy they did, in the name of the Confederacy, in the name of war both sides took what they wanted. Bill was one of the worst of'em, he was cruel. But he was a looker, a charmer and he could read and write and he won over Addie.

Now there are all kinds of stories as to how Bill died, but you see, there's a bit of truth in all of them. These women, they was killin' hogs. You do that in cold weather. It was Jan 28, 1864. He and Addie lived near her folks and they had a hideout on Meadowcreek near where the women were getting ready to skin that hog. Well, some soldiers, on their way home for a few days come through and the women fed them. One of them was from up Rapps Barren. I think his name was John Hoffman. And John Robison and then there was the Johnson boy, Richard or

Robert, some kin of Addie's. They'd laid down their guns and it was the Johnson's boy's pistol that Jim Berry used to kill Bill. Some say he got of his horse and chased the boy others say he just took aim and kilt him. Jim never wrote his own story, he couldn't read nor write, others wrote it for him as he told it, got bigger every time. Now the soldiers were so scared they wrote up what happened but didn't tell all the facts first saying Capt. Dark was wounded, then a week later saying he was dead in their official records from Jan and Feb 1864. It was Johnson who went and got Addie and helped her get out before folks come for her; he never told her it was his own gun that kilt her husband. They spread the word she rode out crossing the Red River. Addie's sister, Mary Jane she married one of the Indian Avey's, Pest, all these folks were kin. She went down to Sylamore then out through Forest Home, crossing the river somewhere there heading on over to Will Akins. I reckon Johnson you might know him. He was riding with Freeman."

Will Aiken, that Missus Addie and her baby boy lived with owned Aunt Lucy's place. He'd bought it from her allowing her to continue living there when she'd fell on hard times a decade after Uncle J.R. had died.

The Union was highly frustrated at having failed to capture Col. Freeman. They had a large camp of men near Burrowsville in Searcy Co for over two weeks raiding and pursuing Confederate partisans. They did horrible things to the local people, both Union and Confederate in their efforts to find and destroy Col. Tom and his men. A large number of our boys were wounded, captured, killed and worse imprisoned: E.N. Herron was sent to St. Louis, Sgt John Baily died of measles in St. Louis prison hospital, James Alexander was sent to Rock Island, Pervine Clark, James Denton, husband of Millie Partee, died at Rock Island prison and his brother John died of typhoid at the prison in Little Rock, Thomas Duty, Lorenzo Edwards and Patrick Gleason all died of diarrhea while in the Little Rock prison. Columbus Lamb, James Lawes and James Riley Rollins were captured. Jim was sent to Rock Island and took the Loyalty Oath then volunteered for frontier service but was rejected because he was only 15 years old. J.K.P. Wheeler died in Little Rock of rubella. Due not only to their outstanding service but to the large number of men lost on Jan 25th M.V. Shaver was promoted to Maj and Shelby to Brigadier Genl. The scouts returned reporting Col. Frederick Brand had been given a proper burial inside the cemetery that lay near the banks of the river. Since he hadn't been in uniform and didn't have any papers on him, he was in an unmarked grave assumed a Confederate.

Given Horn was wounded while trying to cross the Buffalo River near Yellville. He and Doc Campbell, George Maddox, Al Scott and James Stewart tried to steal some cattle near Big Flat and were attacked by the Reece and Treat family. Horn was wounded and told the others to leave him behind, but they refused. Two local boys who had joined them in the effort were found and killed, buried near the Reece house. We figured the

Reece and Treats thought they were shooting Union jayhawkers but it didn't really matter because they were protecting their livestock against thieves.

When Col. Tom learned some of the women insisted this man they killed, our Capt. Brand, be buried in the local cemetery, he ordered half of dozen of the best riders to head with dispatch to Genl. Price detailing the events. They encountered troops of the Eleventh Missouri Volunteer Cav near Rolling Prairie and got into a skirmish with no lives lost on either side. The Union needed to contain our boys and was steadily increasing their efforts against our successes in North Ark. A number of Union officers had been in and out of Batesville during the war. On Christmas Day 1863, Col. Robert Livingston and a small army entered Batesville, sent to re-occupy the city, keep peace in the area and promote Union control. These were the same orders we were receiving except promoting Confederate control. We had them surrounded and had great support in the area. Both theirs and our concerns kept coming from outlaw gangs terrorizing the countryside.

Our discovery at Cooper Valley near Lunenburg, Izard Co, Ark was the result of the capture of picket Bob Porter. He was a heck of a rock thrower and escape artist as well. Joe Hart could have practiced with him. Martin Beem of the Ark Mountain Infantry wrote of Porter's abilities in his official report:

> "Early this morning, unfortunately Bob Porter succeeded in eluding the vigilance of the guard and made good his escape, much to our regret... He is a sharp, desperate fellow... Porter stated that they were all to concentrate at Clinton, 60 miles from the post. Killingsworth, Second Lt, Capt. West's Co is reported near Buck Horn with about 20 men."

Bob Porter had been captured by Yankee's a few days earlier on Jan 16, 1864. He was a big burly man with an arm that was strong and accurate. On more than one occasion, he warded off Federalists' with nothing more than rocks. The boys liked to tell how he alone fought half dozen Union horsemen with nothing more than rocks. Attacked by Porter one of their horses was hit in the chest causing the horse to rear up, the soldier fell to the ground. Porter then pelted the others with rocks until they all fled. When they captured him he was determined to escape. He feigned illness; they didn't believe him and marched on in the bitter cold. He swallowed a plug of tobacco without anyone seeing and soon began throwing up, then the back door trots hit. They took refuge in an abandoned cabin for the night to shield them from the freezing rain falling on top of the already deep snow. As each new attack of vomiting and dysentery struck, the guard would have to follow Porter out into the cold. After several trips, he took to simply running out in his stocking feet and under garments. Finally, the guards stopped following him and told Porter, now seemingly very weak and sick he need not try to escape because they were ordered to shoot to kill. No one thought that any sane man would try to escape into the bitter cold of the night with freezing rain falling in only his underclothes and socks. But escape Porter did. The sentry soon realizing he had not returned alerted the others and they took out after him on horseback, however, Bob had numerous 'stockpiles' of ammunition along the familiar ridges and managed to again knock soldiers from horseback into the cold snow. They abandoned the chase for the crazy man in his underclothes.

He ran about 4 miles through the woods to his sister Susan's. Banging on the door in the middle of the night her husband Sam Blair answered the door finding a frozen, spiked hair, icicled man. Porter was described by Sam as having ice frozen in his eyebrows, hair and chest. Fearing the safety of his sister and her family, he stayed only long enough to warm up, gather clothes and move on. Then knowing the soldiers would be searching for him come day break, Sam and Susan hid his tracks, leading to and from the cabin by brushing over them with limbs. Even though that week in Ark was one of the worst I experienced in all of the War Between the States, I've told the story about Bob Porter repeatedly. Typically leaving out the fact that he was the reason we were discovered.

Jan 29th, 1864 Momma had her 49th birthday. Jesse was in Texas and I was here in Ark. She had no way of knowing how either of us was fairing and I knew she was worried. I knew which ever of us made it home first would bear the worst of her fear for us expressed in anger.

A scout entered our main camp near Milligan's campground, near Strawberry, on the evening of Feb 7th having located a detachment of Union troops out of Batesville moving north camped near Hookrum. After the war, they'd officially name it Evening Shade. Col. Tom, wounded at Rorie's Mill, remained at the home of his cousin John Calhoun Freeman near Big Flats. Col. William Coleman and his men were in camp discussing the situation with the other Col.s and Lt. Col.'s. It was decided a flag of truce should be sent forth with four of the Union prisoners. Capt. Michael Hedrick Wolf volunteered to parlay taking the flag and prisoners to Batesville. The rest of the boys would move into Fulton Co. joining with Joseph Love's troops at Morgan's Mill on Martin's Creek.

Michael Wolf, son of Reverend John Wolf and Margaret Livingston, joined Col. W.O. Coleman's Co, charged with protecting not only their families and those with Southern sympathies but the munitions works in the hills and caves here near his home. He proved himself over and over acting as a scout, familiar with terrain. Wolf was famous for jumping his horse off the high bluffs above the White River out riding, maneuvering and eluding the Union after a skirmish near Mt. Olive. Fleeing Wolf run upon the high bluff on the White River jumping straightaway into the frigid waters escaping his pursuers. The area of his remarkable jump is known as Soldier's Rock. Stories say he waved his hat to the Union soldiers who watched him and his horse float down river, then swim safely out on the opposite banks. While Wolf had eluded them, it had been then July 10th, 1862 Daniel Freeman was killed at Mt. Olive. He had come with the Bigham's when they moved here. He was 27 years old. He joined the 34th Arkansas Regiment, but following Pea Ridge stayed in the White River Valley instead of going west to Shiloh, Tennessee. They buried him near Isaac Jeffery at Flat Rock Cemetery at Mt. Olive.

The Union out of Batesville was doing their best to root our boys. When the two sides engaged it resulted in a running fight on horseback over five miles. Almost no one was injured or seriously wounded and no one was lost in the fight. The Union however tucked tail and run back to Batesville with several wounded. Genl. Dandridge McRae, Col. Freeman and Col. George Rutherford stationed men from Rolling Prairie to Jacksonport under direct orders from Brigadier Genl. Joseph Shelby. Both Union and Confederates were foraging and patrolling the area. Feb 7th, they captured Robert Payton; 9th, Jesse Maness, Joseph Orr and Robert Richie who were sent to Little Rock. Jerry Seward and Lycurus Fallas were sent on to Rock Island, Illinois. Lycurus died of acute dysentery Aug 1, 1864. Jerry was sent to New Orleans for exchange. On Feb 10th, they captured Isaac Ritter, Francis McClinton and Jesse Riggs. They were all sent to Little Rock, with Frank and Jesse sent on to Rock Island. Jesse was transferred to New Orleans for exchange, March 1865. Frank Creswell, Co A, son of Samuel Harvey Creswell and Louisa Lafferty, was captured at his parent's home. His cousin and ours, Lt. Henderson Creswell CO H was at home with his parents, James Lytle Creswell and Margaret Lafferty when they found him. Being an officer Hen was sent to Little Rock, Ark. He was transferred to Rock Island, Illinois then forwarded to Johnson's Island, Ohio. He died of typhoid fever on Sept 12, 1864.

Wild Irishman Arthur McCoy, captured near Pine Bluff, escaped and floated back down river to Shelby at Clarendon. He was just in time to rejoin Col. Elliot to whom most of us remained officially assigned, scouting in the advance for Shelby. While out surveying the area on the 14th, along with 20 other scouts under Capt. Tuck, one of the scouts alerted the others he had seen a black man in Union uniform taking corn from a bin on the farm of Lycurgus Johnson. Taking cover in the canebrake along the lake front they were able to enter the farm at the gin house engaging the sentry. The coloreds formed a line and fired a volley but were unable to reload quickly. McCoy and the others were able to scatter them using colt navy and dragoon revolvers. They located and killed every man in the detachment. McCoy delighted in the fact they took the corpses laid them face down on the ground then pinned them with their own bayonets. There were men among us of whom the war brought out the worst of human nature. It seemed when one would commence with such an atrocity the rest would follow, somehow exacting all the pain inside them upon the dead. I remained sickened by these acts. "Men at some time are masters of their fates: The fault, dear Brutus, is not in our stars, but in ourselves, that we are underlings". Then, there were the times in camp when the Irish boys would sing songs, ballads from the old country.

On Feb 18th, 1864 thirty five wagons escorted by Union Capt. William Castle and 100 soldiers stopped at the farm of Lewis Waugh 10 miles west of Batesville, in direct line with our Blue Springs camp. Several of us had gone with Col. Tom to Capt. Rutherford's camp near Knights Cove across the river. Col. Tom wounded at Rorie's Mill returned after regaining his health. He required a walking stick but rode fine. After being alerted those of us with Col. Tom headed back across the river using Grigsby's Ferry, up through O'Neal to Ruddell to Blue Springs to mount a defensive from the east. Early the next morning under the command of Capt. Rutherford, the Cav attacked the wagon train, killed four, wounded ten and captured thirty two. John Minckin of Batesville was killed.

What brought the Mincken family from Ohio to Ark around 1840 is unknown, but it is clear they were a prominent and wealthy family in Batesville by 1850. In 1844, John Mincken later spelled Miniken purchased 40 acres in Ruddell Township. Married to Jane Ann Middleton, he was a merchant in Batesville with $8,000 in assets. In 1852, John died, leaving Jane with a large household and business to run. The year before the War Between the States, their son William was working as a carpenter, George as a clerk, Charles as a printer and young John had taken up the family business, a clerk in the family store. In addition, the Miniken household included Hellen 21, Jane Ann 16, Lucy Ann, 14 and Harvey L, 9.

Strong Confederates, believing in the states rights to self govern as like so many the Miniken's didn't own slaves. When war was declared sons, George, 28 and Charles, 19 walked 200 miles to Fort Smith to enlist on June 9, 1861 in the 1st Reg, Ark Mounted Rifles for a period of 3 months. William, 32, enlisted in the 7th Reg of the Ark Infantry first known as the "Ragged Seventh" due to their civilian clothes and ragged appearance. They become known as "the Bloody Seventh" following tremendous losses at the Battle of Shiloh. Known as one of the most loyal and fiercest of Co's including William they would fight as far west as the Battle of Perryville, Kentucky. Some of the boys returning home told of camping on Chambers Hill above a deep cut valley about five miles south from where they battled. From the hill they looked one direction toward Lebanon and Samuel's Depot, the other toward Perryville and east toward Danville. There was a fresh water spring in the valley cut between the two hills with plenty of water, and for a night, they felt safe. Those were rare nights for all of us.

Charles Miniken served through June 1863, nearly two years then for unknown reasons deserted and joined the 46th Regiment, Crabtree's Ark Cav. George served his 3 months and in Oct 1861 was discharged. He returned home to care for his mother and siblings and perhaps to assist young John who had remained in Batesville providing information to Emily Weaver, a spy for us. John would take assignments himself under Col. Tom's local militia. He joined Capt. S. J. McGuffins "Popcorn" Co.

Capt. George Rutherford along with Archibald Dobbin's Cav, Capt. McGuffin's Popcorn Co and us boys of Col. Tom's Cav were camped at Knights Cove on Feb 18th, 1864 when the slave girl of Robert Childress, along with one of Childress' daughter's appeared at the camp to tell us Capt. Castle was camped at Waugh's farm west of Batesville. Capt. Rutherford along with about 80 men reached the Federal camp just before dawn attacking with surprise and force taking the enemy completely off guard. They captured 17 and killed 13 including Capt. Castle. Our only casualty was young John Miniken. Bill Chitwood and Nate Turner carried John's body home to his mother. Missus Jane ask them to lay his body out on the table where she carefully washed her son clean. They stayed long enough to help George dig the grave near their home. His sister already an eager aid took up where John left off becoming a stalwart spy for the Confederacy risking her life on a number of occasions.

Most of the Union wagons were confiscated along with contents and horses. Both Union and Confederate leaders disputed whether the shooting of Capt. Castle was an atrocity or battle incident. Capt. Rutherford recovered Castle's watch and pencil case from his men. He returned them to Union Col. Livingston, with kind words for Castle and a request Livingston try to save his recently captured brother, James Rutherford, for a prisoner exchange. Livingston blamed Castle for being surprised, reporting the Capt. "paid the penalty for his neglect with his life." James Rutherford was not immediately released and Capt. Rutherford himself was captured a few months later and imprisoned in Little Rock until the end of the war. The men did not exchange prisoners; both the North and South were holding military trials for deserters, men who had been in their ranks then conscripted into service with the enemy, such as the case of Jody Rorie.

We were getting news out of Texas things were heating up and many of the boys were forming their own companies, including Bloody Bill commissioned by Genl. Price himself as a Col. commanding a 100 of our boys. On Feb 22, 1864 War Chief, Joel Mayes married Martha McNair, also an Indian. They had a white and an Indian wedding and all the boys were invited and went. Doc said Indians can't drink white man's whiskey because their bodies can't handle the sugar and alcohol. White man has been consuming it for thousands of years but not the Indians. So, there's some truth in Indians can't drink without going a little crazy, then you add the war torn young men who wanted nothing more than to let loose a little. Yep, reports out of Texas of wild drinking and shooting escapades of the men, earned it the nickname Helldorado.

John F. Bolin led a group of guerilla Partisans in southeast Missouri. He was considered one of the most feared in Missouri along with Quantrill and Sam Hildebrand. Bolin terrorized the Union and citizens of extreme southeast Missouri from the beginning of the War Between the States up to the day of his capture and execution by hanging on Feb 5, 1864. The Bolin Band was successful in attacking Union supply trains and garrisons. Bolin's capture and hanging by a vigilante mob was news across the state. The Charleston Courier reported:

> John Bolin was captured and incarcerated in Cape Girardeau, Missouri where a mob removed him from custody and hanged him Feb 5th, 1864.

His confession was published in the Cape Girardeau Argus:

> "I was at Round Pond; there were eight men killed, two by Nathan Bolin and one by John Wright. They were killed with hand spikes. I emptied one revolver. At Round Pond I shot one man, and at Dallas I wounded another. I captured eight men on Hickory Ridge; I told them I was going to shoot them, but their soldiers recaptured them before I could do so. I have killed six or seven men; I killed my cousin; I ordered him to halt — he would not, and I shot him down."

On the last day of the month, Feb 28th, Theo Carter was killed in his his Momma, Martha Green Carter's front yard as she watched from the window. The war was brutal with mommas, sisters, brothers, daughters and sons witnessing unimaginable acts upon their kin and themselves.

Andy Blunt stayed in Missouri during the winter instead of going south with Quantrill or joining a regular command. Jim Wilkerson, second in command to Andy, forced Rev Moses B. Arnold to marry him and Miss Barbary Jane Gray at gunpoint. The ceremony was at the home of Judge Gray of Jackson Co March 8th, 1864. It was illegal for Confederate Southerners to marry or preach and being caught doing either was punishable by death. Two days later on the 10th, Andy was killed south of Oak Grove. March 9th, Robert Cartwell was killed at Warrensburg.

Some of the boys ran into Press Fugitt and Fletch Tayler guarding the road from Lafayette Co to Clay. This was the first sign Bloody Bill was back in Missouri. Guarding the roads allowed Bloody Bill and the boy's time to rest, clean their guns, make bullets and otherwise prepare for what lay ahead. When you met Press, a preacher came to mind. He wore a hat some of the boys swore he'd took off an Amish man. He buttoned his collar to the top and wore a full face of hair with his head cropped clean. His demeanor and attire always fooled the Union. Because the boys teased him so often near the end of the war he shaved his beard off in place leaving a goatee. He didn't look so Amish after that but still preacher like.

A number of us left Ark headed home to join Bloody Bill.

Valentine Baker, 1st Sgt William "Billy" Blackmore, Jeptha Bowles, Harvey Brown, Henry Buford, Dolf Carroll, Theodore Cassell, Dock Corley, Henry Coward, Abner Creek, Creth Creek, George Daily, Richard Ellington, Peter Farley, Samuel Finnegan, John Fisher, Tommy Fulton, Garrett Groomer, William Hensburg, Joe Holt, Snowy Jenkins, Silas King, Mars Lisle, Ning Ling, Peyton Long, Rez Magruder, Leon Martinez, Plunk Murray, Pat and Sandy McMacane, Allen Parmer, Cooley Robertson, Doc Rupe, Harvey Rupe in his forties was an old man among us, Ol Shepherd, Bill Stone, Oscar Swisby, Parker Talcott, Nate Teague, Robert Todd, Clarence Tomlinson, Thomas Tuckett, David, Newman and Samuel Wade and Dick West.

On our way home, we moved along the White River to Yellville relaying a dispatch to the boys there under Lt. Col. Joseph Love. They received information ahead of us Orr was moving in their direction. They were confident they didn't need our assistance so we moved on north toward the Missouri border headed toward Springfield. Riding through some dense brush I was happy the ticks and chiggers were not yet out.

On March 15th, 1864, Capt. Bill Chitwood and several of his men were reconnoitering when they spotted a detachment of the Eleventh Missouri Cav near Buckhorn. The boys dispersed without incident. Two of the boys, Frank Petty and Andy Pinckston were captured after crossing the river, found hiding in the William Weaver barn near Ruddell Hill. Weaver an elderly man was an uncle to the Chitwood boys and offered a safe haven. Maj Pace took them to Batesville then sent both Andy and Frank to Little Rock and then to Rock Island, Illinois. Frank died at Rock Island June 3, 1864. After Frank died, Andy was paroled and transferred to New Orleans for exchange Jan 1865. Misinformation was provided as directed in these cases. Andy told us Maj Pace had been residing at the home of John Byer's widow Esther Wilson Byers, mother of little Mary, one of Batesville's belle's and a cousin to Nannie Wilson, wife of Carroll Wood. Missus Esther received compensation from the Union for boarding the commander. Mary kept a journal noting he was a Northern Methodist preacher and she loved arguing with him on the subject of slavery. Andy told how they gave him food but kept Frank from eating trying to get them to turn. Frank got sick with dysentery and died. It was clear from Andy's face there were worse things than dying.

We understood from the numbers of men wounded, captured or killed the Union was taking our efforts seriously. Down in Louisiana on March 21, 1864 Capt. Joseph Lea moved into Tensas Parrish where he and Capts Middleton and Lusk fought Federal soldiers. Cole Younger had stayed with him 3 months at the Widow Amos' farm on Fortune Fork in Tensas Parrish before being ordered west. On March 22, Sgt. Thomas Louis Vandiver on a secret mission north to Canada was captured at Saint

Paul, Minnesota. He was returned to St. Louis to stand trial. Things were getting rough, the Union notorious for taking scalps, something we'd learned from them, were blaming us, Quantrill's men, whether we rode with him or not of atrocities the Union themselves were perpetrating. Some of the boys believed they were supporting the vigilantes who were guilty of some of the worst atrocities. Turner Ashby under Stonewall Jackson crucified men and worse, long before Quantrill had a band. I knew the atrocities of the Union and Jayhawkers had preceded those of the guerillas. These were acts common in the Great War of Independence, these were not sole acts of guerilla warfare but acts of warfare. I wondered how many sons were told by their fathers, uncles, grandfathers, men who'd fought in 1812, the Spanish War and Florida War with the Seminoles, "You survive. You do what you must, but you survive."

Back home in Missouri, March 23, Joel Chiles, Jim Nolan, Ves Akers, William Gaw, Allen Parmer, Jesse Morrow and I went to Camden on the southern border of Ray Co for a little action of our own. We crossed the river in a raft then managed to steal several Federal uniforms, clothing, ammunition and a horse without being caught. William Gaw could be an anxious sort. Returning he accidentally shot me in the face. Now, I did have to go home for Momma's caretaking. She and Aunt Charlotte carefully tended to my face removing bits of powder and metal. Cooking up some of their drawing salve they made sure I kept each spot moistened with it. For days bits of stuff would head up and they would squeeze it out of me. I dare say they appeared at times delighted to be making me flinch.

Back in Batesville, Union Capt. William Orr's Co set up camp. A majority of the local men went home to visit their families. Even though they were local boys, they were Union, so they were ordered, like us, to travel in groups of two or more. Some of Col. Tom's boys attacked a couple of them near Magness Landing successfully robbing them. Orr sent a regiment after the boys capturing Corp. Larkin Turner. He was sent to Little Rock and died Aug 21 of typhoid fever. The boys made it back to cousin Burwell Lee's where they were quartered. Too close for comfort, several commands moved closer to Jacksonport near Akron at Big Bottoms while others moved up the White River toward Yellville with the intentions of cutting off any Union headed back toward Rolling Prairie. On the 26th on the south side of the White River at Oil Trough, across from Big Bottoms, Orr's command came upon a group of the boys out reconnoitering. They held their ground and the losses were about the same on each side. The Union managed to confiscate some horses, guns and a saddle the boys had taken from one of their men. Capt. Samuel McGuffin, who had helped organize the men of Batesville with Capt. Rutherford was killed in the fray.

On the 24th, Capt. Albert Kauffman, Eleventh Missouri Cav Volunteers, Union, moved out of Batesville up the White River to the mouth of Wolf Bayou and Briar Creek. Scouts followed close watching the movement of up to two hundred men. They turned southwest at Coon Creek camping on John McCarn's farm. There they found a harness that had been taken during the battle at Waugh's farm. John's wife, Louisa Qualls McCarn was at home with four young children. They killed her milk cow and ate her. For whatever reason, they did not burn her out. The scouts returned reporting to 2nd Corp. Thomas Smith of their movements. Corp. Smith was pursuing the Union hoping to attack and rescue two of our boys they'd taken captive. Capt. Kauffman caught up with the boys taking them completely by surprise. They killed no one during the skirmish but wounded several of whom they took prisoner; Lt. Wiley Horton, Capt. Bob Trimble, Carl Hughling, Andy Snyder, John Ward, Wiley Horton, 2nd Lt. Will Hancock and several more. They were all sent to Springfield, then on to Gratiot Street, from there to Alton or Camp Douglas prison camps. They all survived except for Carl Hughling who died Dec 8th of small pox at Camp Douglas, Illinois. Robert Tinkle managed to escape. He was married to Mary Courtney Hall, a cousin of Joseph Courtney Hall, neighbors and family in Missouri. She'd been orphaned in Mississippi. Our boys managed to wound one man and kill a number of their horses. Some of the boys watched as the Union skinned out the dead horses, taking both the meat and skins. Two local boys had joined Corp. Smith, just boys, not more than 14 or 15. They were captured hiding in the brush. It was said they had some of the clothing and equipment taken from Capt. Hinkle. These were not soldiers, not even men, just boys. After camping for the night, Kauffman convened a mock military commission and executed the two boys. They left those young boys exposed to rot, but took a family of Union sympathizers with them who had spoke against the boys. Three of the scouts picked up the boys and took them home to be buried. Three others followed along skirting Kaufman's movement watching as the Union burned a number of homes along Coon Creek. The family had a wagon pulled by an ox which had difficulty in the mud and muck created by the troops advance. They made their way back to Batesville crossing the White River near Ruddell at sunset on March 31. Within two weeks, things were so difficult on Col. Livingston in Batesville, not enough local forage or support, constant breakdown in communication and supply lines he vacated Batesville. By May, Jo Shelby reclaimed Batesville for the Confederacy.

I arrived home mid March around the same time things in Sherman, Tex were getting out of hand, robbery, murder, drunkenness and disorderly conduct by our boys left Genl. McCulloch with no choice but to act. In order to get rid of Quantrill, on March 28th McCulloch ordered him arrested.

Quantrill escaped fleeing back to camp pursued by over three hundred Texas Rangers and Confederate troops. James McArtor was with Quantrill. About two hundred of our boys fled with him including my little brother Jesse, crossing the Red River into Indian Territory. There they were able to supplement their provisions and headed home to Missouri. Heading north they broke into smaller units to escape detection. The lack of leadership in Texas had given way to the boys forming new alliances and new guerilla bands under Fletch Taylor, George Todd and Bloody Bill Anderson.

They moved due east from Bonham to Fort Towson, a hard two days ride. There they rested and regrouped before moving north along the Ark border 150 miles north to Fort Smith. Once they felt safe, they were in no hurry, resting and camping, doing a little hunting along the way. They explored the terrain and talked about what life would be like after the war, maybe buying some land and raising cattle in southern Oklahoma, Ark or north Texas. Passing they learned Fort Smith and Van Buren were heavily bolstered by the Union so they moved north and west along the border 75 miles to Fort Gibson. Finding it also occupied by the Union they passed quietly during the dark on April 21st, crossing the Ark River moving toward the home of Confederate Genl. Stand Watie near Spavinaw Creek in Indian Territory. The Rogers settled there. Genl. Sam Houston married Chief John Rogers daughter Tiana, a sister to Lewis Rogers who set up the first mill, a distillery and salt works with the Chief. Lewis and Tiana were siblings of Mary Ark "Arky" Rogers Vickery who was living north of Batesville near Strawberry among the Irish. Genl. Stand Watie's family was among those forced to leave their homes in Georgia by President Jackson. The Cherokee council outlawed the operation of distilleries and the Roger's family lost both their distillery and their salt works, which they partnered with Robert Bean, brothers Sam and John Houston and Jehoiada Jeffery from Ark, from the White River Valley. Robert's father, Capt. Jesse Bean of Batesville, Ark had been made head of the Ark Militia, the first military west of the Mississippi. He led the writer Washington Irving on a tour which he wrote into a travel guide in 1834 *The Tour of the Grand Prairie*. That was before Sam Houston left his second wife, Tiana Rogers and their children heading south to Texas. These lands were all once part of the French Chouteau Territories, lands the new United States bought and called the Louisiana Purchase. Quantrill ever the school teacher and a history buff taught the boys as they moved north from Fort Gibson to find Genl. Stand Watie.

Jacob Croft a Mormon exiled from Missouri enroute to Utah settled at Spavinaw Creek around 1846. Indian, Joseph Lynch Martin hired him to help rebuild the mill which had been destroyed from flood waters of the creek. Then around 1855 a large group of Mormon missionaries from Utah arrived at Crofts. They began trying to convert the Indians which didn't set well when they began trying to get them to move to Utah. Lewis Roger's complained to the council and Chief John Ross. In 1856, they ordered all Mormons out of the Cherokee Nation. It seemed no matter where they went the Mormons weren't welcome by decent folks. They even told the Indians that they would turn white if they converted and baptized in the Mormon temple. They even said black folks would turn white. Maybe President Lincoln simply should have just required the blacks to become Mormons, freeing them when they turned white. I don't reckon I ever knew any person to change the color of their skin. Perhaps if your god lived on Kolob he could do that, but I never saw any proof of it.

In 1862, Chief John Ross was captured by the Union and held as a prisoner of War. Genl. Stand Watie declared himself Chief of the Cherokee Nation. Then burned down Ross' house. John Ross and Stand Watie had their own kind of war that went back to before they were forced to move. Genl. Stand Watie was part of the Treaty Party and Chief John Ross was part of the Nationalist Party, or maybe it was the other way around. They didn't get along and had their own war in Indian Territory. When the boys met up with Genl. Stand Watie, they moved into Seneca lands headed to North West Ark. While there they skirmished with Union and aided some of Col. Tom's and Capt. Love's men in patrol. Camping they shared stories and learned what had been happening while they were in Texas. After a week, they moved on up north along the Missouri Kansas border. Their travels were marked by rain, cold and wet, hard to make camp a number of the boys took sick. The muddy roads made travel difficult and very slow but off roads were worse. This contributed heavily to their route north along the Kansas Missouri line where Quantrill was most feared. Genl. Stand Watie aided the boys safely through Indian Territory then returned south west. Col. William Penn Adair remained with them continuing north. Both enlisted and civilians were guessing where Quantrill and his men would emerge, fearful it would be in their town.

On May 18th, 1864, guessing stopped. Quantrill and the boys entered Carthage, Missouri in Jasper Co. They entered Kansas west of Joplin moved north and then east to Carthage. The town had been burned and the courthouse destroyed in an attack two years before. Quantrill and the boys challenged the Union stationed there to come out and fight. They declined. The Union command conveyed the sighting to other outposts reporting "the guerillas under Quantrill were in Union uniforms." The boys camped outside of town before heading 20 miles north to Lamar on the 19th.

Headed south in the fall on Nov 5th, Quantrill and the boys fell in with Col. Warner Lewis of the Missouri State Guard near Lamar. They made plans to attack the Union outpost there. They rode down the streets to the courthouse where they fought Union Capt. Breeden for over an hour and a half setting fire to over a third of the town's homes and businesses. At dawn on May 20th, six months later, they were about to strike again. The Union under misinformation distributed by the Confederates believed Quantrill and the boys would attack Neosho. They sent a large portion of their soldiers from Lamar to defend Neosho leaving only a small contingent of forty men from the Seventh Missouri Provisional Cav behind. Some of the Seventh were from Lamar and at home with their families and not at the garrison. When the boys attacked, not even thirty soldiers were present, some having breakfast others feeding their horses. Everyone was caught off guard, including Commander Lt. George Adler. They scattered in all directions, fleeing on their horses hiding in the timbers along Muddy Creek. Col Adair, leading a hundred Cherokee soldiers, pursued them toward Fort Greenwood. Quantrill and the boys then attacked the burned out shell of a courthouse not once but three times. Each time the troops holding it forced them back. Union Sgt. Jefferson Cavender and nine men held it. When Col. Adair's men returned reporting most of the Union men wounded or dead, they moved on headed towards Warrensburg, 90 miles north.

SPRINGFIELD. Mo., May 21, 1864.

Lamar was attacked by 100 rebels about daylight yesterday morning, who were repulsed by our troops with the loss to us of a few horses killed only. Enemy's loss not reported. This is no doubt the same force that passed through Granby the night of the 18th instant. There are quite a number of rebel troops north of the Ark River, and they are constantly moving north in bodies of from 50 to 125. It seems utterly impossible with my reduced stock to intercept them or bring them to an engagement; still I will keep trying. No attack was made on Neosho, and the troops there pursued this force north until their horses gave out.

JOHN B. SANBORN,
Brigadier- Genl., Commanding.
Maj. O. D. GREENE.
Assistant Adjutant- Genl., Saint Louis.

FORT SCOTT, KANS., May 20, 1864 10.30 a. m.

This a. m. at 4 o clock the rebels attacked Lamar. Mo., 40 miles from here, and took the place, it being garrisoned by about 25 State militia and the same number of citizens. My orderly and one of my scouts were just outside of town in the edge of the woods, saw the fight, which lasted less than five minutes, and then started for here.

As far as they could hear anything, they heard firing in the town, supposed to be the rebels murdering the soldiers and citizens. The officer at Lamar, in the night, last night received a dispatch from the commanding officer at Newtonia, Mo., 80 miles from here, that at that place they had fought Marmaduke and 500 men all day yesterday, and asking help. In five minutes two companies will be on the road from here to see about the matter. I will keep you advised.

CHAS. W. BLAIR,
Col., Commanding First Brigade.

Brig. Genl. T. J. McKEAN.   FORT SCOTT, May 20, 1864.

I neglected to add to my former dispatch I do not believe it is Marmaduke who is at Newtonia, but if it is, the 500 men are only his advance, as he is not likely to move with less than 5,000 or 6,000.
CHAS. W. BLAIR.

Genl. McKEAN.   FORT SCOTT, May 21, 1864.

It was Adair that attacked Lamar, and after they got clear into the town, the militia rallied and drove them out at 10:30. My troops and the militia are still in pursuit south of that place. Nothing further heard from Newtonia.
CHAS. W. BLAIR, Col., &c.
Genl. McKEAN.

MOUNT VERNON, Mo., May 30, 1864.

RESPECTED SIR : I have the honor to inform you that the town of Lamar is in ashes. The bushwhackers under Taylor, Marchbanks & Co. entered the town at 2 o clock on the morning of the 28th instant and burnt nearly every house in the place, together with most of the household goods, &c. All the books and records of the Co were again burnt. The women and children were sitting outdoors trying to take care of what they saved until help could be sent. I tried to get some assistance at Carthage, but Capt. Walker could spare no men, so I came here, but find the Col. absent. I do not know what the loyal citizens of that place have done that has subjected them to such treatment from the military. We were promised better things; but alas, again we find ourselves the victims of mistaken confidence. I care not for the amount of property destroyed ; the great damage done is that the Co cannot again feel organized in two years. The people will be compelled to go to Kansas or elsewhere where they can have the protection that loyal citizens deserve. I am happy to hear that you condemned the moving of the troops from the town. I hope, Genl., you will see this matter investigated.

Hoping to hear from you soon, I am, Genl., with high regard,
your obedient servant,
NATHAN BRAY.
Brigadier-Genl. SANBORN,
Commanding District Southwest Missouri.

On May 23, Quantrill and the boys attacked a forage wagon on the Little Blue River killing one Union man and wounding another. They burned the wagons, shot the mules and cut telegraph wires between Pleasant Hill and Warrensburg. On the 26th, they attacked the mail route between Pleasant Hill and Warrensburg capturing the Union's orders, directives and letters. The mail route became so dangerous for the Union by land or water it virtually ceased. Similar success by the boys in Ark under Col. Tom had virtually stopped all river travel on the White clear into Missouri.

In Platte Co, Ridgely, Missouri, Union Capt. Fitzgerald in head of the troops managed to keep Fletch Taylor and his men from entering. They finally gave up and headed on to Clay Co.

On May 27th, George Fielding was at home at Marshfield, Missouri east of Springfield when he heard gunfire coming from his neighbor's James Bradley's place. Riding over to investigate he found his best friend John Thomas surrounded by Federal troops. Unaware John was dead he charged full force and was killed. Bill Stone wounded in the right thigh, back and hips managed to crawl to a fence witnessing the whole thing. George Fielding charged into Federal soldiers in order to save John Thomas who was with Stone but was already dead. Fielding was killed. His brother Thomas was killed two weeks later on June 11, 1864 by a Union soldier for his boots, near the Bradley farm as he was walking home. Two weeks earlier on May 15th their brother William Fielding was captured near Ridgely. The Union dug a grave, tied William to a log and rolled it over the grave. They shot him multiple times then cut his body loose letting it fall into the grave. Then they rolled the log in on top of him and left the grave open. William was more of a city boy than a country boy. He liked to dress sharp with a clean shirt and neck string. He had what he called a manicured beard and mustache. Moorehead who we called Moose was killed at Mister Bradley's house.

Chapter 22

I was right about Momma's fear and worry turning to anger. Arriving home before Jesse, I received the brunt of it. Luckily she had received a letter from him stating he was fine and leaving Texas. About the time Jesse left Texas headed back to Missouri, Momma got word from Uncle Marc Thomason, a doctor in Clay Co, his daddy Robert Thomason was sick and dying. Gramps Bob was our step grandfather, the only grandfather Jesse and I had ever known and brother of Uncle Wild Man Bill Thomason, Bloody Bill and Jim's grandpa. I didn't know how to take this. I was overcome with sorrow. Unc, the man most responsible for teaching all of us children, now soldiers, survival skills died in 1858 and now his brother, my Gramps, one of the most important men in my life was dying. We headed to the house. Gramps Bob died April 2, 1864.

Along with Momma and us children, Mattie Thomason, Momma's half sister and the rest of the family was there, save Jesse and Bloody Bill who we were unable to get word to. Gramps Bob had married Mrs. Julie after Gramma Sallie died. She was crying, tears streaming down her face, walking about talking to people. "Get yourself something to eat now," she'd say, "There's plenty." It was like no one could see her tears. Her son John by her first husband was a doctor and attended to Gramps the last few days along with Uncle Marc. Southern funerals are not like burying people in other places. People sit up with the dead who can't be left alone until it is time to be planted in the ground. There's always food, lots of it and singing. People talk all night, men on the porch if the weather allows which it did for Gramps funeral and women in the house in the kitchen cooking and talking. Children run around playing games, preferably outside. Life and death are celebrated. "If you prick us, do we not bleed? If you tickle us, do we not laugh? If you poison us, do we not die? And if you wrong us, shall we not revenge?" I kept hearing Daddy's words from the Bible in my head. Seeing the reality of the war and all the families this war had forever changed, I reached into my pocket grasping my button tight.

Quantrill, the boys and their horses were worn out. Skirting the edge of Warrensburg in Jackson Co, Missouri, about six miles out, dressed in their Union blues they were passing themselves off as Colorado troops when they met a detachment of Missouri Militia under Union Lt. Nash. They spoke to each other from a distance with most of the boys hiding in the brush. George Todd, Dick Kinney, George Shepherd, John Barker, James Little, William McGuire, John Jackson, William Hulse, John Ross, George Maddox, Sim Whitsett, and Quantrill faced Nash killing all but one man. He escaped alerting the rest of the Colorado Second Cav. Traveling on the muddy roads was difficult and early dark found them caught between the pursuing Cav and an infantry unit waiting in ambush. The better choice was to turn and charge the cavalry. Wheeling around, Bill McGuire's saddle broke throwing him into a tree. He staggered to his feet. Todd and Quantrill came through unscathed. A few days later, Bill McGuire and Babe Hudspeth were with Tid Sanders when they were surprised by Feds. Bill took a hit, wounded badly but they escaped to the Sni Hills. The Union tracked them down and killed Bill. Tid had been hit 11 times. When the boys found their bodies, Bill looked like he'd just laid down and fell asleep. The weather was cool enough the flies hadn't blown him yet and the weather hadn't yet warmed up enough to bloat him. The boys buried them.

George Shepherd on his horse
Emory Cantey Collection

Jesse would use all the skills Unc taught us riding with Bloody Bill, moreso than with Quantrill. We'd learned to use a slingshot, tomahawk, clubs, poles, spears, bows and arrows and in the end, pistols, Unc's preferred gun. Each of us learned to skin a rabbit leaving the hides almost completely intact and duly demonstrated it to Unc. We caught snakes bare handed, hung them in trees and skinned them. We milked poison from the fangs of rattlers. Unc used it in medicines and he always had some in a pouch. He said he learned from the Indians more venom was the only thing that could keep you from dying from a bite. We trapped coyotes, black cats and bear. We hunted deer, duck, small game and hogs. With every animal, we learned more and more about how animal instincts are dominated by a sense of survival, defending their young from other animal prey and humans. And, we learned we weren't all that different.

One of the first things that shocked me was how even my dog ate a couple of her own puppies. Unc and Momma explained animals understand when a baby is not going to make it. They kill it or let it die, most typically they eat it. They can't let the scent of death lure in animals that would prey on them, killing them all. Unc showed us how to scalp using animal heads. The feel of the skin of a hog he said was most like that of a man. Things that would repulse most people we learned to do with skill and speed, harvesting the best of the animal if on the run. We had contests of how fast each of us could skillfully cut the shoulders or leg quarters off a deer. The shoulders and shanks of deer could be tossed across our shoulders and carried with greater ease. Unc prepared us to survive. Losing first him, now Gramps, I felt a growing weight of being the man of the house Daddy had proclaimed me to be.

That summer Bloody Bill would let loose all the grief he'd held inside. No matter how they had died, killed, murdered and scalped, burnt out left destitute, small pox, maimed, injured, crushed in the collapse of the Grand Street building, Bloody Bill lost more than his share of family at the hands of the Jayhawkers and Union. After returning from Texas he began killing without mercy. It set heavy on him he wasn't home when our Gramps died, his favorite Uncle. I could see it in his eyes. I held on to that button a lot during the war, but no time like 1864. Now, when Bloody Bill spoke of paroling someone, it meant kill'em, no exceptions. He talked this way not only around each other but whenever he was around our families. Every one saw the change in him.

Just as the Union had their passwords for recognition we developed our own set of words and symbols. Several of the boys, including Col. Shelby, were Masons' so it was easy to expand our symbols using some of their Masonic symbols. We left carvings on trees and rocks, a means of communicating especially when changing camps. Jesse's symbol was two J's back to back like an anchor, mine a J with a slash through it looking like F and J were on top of each other. We used them when leaving messages and marking paths. Some of our signs were old Indian signs, water looked kinda like a snake with no head and such. We incorporated Unc's knowledge of the thong trees made by the Indians. They pointed to water and shelter. He showed us how to cut the young trees so they would grow this way. It was important to continue to mark the trails this way when the older trees would die a new one had to be started to keep the trail marked.

Archie Clements took to riding with only Bloody Bill. He mistakenly believed Bloody Bill's rage was his character. It was Peyton Long and Archie who first begun scalping victims. Peyton killed a Union courier and found two ears in his pouch. The report in the courier's bag said Quantrill's men killed and scalped some of their troops in a skirmish. We knew this wasn't the case. When discussed with Col. Shelby he was against it. Archie suffered the Union scalping members of his own family and decided to take matters into his own hands. Some blamed the scalping on the Cherokee Union, but knowing the Cherokee, Osage, Kaw and other Indians the way I did, the way Unc had taught us, the way Cole Younger, part Indian himself knew and Stand Watie, scalping was not a typical trait of our Indians. It was more common to the Great Plains west of us, lands folks were now calling the "wild west." We first heard of Union scalping men as early as 1862. Now two years later Bloody Bill and Archie Clements pushed the vote and not only actively engaged in scalping but encouraged the boys in it. Eventually only a few of the boys had not taken at least one man's scalp or tried. I witnessed many turn sick unable to finish what they started. Newspapers and the Union, even other southern soldiers who didn't know spoke with certainty that William Thomason Anderson earned the nickname of Bloody Bill because of the scalping. Bloody Bill minded at first but come the summer of 1864, nothing seemed to matter anymore. He and Archie mirrored the worst in each other. John B. Bramlett said, "They are with killing men like most people are with mosquitoes. They squash them." When any one ask me, of either of them, "What's wrong with him?" I could only reply, "The list is too long." The changes in the boys, the men, were becoming more and more evident. George Todd dancing across the dead counten' them come up short face to face with Archie holding a victim's head high. He beheaded the man rather than simply scalp him. Blood running down his arms, dripping off, I saw several of the boys head for the bushes.

Bloody Bill and John Thrailkill were Jesse's best friends. He was riding with the two of them. John was older and had more sense. I was beginning to fear for Jesse with Bloody Bill, not just for his life, but what this change in Bloody Bill would have on Jesse. At Union Mills, Platte Co, Missouri, Joe Macy and John Thrailkill made camps a mile apart near the Harrison farm. A Union column traveling in secrecy stopped at the farm house and Harrison's daughter, Mary, slipped out of the house making her way to warn Thrailkill. She saved not only his life but my little brother who was camped with him. He sent one of the boys to warn Bloody Bill's camp. Thrailkill was ready when the Union soldiers attacked. Joe Macy, was making his way from Bloody Bill's camp when he heard gunshots. He raced to Thrailkill's camp and along with several of the boys from Bloody Bill's camp, defeating the Union. I needed to talk to John about Jesse riding with him more than Bloody Bill, where ever Archie wasn't.

John Thraillkill
Missouri Valley Special Collections, Kansas City Missouri

Todd was growing in his leadership and in some ways was showing the effects of war as well, counting the dead by jumping from body to body, taking ears. Archie's beheading of Unionists at first alarmed him, then he too seemed to find an eerie delight in it. Returning from Texas they found home decimated by war and the people who supplied and aided us, burned out, gone or dead. The few remaining people had little to give. We had to disperse across the region. Bloody Bill held the area north of the Missouri River and Todd to the east. Quantrill became increasingly absent spending time with his child bride, Missus Kate.

Even at rest we were on alert. Jesse and Peyton Long were watering their horses by the creek while Theo Castle and Jim Cummins lounged in the shade of paw paw trees talking. Sort of on guard, they were surprised by Union soldiers. Theo escaped but Jim was shot in the leg while trying to get his horse loose. His horse jumped and ran toward Peyton and Jesse. They all got away but the Union got his horse which had his suit on it, tailor made for him. It was clear he was more upset about the suit than having been shot in the leg. We found out from Ol Shepherd, while they were at the home of Mrs. Fox, in Clay Co, Alexander and Arthur Devers were killed when Capt. Rogers surrounded the home. They buried the brothers in the same grave. When their brother James learned of their fate, he joined us. He was a formal kind of person insisting on being called James. A lot of people with that name were called Jim or Jay. He was a clean shaven well groomed man of stature. Earlier on March 10th, in Jackson Co, Jim Waller and Andy Blunt tried to rescue Otho Hinton and Andy was killed. At Kingsville, in Johnson Co, Jack Bishop fought a skirmish and his horse was shot, when it fell it pinned him underneath. J.C. Ervin was captured and held at Lexington. Each time one of the boys out with the regular troops or other Partisan Rangers bands made their way back, they had news and none of it good. Oth was later captured and executed. We read it in the Lexington Union dated Feb. 27, 1864. George Byron King, a boy, had his left arm blown off at Lexington. He was happy to return fighting with us and told us it was fine we called him Lefty now. The boys were gonna call him that whether he liked it or not, they had a fondness for him and liked getting a rise out of him. He'd grown out a full mustache and was now looking more like a man than a boy.

Sydney Drake Jackman was ordered back to Ark to recruit raising his own Ark regiment. He captured three men and a young boy suspected of being Union guerrillas. He hung two of the men. The boy and the other man "willingly" escorted Jackman to their leader a man named Meeks. Jackman surrounded the log cabin where Meeks and his men were. Running from the cabin 15 of Meeks men were shot down in their nightshirts and Meeks wounded. One man was captured and hung from the eave of the cabin. Col. Sydney Drake Jackman, along with Col. Shelby and Col. Tom were given the commission of Brigadier Genl. before the war was over due to their successes for the Confederacy.

On April 1, Genl. McRae was camped at the Anthony plantation, north of Augusta in Jackson Co, Ark. McRae was watering his horse by a stream when he was nearly captured. After a twelve mile pursuit they stopped to rest near the Fitzhugh Plantation. By then our boys under Col. Tom and Capt. John Bland were over 400 men strong and attacked. Col. Tom not having recovered fully from his Jan wounds received near Rorie's

Mill was using a walking stick. He was wounded again during the attack. The Union fled south of the plantation into a forested area known as Fitzhugh's Woods. There Capts George Rutherford, Jesse Tracy and Jesse Reynolds brought in their forces, now over 550 cavalrymen were striking from the front, rear and left. Both sides ran low on ammunition bringing the running fight to a halt. The Union headed back towards Augusta. The losses on both sides mirrored the other. The Union captured 16 year old John Huddleston, son of William and Sarah Hodges Huddleston from Batesville, Independence Co, of Col. Tom's Co A who had been wounded. He was transferred to Rock Island, Illinois.

On April 2, a command of 1,200 troops under Brigadier Genl. Jo Shelby, Col. Shelby to us boys, attacked a Union supply train of more than 200 wagons at Wolf Creek a mile east of Terre Noire Creek. They were being escorted and guarded by the Twenty-Ninth Iowa rear guard and men of the Fiftieth Indiana. Shelby's men rode in flanking the supply train but were held in check by the Union. Fighting continued back and forth throughout most of the day. Near sundown Shelby's men attacked again forcing the Union to retreat. The Union captured Tom Pridmore. He was sent to Little Rock, then to Rock Island, Illinois on June 23, along with Huddleston. Pridmore was exchanged on March 4th, 1865.

On April 5th at Whitley's Mill in North West Ark troops under Union Brig Gen J.C. Sanborn attacked the boys near the headwaters of the Buffalo River. The Union had sent men into the region to try to put an end to our independent units, irregulars and guerillas. From late March through April our boys skirted their camps along the rivers. Col. Bill Patton captured in Jan, taken to Springfield, died in Dec 1864 at Camp Douglas, Illinois. His men 250 strong were still operating under Lt. Col. William Harris Monroe Cooper, part of Col. Tom's command from Izard Co. Our scouts made aware of the approach were ready. A two hour engagement ensued. The Union wounded Lt. Col. William Cooper. Our boys in turn killed several of their men and wounded several others, capturing Union Private Obie Patty. Lt. Cooper, assigned to the 27th Ark was sent home to recover. We learned of his death on Dec 5th. We had made camp in Cooper's Valley, near their home the night Billy Hinkle joined us.

Lewis "Bulge" Powell's men of the 13th Missouri Light Cavalry in the Missouri bootheel were being sought out by the Union when they found Lucas "Like" Bissell on April 6th killing him. Like was just a peach faced boy. He wore a coat his momma made him. It was big sleeved and would fit over several layers of clothes. He kept good and warm in it. A few of the boys asked about buying it off of him knowing he'd never sell it. He'd puff up with pride when they'd ask. When the Union found Like and killed him twenty five boys from Bulge's command moved on the Union the following morning at daybreak. They were outraged, angry with rage taking over where sensibilities should prevail. It was calamity in the making. Thinking of Like, they were bent on revenge. Unfortunately with no real plan of attack, several died trying to avenge young Like. April 11, 1864, Jackson Bawyer was captured. The Union hung him in Sept. It was worse for some more than others, but I know just because we survived didn't mean we were okay. Some of those boys were shot a thousand times over, every night in their sleep. The pain and fear could be hidden during the day, but at night, the screams of sleeping troops told the truth.

The Federalists have occupied Batesville since Christmas. Our main camp was located near the Milligan's Methodist Campground southwest of Smithville, west of Strawberry. Milligan was one of those red haired Irish that Strawberry was named for. It was a game of cat and mouse with their boys winning a few and then ours winning a few. No real successes or defeats were gained or lost in skirmishes. The boys real success against the Union, was harassing, disrupting communication and supply lines and maintaining the munitions effort safe but most important, keeping the Union busy on the west side of the Mississippi. Following an unsuccessful skirmish at Smithville the 13th, Union Col. Livingston gave it up and moved the majority of the troops out of Batesville to Jacksonport.

Col. Tom wounded at Rorie's Mill and again at Fitzhugh's Woods was able to ride his horse. He placed Lt. Col. Joseph Bell Love, son of Thomas Bell and Elizabeth Barnard of Wright Co, Missouri, in charge of reconnoitering the area south of Batesville, at Big Bottoms, Oil Trough and Jacksonport. Union Col. Robert Livingston set up camp at Jacksonport on the White River with 1400 troops. He was planning to take half of them to Augusta to secure more supplies. Oil Trough lay across the river from Big Bottoms. It had taken its name from the early frontiersmen who operated keelboats in the area, trading with the Indians they secured bear oil in troughs. Jacksonport was five miles east on the White River.

On the morning of April 20th commanding men from several of Col. Tom's companies including men riding under Lt. Col. Christopher Cook, Lt. Col. Love, Col Robert Wood, Capt.'s George Rutherford, Osby Dillard and Bill Chitwood, Corp. John Bishop and 3rd Lt. Bill Arnold and troops of Brigadier Genl. Dandridge McRae engaged pickets near Elgin Road. The boys had been unable to dislodge Livingston from his camp. Union Lt. Col. Baumer who we faced at Rorie's Mill sent out eighty men to battle. Baumer charged the second line Love set up. They were able to disperse the boys who moved to set up a third line of defense further down River Road with Bill Chitwood and a command ordered to destroy the bridge at Village Creek. With reinforcements moving in Baumer was able to push the boys back forcing them to abandon the bridge before it could be destroyed. It took all of Baumer's and Livingston's men to hold the bridge through the following day allowing time for our boys to move to Augusta alerting Genl. McRae's encampment of the Union's movement.

The rainy season was upon Ark and Missouri. Movements were becoming more difficult, especially for the Federalists who seemed to spend a great deal of time bogged down in the mud and mire. We were able to draw them out into skirmishes depleting them of their supplies and stores. Angry returning unsuccessful from Augusta, Col Livingston and his men went on a rampage. Stealing cattle, horses, mules, wagons, food, murdering citizens and killing livestock they didn't want, burning homes, barns and fields. They were too ignorant to salvage the livestock for food. It didn't stop our boys from skinning out the charred animals getting to the good meat. Southern boys know how to survive and the Southerners who had joined the North had little voice or say so. The weather aided our boys just as it had done back in Jan '63, the rain soaked fields and buildings were too wet to fully burn. Between Augusta and Jacksonport, the Federalists stole a dozen slaves from the Shoffner farm "enlisting" them as cooks and dishwashers for the Union at Jacksonport. They captured Robert Blackburn at home. They sent him to Little Rock, he died Sept 4th, 1864.

"The men designated by name took the prisoners, and from the plunder they clothed all who were naked. They provided them with clothes and sandals, food and drink, and healing balm. All those who were weak they put on donkeys. So they took them back to their fellow Israelites at Jericho, the City of Palms, and returned to Samaria." 2 Chronicles 28:15 War has not changed.

I received a letter from Bill Gregg. He was returning from Louisiana intent on forming his own regiment. When he got home, Ben Mead and I joined him with enough boys to make up a regiment, operating under Bloody Bill's command. We met at Uncle J.R. Cole's house to discuss their charge under Genl. Price. Nearly 200 of the boys decided to ride with Bloody Bill. Sandy McMacane, Silas King and Allen and Buster Parmer joined Fletch. Allen had been home with me a few times and was clearly sweet on Susie. They were both 16. Momma insisted Jesse remain with Bloody Bill. I was becoming more and more concerned about that but couldn't fully explain my reasoning to Momma. I needed to talk to Uncle Till or Uncle J.R., soon.

French Indian Anderson Baby, Hamp Watts, his momma Evaline Boone, was the great granddaughter of the famous Daniel Boone, and Joey Holt son of Jeremiah and Elizabeth Green Holt joined up after meeting with Stand Watie and William Penn Adair; Andy, Joe and Hamp were all 16 years old or less we think, lying about their ages to join up. They were big boys so we weren't certain. They were at the home of Capt. Sebree when Federalists surrounded them along with three others, 3 escaped and 3 killed.

Back in Ark Genl. Shelby sent Col. Sydney Jackman to locate deserters bringing them back to camp in the area of the Buffalo and Northern White Rivers. Jackman and his men joined Col. Robert Wood's Missouri cavalry engaging near Poison Springs. The boys talked quietly among themselves about the killing of blacks there, mutilating them, taking ears and scalps as souvenirs. I learned later Wirt Woodson, a cousin and half brother of the great Stonewall Jack, was riding with Col. Wood both at Jenkins' Ferry and Poison Springs. He was married to Clarrisa Cummins of some kin to Little Jim Cummins. He told me of the mutilations in detail. When President Lincoln made this war about slavery he changed what men were willing to do. It had become Mister Lincoln's War.

May 3, enroute from Searcy Co toward Newton Co, Col Jackman enountered 1st Lt Andrew Garner, under Union Col. John Phelps, at Richland Creek. Andy was from Searcy Co, just south of Richland Valley son of John Garner and Ruth Elliott. He served in the Confederacy a year Aug 61-62 then deserted and went home. Captured by the Union he was forced to join or die. He married cousin Becca Cole in Feb. Under orders to seek forage for their animals, he was headed home to Mount Pleasant in Searcy Co with a 100 man detachment with twenty four wagons drawn by mules. Traveling down the north bank of the Buffalo River across from Richland Creek, north of Mt Pleasant, they were stopped by high water.

One of the Snow girls, neighbors of the Garners had seen them and come to camp alerting Col. Jackman and the boys of their location. The boys rode to the mountain overlooking Richland Valley. They could see Andy and his command crossed the creek and was moving along the south banks. Unaware of any enemy presence they were taken by surprise when the boys charged them from the rise running through a fence cutting off the main guard from the rest of the troops. The boys on both sides were fighting hand to hand, using their guns butts and barrels, whatever they could to attack the other. Bill Chitwood was angry when one of his cousins, Jim Hester, was found among the Union dead. He knew he was not a Union man, he too started out with the Confederacy. Andy escaped leaving behind his supply train, moving back north toward Bellefonte and Rolling Prairie. Our boys suffered no losses but killed some 30 or 40 of the Union. The boys said they sat on the hillside watching as Bill Chitwood descended back down into the valley to help in the burial of the dead in Richland Valley. George Maddox said the cries of the dying mules made him sick. It was as awful as a rabbit's scream. I knew what he meant. I thought about the night Jesse and Bill came back to camp with the Momma rabbit and babies, the night Bill was knighted by Unc as Bloody Bill Anderson.

Confident the Union had moved out some of the boys went home to visit family. Capts John Sissell, George Newton and John Hicks Nichols were sent out scouting while others set up camp with fortifications. For a night, all was well. On May 5th, Col. Phelps made a surprise attack. Learning of the defeat of Andy's command he rode all night in order to affect an attack on the camp. Taken completely off guard, our boys lost funds, mules, horses and communications. The rest of boys moved east staying near the Partee's, Arnold's, Dillard's and Jeffery's for a few days before returning back west of the river to continue coverage and recruiting.

Shortly after the boys left, Genl. Watie moved back west. On May 8th, he and his men were pitted against Union Cherokee organized under Col. William Phillips. Union Capt. Hen Anderson, scouting east of Fort Gibson, was searching for Confederate Col. William Penn Adair. They had a skirmish with about 20 men north east of Maysville. Our boys forced the Union to flee back toward Fort Gibson.

Two days earlier on the east side of Ark south of Piedmont, Missouri, Capt. Abijah Johns and the Third Missouri State Militia, under orders from Union Col. John F. Tyler, entered Ark searching for our forces near Pocahontas, north of Milligan's campground. Our boys destroyed the bridges on both the Current and Black Rivers and the spring rains engorged the rivers and outlying areas with water too fast and furious to cross without them. The Union headed north along the Current River in search of a safe place to cross. The advance guard entered Cherokee Bayou, the area between the Current and Black Rivers on May 8th where they engaged a group of our scouts out foraging. Our scouts scattered into the brush leaving their men in the swampy area. One of their men deserted and fled, a local boy known to one of our scouts, he was allowed to go home. We suffered no causalities or wounds, but killed two of their horses. The scouts followed the Union watching as they made their way to Buckskull where they made camp before proceeding north.

On May 5, 1864, Shelby was ordered from his position south of the Ark River to "occupy the valley of White River and to prevent its navigation in every possible manner and fashion." Union Col. Robert R. Livingston had left Col. John Stephens with a small detachment in Batesville. In a letter dated May 11, 1864, Livingston advised Stephens of probable evacuation: "I may deem it best for you to evacuate Batesville, and should you find it necessary to do so, fall back upon this point," being Jacksonport, Jackson Co. Shelby and his troops moved from Clarksville, Johnson Co crossing the Ark River at Dardanelle, Yell Co on May 18. Shelby stopped there joining Col.s John T. Coffee and Sydney Drake Jackman recruiting. Meanwhile, Livingston hearing of Shelby's approach evacuated Batesville on May 20 moving to Jacksonport. Shelby then passed through Van Buren Co, "over rough and sterile roads, over Blue and Ozark

Mountains thru Richwoods," across the ridge descending near Rocky Bayou Creek down through the farm of Col. Thomas Black toward Buck Horn.

Maj Genl. Sterling Price and Shelby ordered Col. Jackman to station at the base of the Boston Mountains some 40 miles from Buckhorn. He was to continue recruiting in the area raising a regiment of cavalrymen, Jackson's Missouri Cavalry, though half of them would be Ark boys. They camped north of Burrowsville in an old Indian settlement. This was home to Federalist Chris Denton's Mountain Boomers. He had been killed but his men continued to pillage and loot under the guise of protecting people. Many of the local boys had served their time in service to one or the other, Confederacy or Union, only to be captured and forced to serve again on the other side. Many of our boys, sent home to care for the women, were ordered to aid in the Confederate Nitre and Mining Bureau munitions efforts. They happily did so, glad to be nearer to home.

Months earlier the Union camped here, wrecking havoc on the area from Batesville, to Mt. Olive, Sylamore and Riggsville, torturing, mutilating, killing and burning people alive. They destroyed homes, mills, barns and fields. They burned the courthouse and most of the town of Burrowsville before moving out setting up command centers at Rolling Prairie and Berryville. Again, they were charged with finding and eliminating the guerillas in north Ark. The mountain terrain was unknown to them. The broken hills, impressive mountains and valleys were the exact locations we needed to hide and to set up ambushes. Jackman recruited companies already operating in the area and independent groups to join him, including Capt. James H. Love's Co C of the Seventh Ark Cav. The drought in the fall of 1863 and spring of 1864 had as much impact on the availability of food as the slash and burn policy of the Union, who were now suffering as much as our boys were. We were hearing reports of the Union boys donning Confederate uniforms taking cattle and other animals from families to feed their troops. They had almost decimated the area around Rose Mountain over a week's time.

On May 13th, preparing to head toward Batesville, Shelby was faced with the same problems of high waters near Lewisburg 30 miles west of Little Rock. The Union was encamped on both sides of the Ark River. Genl. Shelby planned to use two boats to cross the entire command to the north shore when near sundown his pickets were attacked by over 400 Federalists who had taken Lewisburg. In order to keep the Union from realizing the number of his troops, he reinforced the men who were engaging the Feds at intervals. They ceased fighting as darkness fell. Shelby reported killing and wounding some 40 Union with no causalities on our side. The Union destroyed the encampment on the north side of the river. Shelby moved the troops further west towards Dardanelle.

Camping on the night of the 16th with plans to attack the following morning the Union made a surprise attack during the night. Shelby's men responded capturing some 100 Unionists and a large amount of their supplies. The Union fled crossing the swollen Ark River. Shelby and his men began crossing the river and by the following morning had gotten the entire command across to the north banks. They made camp at Norristown where Federal troops from Lewisburg attacked the pickets. They were now aware Shelby had crossed the river to the north allowing them time to evacuate Lewisburg 30 miles east. Shelby's men were able to retake Lewisburg. The Union suffered greatly due to a smallpox epidemic that claimed many of their men. Huge numbers of Confederate prisoners were found sick and infected. The dead had been left unburied, among them young Andrew Rorie who had been forced to join the Union or be killed. Everything had to be burned and buried in order to eliminate the risk of the small pox spreading. A regiment was left to complete the task and bury the dead with orders to join Shelby near Batesville.

Genl. Shelby sent Capt. David Williams and 50 men ahead as advance guard. On May 25th, 1864 they encountered Bill Williams and his vigilantes, Union deserters and Mountain Boomers, near Buck Horn on the ridge above Walls Ferry, where they were camping. Williams and his gang had taken advantage of the local men being away at war and were terrorizing the area. Mention of Bill Williams' name reportedly "sent chills of terror into the hearts of people who were helpless against him; he and his men stopped at nothing." From his camp near Wall's Ferry, he stole, plundered, and murdered. He was able to move north and south across the White River with ease. Shelby described him as "the notorious Bill Williams who commanded a hybrid of deserters, Negros, women ravishers, and Feds." Local militia under Col. Tom, Jim Anderson, Bill Chitwood, Will Jones, John Younger, Henry Moore, Bill Knight, Charles Grigsby, John Freeman, Ike Flannery, Bill Arnold, Elbert Benbrook, Ben Gill, Bill Blankenship, John Byler, Ril Gillihan and others, were allowed to stay or return home due to impending evacuation of Batesville. Freeman left a Majority of men at home to protect against Williams and to secure the munitions efforts. Many were upset over the capture of Franklin Creswell in Feb and Henderson Creswell in March at the hands of Williams. Both men had been helping their family prepare for spring planting. William's had handed the location of our men to the Union.

In the fight between Shelby's men and Williams, forty-seven of William's men were killed. Two were captured and executed the next day. Shelby's report described the relief felt by the residents: "Young girls and old women met us the next day and called down Heaven's blessings on my command for what they termed a glorious and righteous deed."

Shelby moved toward Batesville crossing the White River at Grigsby Ferry on May 26, 1864. Control over the White River remained the main objective in the area. Rugged terrain and lack of provisions made the White River valley an undesirable place to do battle for the Union. More people had been killed in the Skirmish at Buck Horn than in any single battle anywhere near Batesville. As Shelby approached, he got word Livingston was in Jacksonport. He pushed his men riding through the night but was too late; Livingston evacuated Jacksonport on May 26.

In the White River Valley, Southerners were riding high. There had been no significant causalities for our boys. Shelby ordered the rest of our boy's home ahead of Genl. Price's plans to move into Missouri. Orders were to continue wrecking as much havoc on the north as possible, driving attention to away from the path Genl. Price would be taking. His goal was to take Saint Louis. We learned from The Louisville Courier Journal that Basil Duke a brother in law of Confederate Brig Gen John Hunt Morgan had taken over John Hunt Morgan's command following his death. Shelby set up headquarters at Batesville.

News spread like wildfire among the Union, Quantrill had been killed on May 28th. James, John and Tom Kelly were carrying letters addressed to Quantrill when one of the boys was killed near Salem in Fulton Co, Ark during a raid on a wagon train. They thought they had him until it was confirmed Quantrill was alive and well raiding Missouri. He enjoyed the news and used it to his advantage on more than one occasion claiming, "I'm not Quantrill, that fella's was dead, Union dead".

May newspapers reported successes of Union Genl. Grant marching across Virginia against Genl. Robert E. Lee. They reported horrendous losses: the Union over 3,000 dead, 21,000 wounded and 4,000 missing in the Battles of the Wilderness and Spotslyvania. The dense forests of Virginia should of offered southern troops an advantage but Lee retreated.

June 1st, Bloody Bill and about 60 boys under him arrived at Momma's. For a few hours we were soldiers swapping stories, then we were boys again at Momma's table enjoying sorghum molasses and sweet butter on hot cat head biscuits with cold milk from the spring. The boys with Bloody Bill were refreshing their horses and enjoying relaxed time just wandering around the farm. They killed more than a few squirrels and Aunt Charlotte made a huge kettle of squirrel dumplings. One of the boys cut off all of the heads of the squirrels boiling them in a hanging pot over the fire. When they were done, he proceeded to tap each head sucking out their brains. Aunt Charlotte offered she could fry them up with some eggs but he didn't want to share. The boys started tossing the squirrel skulls around like they were balls, juggling and playing. Momma sat on the front porch watching. I saw her smile and for a moment all the world was right.

Some of us, Peyton Long, Jim Bissett, Jim and Bloody Bill, Fletch, Jesse and me took a ride around the farm on the 4th. We come upon neighbors, childhood friends, Brantley York Bond and Alvis Dagley. Boys we had grown up with, we had been friends, neighbors, who sat on the same pews at church, swam, fished and rode horses. We had learned with certainty it was Brantley and Alvis who had lifted Doc to be hung by his neck at our farm a year earlier. Momma and Susie had seen them. We had known the day would come when we would encounter them. Revenge is best served up cold. Bloody Bill wanted nothing more than to kill and scalp them, threatening them as we all sat astride our horses side by side on the road near Haynesville. I saw a side of Jesse I'd not seen before. He was smooth insisting their innocence to Bloody Bill who immediately caught his drift. Calming them somewhat, they drew closer to Jesse, thinking he believed their proclaimed innocence, thinking maybe he hadn't seen them that day. With a nod of Jesse's head, we all drew our guns, except only him and me, fired. He shot Brantley square between the eyes. The bullet I shot went clean through Alvis' head, in one ear and out the other. Peyton Long jumped from his horse and put another shot through Brantley's twitching body. Alvis had been working on the Travis Finley farm not far from Momma's. Bloody Bill was outraged because he thought they needed to suffer, instant death was too good for them. He wanted it to look like they hadn't been killed together so he loaded Alvis back onto his horse leading him to a bank near the Travis farm. He acted as though he was going to scalp him but mostly we simply listened to his ranting the rest of the way to Momma's about what he could of, should of done. They got their due. "Patience, a virtue."

The Bigelow's lived about 6 miles away from the farm. Momma was certain they were providing information to the Union. They were known to slip off, fight awhile and come back, similar to the manner in which most of the Southerners fought but they couldn't be found in any of the units of the Confederacy and no one had fought alongside them. Fletch decided they needed taught a lesson. We rode over to their place with the intention of setting fire to the farm. It was a brisk June day and the strong breeze would carry the fire. Since the Union made the most of setting fires, it could be blamed on them. When we got close John, who had been out hunting was making his way back across a field caught site of us. He ran toward the house a clear sign he was guilty of something, Momma said later. They were firing upon us before we reached the outbuildings. We dismounted, taking cover. Jesse was proving himself over and over, darting closer and closer to the house he pushed through the front door attacking them in hand to hand combat. A fight ensued worthy of a bar room brawl with furniture being bashed over the backs of attackers. By the time I made it in the house, Jesse and Fletch were standing side by side both Simeon and John Bigelow dead in a pile of broken furniture. After emptying their guns they started fighting with chairs, stools, anything they could to defend themselves. Some might say it was a sorry fight, others might call it valiant. I knew it was just the way things are when people fight on opposite sides. This was war, even if it was friends and family, neighbors. "Some rise by sin and some by virtue fall." I felt the shame the Bigelow boys, Alvis Dagley and Brantley Bond, should have felt. They had been taught by Unc. "Vengeance is mine, saith the Lord." Again, we felt righteous.

Genls Sterling Price and Marmaduke planning a raid into Missouri, ordered a large number of Col.'s and Capt.'s to move into the areas of north Missouri to harass and engage the Union keeping their forces away from the southern border where Genl. Price would enter the state. He ordered a meeting of all the Col.'s and commander's of regular, irregular and Partisan Rangers. While Shelby was recruiting and gathering men in Ark, we were to do the same in Missouri, paving the road north, securing support among the civilians and adding new recruits to the ranks. Col. Shelby had been promoted to command all Ark Confederate forces north of the Ark River.

Lt. Col. Osby Dillard and several of Col. Tom's men rode in for the meeting. They brought us up to date on Ark. At Moccasin Bend a major crossroads for travelers between Little Rock and Batesville on the Little Red River near Searcy the Beeler family operated a ferry. Their large 500 acre plantation was located on the east side of the river. On June 6th, Shelby sent a detachment of 40 men to lay out an ambush for a Union foraging party sighted nearby. The men waited but grew restless and crossed the river where they found twenty five Unionists. Tom and Pollie McGaw Cullum were neighbors of the Beeler's. All the families were loyal Southerners and had hid a great deal of stores, ham, bacon and other provisions as the Union moved in. The Union foraging party confiscated the Cullums' smokehouse chickens and meat along with corn and goods from the house, including clothing and quilts. The Union and Shelby's men skirmished at the Cullum's house, kin of Shelby's. Their daughter Nancy was being courted by one of the local Cherokee, Samuel Lowery, great grandson of Maj George Lowery and Lucy Benge, niece of Duwali, Chief of the Ark Cherokee, sister of Sequoyah, Chief John Jolly Due, Chief Robert Benge and Bloody Fellow, Native American Lords and Ladies. The skirmish took place right in front of the Cullum's home.

Union Capt. Wagner boasted he could go anywhere in Jackson Co with the right 65 men. George Todd and Ike Flannery, Bill Basham, Lafe and Hence Parvin and Henry Porter met him and the 2nd Regiment Colorado Cav on the Harrisonville Road about 7 miles south of Independence on Wed June 8th. Wagner and 27 of his handpicked men were killed. Polk Bradley was wounded but not seriously. Henry Porter was wounded in the left leg. Wagner and his men were buried in the local cemetery by local women, a far better fate than they would have had for our boys.

Union Capt Fitzgerald was head of the troops stationed at Ridgely, Platte Co, Missouri. On June 11th, Fletch Taylor and the boys unsuccessfully tried to get into town. After five attacks Fletch finally gave up and went on to Clay Co. News of what was happening around us filtered in. All of the boys dressed in their Union blues, mounted and headed to Johnson Co with the goal of attacking and killing the first Union they met. Union Sgt. J.V. Parman and 14 troops of the 1st Missouri Cav were out scouting between Holden and Kingsville when led by Fletch we encountered them, killing 12. Of our boys, we lost Billy Oldham. The Union was stripped of their uniforms and packs. Ammunition and supplies were gathered. The Union horses were not only branded but were skin and bones. We had to kill'em all. The order that allowed we should be treated as criminals, outside the tenants of soldiers had changed most of us. Decency did not describe the Union and we were retaliating in like kind. We left the dead there on the road. This was becoming easier to do. I read my Bible more and found throughout it a righteousness I have come to understand boiled not only within me, but the likes of Union men, each of us believing God was with us if not leading. I reckon mankind can justify any act if they believe themselves righteous in the act. Col Coon Thornton and his men fought with Union Capt Benjamin F. Poe of the 89th Enrolled Missouri Militia from Plattsburg with similar outcomes. Col Thornton received word Quantrill along with his wife Kate had went to Howard Co and John Ross was with them. Frank Gregg was wounded trying to get to the Missouri River and Lt. William Greenwood was shot in the leg at California near Jeff City. Here we joined ranks with Col. Thornton.

Two days later on the 13th of June, we attacked a wagon escort of 30 Union, 12 miles south of Lexington and Thornton's men held up the Independence Warrensburg stage. The boys were moving along the road tearing down the telegraph lines when the stage appeared on the road. They captured two wagons and killed 15 of mules and eight soldiers from the escort. Tuck Hill was voicing concerns about how he viewed Bloody Bill which didn't set well with many of the boys who understood his rage and his sorrow. Momma always said there is no right or wrong way to grieve. Albeit I doubt she understood all Bloody Bill was doing, she loved him and she would always be there for him. Tuck left and joined up with Fletch Taylor. Dr. Lee Miller took leave of us, joining a wagon train as wagon master headed to Salt Lake City. We could tell things were heated on both sides and our efforts were exacting trouble for the Union as set out by our commanders. But, the lack of recognition by the commanders was hitting home with many of the boys.

We'd entered this war innocent, having heard the stories of men in our families, grandfathers, uncles who fought in the War of 1812 and Indian Wars. Now, we were changed, no longer innocent. No boy should have to bury a friend, especially a brother or cousin. We should be considered unfortunate and our lives changed should we bury more than one, sit in church, hear the preacher deliver his message then carry that casket to the grave. Now we hid in caves, barns if we were lucky. We watched our friends suffer with gangrene only to lose a hand, arm, leg hacked off in an attempt to save their lives, which more often than not was unsuccessful. We witnessed the ravages of disease and sicknesses. We may not be the stuff of men, but we certainly were no longer "the boys" we called ourselves. Words were heard less often than silence as shovels cut the earth to lay another friend to rest and laughter was only something we remembered.

In northwestern Ark and southwestern Missouri our boys were being used to keep the Union from discovering and destroying the munitions efforts. Federal forces were determined to find and stop us. Col. Tom sent word amongst the other Col.'s of a meeting at Cross Hollow. On June 20th, Capt. Powell of the Union's Second Ark Cav was ordered to move from Cassville, Missouri on a scouting mission into Ark. One of our spies riding with them learned of their movement near Sugar Creek. Thomas Nail under Col. Tom and his Uncle Charles Nail had been captured, but Thomas managed to escape. Charles signed an oath of allegiance and rather than parole him, the Union forced him into service under Capt. Powell. He managed to escape returning home to Ark and now Powell was determined to find him. The Union allowed he was to be shot when found. They moved toward Cross Hollow there turning south to Fayetteville then to Bentonville. The third day out one of the Cherokee Scouts returned to inform our boys Powell had found Nails' wife. She told him he was trying to locate Confederate Col. Brown but that's all she knew. Powell continued his search coming upon four or five of the boys surprising them. They captured one of the boys who provided misinformation to lead them to the area of the planned attack near Walnut Springs. An ambush was set up however it became clear a number of our boys were sick with small pox. Rather than follow through with the attack, Col Brown sent most of them home, engaging with Powell then dispersing. The Union always took this as fleeing but hit and run attacks were part of our maneuvers. Desperate for clothing and blankets, some of the boys had kept the pox infected items found earlier which infected and spread among them. The boys left behind pox infested overcoats and blankets previously captured from the Feds and Confederate prisoners which they knew the Union would use just as our boys had. They also left behind two horses that weren't going to make it much longer. It's always interesting to note the discrepancies between what happened and what the Union reports say happened. When we'd capture them, we'd hoot and holler them.

We successfully interrupted mail routes and telegraph lines, goaled toward stopping river travel. The riverboats became targets, a moving shooting gallery. Tom Bell volunteered to swim the Missouri River in Carroll Co below Waverly, a cramp seized him and he drowned. After fighting at Vicksburg he'd come home to fight with us.

We learned the people of Kansas City, the largest city in our region, had been called to a mass meeting to discuss our activities. Civilians, Union and Confederate sympathizers were present, a common fear of another mounted attack on some post or city, as had occurred at Lawrence, Kansas uniting them. We understood this. The Border Wars and the attacks from Kansas had united our families, bleeding onto our generation hatred and desire for revenge. The men of Kansas City were supplied arms for defense of their lives, homes and the city. The Union concern for an all out attack on Kansas City and the growing alarm under which citizens were acting led Union Gen Rosecrans to mount a response campaign against us.

Quantrill chose his new bride over the men and remained in Howard Co. The remaining Col's Coon Thornton, Fletch Taylor, Clifton Holtzclaw, George Todd, Bloody Bill, Dick Yeager and Dave Poole under which we were riding set out breaking into smaller groups of 25 to 30 operating on our own, complying with the overall orders of Genl. Sterling Price to wreck havoc in anticipation of his move into Missouri. Brown pursued us with a vengeance of his own throughout the rest of June. He succeeded in murdering 22 of our boys. The Union set up signs and countersigns for accurate identification when encountering "men in blue" while out reconnoitering and scouting. Bloody Bill and George Todd secured the list under which they were operating, learning the signs turning the Union's efforts against them.

On July 3rd, in Platte Co, six miles north of Platte City, Fletch and his boys were surrounded by Union, several killed on both sides. The next day we heard Bill Wilson held a little skirmish on his own in Clay Co. He rode back and forth, back and forth through the damp soil making it look like there was a dozen or more men, enticing the Feds to pursue him. When they did, they launched from the edge of the bank into a quicksand. The more they struggled on their horses the more vulnerable they were. One by one, Tom picked them off. In celebration of our nation's Independence Day, skirmishes were fought in large numbers between small groups of our boys and the Union across the entire state. On July 4, 1864 we were in Clay Co, Missouri. Hiram Guess joined us riding under Bloody Bill.

On July 6th, the boys with George Todd skirmished on the Little Blue River ambushing a patrol of the 2nd Colorado Cav killing seven men including the Capt. A copy of the Kansas City Journal newspaper was found among the items. Todd was delighted with it:

"Quantrell is a regularly commissioned officer of the Confederacy. His murderous raid on Lawrence was openly defended by the rebel papers in Richmond, and there is no doubt that his operations and those of his companions are under the Genl. direction and control of the Confederate government. They are rebel forces employed, sanctioned and kept up by the rebel government. The regular forces of the rebellion were long since expelled from the state. The rebel lines are hundreds of miles from our border. There was never a more atrocious system of arson, robbery and murder, set on foot anywhere than the Confederate authorities have inaugurated and sustained in Missouri."

July 7th near Parksville on the Missouri River, we were joined by Col. Coon Thornton along with 20 or so men of the Paw Paw Brigade. Three days later we hit Platte City capturing over 300 Missouri Militiamen. Upon realizing they were going to be killed they downed the Union flag and hoisted a Confederate banner in its place. Although Fletch was suspicious as to why they had a Confederate banner in the first place, the rest of us were satisfied these men were with us. Later, Coon told us it was staged because they had wanted to join us but couldn't or they would be shot as deserters. The men wanted to prove themselves suggesting we pay a visit to Charles Morris. A Methodist Minister with known Union ties and a strong abolitionist, he might seem a likely target but like women and children, Jesse and I protested stating men of the cloth should not be included as targets. Fletch led the way there allowing some of the captives to prove themselves. After setting the house on fire, three men, among them Charles Morris attempted to escape and were gunned down, riveted with bullet holes fired from probably 100 of the boys. Jesse and I stayed back watching.

The Kansas City Journal reported we were operating under Genl. Sterling Price and were included in his numbers of the Army of Missouri, which Union Genl. Rosecrans had difficulty believing. Genl. Price actually opposed secession from the Union but had been put in a position he had to choose sides. In 1838 he was sent as part of the delegation investigating the Mormon Wars in western Missouri, mostly around Liberty. At first he had sided with the Mormons reporting back to Gov. Lilburn Boggs they were not guilty of the charges made against them. Gov. Boggs ordered him to aid and protect the Mormons from the Missourians when they surrendered in Caldwell Co. Genl. Price was a man of reason who understood what fighting meant; he understood guerilla warfare, irregulars and Partisans. He understood righteousness, acts unholy and otherwise, believed righteous.

The Union captured his son, Genl. Edwin Waller Price. He was distracted by the fact his wife, Missus Kittie Bradford was experiencing a difficult pregnancy. Many Southern women rushed to her home in Brunswick, Chariton Co, to aid and care for her in his absence. She had three small children in the home, Katie, 5, Sterling, 4 and Austin, 3. Heavy with child, she was due the following month in Aug. The heat and war was taking a toll on her requiring confinement to bed until the baby came. Genl. Rosecrans sent his captive Genl. Edwin Price to determine if the guerillas were in fact operating under his father, Genl. Sterling Price and if they had been commissioned. He was allowed to parlay with Col. Clifton Holtzclaw who confirmed we had all been commissioned under orders from his father, Brigadier Genl. Sterling Price, most while in Ark at the Dripping Springs camp. Col. Holtzclaw further informed him he himself had been ordered to Missouri with specific goals of recruiting in Howard and Boone Co and was authorized to commission men. Although our numbers were not exact, he told him we had upwards of 10,000 men to aid his father in his goal of securing Missouri for the Confederacy. This information was not far from accurate and had been part of the orders Col. Holtzclaw was given. He was a big bulk of a man with a shock of black hair and a long beard. His eyebrows were thick and furrowed at the brow between his eyes. He had the look of a man you did not want to mince words with. Should I ever of imagined what a pirate might look like, I would have Col. Holtzclaw in my mind. He had a handsome homemade gray coat made to fit his broad shoulders. He was a commander in every sense of the word. Union Genl. Rosecrans made it clear, he would not be retaliating against all Confederate prisoners but he would not recognize irregulars nor guerillas. When word of the meeting between the two reached Genl. Sterling Price, he sent communications ordering a war conference be held sending direct orders to each Col. including Quantrill and Bloody Bill.

Church was a good means of getting word out. Women, sisters, wives and mothers would be at church and Sunday morning services were considered safe by both sides. Then on July 10th, 1864 while attending church services at Warder's Church, Wellington, Lafayette Co, Jeff Wilhite and 4 other guerrillas were killed. Jeff was shot with 28 minie balls, some passing completely through him. John Prock who couldn't swim, escaped by holding on to a cow's tail crossing the nearby creek. Quantrill and Kate were at the home of Evan Hall in Howard Co resting when Patrick DeHart, one of Cason's men found him delivering the news of the attack on Warder's Church and the war conference. DeHart joined us.

The following day, July 11th 1864, Col. Calhoun Thornton ordered Capt. Overton and 9 men to eliminate Capt. Fitzgerald commander of a Co of Union militia near Ridgely, Platte Co. Our boys were surprised to find the Unionists awake and armed. They tried to catch Fitzgerald off guard and kill him unfortunately Capt. Overton was killed. Fletch and his boys joined us riding with Bloody Bill in raiding Lafayette, Saline, Carroll, Chariton, Randolph, Monroe and Shelby Counties. Before we rode back to Carroll Co and entered Ray Co on July 12, Johnson "Jock" Barbie, Jesse, George and Ol Shepherd, Bud Pence and Cooley Robertson and I planned a little ambush ourselves, luring some Unionists into a trap. James Justice volunteered to lure the Feds into the ambush was killed. Hiram Guess, Archie Clements and Woot Hill all had horses killed. Left behind to find horses on their own, they quickly caught back up. Jesse took Jim Justice's revolvers off him while Dolf Carroll shielded him from Union fire. He rode with Jim's body across his horse and got Momma and Missus Bettie Robertson to bury him that night. If the Union found out they buried him, there could be severe reprisals, but this boy was only 17, same as Jesse and a neighbor to us. He hadn't lived long enough to do much wrong.

Quantrill spent most of June and July with his new bride Kate in Howard Co. With news from DeHart of the war conference, he located John McCorkle and John Barker ordering them to find Bloody Bill. They found us near Boonsboro. Polk Helms and Willie Reynolds didn't want to ride with Quantrill. When Bloody Bill left heading to meet Quantrill they went to Clay Co joining up with Fletch Taylor.

When they were very young, Bloody Bill and Jim had lived in Huntsville, the Co seat of Randolph. On July 15th, while wearing Union uniforms our boys killed a man, robbed the local stores and took nearly $45,000 from the bank. When we gathered back up, no one wanted to say just what had happened because we figured they didn't want to add the money to our operating coffers.

Chapter 23

Col. Coon Thornton was in the area recruiting, commanding his own company of men when the decision to raid Plattsburg was made. They attacked Arnoldsville a month earlier with success then moved west and north to join our efforts attacking New Market. There we secured a number of goods, horses, guns and money. The goal of clearing the area in preparation of Genl. Price's march into Missouri was proving successful and the larger town of Plattsburg in Clinton Co was next. Col's Thornton and Thrailkill with whom Jesse and I were riding, along with Bloody Bill and the rest of the boys, moved into Caldwell Co attacking Kingston. In early July, Union Capt. Poe, commander of Co B of the 89th Enrolled Missouri Militia at Ridgely was ordered to move to Plattsburg along with Capt. Turney of Co E. Together they had 100 men. Poe and Turney were over the garrison at Plattsburg. Union Capt. Sessions, head of the garrison at Richfield was at Plattsburg. We were riding nearly 500 men strong. Col. Thorton increased our numbers with the Paw Paw's, former Confederate soldiers and southern sympathizers who joined him in both Parkville and Platte City. They brought a large number of arms. Col. Thrailkill was having similar success in numbers. One of the boys learned from a local woman at Camden Point there was a large store of gunpowder and supplies to be had. Camp was made in an open pasture north of the village. We suffered a surprise attack that didn't amount to much. On the 17th Col. Thornton and Col. Thrailkill skirmished with the 2nd Colorado Cav between Fredericksburg and Excelsior Springs on the Clay-Ray Co line.

On the 19th, Capt. Poe was alerted by scouts that Thrailkill was leading 400 men on horseback headed towards Plattsburg. Capt. Poe sent a patrol under Capt. Turney out to reconnoiter with the goal of locating us. On the morning of the 21st, when Capt. Turney saw our approach he realized we carried a flag of truce. Around nine o'clock on the morning of the 21st, Col. Thraillkill's messenger delivered to Col. Poe a demand to surrender the town.

"I hereby demand an immediate surrender of the town. We are not bushwhackers, but Confederate soldiers. Your men will be treated as prisoners of War.
John Thrailkill Maj, Commanding Confederate forces.

Maj. John Thrailkill: July 21, 1864
Sir: We are not here for the purpose of surrendering, but to defend the flag of our Country.
B.F. Poe, Capt., Commanding Post.

Not pleased with the response Col. Thrailkill ordered John Jackson to prepare the advance guard. In the first charge Union Capt. Turney was killed. His men fought a heated but short encounter under Lt McCulloch who realized they were at risk of being cut off and fell back, taking Capt Turney's body with them. The Paw Paw boys were ordered to flank Turney's Co. Capt Poe hearing the exchange believed Turney's men to be captured ordered a retreat. When he saw McCulloch returning he ordered an attack, however most of their men had already fled in retreat.

A large number of armed citizens joined Capt Poe surrounding the court house prepared to defend it. One of our scouts rode in alerting Col. Thrailkill of a rested well armed force out of Cameron moving toward our rear. He ordered a retreat withdrawing toward Haynesville. Losses were minimal on both sides. The boys had taken $10,000 of Missouri bonds and destroyed a large amount of guns. Fletch Taylor and James Little took about $6,000. Gregg demanded Fletch split the money. Todd and Quantrill said they had a right to keep it causing a trouble between Taylor and Gregg.

Plattsburg was the home of David Rice Atchison, U.S. President for one day. Zachary Taylor was to be sworn in March 4, 1849, but because it fell on Sunday he refused. Vice President George Dallas resigned on March 2, 1849 and because of the order of succession Senate Pro Tem Atchison became president for the day. One of those things you remember from school. I wondered what had happened to Mister Bird. He was an entertaining teacher who made learning fun for all ages. The idea of taking up teaching when this blasted war is over seemed more and more appealing.

On July 22, 1864 Bloody Bill and the boys burned the North Missouri Railroad depot at Renick in Randolph Co and destroyed telegraph wire for several miles. There were minor skirmishes in and around Momma's farm throughout the summer but mostly Jesse and I stayed home and worked, occasionally joining Jesse's best friend Col. John Thrailkill. We got word to meet up in Lafayette Co in Aug for the war conference. Meanwhile Bloody Bill was becoming more crazed with each kill. His "scalp belt runneth over," Doc said. Bill Marney riding with Bloody Bill was killed when the boys burned a 150 foot bridge of the Hannibal and St. Joseph Railroad over the Salt River. At the war conference we heard Bloody Bill demanded Lexington, Missouri surrender. Jesse and I had been with John Thrailkill, his best friend, at Plattsburg and Jesse told how Thraillkill had ordered a surrender.

In eastern Missouri even after the execution of Col. John Fugate Bolin, Bolin's Band continued to operate after his death. Richard Elijah "Lige" Clarke, a Lt. Col. under Col. Tom moved north to aide Bolin's band after Bolin's execution in Feb. In the fall on Oct 30th Lige was captured near Fair Play in Polk Co couriering information between commands. He was sent to St. Louis to the military prison. From there he was transferred to Point Lookout, Maryland for exchange. During late July 1864 riding with Bolin's band in the bootheel of Missouri and northeast Ark recruiting and raising Southern support they were attacked by Union Lt. Col. John T. Burris at Scatterville. Outnumbered they attempted to flank the Union without success, fleeing. Several had minor wounds. Col. Burris burned most of the town before leaving Scatterville advancing further into Ark. They were in a skirmish at Osceola, Ark near the Mississippi River on Aug 2 and at Elk Chute in the bootheel of Missouri in Pemiscot Co on the 4th. On Aug 7th, Stephen Hodges was captured after his horse went lame chased by Union boys on horseback. He was caught near the home of William J. "Indian Bill" Davis near Hesstown. The Union tied Stephen Hodges behind one of the soldier's horses. They tied his horse to another soldier's horse and walked them to Batesville. Once there they shot and killed his horse and ate her. Word was he didn't tell'em nothing. He was sent to Little Rock, Ark. then forwarded to Alton, Ill. Military Prison Nov 17, 1864 where he remained until the war ended. At war's end, President Lincoln ordered prisoners be sent back to the closest city nearest their homes. Stephen was sent back to Jacksonport, Ark where he enlisted. His family had moved to Missouri. After President Lincoln was shot and killed, southern boys were put off the trains and boats. Stephen walked from Jacksonport to Batesville. From there he was able to get a ride with people he knew to Riggsville. There, he stayed with the Halpain's near Col. J.J. Kemp's until he got better. His wife Jane came down and for a year, they lived in Richwood again.

Some of Bolin's Band moved south aiding Col. Archibald Dobbins as men from the south from the other Col.s' moved north to reinforce the forces in the bootheel, faces were becoming too familiar in home territories. The Union predicting success in the war was implementing a new kind of experiment on the Ark plantations along the Mississippi River delta, freed blacks working land; ready Confederate targets. Col Archibald Dobbins destroyed a number of plantations, including the one belonging to the Lamb family. He captured 300 former slaves and over 200 mules, as well as goods and clothing with some 75 wounded or killed in the action. The Feds low on men and supplies didn't attack, destroying the plantation would leave everyone without winter food. Our boys captured all the livestock and farming tools.

Capt. John Chestnut was sent by Genl. Price to find the Partisan Rangers and guerillas with orders to gather them together for a war conference to be held in the early hours of Aug 9th. The boys had begun assembling. T.C. Kelly, a scout for Union Col. James H. Ford located us, reporting back to the Union:

"All the guerilla leaders, Quantrill, Todd, Thraillkill, Anderson with three to five hundred men were in the Sniabar Creek timber about 12 miles from Chapel Hill in Lafayette Co. They held their war council then broke up departing in groups of 25-50." He advised Ford it "appeared the guerillas were waiting on instructions from Genl. Shelby and were planning a great raid into Kansas. The raid would commence out of Ark."

Men moved north of the Missouri River. Before the war conference Bloody Bill raided Clay Co, taking money, arms and the best horses on the 5th. On the 12th moving east toward Fredricksburg, Ray Co, Bloody Bill and 70 of the boys attacked a patrol of the 51st Missouri Cav led by Capt Pattern Colley out of Richmond. They scattered the patrol killing four men.

Doctor Edwin Price, Genl. Sterling Price's brother, moved his son Edwin's wife, Missus Kitty, to his home at Brunswick, not far from their home in Keytesville. On Aug 12, she delivered a baby girl, Martha, a blue baby. I'd always thought blue babies were called blue because somehow they were blue skinned, marked by something. But Momma said it was because her air was cut off and she didn't breathe right when she was born. She come out feet first too, breech. Little Martha was pulled out hard and hurt bad while being born. She lived one year and one month.

Along with about a dozen men, including William Gaw, John Johnson, Jim Wilkerson, Jake Freeman, Dick Johnson, Jesse and I went with Capt. George Shepherd to the Lotspeich Farm on the 12th. At Fredricksburg in Ray Co, at the Conrow House, Garrett Groomer fought Capt. Moses who was the head of the Colorado troops. Capt. John Chestnut, who had brought the news to gather for a war conference and the assignments from Genl. Price, fought with Anderson and Fletch Taylor, along with Silas King, Si Gordon and Thrailkill. I know Momma hadn't wanted Jesse to join up, thinking him too young. But we had boys, I mean real boys among us. Leon Martinez, A.J. Luckett and others among us couldn't be sixteen. Those three looked like babies, like they weren't yet even twelve year old. Not one was coming close to having any hair on their faces and their voices were still boys. None survived the war.

Theo Cassell and Jesse captured a courier with a dispatch warning all the posts from Richmond to Chillicothe of Anderson and his men. Peyton Long captured two couriers who were carrying information about the Fredricksburg skirmish warning all posts of impending danger. The couriers were killed. Col. James Nichols, Joseph Nicholson, Allen Parmer, Bud and Henry Pence, Gooly Robinson, Doc Rupe, Zack Southerland and Bill Stone used the information attacking the troops.

Aug 13th at Flat Rock Ford, Hiram Gist was on guard duty when 150 Missouri Militia and Kansas Red Leg under Col. Catherwood attacked. Hi was the great grandson of Christopher Gist, American Surveryor, he and Col. Shelby were cousins, and to Sequoyaht. Their families moved from

Kentucky to Missouri together. Hi's grandma, Mary Jarrette was of kin to John Jarrette. Jesse and Peyton Long saw Catherwood and his men coming with enough time to warn us. Bloody Bill ordered half the boys to saddle up and the other half to fight standing. Sandy McMacane was killed. In the third volley, Jesse was shot just close enough to jar him. Dropping his pistol, he grabbed a second one when he was hit with a shot from Spencer rifle on the right side. Knocked unconscious Arch Clements and John Jarrette carried him to safety. Moving Jesse, Arch was shot in the leg. We defended our ground and the Feds finally retreated enough we could get away. Seventeen year old Doc Rupe was killed. Calvin "Cave" Wyatt was wounded. Ben Rice, Nathan Teague and Gooly Robinson took Jesse to Capt. Rudd's. Rudd was serving in the regular army under Genl. Shelby. Gooly lived near us. He'd been a good friend a long time. He was a medium built fella but he could wrestle a bear to the ground. You didn't want to mess with him. He had curly brown hair and a trimmed out mustache, no beard and short trimmed hair. He said he didn't want no body yanking on his hair. Gooly was elected 1st Sgt.. When Ben McCullock a federal spy, not Union Genl. Ben McCulloch, burned down Gooly's widowed aunt's home, stole her horse and drove off her livestock, Gooly found McCullock, rode right up to him and shot him with both barrels of his double barrel shot gun, killing him. We knew we could trust Gooly. Although at first it appeared Jesse had nothing more than a scrape, Nathan Teague was worried and went with Gooly making sure Jesse was okay. Jesse struggled to breath and was certain he was going to die. But this was nothing new for Jesse. Even the slightest of colds, he was always certain he was dying. Dramatically, insisting he was gonna die, he gave his ring to Peyton Long to give our little sister Susie should he not make it. Maybe he feared making it home only to be treated with more skunk grease. Peyton had his horse shot out from under him in the battle. The next day Castle and Hiram Gist were on duty when the EMM and Kansas Red Legs attacked the camp. Castle and Gist were cut off from the camp but managed to escape. A wounded Archie Clements saved Quantrill by pulling him up behind him on his horse. My horse "Little George" was killed in the skirmish. Willie Reynolds broke his left arm.

Si Gordon and Thrailkill rode 50 miles to Keyesville, Chariton Co. Bloody Bill anxious to find out how Jesse was doing headed toward Carroll Co. He and the boys were spotted and pursued by Union militia. For two days he engaged in rear guard skirmishing with the militia Cav, killing eight more of them. Due to exhaustion they gave up the chase near the Grand River on the Chariton Co line. A scouting party consisting of Jacob Mead, Ol and Frank Shepherd, Dick Kinney, Dan Vaughn and Press Webb were attacked by Federal troops at Rush Bottoms in Lafayette Co. They escaped.

At Cassville, we heard of Genl. Price's difficulty at Pilot Knob east of the Wire Road in Ark two hundred miles south of us. The Union was garrisoned there using it as a departure point for excursions throughout north Ark and southern Missouri. A Maj task for Union troops was keeping the supply road between Springfield and Fayetteville open. We called it the Wire Road as this was the main telegraph line from Missouri into Ark. On Aug 23, the Union left Big Springs near Cassville headed to Fayetteville. They moved to Little Sugar Creek in Benton Co making camp. The next morning they passed through Cross Hollows and Mud Town, a place with a tavern and two stores. Prior to the poisoning of forty two Union Benton Hussars, a German regiment, on Feb 20th, 1862, it had been a stagecoach stop. The Unionists consumed food and drink believed to have been poisoned by rebels.

During the week of Aug 20 we joined Clifton Holtzclaw, Capt. Tom Todd and their men in the wild Perche Creek hills of northern Boone Co. Bloody Bill and the boys made their way through Chariton and Howard counties, using signals and passwords they had obtained from the Union enabling them in their attack on the steamboat Omaha, 12 miles below Glasgow. We moved in groups of 10 to 100 every day moving out with newly established targets. Bloody Bill decided riding with 100 men was too risky, a move not unlike what Quantrill done in June. Bloody Bill disbanded his men on Sept 2, ordering them to ride in smaller groups, no more than 25. John Mead a new recruit rode with John McCorkle. John Hope joined Jim Anderson. Plunk Murrary was on his way home when he was attacked by Federal soldiers who shot him in the arm. He escaped. He tore his nice red shirt made by the ladies. Plunk had a shock of black hair, clean shaved, ash white face with red checks that looked like a crazy old aunt pinched them pink.

On the 24th, Gooly's wife, Wealthy Austin, daughter of Willie and Anna Haynes Austin, was arrested for aiding the Southern cause. She had three babies in the house, Maggie 4, Willie 2 and baby child Lee. The Union took her to the Women's Prison on Gratiot Street in St. Louis. Her sister's were able to get the children keeping them safe. Missus Wellie was moved to the jail at Warrensburg and died before the year's end.

On Aug 28th, 1864 Genl. Price left Camden, Ark on his Great Raid into Missouri astride his horse Bucephalus. The next day two more divisions joined him. Along the way men, boys, farmers, sons, fathers, brothers, husbands joined his ranks with whatever they had. When they got to Pocahontas a third division joined them. There were skirmishes and battles throughout the march into Missouri.

Bloody Bill and Holtzclaw attacked a 40 man patrol of the 4th Missouri Cav from Boonville on the 28th. Union Capt. Joseph Parke had been boasting for days how he and a handful of his man could run our boys into the ground. When the Union departed Boonville a few shots rang out from the east bluff above Moniteau Creek. The Union were ambushed as the boys descending upon them. Capt. Parke reported half a dozen dead, another three wounded and three missing. Of those, three joined us. Archie and Bill had scalped the dead before anyone else could dismount. Throats were cut on three not dying but not dead.

Alarmed, fifteen miles east in Columbia, the citizen's home guard, The Tigers, were called to duty and stationed at the courthouse. It was fortified and barricaded along with the University of Missouri building and a blockhouse in anticipation of an attack. R.B. Price, Genl. Sterling's nephew had been alerted and removed all the gold from the Boone Co National Bank of which he was President. He buried it under fence posts where it remained until war's end.

Genl. Shelby headquartered at Jacksonport, about 40 miles southeast of Batesville. Hundreds of recruits were flocking to the irregular troops, joining the Partisan Rangers both in Ark and in Missouri. The Union's only goal in Ark was to now drive Shelby out of Jacksonport. They didn't realize he was planning to move north soon anyway. Both sides skirmished throughout the summer and then on Aug 30, Gen Shelby left Jacksonport marching north toward Smithville to rendezvous with Gen Price. Their raid into Missouri was to commence mid Sept. Col Tom along with the other Col.s, their Lt.s and Capts were to keep Ark busy throughout the coming fall preventing the Union from mobilizing to move north on the rear flanks of Shelby and Price. Jim Cummins was sent by Genl. Shelby couriering coded orders when to move north as a rear flank joining the march into Missouri. Col. Tom sent him to Capt. William Stuart with orders to join Bloody Bill at Boonville.

Aug 30th the boys attacked Rocheport. John Brown Ward, Co F of Col. Tom's men had stayed riding with us, along with his brother Joseph Brown Ward, they lived near old man Ike Flannery across from Langston's Landing down river from Aunt Lucy's. They had worked a little on the steamers and were able to relate information aiding in the seizure of steamers. The boys captured the docked steam tug Buffington which belonged to the Jeff City penitentiary. They proceeded to stoke up the boilers then rode up and down the Missouri hooting and howling, shooting off their guns. Most of the boys had never been on a steamer and Bloody Bill took any opportunity he could to give them a minute of laughter. Bloody Bill and the boys stayed around Rocheport for a week. They ambushed the steamboat Yellowstone. Two of the boys rowed a skiff out to meet the Mars demanding it surrender. They were fired upon and one of them killed. The steamer retreated to Jeff City. The boys were tearing down communication lines when the North Missouri Railroad was heard in the distance. They attacked securing four carloads of Union horses.

Saturday Sept 3rd, 1864 Union Commander Rosecrans received several warnings from Genl. Washburne Commander at Memphis, Tennessee that Genl. Price and Shelby were intent on invading Missouri. Genl. Kirby Smith had ordered Price to recruit loyal Southerners and to avoid "wanton acts of destruction." I'm certain he was thinking about the past winter in Texas with Quantrill. Genl. Price continued to be a supporter of guerilla warfare. He involved our leaders, our Col.s when planning the raid. He planned with us to prepare Confederate sympathizers in North Ark and Missouri to join in the invasion. The Knights of the Golden Circle and Copperheads supplied Price with information and many rode in from other states, Iowa, Illinois, Kentucky and Ohio to join the invasion. Thomas Reynolds joined him at Camden. He entered Missouri with over 12,000 men, our duties to keep the Union soldiers busy, cut transportation lines and destroy all bridges, kept them busy in Missouri and Kansas and out of the south east. Genl. Price's main goal was to confiscate Union warehouses in St. Louis. Then to capture the capitol Jeff City and live off the land much like Union Genl. Sherman did in his march to Atlanta. The new recruits he enrolled and the supplies he was to capture would be sent to Robert E. Lee.

Chapter 24

Sept 5th Jesse was turning seventeen. He'd been back a few days and I could tell he was worn down. I used the excuse of his birthday and needing to see Momma to head home. Riding toward Liberty Jesse spied a saddle on a fence he decided he wanted. It would be his birthday present to himself. Unbeknownst to us, the old German farmer Heisinger was not going to let his saddle go easily. At work in the fields, he heard us coming. He took aim shooting Jesse hitting him in the right lung. A few shots were returned but realizing Jesse was hurt, we fled. It was still a two day ride home. Nate Teague and I stuffed Jesse's chest full of linen from a shirt in my pack and headed home to Momma.

I was quiet most of the way, listening to Jesse's breathing. It was at times labored and other times gurgling. I thought of the boys who I watched die swallowing their own blood and the sound that made. I couldn't rest on that, my mind had to stay on Jesse. By the time we got home, he was slumped forward on his saddle, hugging it and his horse's neck to keep from falling off. Uncle Tom, Daddy's brother brought fellow Kentuckian Doctor Isaac Ridge to care for him. His arrival didn't stop Momma and Aunt Charlotte from concocting their own remedies. Bloody Bill and I knew Jesse was in it, when Aunt Charlotte told us to go bring her back a polecat. Whether you were the recipient or not you didn't defy Momma and Aunt Charlotte when it come to their doctoring. Some of the boys with us were shaking their heads assuring Bloody Bill and me they need not be on this hunt. We had to agree, tracking down a pole cat doesn't require a herd of boys. We didn't have time to put out traps and we knew we'd have to bring back the polecat without it letting loose its noxious spray, the prize for Momma and Aunt Charlotte's intended concoction.

We found a female with some babies in a den near the creek. We knew the old male was somewhere nearby. We put out some chicken innerds as bait and sat waiting. It was a few hours and we were about to give up when Bloody Bill caught sight of the old fella moving our way. We had a net ready to catch him with and a club to knock him out with, hoping like the dickens we didn't get sprayed. We lucked out this time, which hadn't always been the case when out gathering supplies for Momma and Aunt Charlotte, be it skunks or ginseng roots. I had brought a cord sack to put him in, we got him in there and headed back.

Anticipating we wouldn't come back to the house empty handed, a hot fire was going and the water in the kettle boiling. We watched as Aunt Charlotte's skilled hands skinned him out, dropping the gutted little fiend into the hot water. She set his guts aside carefully working through them to find the stink sac. After he had been boiled down good, us boys had to carry the kettle, skunk and all to the spring. There we sat the kettle in the cold water which made it cool down faster. We watched as the bones, meat and juices settled and the grease started rising to the top. We had to get it back to the house before it was completely cooled, so we hoisted it up again carrying it to the back yard. Aunt Charlotte ladled the grease into another smaller kettle then added the stink sac stirring it into the grease. Her stirring cooled it, but we didn't know how she could stand the smell. Maybe that's why she was rarely sick.

Dr. Ridge wasn't about to argue with these women when they presented him with their notion of rubbing Jesse down with the skunk grease concoction. They reckoned rubbing it all over Jesse's back and chest it would penetrate his skin going into his lungs helping to clear them up, driving out any infections deep inside his lungs. Dr. Ridge protested only when they were going to have Jesse drink some of the hot water and skunk grease oil. He insisted what was wrong with Jesse would not be aided by the vomiting drinking it would cause. Instead the vomiting could cause him more harm. Only with that argument did Momma relent.

Bloody Bill spent a couple days at the farm with a little side recruiting and visiting. He convinced Jesse when he could ride he would be part of his company, again. Bloody Bill would not be riding with Quantrill nor taking orders from him. They would be riding completely independent. Doctor Ridge said Jesse was in great pain and in a dangerous situation since he had had no medical attention other than cleaning of the wound. The old German had shot him with a minie ball the size of a man's thumb. It had hit him above the nipple on the right side passing completely through his body. When Doctor Ridge confirmed a broken rib, Jesse was delighted to have been right about it. He attended Jesse almost daily perhaps in part to make certain Momma and Aunt Charlotte didn't subject him to any additional home remedies. Uncle Till and Aunt Lizzie arrived and Doc felt he could care for him with their help. Although it makes a fine story Jesse got the worst of his chest wound during battle, the truth is the wound to his right lung was from an old man's rifle, both he and Jesse coveted.

Nate Teague was our assistant doctor of sorts and he had taken a likening to Jesse. He cared for Jesse both this time and the last making sure he was okay. Nate, like Jesse Riggs, was a relative of Samuel Clemons who made a fortune after the war writing about a Missouri that didn't exist for us. Nate was the reason Jesse was able to expand on the story of his having been wounded at Flat Rock Ford, shot twice, wounded in the chest, near death. Nate and Jesse both were about as good as any man when it came to stretching the truth. Nate was part of the Kentucky ex pats. Jesse would say something and before he could finish Nate would take up stretching the truth until it was unrecognizable.

Born to Joshua Teague and Martha Elizabeth Clemens, Nate's cousin Isaac Teague was homesteading the area above Sylamore in the 1840's as Nate's parents settled in Missouri. Men traveled long distances searching out new land; how long they were gone marked in the space between the births of their children. Isaac Teague married South Carolinan, Margaret Miller in Alabama with their first 3 children born there. It was here Teague met Thomas Riggs and wife was Rhoda Casey. Jesse Riggs was a fellow soldier with Col. Thomas Freeman. In 1819, Thomas Riggs settled Riggsville. We stayed in Riggsville on many occasion. It had a blacksmith, livery, tavern, school and both a Methodist and Baptist Church. Born a year apart, Clemens' grandmother Margaret Peggy Casey b 1803 was a cousin of Rhoda's b 1802. Peggy married Ben Lampton; their daughter Jane married John Marshall Clemens in 1823. Samuel was a young boy of only 11 when his daddy died in 1847. He was sent to Ark to stay with family for awhile, a place he would return to throughout his life. Raised at Hannibal, Missouri a port on the Mississippi on the eastern side, Samuel Clemens traveled by steamer docking at Sylamore. This was during the days when steam boats plied the waters with horns whistling and bands playing. Samuel Clemens and his cousins, the Riggs, Teagues' and Tandy Casey from Rapps Barren spent time at Sylamore Landing watching the fancy boats and merriment aboard them. War had not yet come to the hills of Ark. Taking Mark Twain as his name is not lost on people who have been raised along the rivers. The depth of the river was sung in a sing song cadence by men who stood at the bow of the boat. Measured not in feet but in terms that were understood in the wind, hail and storms by the cadence of the songs as shallow depths were short while the deeper the river the more prolonged and drawn out the cadence. A depth of 12 feet was a mark 'twain', mark three pronounced as a long thi-ree, was the call for 18 feet and mark four 24 feet. Water deeper than 24 feet was a "no bottom."

It was remarkable the resemblances in that family, a lot like the Younger's, they were tall, lanky people. Samuel and his cousin Tom Teague fooled people as to who was who. I also never really understood all the nicknames in these parts. The Younger's never went by their names. John Bomar Younger was Cole and Thomas Coleman Younger was Bud, then there was Scooter, Red and Pete who had nothing in his name like Peter, go figure. Tom's daddy, Isaac and Samuel were first cousins. They lived on the land on North Sylamore Creek during the War Between the States, near Gunner Pool.

Jackson Bawyer one of Holtzclaw's men was court martial on Sept 8th. He threw himself on the mercy of the court. They hung him. Capt. John Chestnut found George Todd and Allen Parmer in Jackson Co at Judge Gray's near Bone Hill. Capt. Chestnut had additional orders and commissions from Genl. Price. Of the numerous commissions, Peyton Long and George Todd were made Capts in the regular Confederacy.

With Sept half over, fall was coming with mixed reviews, hot one day as if Aug had not yet passed and cold the next suggesting Dec was around the corner. The trees a mix of orange, reds and no artist could do them justice. On the 15th brothers, Woot and Tuck Hill were sent to lure the Union into a trap near Boonville in Cooper Co. Capt. Peyton Long, Zack Southerland, Ben Broomfield, Archie Clements and Silas King were to lead the attack. The Capt. had been boasting he was after Anderson and had robbed, killed and looted some southerners. Archie being Archie jumped the gun, attacking and killing 23 troops and capturing 40 horses. Bloody Bill was so angry he took Archie down in front of all the men, humiliating him. Dick West was with them and heard the entire thing. Archie never took well to criticism from anyone and being demeaned in front of the boys was something he'd never forget or forgive. Jim Cummins and John Maupin left riding with Archie. John and Archie stayed friends and both went to Texas with George Shepherd when we left with Quantrill for Kentucky. John, Thomas and Archie together killed a Federal soldier, a man named Harkness, who led the Union to his Momma's killing his brother and burning his Momma's house. By mid Sept stages had been robbed and all mail stopped between the military posts at Fayette, Franklin and Renick. Union Maj Austin King had been skirmishing with the boys for days. They reported widely they killed several of guerillas, taken 12 revolvers and one bridle braided with human scalps. Allowing the Union to believe their successes made certain they continued their pursuits of us.

Several of the boys found themselves surrounded by a militia unit. Joe Holt told them he was just a local farm boy who had been pressed into supplying the guerillas food. The Union released him. His fast talking allowed the boy's time to gather their thoughts saving Plunk Murray and Ed Phillips. Robert Todd, Jack Wilson, Harvey Brown, Tommy Fulton and Dolf Carroll weren't so lucky, they were killed. Dolf wore his hair cropped short. He was clean shaved and had a face like a French painter might chose to paint. Harvey Brown might have been eighteen, but he didn't have no hair on his face. He was a pretty boy, always happy and smiling. He had the biggest hands of anybody I ever saw. The men joshed him about his hands, his feet and his man parts, if they were of similar proportion. Plunk and Ed were able to save themselves but were unable to help the others. When they knew the Union had moved on, they found the other boys were not only riddled with bullets but all of them had been scalped. Tommy Fulton was still alive but lasted only a few more minutes.

Jesse couldn't wait to get back in the saddle and when he did, he headed out with me to find Bloody Bill. We should have known Bloody

Bill would go off the deep end. His little brother, Jim had formed his own band in early Sept and many of the boys were more willing to ride with him. We had all learned the art of war under our Unc, their grandpa Wild Man Bill Thomason. Wringing the neck of a chicken or chopping it off, killing hogs, lambs and goats were routine farm life, even for the women. At an early age we had learned not only to skin a squirrel but to take its head off with one stroke. We had learned how to skin a snake preserving its skin completely intact. Bloody Bill proved his skills with the capture of a number of gentleman rattler's on more than one occasion, tanning and trading them to the mercantile that got a good price for them. Men who couldn't likely shoot and were even more than likely to mess their pants if they came upon one of these Diamondback or Timber Rattlers wore them as hatbands or belts. Bloody Bill had known his grandpa had taken scalps while living with the Indians. The oldest of all us kids, he had shown him more details on how to hone his skills than the rest of us. Bill had not been taking scalps or allowing it with any regularity until Centralia. One of his boys had braided Union scalps he'd taken into his bridle. Bloody Bill was okay with that but I don't know how he stood the smell.

Thrailkill, Todd and his command crossed into Clay Co north of the river near Liberty. By the 16th of Sept, Todd was well into Ray Co. A citizen informed Todd a Co of forty-five militia was stationed at Shaw's blacksmith shop in the northeastern part of the Co. John Jackson, Dan Vaught, Andy McGuire, Andy Walker, Dan Vaughn, Ben Morrow, Hence Privin, Harrison Trow, Si Gordon, Dick Kinney, Sim Whitsett, Ol Shepherd, Jesse and I, with a few others under Col. John Thrailkill headed out as the advance for Todd's group. We were to make seven and a half miles an hour no more staying half a mile in front of Todd's group. When we spied the Feds Dan Vaught and Si Gorden returned informing Thrailkill. The Union was camped in a black oak grove with a corn field on one side and a meadow on the other. A wide lane ran between the two fields. Todd's entire guerrilla band emerged into the open entering the lane at a walk. The Union mistook the boys as fellow soldiers and allowed them to ride up within about 300 feet of the camp. Someone let out a rebel yell sounding the alarm for us to charge. In the front rank George Todd, John Thrailkill, Andy Walker, Dan Vaught, John Jackson and Dick Kinney rode abreast, followed by Sim Whitsett, Hi George, Ol and Frank Shepherd, and Ben Morrow. One of the Hudspeth brothers, John Koger and Andy McGuire, followed by James Hendricks, William Gregg, Si Gordon, Hugh and William Archie, William Hulse, Jesse and me came in behind them. Within a minute a dozen of the Union militia were killed with others running scared into the fields. Running on foot we rode our horses after them, mowing down the corn stalks in our charge. It was like bird hunting with Unc, flushing out quail, except we were on horseback. John Jackson, Dick Kinney, Jesse and I flushed out four at once, killed them and moved on. One of them managed to raise up shooting John Jackson in the back. John mortally wounded from the minie ball of a Belgium musket fell from his horse. Jesse turned and shot the Union attacker dead with two quick shots to the head. John Jackson was dead within the hour.

George Todd and John Thrailkill with 150 men moved north of the Missouri River just below Dover in Lafayette Co at dawn on Sept 19th. They threatened Carrollton, the Co seat of Carroll Co, and then went east into Chariton Co riding over 40 miles in a day and night.

On Sept 20th we roared into Genl. Sterling Price's hometown of Keytesville, the Co seat of Chariton Co surrounding a Union garrison of 35 militiamen ensconced in the fortified brick courthouse. Thrailkill went in with a white flag of truce stating he was a Confederate Maj acting under orders from Genl. Price. He demanded Lt. Anthony Pleyer surrender the garrison and he did. The courthouse was burned and Keytesville looted. Money taken from citizens was ordered returned by Thrailkill. Robert Carman, the Co sheriff and William Young a prominent Union man were marched out of town and shot. Most folks believed them both to be Union spies, especially Young and weren't sorry to see them killed. Seven of the militia men joined Thrailkill stating they had been forced to join the Union.

That evening, Sept 20th, we sat around talking. We were all smiles talking and thinking about Payne Jones having married Belle Evans today. Marrying was against Union law for Southerners, but that didn't stop our boys. Weddings were important, signs that life continued, just as announcements of impending births brought out slaps to the back and births a celebratory smoke. Joining forces in Boone Co our boys under Todd, Bloody Bill and Thrailkill struck a mighty blow on the Union on the 23rd. Riding over 300 in number, we attacked and wiped out a twelve wagon military supply train ten miles north east of Rocheport. The train escorted by Capt. James W. McFadden and 35 troopers of the Third Missouri Cav was on its way from Rocheport to Sturgeon. At sunset McFadden was met by Capt. James Roberts and a patrol of an additional 25 men of the Third Missouri. They had just come together and were discussing the quietness of the day when we charged. They fled in disorder leaving Bloody Bill and us boys to haul off eighteen thousand rounds of ammunition, a wagonload of Union uniforms and a thousand rations. That evening, Brigadier Genl. J B Douglas who had just arrived by boat at Rocheport with five hundred men went north after Bloody Bill but couldn't locate him. Union Maj Reeves Leonard with a Co of the 9th Missouri Cav arrived from Fayette.

Maj Leonard found the carnage and took out after us. They wounded Allen Parmer but he escaped. Fletch Taylor was severely wounded, his arm mangled, shattered by a minie ball. It was several days before we could get him seen to. A half dozen of the boys went into Wellington, not really capturing but certainly persuading with threats, Doctors Murphy and Regan to treat Fletch. They amputated his arm in the woods. Murphy was later arrested for treating a guerrilla but released. Joe Davis and my friend, Garrett Groomer were killed. It was Garrett's grandpa Jacob Groomer who built the house I call home. Garrett was married to Sarah Francis "Fannie" Pence, Bud and Donnie's older sister. Garrett and Fannie had Robert Woodson, 8, Elizabeth 7, Margaret 5, Lucy 3 and Garrett was just a baby child. The next year, Missus Fannie married James W. Corum, another one of our Partisan Rangers. Patrick DeHart fought, was captured and escaped. John M Taylor who rode with Capt. Cason was wounded. We returned to Preacher Thomas Todd's recruiting camp at Dripping Springs, Missouri. Fletch was an incredible man, still recovering from the amputation he was able to return joining Genl. Price's great Missouri raid two months later in Oct. While Leonard was moving toward Genl. Douglass the boys circled him and at dawn of the next day were on the outskirts of unguarded Fayette in Howard Co.

While we rested with Bloody Bill and George Todd in the hills south of Fayette, Quantrill rode in with a couple of the boys. We assumed he returned bored by married life. Together we discussed raiding Fayette. Todd and Bloody Bill felt the town was almost void of Union and wanted to attack. Quantrill argued the situation with the brick courthouse, something he'd had significant experience with. After heated discussion including several of the Lt. Col.s and Capts, the vote to attack was approved.

On Sept 24, we met in a grove of timber south of town. A majority of the boys were riding the famed Missouri Fox Trotter horses, famed for the horse's ability to traverse the rugged terrain yet pull a carriage with grace and style. They had been in the Ozarks since these lands were part of the Missouri Territories and retained the name, Missouri Fox Trotter. We proceeded at a beautiful fox trot up Church Street past the cemetery. At the edge of the sleeping town we broke into a gallop yelling out the Rebel yells, fierce and haunting descending into the court square. We were fine riding into Fayette dressed in Federal uniforms, we looked as though we might be coming as a parade, a returning triumphant unit. The ruse worked until one of the boys saw a colored man in Union uniform and fired on him. Then people started running, screaming and firing off weapons. The 9th Cav under Lt. Joseph Street and Thomas Smith holed up in the courthouse and a heavy railroad tie blockhouse on the north side of town, were ready for a fight.

I tell you, pride makes most of us do many things we wouldn't do otherwise. Many men would have run away in that battle if the others weren't watching them. Ol Johnson was wounded on a rise not far from the blockhouse, Dick Kinney, Sim Whitsett and I went in after him but got pinned down by gunfire. We hugged the ground as they peppered us with shot. The blockhouse was like charging a stone wall that belched out lead. Dick managed to get close enough to get a blanket over Ol, inching him to where we could pull him out staying close to the ground. I was honestly afraid I wasn't going to make it out of this one alive. Lee McMurtry had been shot and lay even closer to the blockhouse. Whilst we were trying to get Ol out, Jesse went in and pulled Lee out. I saw Jesse's shirt soaked with blood, the others thought it was from the wounded but I knew, Jesse's wound had opened up.

Quantrill was so disgusted he left before things were over. George Todd seeing him riding out shouted obscenities. Kicking and screaming he blamed Quantrill for the fiasco when it was him who hadn't wanted to go in at all. Ordering a retreat, Bloody Bill, Percy Boulware, Al Carter, Patrick DeHart, Archie Clements, Cy Gordon and John Dickerson brought up the rear guard. Al Carter was a hard man who had had a hard life. He wore his hair long tucked behind his ears, pushed back it parted a little on the side. He was a good man, trustworthy. He could pass for Bloody Bill. In fact he was apprehended more than once having been mistaken for Bloody Bill. He was arrested on Sept 12, 1864, mistaken once again for as Bloody Bill. This time they scalped him and shot out both eyes. We lost several men killed and about 30 wounded. We left town with the dead and dying on their horses. The wounded were taken to homes of supporters to be cared for and a burial unit saw to it the others were buried in a cemetery.

When we met up that evening, the boys were upset; everyone had something to say to each other and their immediate commanders. We had lost almost 20 boys and twice that many were wounded, some would die among them Lafe and Hence Parvin, Capt. John Rains, Robbie Stewart, Ben Aden, Capt. Tom Garrett, young Will Akin, George McMurtry, William Hulse, James Anderson, Garrett Groomer, William Hayes, Newman Wade, Tom Grosvenor and Capt. and Preacher Thomas Todd. The Union had scalped Capt. James Bissett. Wounded but surviving, Silas King, James Little, Sandy McCane, Tom Maupin, Lee McMurtry, Jesse Morrow, John McCorkle, Lawrence Wilcox and Jack Will. Peyton Long had his horse shot out from under him but turned shooting a Union man from his horse, he mounted it. Col. Caleb Perkins had been with Genl. Price at Glasgow, helped Poindexter's disbanded men cross the river just two days before, was wounded. Harrison Trow stole a shotgun and fired so fast at the Union boys shooting from the Academy building they abandoned one window. Our only order was the orders we received from Genl. Price, everything else was disorder. And, like it or not, Quantrill was our most brilliant of leaders. Momma said leading us boys was like trying to herd cats.

The boys were disgusted with Quantrill having gone off again; saying things about love having made him a coward and now his distractions were getting us killed. I looked at Bloody Bill. When his eyes met mine his stare stung like a bullet nick. It was clear the boys wanted a new leader, someone other than Quantrill and not likely Bloody Bill either. When the vote was done, it was George Todd who would command. Before dark, Todd and Thraillkill left taking most of the boys with them. Jesse went with John Thrailkill. I'd pulled John aside telling him my fears of Jesse's wounds opening up. He'd promised to watch after him.

As much as I feared for my little brother, I was gravely concerned about Bloody Bill. Along with about 50 men, I remained with him. I was watching Bill die right before my eyes. His grief and pain at the personal tragedies this war had were winning, his decisions weren't sound and he wouldn't go home, not even with me to Momma's. I tried to use Jesse as an excuse but even that hadn't reached him. He was crazed. Momma always said there was no right or wrong way to mourn, but I knew she didn't mean this. Jeremiah David Helton and James Little had left with Quantrill, part of his trusted body guard. I could see the betrayal on his face.

By Sept 26th Todd moved south toward Renick where he vented his rage by pulling down miles of telegraph wire along the North Missouri Railroad. John Thrailkill knowing the situation with my little brother Jesse decided they all needed some rest. They went to the farm of brothers Middleton and Leonard Singleton in Boone Co, four miles south of Centralia. George Todd and his boys joined them there.

Riding with Bloody Bill, we headed north and east into Audrain Co. The command at Paris in Monroe Co had been alerted of our movement. Maj A.V.E. Johnson mounted his men and rode to intercept us. Around noon on Tuesday Sept 27th, we ran into Johnson's scouts, we turned and moved south, crossing the rail of the North Missouri east of Centralia in Boone Co about fifty miles north of Jeff City as dusk turned to dark. Our scouts confirmed both George Todd and John Thrailkill were camped at the Singleton Brothers farm. We headed to the Singleton farm ourselves. Riders came in from the southeast alerting us Genl. Price had entered Missouri at Mammoth Springs and was camped near Doniphan headed toward St. Louis. The defeat of Fayette became a memory with the excitement of commencing of the Great Raid into Missouri.

By daybreak about 250 men were preparing to move east toward Pilot Knob to join Genl. Price. Movement was casual and easy about the camp, fires flickering boys warming themselves, having a smoke and making coffee. Bloody Bill was anxious, nervous and restless about news of Price's movements. We were still dressed in our Federal uniforms when about 30 of the boys joined Bloody Bill to ride into Centralia to secure newspapers, including Jesse, his chest wrapped tight with linen under his shirt. The town was made up of a dozen home, a couple stores and two hotels. It was a haven of Southern supporters, safe and a good place to get supplies. I'm not sure what happened, there was no plan, just all of a sudden Bloody Bill let out that Unc Wild Man yell and the rest joined in. Shooting off his pistol the others soon were of like mind, racing into town.

For nearly 3 hours the boys sauntered around town demanding breakfast, especially from the pro Union inhabitants. Archie Clements discovered whiskey in one of the stores which was soon consumed by a half dozen of the boys. Drunk they were shooting off their pistols when they decided to set platform serving as the depot on fire. Whether intentional or accidental, I'll never know with certainty, but some of the boys were trying to put it out while others were fanning the flames laughing. Things were winding down, the kick had about worn off when near 11 o'clock the stage rolled in. Several of the boys surrounded it on horseback holding the led horse bringing it to a stop.

U.S. Senator James S. Rollins on his way to a political meeting was among the first hauled off. He immediately started with some fancy talk passing himself off as a local farmer and an ardent Southerner. He walked away headed to the Sneed hotel. The boys rifled through the valises and trunks of the passengers, putting on some of the clothing and taking other items for the women in their family. The boys relieved the passengers and robbed them of their personal items and anything else they wanted. Some of the men were tossing the clothing found in trunks about in the air, women's dainties atop one boy's head brought roaring laughter. One of the men found a barrel of whiskey, rolled it into the street and opened it. Already crazed, this drunken bunch convinced themselves they could do anything. There had been talk because Centralia was a known Southern town that the Union was going to send in troops to nullify it. Meaning the townspeople were going to suffer badly. We saw no indication there was going to be any trouble, but we were keeping an eye out for any northerners. The men now fully intoxicated had begun looting the stores in town telling the storekeeper they were taking supplies before the Union came.

Again things were winding down when the whistle of the incoming train was heard. Some of the boys rushed to the tracks placing staves from a nearby pile onto the track. Stepping back they waited for the train to approach. The staves would derail it if the conductor failed to yield, either way, it was stopping for them. About half past 11 o'clock it screeched to a halt. The engineer, one James Clark, had seen the smoking timbers of the depot but made no effort to reverse his engines. Later we learned a train loaded with gravel was on the same track behind him. As the cars pulled up to the depot, the boys surrounded the train, firing their pistols just above the windows. The passengers were removed from the train at gunpoint. There were about 80 of the boys by now including Bloody Bill and Jim, Archie Clement and Jesse. I rode into town with George Todd and about 60 more in the midst of this. The train was out of Saint Charles and would likely net us additional arms and supplies we needed. There was no stopping to plan or think. The boys lined the passengers up against the car of the train, each one approached with a bag to deposit their valuables into. Archie discovered Union troops on board and held them at gunpoint until all the civilian passengers had been robbed. He then proceeded to march them off the train and a half dozen of the boys instantly moved up to guard them. Bloody Bill rode up watching the procession of Union captives emerging from the train then began questioning them. It became clear most of them were on furlough. Bloody Bill ordered them to strip stating we needed their uniforms. By this time each prisoner had one of our boys standing with a gun to their head. They did as Bloody Bill told them, they stripped. I thought of the Mountain Meadows Massacre and for a moment, I wanted to protest. Their uniforms were more valuable without bullet holes or blood all over them. Some of them were wearing undergarments; others were naked. They were young. I felt their fear and shame in being naked in front of the passengers, some of whom were women. They tried covering their manhood with their hands, some of them barely had any body hair. It was moments like these my stomach felt sick. I felt my heart quicken. These boys had no idea they were about to die. Bloody Bill was determined to learn if any of them were officers, commanders, commissioned or non commissioned. He told our boys to cock their guns. They all stood silent then one man, maybe 25 years old, stepped forward. He said his name was Thomas Goodman. I'm certain he thought he would be shot hoping he could spare the others. He stated he was a Sgt. of Missouri Engineers. I was certain since the Engineers were charged with rebuilding the rails Bloody Bill would kill him. None of us were shocked when he told Goodman to step out of line. We knew he was going to kill him. He told Archie to muster them out. Each man stood by their soldier waiting as Archie trotted down the line, one by one shooting and killing each of them. A few of the boys killed the young men at the end of the line, perhaps it was instinct to prevent them from suffering, perhaps it was their own survival. Our boys and these all had a stunned look of shock and amazement on their faces as Archie trotted along the line murdering them point blank smiling. Only one of them bolted from the line attempting to get away. He crawled under a wooden dock adjacent to the platform not fully burned. The fire was fanned and the flames forced him out. He was shot as soon as he reared his head into the open. Just as Archie shot them point blank in the face moving down the line, he went back up the line scalping each of them. He carried their scalps on his bridle. Archie once used a German by the name of Eisenhower as a guide, killed him, cut off his head and laid it on his chest with his hands crossed. Maybe he should have been born a Wild West Indian warrior, his actions sickened most of us.

Some of the boys jumped aboard the train stoking up the engine and securing the whistle, others moved the staves from the track. The wooden stock cars were set on fire and the train sent down the track toward Sturgeon five miles away. A few passengers had hidden themselves on the train jumped off when they realized they were on a burning train. The burning cars sent columns of smoke into the clear blue sky, seen from miles away, several of the boys from camp rode up to see what was going on. A crate of boots had been secured and a few of the boys filled theirs with whiskey from the keg. Others were simply delighted to have new boots, slinging them across their horse's neck. Sgt. Goodman was secured, tied and bound to a horse and taken captive. We headed back toward Singleton's farm.

The billowing smoke from the burning platform and train alerted Union Maj Johnston. With 250 raw recruits, Johnston arrived around four o'clock in the afternoon. People were still in shock, women and children crying, men standing around in disbelief. They saw the bodies of the dead at the train depot. Some of Johnston' had no guns at all, some had old muzzle loading Enfield muskets. Johnston decided to take after us and to make us suffer for what had been done. Leaving left behind about a third of his men to help restore order in the town, the people of Centralia tried to tell him not to go after us.

Most of the people were Southerner's supporting the Confederacy, including Leo Singleton who angrily told us never to return. Bloody Bill threatened him but George Todd and John Thrailkill who had secured use of his farm prevented Bloody Bill from following through. I pulled Jesse aside insisting he remain with John Thrailkill. He understood with nothing more said. A scout came in informing us Maj Johnston was pursuing us. An ambush was set up outside town in Mister Fullenwider's pasture. Not only could Bloody Bill and Jesse bring out the worst in each other, I was about to understand, Thrailkill and Jesse could be each other's worst enemy. With Jesse by his side, they rode out to lure in Johnson. Tuck, Jesse Morrow and Peyton were right behind them. They rode out facing Johnston then turned racing off to lure him back. Johnson did as the enemy always did, he came racing after them. There was a gentle rise in the road just before it reached the Singleton Brother's farm at the edge of Mister Fullenwider's pasture. When Johnston and his troops topped the rise they were faced with over 200 of us standing by our horses, guns in hand. Johnston dismounted his men forming a 60 foot line of men to face us. Heard up and down our line, John Koger said, "The fools are going to fight us on foot." These young recruits had been trained to fight hand to hand on the ground, not from horseback armed with Army issue Enfield rifles. I immediately realized unlike our pistols these long barreled single shot rifles couldn't have easily been shot from the back of a horse. Johnston had no other choice but to dismount his troops to fight. "God help'em," John added as George Todd roared out to us to mount. Led by George and Bloody Bill in front, we charged Johnston's line running completely over and through them. Even now I can see them on that ridge. They didn't know what hit them, just boys. It was war. I keep telling myself that. Johnston's troops fired one volley hitting only three of our boys. Hank Williams shot dead fell from his horse. Dick Kinney was hit. Frank Shepherd, riding to my right was shot through the head, his brains and blood covered my leg. Harrison Carter, brothers, Bud and Thomas Maxwell and Lee McMurtry were all hit but continued fighting. Capt. John Chestnut, Price's unit, James Cummins, Capt Ning Ling, Johnson's men, Creth Creek, Ike Flannery, William Gaw, Press Webb, James Little, Thomas Little, Hiram Litton James Gibson, Joe "Pink" Gibson, who had been burned out, Richard Glasscock, Si Gordon and Frank Gray fought without injury. Dr. Lee Miller back from Salt Lake City joined us. Dave Poole, Cyrus Porter, Henry Porter, Marion Prewitt, Chat Renick, Willie Reynolds, Jack Rupe, George Scholl, Albert Scott, George Shepherd, Ol Shepherd, Otho Offutt, Allen Parmer, Gabe Parr, Mike Parr, Lafe and Hence Parvin, Bud Pence, Col. Caleb Perkins, Bill Carter and Theo Cassell also fought without injury. Creth Creek's brothers were with us. Creth he had straight slick hair, he kept bear grease on and a full beard. Momma said the bear grease kept any head or bed bugs from attaching. She tried to get me to use some but I was more afraid of her concoction than any bugs.

It was war. I kept telling myself. It was war. This is war. I repeated it to where it's all my brain could hear. We rode into their lines shooting our guns scattering men and horses. I saw young men biting off the ends of caps trying to reload, frightened, and killed with terror on their faces. Some fixed their bayonets, others ran and worse some were frozen in their tracks. Within minutes most of them were dead. We knew guerilla warfare. We understood our hills and how to use them to our advantage. We completely slaughtered the Union soldiers. Boys were lying about wounded and dying. Maj Johnston grabbed his pistol firing. Jesse having ridden past the main line was behind him. He shot Johnston in the head. Twenty four days before on Sept 3rd, Jesse had been shot. Sept 5th, he'd turned 17. Now, here was Jesse, one of the youngest in our group killing several men without a thought, without a flinch or hesitation. Bloody Bill went crazy, whooping and hollering, several of the men followed his actions, mounting and scalping the men, including Jesse who claimed Maj Johnsons for his own. I didn't recognize my little brother in that moment. I didn't know if I feared more for him or Bloody Bill or feared them.

Retreating Richard Ellington was wounded in the shoulder and leg. Rufe Hudspeth, Robert Napoleon Hudspeth, Moses Huffaker, Henry & William Nolan, Payne Jones, and Silas King left with the rear guard. Frank Gregg and Jesse were in the rear guard along with Lt William Gregg, Hiram Guess, Jeremiah David Helton, Dick Burns, Jeff Emory, brothers James "Pony" Hill, Thomas, Tuck and William Hulse. Ed Hinks, Clarke Hockensmith, Clifton Holtzclaw and John C Hope who had fought at Van Buren, Ark were here with us. Plunk Murray wounded in the left arm earlier in the month when attacked by Feds got his right arm broken at Centralia. Retreating for cover he took a bullet in his left side. Ben Broomfield was killed trying to protect Plunk. When they left, Bill Stewart and Jesse Morrow rode in Holtzclaw's rear guard. Hi Litton escaped with Plunk. Capt William Stuart was wounded. He stayed behind to help tend to Plunk then he and Ben were attacked. Ben was killed but they delayed the enemy which allowed Plunk and Litton to escape. Zack Southerland left in the rear guard. Nate Teague, Capt George Todd and his men, Capt, Preacher regular CSA Thomas Todd whose main camp was at Dripping Springs, Bill Toler, Lou Welch and Si Whitsett. While camped on the White River in Ark a hog wandered into camp and Dick West accidentally shot Sid Creek in the mouth. It was serious but not fatal. Sid Creek, John McCorkle, Andy McGuire, Simeon Davis, Patrick DeHart and Capt. William Downing, part of the Cherokee CSA were all part of the rear guard.

John Payton, Hank Williams and Frank Shepherd were killed. We buried them in the Pleasant Grove Cemetery on the Silver Farm about 4 miles from Centralia. The bodies of the Union were left where they lay as a warning to others. The boys headed back into Centralia for the rest of Johnston's men. Capt. Theis left in charge with some 60 troops managed to get to his horse along with two dozen more of the troops. They fled west toward Sturgeon, Bloody Bill shouted out for Archie and me to follow, maybe half of them reached Sturgeon.

Before returning to the Singleton farm, the boys killed the wounded Union at Centralia then returning to the farm killing any wounded they found along the way. Jesse told me Dave Poole looting the bodies of the dead began jumping on their bodies near Singleton's, crowing as he counted them. Thrailkill objected and Dave said, "If they are dead, I can't hurt them, I cannot count'em good without stepping on'em. When I get my foot on one this way I know I've got him." Jesse looked at me, "Momma can't know about this." I understood what he was saying. He'd scalped his first man today. These were boys his age, most of them forced into Union conscription. He looked pale and sick, his wounds weren't healing as they should but I wondered if his paleness was a result of his own actions. I walked among the dead. I was worried about Jesse and ask John Thrailkill about my getting him home without shaming him. I hadn't liked what I had witnessed today but John was Jesse's closest friend. We headed into Howard Co and from there dispersing into the smaller groups of 20 to 30. Bloody Bill held Goodman captive, three nights later on Sept 30th he escaped while we were crossing the Missouri River. Renick ordered Riley Crawford executed in Jackson Co on the return trip from Centralia. Riley was shot in the guts with buckshot and died later that night. I thought about his momma and how hard this news would be on her. "And fear not them which kill the body, but are not able to kill the soul: but rather fear him which is able to destroy both soul and body in hell." Matthew 10:28 I could see the boys souls, perhaps my own, has been compromised by the war, committing acts the most horrible of dreams had never revealed. I doubted if any of us any longer feared hell, I knew the Unionists didn't.

One of the boys I'd grown up with, remained close to was Dick Kinney. He had been mortally wounded at Centralia. He died of lock jaw three days later. I kept his pistol. He had carved 48 notches in it.

Jesse was finding himself short of breath and his chest continued to erupt bloody pus like an infected thorn trying to get out from under your skin. He found himself very sore and aching, his abscess giving him considerable trouble. He hurt when he breathed. We weren't certain how we were going to get him home, he insisted on remaining with us riding with John Thraillkill.

Communications intercepted:

"GENL.: Anderson and his friends captured the train from Saint Louis today at Centralia Station, killed 21 soldiers who were on the train, robbed the passengers, and burned the cars" "...my telegrams have advised you of the disasters at Centralia, the capture of the railway train, the inhuman slaughter of the defenseless soldiers thereon, the robbery of the passengers, the burning of the moving train, and the indignities visited upon helpless women must be regarded as one of the chief barbarisms of the war."

Richard Stevenson, a cousin to Uncle Till, drank to Jeff Davis and Sterling Price in a saloon in St. Louis on the 27th. He and Hart were arrested the next day at the Myrtle Street Station. They were asked if they were "Union or Rebels." Stevenson responded boisterously "a wolf and a bushwhacker, by god." He told the prison guards the same thing. The guards wanted to hang him but were stopped.

Genl. Price's invasion into Missouri had begun and would take over a month. He had entered Missouri just days before and we had been exuberant with the news. Then news arrived Genl. Price battled at Pilot Knob, Fort Davidson in Iron Co against Brigadier Genl. Thomas Ewing's command losing 1500 men to Ewing who lost less than 200. Union Genl. Washburne, commander at Memphis in Scotland Co, early in Sept had gotten pieces of information that suggested Genl. Price was intent on invading Missouri. He had sent word to Union Genl. Rosecrans of what he believed was Genl. Price's goal of taking St. Louis. Rosecrans had moved by rail with reinforcements to Ironton to intercept him. While our boys were at Centralia, Genl. Price attacked Ewing's command, driving them back into Fort Davidson. During the night the Feds evacuated the fort blowing up the powder magazine, destroying everything. Genl. Price had intended to march through Missouri both foraging and securing supplies from the spoils of war following in Union Genl. Sherman's march to Atlanta. This was not a good omen.

Chapter 25

The boys were a mess after Centralia, fighting and arguing with each other. It impacted even the most hardened among us. Oct 1st, Joel Frank Chiles killed William Ridings. Chiles was so angry and out of control he shot Fletch Taylor and Bill Basham wounding both. Bill in turn grabbed his gun, shot and killed Joel. Fletch was still recovering from a previous wound or likely he'd of been Bill to the draw killing Joel himself.

Oct 5th we received word from Genl. Price to join Todd and meet him at Boonville. We crossed the Missouri River at Rocheport. Jesse Morrow went with George Todd to Howard Co to hunt for Quantrill again absent. Todd sent Jesse Morrow, John House, Trow, William and Henry Noland and me into Jackson Co to alert the guerrillas of the status of Prices raid into Missouri. Genl. Marmaduke made camp at Hermann, a German community in Gasconade Co. The Union had moved troops to Jeff City and Rolla leaving Hermann undermanned. The older men in the town used multiple shots from a single cannon giving the impression the town was heavily guarded. Known for its winemaking vineyard, the men enjoyed the barrels of hard cider. When they started getting tipsy, they were ordered to pour the wine casks into the Missouri River.

Sunday, Oct 9th George Todd ordered Si Gordon to lead the attack on German militia at Blackwater in Lafayette Co. Ves Atchison, Bud Pence, Levi Potts, Frank Gray and Ed Greenwood rode with Poole. Jobson and Hiram Masterson were killed. Lt. William Greenwood, Frank Gregg, Andy McGuire, Albert Scott and Jesse rode with George Todd killing some discharged Union soldiers and civilians; all men of German ancestry. Even though they were warned of our approach we were able to force a retreat. Todd ordered Dave Poole with ten men to go out and hunt up any Federal troops around. If they found any they were to lure them to camp. On Oct 10th, 1864, Price's men arrived at Boonville. We got there on the 11th finding Price's men were looting and stealing which did more to turn the townspeople against them than help, especially since Boonville was pro Confederacy. Union Genl. John Sanborn, a brigade forming part of Rosecran's force was pursuing Genl. Price from Jeff City collided with his rear guard on the outskirts of town on the 11th where he was pushed back by Marmaduke and Fagan, withdrawing to the south banks of Saline Creek.

It had been nearly two weeks since Centralia. When Bloody Bill met with Genl. Price he made him remove the scalps from his belt before he would talk to him. When he saw other men among us had scalps hanging from their horses, Price ordered the men to remove them in front of Bloody Bill, effectively shunning him, demeaning him in front of his men. I thought of Unc talking of the proud Indian warriors, braves like Geronimo who proudly wore his scalp belt. I prayed for Bloody Bill but mostly I wished Unc was here to explain things. Shamed in front of his men, Bloody Bill was thinking and that could be dangerous. Gen Price gave Quantrill, Bloody Bill and George Todd instructions to destroy certain rail road lines. Todd went south and Bloody Bill was ordered to destroy the Hannibal and St. Joseph Railroad to prevent enemy from maneuvering to move in front of Price from St. Louis. They chose to respond to Genl. Price's orders in their own way. I stayed under Shelby. On the 12th we learned Maj James Blunt was on his way to block Price from crossing the Missouri river into Kansas at Westport. We didn't know where Bloody Bill had gone with his men. And, since I didn't see Jesse, I figured he had likely joined him. Genl. Price didn't realize the efforts of Bloody Bill and George Todd had already brought rail traffic to a halt in Western Missouri. Bloody Bill left with a group of men attacking and looting small towns north of the river. When Todd returned Genl. Price assigned him and his men was assigned by Price to be scouts for the main army.

On Oct 15th Genl. Price sent a detachment under Genl. Shelby and John Clark to Glasgow to find, capture or destroy the weapons and supplies in the garrison there. Bloody Bill and Quantrill's commands joined us along with other irregulars from across Missouri. Before dawn the artillery boys had opened the routes into Glasgow forcing the Federalists to retreat. A mounted Cav and artillery force laid siege to the fortifications on Hereford Hill. The Federalists formed a line of defense but Col Harding realizing they could not withstand our force, surrendered. At Glasgow a garrison of 400 Union soldiers was captured along with rifles, overcoats and horses. Many of the troops stayed around the town for several days resting and replenishing their provisions and weapon supplies. There wasn't much difference in our Partisan guerilla tactics than that of the Union or Confederate soldiers. Whenever supplies were needed we backed our horses up to the doors, spurred them and the horses would kick down the doors. We took whatever we wanted and needed.

At Glasgow, Genl. Price sent Genl. Jeff Thompson with 1500 men to attack Sedalia. Quantrill and the boys along with Bloody Bill and 150 of his command joined Thompson. I was happy to learn Jesse was not among them, hoping John had gotten him home to Momma. We overpowered the Missouri militia capturing the garrison of some 400 Union soldiers guarding the town then began to raid and loot. Thompson ordered the men to stop, keep only the weapons, equipment and horses. He paroled and released the captured men. We heard Quantrill had successfully robbed a banker in Glasgow of over $20,000, then disappeared, again. George Webb, one of the commanders of irregulars who joined us for the attack was seriously wounded along with James "Tuck" Tucker. On the 16th some of the boys robbed the citizens of Ridgely of $2,000 and the next night burned down Smithville. Quantrill was coming and going, disappearing to be with Kate as often as he appeared to be with the boys. After Ridgely, Bill Jackson started riding with Bloody Bill.

The 4th Kansas State Militia created 10 days following the attack on Lawrence, Kansas to deal with "the guerillas" was trying to enter Independence. Led by Genl. Shelby we pushed them back to the Little Blue River 9 miles east of Independence. Genl. Shelby and his Iron Brigade were leading the advance for Gen Price. George Todd and his men including me rode as Shelby's advance. Under Shelby and Price we crawled westward. We had been excited to join Genl. Price, but moving slow and uniform was something us guerillas were not used to.

Union Genl. Rosecrans and Genl. Curtis were cut off from communicating with each other to formalize their plans of attack against Price. Curtis continued having problems dealing with his men from Kansas refusing to step foot in Missouri. Genl. Blunt headed east to Lexington about 30 miles from Kansas City. On Oct 19th Genl. Price approached Lexington colliding with Union scouts and pickets at two o'clock in the afternoon. They drove them back engaging in battle. Price's army eventually pushed them through town to the western outskirts pursuing them along the Independence Road until nightfall. Without Curtis's entire force, the Union could not stop us, Price's army.

Near Waverly, home of Jo Shelby, Genl. Price exuberant over our successes and the return of many of the boys, proclaimed amnesty for his bushwhacking deserters declaring he'd "promote Quantrill to Brigadier Genl.." But Quantrill had vanished again. He had been absent more than present since marrying. When Genl. Price sent word to us, it was directed to George Todd. It was Todd who reached out to Bloody Bill, John Thrailkill and Quantrill that Genl. Price was making a second march into Missouri. Everything we did good or bad was credited to Quantrill, whether he was with us or not. Two of "Quantrill's men" R.W. Morgan and Will Morgan, both privates in Co I of Col. Tom's command were captured by Capt. McConnell on the 18th. The boys were growing more disenchanted with Quantrill, upset he was with Kate at a time he was needed.

After the battle at Lexington, Jeems Snider, an expat from Kentucky, went to Col. Shelby requesting leave. His wife, Missus Margaret had fallen ill after the birth of their baby girl Maggie in Aug. Although her parents, Harvey and Mary Wilson Paulette lived in Andrew Co, Jeems thought it best to get her back to Kentucky. He was afraid for her arrest and detention, possible expulsion and should something happen to him, with three young babies in the house. He need not to have worried, Shelby was more than willing to not only grant him whatever time he needed but willing to send a couple of the boys with him to aid in packing up their belongings. He and his brother Jake Snider had been fighting with us. Jake's wife, Fannie Foster Snider, remained in Kentucky and Jake was going back with Jeems.

Blunt reached the Little Blue River on the 20th. Genl. Curtis ordered Blunt to return to Independence only to order a return to the Little Blue the following day. When Blunt approached he found Union Col. Thomas Moonlight and his forces burning the bridge and fighting with Genl. Price's main force. Once again Genl. Price was able to force a retreat. Things were about to change. Oct 21 and 22nd we fought at Westport, the Battle of the Little Blue River. I had just met a young man from down in Ark. Abraham Wood Blythe only 16 years old from Marion Co. He walked all the way to Batesville to join Genl. Price for his raid into Missouri. He survived by killing what he needed to eat, making his own fire and taking shelter in the caves and overhangs when there were no nearby houses. He talked about how the Indians had lived in Yellville and many were still there, married to the whites. He loved home. We talked his momma Clarinda Wood from whom he got his middle name and his daddy Jackson Blythe. I told him, should we survive this fight, I wanted to meet his momma and daddy and I wanted him to meet mine. I had taken an instant liking to this young fella. When the fighting started, he fought bravely. I saw him fall but couldn't immediately go to him. When I tried to get back to find him he was gone.

Genl. Price moved west up the Missouri River with successes at smaller outposts. Oct 21st began as a beautiful fall day. The leaves, bright hues of yellow, orange and red, edged in greens were beginning to fall from the trees. Days were warm and nights could be cool. After having secured Independence we camped in along an unfinished rail road west of town. Union Gen Samuel Curtis was at Westport further north and west when we learned more Union was moving in behind us from the south and east. Gen Curtis' Army of the Border assembled in and around Westport and was blocking our way west. We were moving with 500 wagons and finding a good place to ford the Big Blue River was critical. Byram's Ford was the best ford in the area. Genl. Curtis constructed breastworks and rifle pits near the river placing over eight thousand troops there.

Union Maj Alfred Pleasanton and his Cav caught up with us at dawn on Saturday the 22. Pleasanton crossed the Little Blue attacking from the northeast, hitting Genl. Price from the rear. Marmaduke's division engaged with the Union about 2 miles west of Independence, managing to push the Feds back and hold them until the morning of the 23rd. Richard Glasscock's horse was shot out from under him. One of the most hated men in Missouri, Union Col. Jennison was ordered to keep pickets posted near

Independence. Col. Sydney Drake Jackman led a Cav brigade in advance of Genl. Shelby making the first attempt but was unsuccessful in crossing the Blue. Bloody Bill sent Wild Irishman Arthur McCoy to see if a large steamboat could carry Genl. Shelby and his men across. McCoy rowed a boat out to check on the large steamboat. He rowed out and back, under fire, unharmed. Around ten o'clock in the morning Col Jackman found an unguarded cattle crossing we were able to cross over and flank Jennison. At first Jennison was forced to fall back but was joined by reinforcements. The battle lasted over 8 hours. Colly Chiles family brought food. Chiles wounded and captured at Helena, Ark, escaped rejoining Langhornes Co under Shelby. Colly was an interesting fella. He'd stand with his arms crossed listening to everyone talk, banter about any subject, then he'd announce with a finality what he thought. In most cases it put an end to the discussion as if his point was the only one to be had. He had nappy long hair. One of the boys told him he had a black snake in the wood pile somewhere back there. Only his hair looked like that. He'd had mutton chops but let those grow out and now you couldn't tell where his long hair ended and his beard began. The only thing he shaved was his mustache which he trimmed to a little rectangular shape, the rest was untouched. I liked Colly a lot, his family was one of those families a person could rely on through thick and thin. Colly spent most of his time with Shelby but rode with guerrillas when he was home.

The heavy fighting on Saturday bled over into Sunday when running out of ammunition retreat became the only option. Over 6,000 men were lost, some were calling it the Gettysburg of the South. Of our immediate group, Alex Cates was wounded and captured. He died in Kansas City, Dec 15th. James Wormack was sent to Gratiot Street, released at war's end. Bob Ratcliff was sent to Gratiot, then transferred to Alton, Illinois where he died Dec 16th of chronic diarrhea. Lafayette Tice who rode north with us from Ark, was captured, sent to Gratiot, then to Alton, Illinois and finally to Point Lookout, Maryland for exchange. James Brady was captured, sent to Rock Island, died Dec 23rd of chronic diarrhea. J.M.R. Brown was captured and sent to Gratiot. John Brown, Joseph Bryson, Robert Chrogmorton (died of Variola in Jan), John Clinkenbeard, William Clinton, James Coggin from Evening Shade, John Counts (died Jan 16th in Alton), John Cox, A.J. Qualls, William Dowell (died Dec 3 of bronchitis), William Everett, John Frazier (died from wounds Dec 12), G.H. Goodwin (died of pneumonia Nov 30th), JJ Gordon (died Dec 26th of Variola), James Machan, Robert Jarrette, Ed Johnson (died in prison hospital with measles), John "Sam" Jones, Horatio McFarland, James Mitchell (died Jan 5th), Barney Morgan (died Jan 2 of pneumonia at Rock Island), Richard Partee who had come north with us from Izard Co, Maj Will Perrin also from Izard

Co, H.D. Pulley, Daniel Rhodes, Andy Smith (died Jan 3rd Rock Island), Alexander Stewart (died Jan 14th of diarrhea at Rock Island), Kit Tate (died Nov 27th of diarrhea) and William Taylor who had come north with us from Batesville, Robert Walker and Charles Wellencamp were all captured on Oct 24th. Col. James Nichols had been killed in the battle and Henry Porter was shot in the right leg.

Like any other battle, skirmish or engagement in wartime, it was awful. I saw the youngest among us fall to their deaths. I was heart sick over the death of young Abe. I was glad Jesse and I were the only ones in our family old enough to fight. George Todd was killed Oct 21st. I hadn't known it at the time, but Jesse was riding right up front with him. They were stopped at Sugar Creek watching the retreat of Capt. Herman Wagner, Commander of the Union's 2nd Cav when George was shot through the neck by a sniper's bullet from a Spencer carbine. He rose up in his saddle for a better view and the sniper shot him. The ball shattering his neck knocked him from his saddle. Jesse and Dick Maddox dragged him to safety. Securing an ambulance they took him to Mr. Burns's house where his wound was dressed. Todd was 25 years hold and strong as an ox, but he lived less than an hour. During that last hour one of the boys of the Roman Catholic faith sat with him talking about confessing his sins. Todd became a Roman Catholic in his last breaths. Jesse found me with Col. Shelby. Upon hearing of Todd's death he put Dave Poole in charge of his men then wired George's wife of his death. We took Capt. George Todd home to Independence to his Momma, Martha Morris Todd. When we got there we learned she had just buried her husband, George's Daddy just days before. George died never knowing his daddy was dead. With war all around us, it remained illegal to bury guerillas. Genl. Price made certain we carried papers we were transporting him home for burial, a regular soldier in the Confederacy under Genl. Price. George's momma and daddy were from Scotland and he was their only son. I stood watching Missus Martha as she placed flowers in boiling water then bathed and dressed her son. She cried silently dutifully cleaning every inch of his body. He was quickly buried at Woodlawn Cemetery. Afraid of the Union's retribution even against the dead, regular enlisted or not, we buried him in the Beatty family plot. The Beatty's protested but relented. Andy McGuire, John Thraillkill, Allen Parmer, John Ross, Lafe Parvin, Harrison Trow, Press Webb, Sim Whitsett, Dick Burns and Dan Vaughn attended to his funeral along with Jesse and me. Dick Burns vowed vengeance to George's wife Catherine and 18 month old daughter, Mary. After Todd was buried, Dan Vaughn announced he was putting together a command, a small group of the boys joined him including Sim Whitsett. We were given a meal and visited, but no frivolity. Returning on the 23rd we had missed the fighting on the 22nd. Riding back

Jesse and I talked about Momma and Daddy, all that our lives had seen and endured but mostly we laughed and talked like two brothers who might have just been out for the day at the cattle auction, hunting or fishing. We couldn't talk of the death around us that would make it to real, even for us. Dave Pool in command of Todd's men retreated with Price. Price's wagon train and 5,000 head of cattle crossed the Blue River at Byram's Ford headed southward toward Little Santa Fe and temporary safety at Fort Scott. Genl. Price fled toward Ark defeated. The Union pursued him into Kansas. Catching them camped on the banks of the Marais des Cygnes River, Trading Post in Linn Co. After an artillery bombardment that began at four o'clock in the morning the Union men launched a furious assault. Price ordered his troops to cross the swollen river, leaving Fagan to hold off the Feds until he could get his wagon train across. Although the Union captured two cannon and several prisoners, they didn't prevent the retreat.

Samuel Bigham House (Arnold Homestead NRHP Izard Co)

Pleasanton continued his pursuit catching up with Genl. Price again at Mine Creek where they engaged briefly. Price continued towards Fort Scott. In the late afternoon of Oct 25, his supply train had difficulty crossing the Marmiton River ford and just as at Mine Creek earlier that afternoon, Price had to make another stand. Union Brigadier Genl. John McNeil rallied troops from the commands preparing for an all out assault, but it seems there was some humanity in him. When he realized a good number of the troops under Genl. Price were not only without arms and ammunition, but were without shoes, his assault was not much more than a sound statement the Union had taken Missouri. Over 600 of our men had been killed, wounded and captured including Genl. Marmaduke. A great many of Col. Tom's men who had come north with Genl. Price were captured in Kansas. John Vickery, captured, transferred to Ft. Leavenworth, then to Camp Morton, Indiana. He died there Feb 20th, 1865. W.F. Frazier captured died Jan 31st of diarrhea at Alton, Illinois prison. Sgt. Samuel S. Bigham from Mill Creek, Ark Co A of Col. Tom's men was wounded in the right side of his body and hip at Mine Creek. We had spent many a night encamped on the fields behind his home, near the springs. He and Bill Arnold were close friends. Captured, gangrene set up from the gunshot wound and he died, three weeks later on Nov 10th, 1864. They buried him at Mound City, Kansas. Bill Lawrence and Bill Arnold were both charged with getting word to his family, his wife, Susannah Woods, daughter of James Baldridge Woods and Margaret Finger. She would send word to his parents, Elihu Hall Bigham and Polly Lisenby in Tennessee.

This was 14 year old Clell Miller's his first battle. He was wounded and captured, taken to a Union prison at Chillicothe from there to Macon, charged with aiding and abetting Bloody Bill. He was then taken to St. Louis to Gratiot Street Prison. His daddy and neighbors from Clay Co testified for him gaining his release in April 1865. Most think it was the fact he was only a boy. Col. Tom's men who were riding with us; Harmus Benix Criswell had been captured at Lexington on the 20th then sent to Alton, Illinois. He was the son of James Lytle Criswell and Margaret Lafferty, children of the first settlers of the White River Valley above Batesville, John Lafferty who arrived in 1798 and Momma's cousin, Sarah Lindsay Lafferty. He ran a keel boat operation out of the Ark Post up to the Buckhorn where he settled with his family. They were the first people to apply for a land patent. Will Harmon was captured by Col. Blandon on the 20th and Ben Childers on the 21st. Will died in Gratitot Street Military prison. Col. Blandon captured Calvin Archer and W.M. Hennan, both in Co B on the 22nd. Cal died in Jan at St. Louis prison. J.W. "Jdub" Blankenship was captured on the 21st in Jackson Co, along with Solomon "Rutch" Smith who was wounded. Rutch had been fighting near his brother in law Green Walker when his left leg was mangled from the blast of a gun. He had to have it amputated. They were sent from Kansas City to St. Louis. Rutch remained there until war's end when he was paroled. Neil Walker, Wood Valentine and Lt. Col. Joseph Love were captured in Jackson Co on the 22nd, Battle of the Big Blue. Love was sent to Gratiot Street Military Prison in St. Louis then while being transferred to Johnson's Island, Ohio, escaped along with a couple other fellas. Capt. McConnell, captured brothers R.W. and William Morgan. We understood William got measles and died two weeks later on Nov 2 at the prison hospital in St. Louis. The Union was out with the sole goal of capturing and killing as many of Genl. Price's men as possible. When the Union forces found men among their dead and dying had been scalped, they began to focus on Bloody Bill. I'm not sure what made Jesse and me stay with him rather than go home or join with one of the others, most likely it was those childhood alliances were the reason. I think for me it was the only way I could keep an eye on both of them, both of whom I was terribly worried about.

Leaving Genl. Price, he thanked us all for having served with him. Commending us on our skills and encouraging us not to take his defeat as our own. We needed rest and made camp at Albany, about a mile north of Orrick in the lower part of Ray Co. It was there a farmer's wife reported our location to the Federalists who set up an ambush on Thursday the 27th. Maj John Grimes of the 33rd Missouri Infantry ordered Maj Samuel P. Cox of the 31st to form a battle line across the road leading into Orrick while Grimes men hid waiting. We had no warning, the exhausted pickets and scouts had seen nothing. Bloody Bill was riding out front when we saw Cox. It was our ambush and we should have recognized it as such but tired of mind and body, unsuspecting we gave chase. As soon as Bloody Bill was even with Grimes' men the volleys rang out, killing Bloody Bill, Young Simmons, Sgt. Willy Tarkington and Johnson C. "Mack" McIlvaine, wounding McKitrick and others. Jim Cummins and a few others had just left out heading back to Clay Co when they heard the shots and returned.

Hank Patterson, AJ Luckett, Hedge Reynolds, Jasper Moody, Bill Smith, Paul Debenhorst and Anson Tolliver were killed trying to retrieve Bloody Bill's body. Our cousin, Dick West was seriously wounded when helping Tuck and Woot Hill get Bloody Bill's body on a horse but then the horse was killed. When the horse fell, it pinned Bloody Bill's body underneath. Sgt. Smith Jobson and Billy Winchester were killed trying to save Bloody Bill after his horse had pinned his body down. I retrieved Smith's hat. He had a bolero hat he called it, wide brimmed, it was a smart looking hat. He wore two holsters for his guns and his jacket had special embroidery his momma maybe had done for him. He was a good looking young man. When he shook your hand, his big warm hands swallowed most fella's. This was John Thomas Warren's first battle. He was wounded four times. William "Billy" Winchester he wore a little speck of hair on his chin, called a goatee because it looked like the chin of a goat. And, he had a trimmed out mustache. Both were dark fine hair, peach fuzz. He wore his hair trimmed out short. He was a good looking young man with a great smile. Both of them were just boys. Col. John Holt had his horse shot out from under him during the ambush. William James was wounded by not killed. Peyton Long had 'another' horse shot out from under him. This was the first battle for Arch Nicholson, brother of Joe. Their other brother James had been killed because Arch and Joe joined up with Price.

William "Bloody Bill" Thomason Anderson
Missouri Valley Special Collections, Kansas City Public Library

Col. Caleb Perkins, Capt. A.E. Asbury CSA and Capt. John Rains were with us. Jim Crow Chiles had his horse shot out from under him. Seeing the situation for what it was, we fled, headed to Uncle J.R. Cole's house. Archie Clements took over Bloody Bill's command and Peyton Long and several others chose to join up with Fletch Taylor. Archie and the boys found Col. Groom of Shelby's command seeking to join up with the regular Confederacy but Groom refused them. Archie was so angry he and the boys killed Groom and 54 new Confederate recruits.

The flag given to Bloody Bill by 1st Sgt. Francis Marion "Gooly" Roberson, made by his wife Wealthy was found on his body. They found a letter from Bloody Bill's wife, a lock of hair and money. The Federalists paraded Bloody Bill's corpse through Richmond. Then Maj Samuel P. Cox took Bloody Bill to a photographer in Richmond to document his death. People started gathering and many had their photographs taken with his body, of which they were charged for. Then Cox ordered his head cut off. One of his men climbed a telegraph pole on the court house lawn with Bloody Bill's head placing it atop for all to see. Then Union militiamen drug his headless body through the streets of Richmond. While the actions were both applauded and condemned by people, especially civilians, for us, we felt like the actions were deserving of a man like Bloody Bill. Actions he would have relished, that he himself might have perpetrated upon the Union. It was that day Jesse vowed revenge on Samuel P. Cox.

Sometime in Oct 1864, Charles "Charley" Miniken was captured by the Federalists. Whether it was intended to deter or retaliate, each side would be guilty of such 'military' tribunals and executions. On Oct 29, 1864, Charley Miniken and Bill Blackburn of Batesville were summarily executed. Charley's last words as the rag was being tied over his eyes were reported to be "Boys, when you kill me, kill me dead." Some days later their bodies were found by a local woman returning on horseback from visiting her own husband, a prisoner of war at Rock Island Prison, IL.

On the night of Oct 28th, Union Genl. Sanborn ordered Capt. Roberts to take some men scouting seeking to find and destroy Genl. Shelby who was moving south after the defeat at the Blue. Near Marionville they encountered Shelby's pickets. They engaged in a running fight over some 10 miles along Cassville Rd culminating at Upshaw Hollow. The Union captured twenty of Shelby's men, moving back across the area they had fought the Union reported over sixty men dead. They made camp at Mt. Vernon. The following morning Sanborn ordered a squad of men to return for the dead and bury them. The Union dropped nearly 40 of the bodies of our men into a well. A Mister Wilkes came by the following day and saw the bodies stuffed into the well. He heard a man call for help. Searching he found a man with a bone protruding from his leg stuck into the ground pinning him in place, dead bodies had been piled on and all around him. He took him to Mt. Vernon to be cared for.

The following day more were captured at Mine Creek, W.F. Frazier, died Jan 31st of diarrhea and John Vickroy, died Feb 20th at camp Morton, Indiana. Two more were captured toward the end of the month, Richard Elijah Clark, Oct 30th at Fairplay and Augustus Lapee, Oct 31st at Greenfield. Each of these men was originally sent to St. Louis before being transferred out to northern camps.

Chapter 26

Jim Reynolds and his brother John left out for Colorado. We learned they was captured and convicted of robbery in Colorado. They were taking them to prison when Jim was killed by Union Abner Williamson near Ft. Lyon, Colorado. We figured he was trying to escape. David Goforth was captured near Fair Play, Missouri on Nov 1. Lemuel Lashley, John and Ike Reed in Co B of Col.'s Tom's Regiment were captured at Marshfield on Nov 1. They were taken to Springfield then sent to Rock Island, Illinois on Nov. 24th. Lemuel died on Dec 9th and John on Jan 11th, they are buried at Rock Island.

On the 5th, Dick Jones of Col. Tom's Co C was captured at Buffalo, sent to Springfield and released June 5th, after war's end. Several of our boys some of Col. Tom's men surrendered at New Madrid on the 20th. The Union made a list of the boys saying they claimed to be deserters among them John M Crowder and Benon Sappington. But that wasn't true. They fought at the Little Blue and survived; Genl. Price told us to go home. And, John and Ben were trying to get back to the White River Valley.

In the midst of Genl. Price and Genl. Shelby's retreat, Bill Gregg got married! On Nov 3rd, he and Lizzie Hook surprised us all. None of us knew he had a girl, much less one willing to marry a man fighting a war, one that could make her a widow any time. Bill announced it to several of the men under his command, asking a dozen or so join him. Wearing their best attire they went to the home of the bride where Bill and Lizzie were married. Even my best friend, his brother Frank, hadn't said a word if in fact he had known of it. I heard from several of them they had a fine meal, stood guard all night around the cabin where newlyweds spent the night and then all had a great breakfast before preparing to head back to camp. Much to their surprise, Lizzie joined them. Bill had made the decision to head south to Texas for the winter.

We got word on Nov 6th, Genl. Price and Shelby reached Ark but Union Genl. Samuel Curtis who defeated us at Westport had continued his movement from Kansas into Ark following after them. Genl. Price had employed guerilla tactics, dispersing his men to move south in smaller units, foraging and subsisting made easier with fewer to feed. At Cane Hill, Ark, Genl. Price was ahead of Curtis sufficient enough to allow the larger group of men with him to round up several head of local cattle and skin them out for cooking. Curtis camped near Prairie Grove leaving out at daylight marching toward Cane Hill. There were about 50 of the boys sick and in need of medical attention. They were left behind when Genl. Price moved out south leaving a rear guard who engaged with Curtis' advance. Having been left behind before, sick and captured, I knew how these men would likely be treated, shot and killed or sent home. Unlikely they would be taken prisoner infecting Curtis' men. Somehow Genl. Price left the bag behind containing Union Genl. Blunts flag Quantrill captured at Baxter Springs, Kansas the year before. The flag had been carefully cut into pieces with the intention of giving pieces of it to other southern commanders as tokens of the defeat. But, with the change in the tide of the war to the Union, most of the flag pieces remained in the bag when found by Union Genl. Curtis' men. They made camp Cane Hill continuing their pursuit of Shelby the next morning.

Needing to avoid Fort Smith, Ark, Price swung west into Indian Territory and Texas before arriving safely in to Ark on Dec 2, 1864. He had 6,000 survivors, half of his original force of 12,000 enlisted men. He reported to Kirby Smith that he "marched 1,434 miles fought 43 battles and skirmishes, captured and paroled over 3,000 Federal officers and men, captured 18 pieces of artillery ... and destroyed Missouri property ... of $10,000,000 in value."

On Nov 13th, we got word to meet up. Bill Gregg and George Shepherd decided to go to Texas with about 30 of the boys and their wives. Silas King went with them. Harrison Trow led their advance as they headed south. Nov days were still warm but nights were cold, troops on both sides were suffering. The droughts had left little food for animal or man. Abraham Lincoln was re-elected by the North. Southern states were not allowed to vote. Savannah fell just before Christmas. After arriving, camped near the Yokum place at Sherman, Silas King and Arch Clements were cleaning their guns when Silas' pistol accidentally discharged, killing his best friend Perry Smith. Silas caught the fever and died two weeks later. Adam Yokum buried Silas.

Nov 16th, Bill Stewart was killed near Boonville by Capt. W.H. Susford from Johnson Co. Susford was riding with Clifton Holtzclaw. We didn't get the details of what happened just that Bill had been shot. On the 18th, Capt. Ryder, Jim Anderson, Capt. J.W. Hawkins and Jesse were at Brunswick, Missouri. Jesse didn't want to go south but he didn't want to go with Quantrill to Kentucky. Momma wasn't certain about any of it, but she felt Jesse was safer remaining with Jim.

We got word of the Sipe brother's murder. In July and Aug 1862, the sons of Germans, Jacob and Nancy Caroline Yount Sipe from the Barrens, neighbors of Bill Chitwood's family in Ark, had four sons join the Confederacy; Marcus Philo, 29, Rufus Monroe, 25, William Sidney, 21 and Jacob Pinkney 19. Each of them enlisted for a year of service in the regular service of the Confederacy. Each of them enlisted for a year of service in regular service of the Confederacy. Marcus fell ill and was hospitalized in Monroe, Louisiana in Aug 1863. Rufe served his term of one year and left to go aide his brother getting home to Ark. They learned their little brother Miles Henry 2 year old died in June of the fever. In late Sept'63 on their way home they were captured by the Union somewhere on the Ark Louisiana border. They signed the oath of allegiance and were forced to join the Union or be shot, no parole offered. As soon as the opportunity arose they fled continuing on home. Marcus married Evaline Blue and had two children. Miss Evaline was the great great grand-daughter of Chief Blue Jacket and Clear Water Baby. They come to Ark from Tenn. Clear Water Baby was the daughter of the great Canadian Frenchman Jacques Duperon Baby that our teacher Mister Bird Price Smith taught us about. He had been an aide and confidant of the Indians who were fighting in the War of 1812. One of his daughters, Mamete Baby married Tecumseh. Abe Ruddell of Batesville had lived 20 years with Tecumseh as his brother. These families had lived through Indian attacks only to fight this war.

Rufe and Marcus made it home and when found out were forced to join Union Elisha Baxter's Co or be shot. They joined Baxter on Jan 1st, 1864. Marcus' youngest daughter was born in Sept 1864. The next month on Nov 18th, Marcus was hung from a tree by his fellow troops for aiding the Confederacy. Rufe was married to Eliza Ray. On Dec 18th, 1864 two Union jayhawkers that lived in the area caught their brothers William Sidney and Jacob Pinkney Sipe at home. They were in the field hunting when Jayhawkers saw them, chased them down shooting both of them in the back killing them dead. A little boy George Caraway was down by the creek playing and saw the killings. He hid until they had left, and then went to Rufe and their parents telling what he'd seen. They found the boys bodies and buried them next to Marcus at the Blue Church Cemetery. The boy knew two of the men but the Sipes were afraid for all their safety and told him to never tell anyone who the men were or what he had seen.

On Nov 8th, President Lincoln won the election remaining the President of the United States. He ran against former Union Genl. George B. McClellan who he soundly defeated. Of course, no southerner's were allowed to vote. Quantrill was ranting about going to kill Lincoln. A prospect many of us had thought about, prayed someone would be brave enough to do, but dared not speak aloud. Quantrill sent John Barker out to notify us to meet at the farm of Bud's Momma, Gramma Mary Fristoe Wigginton, five miles south of Waverly, not far from Genl. Shelby's home, on Dec 1st. John came by the farm along with Allen Parmer, sweet on Susie. Allen told us a Federal Lt. had pulled a gun on Quantrill and John was able to convince the Lt. that Quantrill wasn't "Quantrill" by pulling a gun on the Lt. He told him these "papers" proved he wasn't who he thought he was and the more he showed the papers the more people realized it wasn't him. The Lt was so convinced he offered to buy them a round of drinks at the next town. Allen asked John about something he'd heard about Kate, Quantrill's wife, going to Saint Louis taking loot from our raids to finance the re-grouping of the men. John confirmed what he'd heard and informed us of the meeting. He told us Quantrill was planning on going east to Kentucky, possibly even further to find Robert E. Lee.

We joined Allen and a dozen others riding to meet up with Quantrill. We found Peyton Long at Mrs. Hamlet's place at Tuscumbia in Miller Co. He told Peyton he was looking for twenty five men to go with him to Kentucky. It was bitter cold. Quantrill had captured and killed a Colorado Cav officer whose uniform and decorations he carried. Quantrill was wearing the uniform passing himself off as the commander of a unit from the Second Colorado Cav. It was around nine o'clock in the morning when we rode into Tuscumbia, right up to the headquarters where Quantrill introduced himself to Capt. Brown as Commander William Clarke. He requested feed and respite for the horses and the men. A large fire was built inside the Inn they had commandeered and was using as a headquarters. Filled with Union men, we were allowed to go in to warm ourselves. We moved about taking turns truly warming ourselves but also positioning ourselves between the Union men and their arms which were leaning up against the wall. With Quantrill's raised voice telling Capt. Brown to surrender we drew our revolvers out telling the Union men they were now our prisoners. All but one immediately held their hands up, one fella tried to escape through the window. I knocked him in the head with the butt of my pistol telling him to get back inside. We marched the men outside and held them while John Ross took the guns that might be of use. Those that weren't had the stocks broken off of them and thrown in the river. One of the Union men, either drunk or just a jolly kind of fella, said, "why are they doing this, they are Union men?" Their commander replied, "You damned fool they are Southern men and we are their prisoners." Quantrill then ordered the Maj and his soldiers to report to Rolla under arrest of Capt. Charles Moses of the Second Colorado Cav.

About a hundred of the boys agreed to go with Quantrill to Kentucky, Jesse and I among them. Dr. Lee Miller chose instead to head west to Colorado. We headed east in Dec disguised as Feds. We learned Lt. Col. George Thilenus of the EMM was on an expedition from the Cape to Ark with engineers to clear and restore communication lines in Missouri. Quantrill decided our path would take us through Ark giving us the opportunity to destroy whatever success the Union had. When we arrived at Pocahontas we learned Col. Timothy Reeves had camped at Cherokee Bay after skirmishing with Thilenus two weeks earlier near Buckskull on the Missouri Ark border. Our boys were stationed along the Current River near Pitman's Ferry protecting it from Northern occupation preventing their communication from the Cape south. Thilenius moved with some 300 men into Pocahontas on to Powhatan then back north to Pilot Knob returning back to Poplar Bluff arriving at the Cape. Some of the boys had come down sick and talked of heading back home including Jesse. It was a blistering cold day without much prospects of any better in Kentucky. Henry Akers, Rufe and Bob Hudspeth, John William Koger and Ol Shepherd decided to head south to Texas. We heard Frid Fridley and his son, tired of fighting and with Bloody Bill dead, were walking to St. Charles to stay out the rest of the war when they were arrested by Union Capt. George Smith. He told them he'd take them to St. Louis but just west of New Florence at Dryden's Mill he shot them in a peach orchard. Their bodies were found and buried. The papers on Frid's body identified them. After discussing it both Jesse and I agreed, Momma would feel better if he joined the boys headed to Texas rather than going on with us to Kentucky.

Gid D. Powell of Col. Tom's men was headed home when he was captured in Fulton Co on Dec 24th. He was sent to Cape Girardeau, transferred from there to St. Louis where he died February 3rd of small pox in the U.S. Genl. Hospital. They captured Henry B Smith Co B of Col. Tom's men the next day in Lawrence Co. He and Gid were sent together to Gratiot Street Military Prison. After Gid died they sent Henry on to Alton, Illinois, then to James River, Virginia for exchange. Allen McReynolds aided us boys giving us food and shelter at his place on numerous occasions. He was killed on Dec 24th between his place and the Grand Pass Church. Some of the boys went to his house seeking dinner. After they left men of the EMM under Union commander Box showed up asking about them. He pointed them to the road. They forced him to go with him down the road where they shot him in the head. Our boys turned back found McReynolds and buried him in the field of Baltimore Thomas.

The day after Christmas, near Pocahontas, John William and William Hoard, of Col. Tom's command, were captured. Sick, they had decided to go home. We were surprised when we learned the Union had sent sick captives to the prison. That was almost certainly a death sentence, if not for them, those weak and sick at the prison. They were sent to the Union Prison at Gratiot Street in St. Louis. One of the boys who had been there and released said it was part of the Union's plan, to starve out Southern loyalists, breaking them down to the point they got sick and died.

We heard talk of a new war starting in the west. The railroad's wanted land in the west and were financing the relocation of Indians who were fighting back. We understood relocation to mean about the same as our paroling Union captives. They were killing them. We weren't sure if it was an exaggeration or the truth, but I knew none of us wanted to believe it to be true. On Nov 29, while waiting on terms of surrender, Cheyenne and

Arapaho Indians were attacked by 900 cavalrymen at Sand Creek. The Union killed the entire village of people, almost 500 unarmed men, women and children from tribes prepared to surrender.

The Carson family was among the Kentucky expats who moved to Missouri. They settled at Boone's Lick, not far from Fayette, in Howard Co, Missouri. Their youngest, Kit Carson was about one year old. The family settled on a tract of land owned by the sons of Daniel Boone, who purchased the land from the Spanish. The Boone and Carson families became good friends, working and socializing together and intermarrying. Lindsay's oldest son William married Boone's grand-niece, Millie Boone, in 1810. After the birth of their daughter, Adaline, Millie died and William married her sister Cassie. Adaline became Kit's favorite playmate. Cassie and William Carson had nine children of their own. The War Between the States split their families, some of the boys joined the Confederacy and others, like Uncle Wild Man's friend, Kit Carson fought with the Union.

'Jis to think of that dog Chivington and his dirty hounds, up thar at Sand Creek. His men shot down squaws, and blew the brains out of little innocent children. You call sich soldiers Christians, do ye? And Indians savages? What der yer 'spose our Heavenly Father, who made both them and us, thinks of these things? I tell you what, I don't like a hostile red skin any more than you do. And when they are hostile, I've fought 'em, hard as any man. But I never yet drew a bead on a squaw or papoose, and I despise the man who would." – Kit Carson

Some of the Indians cut horses from the camp's herd and fled up Sand Creek or to a nearby Cheyenne camp on the headwaters of the Smoky Hill River. Others, including trader half breed George Bent, son of white man William Bent and Owl Woman, a Cheyenne, were in the camp when the attack happened. He fled upstream and dug holes in the sand beneath the banks of the stream. They were pursued by the troops and fired on, but many survived. Cheyenne warrior Morning Star said that most of the Indian dead were killed by cannon fire, especially those firing from the south bank of the river at the people retreating up the creek. William Bent's daddy, George's grandfather, Silas Bent, had been on the Missouri Supreme Court. The Union was murdering innocent people for the land with the gold claims and the rail road barons. These men who slaughtered these people, they were heathens.

Our hearts were heavy with the news of Col. Chivingtons' Massacre at Sand Creek. We didn't talk much. I made the decision we needed to go to Powhatan some 15 miles south to momma's own cousin, John Anthony Lindsay's, son of Gramma Sallie's brother Jesse Cole Lindsay. We were tired and I needed to assess for myself if Jesse could make it on to Texas. Speaking with an elder of the family might serve us both well. Cousin John moved from Kentucky to Ark when as a young man of eighteen, in the year 1838, just as the Indians were being forced from their homelands. Like

Gramma Sallie, he married his own cousin, Martha Ann Ficklin, daughter of his momma Priscilla Ficklin's brother Asa. Priscilla and Asa's parents, John Herndon Ficklin and Anna Herndon, were own cousins as well, children of siblings Mary and Samuel Herndon, children of Capt. John Herndon and Jane Banks. Cousin John and Missus Martha's son Asa joined the First Ark Mounted Rifles in May of 1861 and fought with us at Wilson's Creek. Cousin John had established a ferry and laid out the town of Powhatan named for the Indians who lived there before him, descendants of Jamestown's Chief Powhaten and the Cornstalks' known to be tall blue haired Indians, intermarried with the white. Cousin John had been commissioned a Capt. at the onset of the War Between the States, having recruited sufficient men he was commissioned a Col. He joined Genl. Price's march into Missouri acting as a guide and an advance through the northern part of Ark. He had delighted Momma showing up unexpectedly for a days rest, sleep and a meal. He had known not only would it be safe but he would be welcomed.

I needed to visit with cousin John about Quantrill. He had lost all sensibilities, talking of killing President Lincoln. Some of the boys were becoming alarmed by his rants while others fell on his every word. We had headed south from Pocahontas when we were met by several men who conveyed indeed Union commander Thilenius and his men had moved back north. We arrived at Cousin John's place on the banks of the Black River. He had a very large comfortable home, one of the nicest I had ever seen, two story painted white. He once owned nearly 10,000 acres here but in laying out the town he'd sold off portions to incoming settlers. Although the war had taken its toll, his estate remained large and prosperous. He was happy to see Jesse and me. He told the boys to tend to their animals and supper would be at precisely six. We had had a good days ride reaching his place and the rest in a secure location was needed before heading east on the Trail over Crowley's Ridge. Cousin John complained about having not been paid for the provisions and supplies he provided to Genl. Price and his troops. He was seeking reimbursement but feared it was for naught. We discussed the position of the South should news continue to come forth of Union triumphs in the east. In consideration of all, Cousin John felt it prudent both Jesse and me head to Texas but I could not abandon Quantrill.

Cousin John provided me clear directions to the homes of Jesse Cole Lindsay, Gramma Sallie's brother, in Ghent, Carroll Co, Kentucky on the banks of the Ohio River and to Elizabeth Lindsay Calvert and husband Obadiah in Stamping Ground in Scott Co. Stamping Ground was named for the herds of buffalo that were once in the area, before that it was named Herndon after the Herndon family. Uncle Jesse Cole Lindsay married Priscilla Ficklin, her momma was a Anna Herndon. Grand Aunt Ann and husband Abner Landrum along with Grand Uncle Richard "Dick" Lindsay moved to Missouri with Gramma Sallie. Most of Grand Uncle Dick's children still lived in and around Scott and Carroll Counties. I believe Cousin John felt better knowing I had by way of him introductions to our family in Kentucky. I was thankful Momma implanted into my head and heart the importance of family. I was excited thinking of meeting family I'd never met. Cousin John told me Carroll Co was at the confluence of the Ohio and Kentucky Rivers. Most all of Daddy's brothers and sisters had moved to Missouri, other than Aunt Nancy Gardner James and her husband George Burns Hite. They lived in Adairville, Logan Co, Kentucky on the Tennessee border, about as far south as Momma's family was north. With both Cousin John's blessing and mine, Jesse headed south with half the boys. The remaining fifty of us headed east toward the Mississippi. Cousin John held his reserve when it came to Quantrill and in private expressed his concern for not only my safety but the others with us.

Charles "Buster" Sanders
Missouri Valley Special Collections, Kansas City, MO

We were traveling in our Union uniforms. We reached the banks Mississippi about half way above Memphis, Tennessee and Paducah, Kentucky. The waters were high and swift, much too treacherous to cross on horseback and at night. We moved back up the river where we found a yawl hidden in the swamp. It needed only minor repair which we were able to accomplish. We crossed the Mississippi on New Year's Eve with the horses swimming alongside. We made it to the east banks of the

Mississippi fifty of us dressed in Federal uniforms secured from the 4th Missouri Cav: Ves Akers, John Barnhill, Bill Basham, Jack Bishop, James, Tom and John Evans, William Gaw, James Gibson, Joe "Pink" Gibson, Richard Glasscock, Jack Graham, John Tyler Burns, Isaac "Jude" Hall, Tom Harris, Jeremiah David "Dave" Helton, Jim and Benny Poteet, Clarke Hockensmith, William Hulse, James Lilly, Jo Lisbon, James Little, Peyton Long, Billy Magruder, Andy McGuire, Lee McMurtry, Henry & William Nolan, George Nolan, Chris Palmer, Allen Parmer, Bud & Donnie Pence, Capt. Henry Porter, Chat Rennick, George Roberson and his father Bill Roberson. John Ross, Buster Sanders, Albert and Clarence Southworth, JB Toley, Henry Turner, Bud Wigginton, John Jack Williams, James "Jim" Williams, Jim Younger, Quantrill and me.

New Year's Day, 1865, we headed north and east toward Mayfield. Robert Harrison Fristoe heard a group of southerner's was camped nearby. He sent Rachel Thomas, his third wife, to find us to see if there were any Fristoe's in our group. They were living on their farm near Folsomdale, Kentucky between Paducah and Mayfield. Robert was eldest son of Daniel and Margaret Harris Fristoe. He had enlisted shortly after the war began. Serving as a surgeon in the Eighth Kentucky he performed both successful surgeries and recruitment. Captured twice, he lost an arm to amputation after being wounded on the battlefield. "Aunt" Rachel was delighted to find among the group, not just Fristoe's but nephews of her husband.

John McCorkle, Bud Wigginton and Tom Harris all were equally happy to meet their Aunt Rachel and visit their Uncle Robert, brother to John's momma Rebecca, Bud's momma Mary Ann, whom we all called Gramma Wigginton and Tom's mother, Laura. Jim Younger's momma, Bersheba Fristoe, was also a sister of Robert's but he had spent time in their home so this wasn't the first time he'd met them. Uncle Robert had lost an arm on the battlefield but it hadn't stopped him. But after losing his right leg about six months earlier, he'd returned home. It was a joyous reunion providing much needed rest and comfort.

Little did we realize what was happening back in Missouri. A Special Order was issued specifically banishing several families including my Momma and Doc, Jim Cummins momma "Ellie" Crossett Cummins, Lurena McCoy, Wesley Martin and Capt. Kemp Minor Woods whose son 19 year old son Skinner had been killed by the Union in Nov. Fellow Kentuckians John Ecton, Missus Mary Ann Duncan Ford, wife of James H Ford, and Mrs. Sarah Rupe mother of Docky Rupe, who had been killed at Flat Rock Ford, only 17 years old. He had ridden with Bloody Bill but served under Col. Thornton since he was about 14. Mrs. George Washington Taylor (Ana Elliott) and Mrs. Sears whose house was six miles from Pleasant Hill. It had been at Missus Sears farm Union Maj James

Gower's men attacked and killed several men who were headed home. They had been captured and paroled. Gower's men left their signed oaths of allegiance on their dead bodies.

Across Missouri, north of Kansas in the edge of Nebraska was the Nemaha Half Breed Reservation, descendants of people of Omaha Indian ancestry. Antoine Barada, born in 1807 across the Missouri River from St. Louis, Missouri, was kidnapped as a boy of 6 by the Lakota. This was in 1813, during the War of 1812. It took his daddy Michel Barada six months to negotiate a trade. He paid a ransom of two horses to get him back. He then sent him to St. Louis to live with an aunt. Three years later, he returned to the Plains. He married a French woman and settled in Nebraska. Because he was a half breed himself, he was eligible for land from the U.S. Government. He helped establish the Nemaha Reservation and set up a fur trading post. He was a large man, huge, Momma said, very strong and an excellent marksman. He could shoot quail, pheasants, and prairie chickens on the fly, from horseback. Now Momma said it was a tale, but it was told while working on the rail road he got mad, grabbed a drop hammer then threw it across the Missouri River. Where the hammer fell the earth buckled creating Nebraska's Missouri River break. This is the stuff of Unc Wild Man's life and tales. Having been held captive as a child, Antoine helped a number of black folks moving north from Kansas into Nebraska, by carrying them himself across the Missouri River. That's not to say he was an abolitionist. He was a humane person, not given to violence. The area he and his wife lived was his town, Barada, Nebraska. Only a few years before the War Between the States broke out, on land that was mapped out during the 1830 "Prairie du Chien treaty", Old Charley Rouleau and his wife Amerial Menard, a Yankton Sioux Indian settled about 20 miles north of Antoine Barada. Their town, Rouleau, Nebraska, about 100 miles from Liberty was where Momma and Doc would go.

The order was given by Genl. Greenville Dodge. Momma and Doc moved up river to Rouleau, Nebraska where Momma's brother Uncle J.R. and Aunt Lou Cole live. By the time we heard the news Momma was teaching school on the Nemaha Reservation for Mister Barada to bring in a little extra money. Doc was again practicing medicine as best he could but clients were limited and money even more scarce. Bartering goods, animals, and services is the norm for most folks. Just enough farther north they faced a bitter cold that jarred Momma to the bone. I wondered if Momma remembered Antoine Barada aided in the Underground Railroad or if she cared by now.

On Jan 1st in Northeast Missouri, Henry Vanslyke was captured and sent to Gratiot Street. He was transferred to Point Lookout, Maryland in Feb for exchange. Jim Nesbitt of Co C of Col. Tom's regiment was captured some time later in Shannon Co. They sent him to Gratiot Street and from there to Alton Military Prison in Illinois in March. Circumstances were so horrible within the prison he signed the oath of allegiance and joined the 5th U.S. Volunteer Infantry on April 14th rather than starve to death or die of disease.

We used Richard White's house near home in Jackson Co numerous occasions. In early 1865 Federal soldiers surrounded the house firing on Samuel Constable, Ed Hink, Frank Gregg, Thomas and Ambrose Maxwell. Sam Constable was wounded and Frank Gregg saved him. Bud and Thomas Maxwell escaped. Ed Hink was killed instantly in the fight. While Frank Gregg tended to Sam Constable, Ed Hink's lifeless body lay nearby. The Feds chased after the Maxwell brothers removing them from the area around the house, saving Frank and Sam both.

In Kentucky we learned at a local farm the state of Kentucky had an order to take no prisoners with full authority to shoot and kill, executing as it was all guerillas. A Union officer by the name of Bunbridge was, taking 4 random captured guerillas, daily executing them for each Union man he heard was captured. No blindfold, no warning, just walking them out in the open and firing until dead. It was said he left their bodies laying for all to see. Such was the Kentucky we entered. From Paducah we rode toward Mayfield. After spending a few days with the Fristoe's we moved on east. On Jan 10th we rode into Harrodsburg, Mercer Co. There we were attacked by Col. Bridgewater. Henry and William Nolan were killed. John Jack White was captured but on the way to Louisville he managed to escape.

We heard Capt. Marion the leader of the guerillas in Kentucky was camped near Worthville, Carroll Co. Some of the boys wanted to join up with him since we weren't familiar with the territory, but upon meeting him, most didn't trust him. He didn't trust our boys any more than we trusted him. In fact, he so distrusted us he posted pickets to guard us at night. Quantrill decided we should leave him behind and no one disagreed. We watched from the banks of the river as Marion and his men crossed the Kentucky River riding straight into an ambush by Federal troops.

Near Hopkinsville, Christian Co dressed in our Union blues we approached a house where Federal soldiers were. They had changed their signs and failing to give them the most current of the counter signs they fired on us. Chat Rennick volunteered to set fire to the house. Hulse, Chat, Peyton, Andy McGuire and me provided cover while he set fire to the house, then three Feds voluntarily surrendered and were paroled. James Little was hit in his right thigh, breaking it. He managed to get back to Missouri but died from septic poisoning from the injury. Andy McGuire was captured by Col. Bridgewater near Nicholsonville in Jessamine Co. He was sent to Louisville to prison but managed to escape, surrendering at Samuel's Depot on July 26th.

We arrived on Sunday, Jan 22nd at Hartford in Ohio Co. Quantrill was posing as Capt. Jasper Benedict of Smith's Corps. Union Capt. Barnette with thirty soldiers was combing the area looking for Quantrill's men. Dressed in our Union blues, Richard Glasscock had the idea that we fall into line with them, killing them from the rear. One at a time the Union was killed. As a man was killed, our boys would move the dead and their horse from the line with one falling into step in the dead man's place. Glasscock moved up riding next to Capt. Barnette with Quantrill falling in behind him. Barnette asked Quantrill and Glasscock where his men were as he could see Capt. Benedicts men but not his own. Richard Glasscock replied they were all out scouting. Quantrill moved out of line and I rode up behind Barnette killing him. Richard Glasscock went crazy screaming and shouting he had come up with the idea and should have been the one to shoot him. We had littered the route with Barnette's men but Dick was crazy over the issue. Another Co of similar size to ours met us about halfway between E Town and Hopkinsville. We engaged in a short skirmish killing 25 of their men, the rest fled.

On the 28th, about eight miles outside of Fort Harrodsburg on the road to Perryville, we set up camp. He ordered a group of the boys to head out foraging. We had passed an old house within a few miles of the fort and several of the boys returned to see what they might find. Col. Bridgewater attacked them, killing Foster Key, John Barker and the Nolan brothers, capturing several others including Richard Glasscock and Andy McGuire. When Dick was ordered to surrender his pistols he refused. One of the soldiers tried to take them from him getting pistol whipped in the process. Col. Bridgewater was so impressed with Dick's bravery or astounded by his stupidity, he told Dick either he would take them off or he would remove them for him after they paroled him. Dick understood and removed his gun belt. They were taken to Louisville to prison. Several of them managed to escape but only Dick made his way back to join up with us. He told us they had buried Foster Key, John Barker and the Nolan's at the Oakland Church Cemetery. Bridgewater located our camp after we had vacated, but was again soon on our trail. After having suffered at the hands of Col. Bridgewater at Harrodsburg, John Barnhill, Bill Basham and Jack Graham helped to lure him into a trap. Isaac and Robert Hall, Tom Harris, Jeremiah David Helton, Clarke Hockensmith, William Hulse, Payne Jones, James Lilly, Peyton Long, Allen Parmer, Bud Pence, Capt Henry Porter, Bud Wigginton and Jim Younger hid their horses off the side of the road waiting on the three to lead Bridgewater into the ambush. We killed several of his men, sufficient enough he backed off but continued following.

Between Jan 28th and Feb 1st, 1865 we moved between Georgetown in Scott Co and Chaplaintown in Nelson Co. On the Lebanon Bloomfield Road we fought with Kentuckian guerilla Capt. Edward Terrill. He retreated and returned to Chaplaintown. Quantrill decided we had to join with a Kentucky group in order to maneuver better. No one liked Capt. Marion nor trusted him but no one argued with Quantrill. On Feb 2nd we skirmished with some Union near Lawrenceburg. Thomas Henry, one of Marion's men riding with us was seriously wounded. He fought like a Jackson Co man, shot in the face twice, he kept fighting killing the Federalist closest to him before falling off his horse. We thought he was dead but he wasn't. He survived after managing to crawl to a nearby house who attended to him.

We were with Marion's boys at a known Union man's farm where his boys and ours were talking much too freely with the farmer who believed we were Union. His daughter slipped away to nearby Georgetown warning the soldiers there of our presence. Momma had always said, its' better to say to little than to much. Listening and watching, I realized the girl was gone and asked the farmer where his daughter might have gone. Alerting the boys one of them shot the farmer. Mounting to flee we saw a squad of Union advancing on us. Four of our men were wounded in the retreat. Peyton Long carried the flag.

At Midway in Woodford Co, we burned the railroad depot and stole fifteen blooded horses. On Wed, Feb 8th, at New Market in Marion Co, south of Lebanon, we captured a wagon. We traveled two days good ride all day on the 8th. On the 9th at Hustonville in Lincoln Co, Allen Parmer took a horse from a Federal garrison and killed a Maj there causing a skirmish to ensure. George Roberson surrendered to Col. J.K. Bridgewater who charged him with the killing. He was taken to prison at Louisville, escaped and was recaptured and taken to Lexington, from there he went back to Louisville where he was hung for the killing in April 1865. Thomas Evans was captured and suspected of the killing. He was held prisoner at Lexington chained flat of his back. The following day Thursday, Bridgewater hit our camp on Little South Fork west of town, four guerillas were killed. Joe Lisbon was captured. He had brown hair and eyes. He wore a mustache and beard and had one of the finest red and white stripe shirts of all the men. Some of the boys had even joked about killing him for his shirt. His captors killed him in April. I hated the idea someone probably stole his shirt. Jim Younger was wounded severely in the right shoulder and right breast; his horse shot and killed. William Merriman was shot trying to save him. Jim and Bill, along with James Evans were taken prisoners of war to Louisville. Rennick was captured and taken to Lexington where he was killed. Ves Akers wounded and captured, was taken to Louisville to prison where William Gaw, Dick Burns and he escaped. James and Tom joined Bloody Bill and Quantrill after the EMM killed their 80 year old father Pleasant Evans. The 15 horses we stole belonged to Col. Alexander. After escaping an attack near Lawrenceburg, Marion returned to Quantrill. He persuaded Marion to return Alexander's horses. We had always loved horse racing and understood what these blooded horses meant to this man. Quantrill decided he and I alone would return the horses. Col. Alexander was so thankful he gave Quantrill and me each a horse. Peyton Long was upset over the whole thing he left us and joined up with Jerome Clarke.

By the end of Feb things were falling apart in Kentucky. Quantrill was talking of assassinating President Lincoln and of going to Lexington to surrender. Some of the boys wanted to go home. Quantrill relented and we started back home headed toward Paducah. On Tuesday Feb. 28th, with some of Ike Berry's men we robbed several towns in Hickman, Kentucky for needed supplies for the trip. Quantrill announced then he was headed to Richmond. He asked us to join him but anyone that wanted to go home could. About half of the boys headed back into Missouri, I turned around and headed east with Quantrill. At Brewleyville, located about half way between Owenton and Louisville, we got into a skirmish. Peyton Long was shot in the gut and killed March 1, 1865 at Brewleyville, Meade Co. I wired his parents, Kentucky ex pats, Garrad and LizBeth Peyton Long in Liberty. They got family in Kentucky to attend to Peyton's body. He was embalmed and shipped home, buried back at home in Fairview Cemetery. We pressed on west and north.

On the 12th, Billy Magruder, Jerry Metcalfe and Jerome Clarke were captured in a barn near Webster on the Meade-Breckinridge Co line. The Breckinridge Co courthouse at Hardinville had been burned by local guerilla's while under occupation by Union troops. Locals were able to save most of the records. They refused to surrender unless they would be treated as soldiers, according to the rules of war. The Union agreed but when the boys were interrogated they were stripped naked and beaten. Clark allowed no defense and was hung three days later on March 15th. People watching were sickened, vomiting on site as he was slowly strangled, hoisted down rather than being dropped through trap door. The Union wouldn't listen to his statements insisting he was not Sue Munday. George Prentice with the Louisville Journal wrote about Sue Munday making him a hero of sorts to the Southerners of Kentucky. He was reported to have been a Lincoln man with the Federal military who had fallen out with them to form his own band thwarting the Unionists at every turn. After the torturous hanging the newspaper man admitted he wasn't a real person. Clarke asked to see a minister and parishioner Reverend Talbot was brought to him. He heard his confessions and baptized him before he was hung. He tried to tell the Unionists they didn't have Sue Munday that this man before them was a regular soldier who had gotten separated from his Co. Reverend Talbot insisted Clarke had fought at Fort Donaldson under Genl. Buckner and rode with Morgan. These proved true after his death. Billy Magruder had ridden with Capt. Marion but had joined us along with Clarke near Lebanon at Doctor McClaskey's. Billy had rescued Clarke when he had gotten pinned under his horse in a skirmish at Bradfordville. Billy was hung on Oct 29th, 1865.

Back in Missouri, on March 14th Archie met with the boys along with other bands to discuss surrender. The next day the group went to Lexington to discuss terms with Union Provost Marshall J.B. Rodgers. They were told they would have to lay down their arms, turning over all their guns and ammunitions, something they were not willing to do. Fleeing they were fired on.

On March 17th Shelby had William Bolton "Squirrel Tail" Edwards shot and killed after learning he was a Mountain Boomer and spy. Squirrel Tail had been promoted to Capt. under Shelby. He was robbing the local people telling them he was requisitioning whatever he was taking on orders of Shelby. When the people came to Shelby to complain about why he was taking their horses, cattle, goods, and such Shelby sent Col. Freeman and some of his men to find out what was going on. It was learned he wasn't an Indian at all, but rather a spy and Mountain Boomer robbing people regardless if they were Southern or Northern. This was happening more and more, across the South.

Frank Gregg had stayed in Missouri. He and a few of the boys found themselves surrounded by Union soldiers. Sam Constable's horse was shot out from under him pinning Sam down. Frank managed to get him free saving his life. Frank's hat was knocked off, he walked over, picked it up, dusted it off placing it back on his head. Then got back on his horse and rode off. I imagined Annie's eyes as Frank told his story.

Doc Sanders had been wounded and hospitalized in Little Rock in Dec 1862. He returned to fight and was wounded at Hopewell Church in Lafayette Co in March 1865. He was recuperating at the home of Dick Kinney's wife in Jackson Co when Capt. J.W. Sheets and his Co of troops found and killed him.

Doc Campbell led a group of men from Yellville, Ark including Given Horn, Al Scott, George Maddox and James Stewart; they undressed, put all their ammo, guns and clothing on a raft to stay dry while they swam the river. They were fired on by Federal soldiers. Given Horn was wounded trying to cross the river. Doc Campbell and George Maddox swam after him rescuing him. He told the others to leave him behind but they weren't about to do that.

Chapter 27

We could tell Quantrill was tiring of roaming the Kentucky countryside. Capt. Marion and his men re-joined us in mid March and having them about wasn't conducive to the environment of trust we had among our boys. Quantrill got a letter from Kate and became even more depressed and ever more determined to get to Genl. Lee. Word was circulating the war was over, that on April 9th, Genl. Robert E. Lee surrendered to Ulysses S. Grant at Appomattox Courthouse in Virginia. Then five days later, on April 14, President Lincoln was assassinated at Ford's Theater. Although we continued to operate for several more weeks, into May, we made a collective decision to surrender. Terms were we would surrender our arms, sign the oath of allegiance thus enabling us to return to a peaceful life. Should we not surrender, the penalty was death and bearing arms after the end of the war was subject to be shot on sight. After surrendering we would head home to Missouri. We voted we would then return to the farm of Robert Fristoe who we were certain could help us know the right people who could get us safely home.

We needed to get our horses seen after, shoed and feed, first. We stopped at Eddyville. Robert Hall and Jack Graham were working on Quantrill's horse "Ol' Charley", the horse he'd ridden throughout the war, one of them cut one of Ol' Charley's tendons. This was a side to Quantrill many of us had never seen, crying blubbering and angry at the same time, he put his horse down. The stir it created among the men was evident. Quantrill told everyone they could go home, retreat, charge forward, whatever they wanted, he understood. Stunned, we really didn't know what to do, but many did leave. Quantrill announced anyone remaining with him must understand we were headed to surrender.

We had crossed the Cumberland River at Bloomfield when we were attacked by Capt.'s Penn and Ed Terrill under Union Maj Wilson. They had been granted the authority by the Union to hunt us down and kill us if they couldn't bring us in. Capt. Marion was killed. Jim Younger who had been wounded at Hustonville had gone to his Uncle Robert Fristoe's to mend. He had returned catching up with us just a few days earlier when we got into the skirmish. He was captured and taken to Alton, IL Prison. He was held there until the fall of 1865.

In Missouri Theo Cassell, John Maupin and Jesse captured a Federal soldier named Harness in Benton Co on the 15th of April. He had been responsible for the death of Archie's brother and the burning of their mother's house. Jesse, Theo and John held Harkness while Archie cut his throat and scalped him. The next day, the boys elected Archie Capt. and William Greenwood First Lt. under Dave Poole.

On the 29th, Capt. Jim Jackson stopped a stage coach about 10 miles outside Columbia, Missouri. Less than a month and a half later on June 13th, he and a dozen of his men surrendered to Capt. H.N. Cook at Camp Switzer near Columbia. He was paroled then captured again in Pike Co a few days later. The boys that captured him were vigilantes. They shot and killed him.

During the first week of May, Union Genl. Granville Mellen Dodge informed Col. Chester Harding as to the terms of surrender for any guerrillas wishing to peaceably turn themselves in. David Poole and his first Lt Lon Railey gathered their men. They voted to surrender. I hadn't heard where Jesse was. I hoped he had gone to Nebraska and was with Momma.

On May 21st, Poole returned with eighty five more of the boys who were willing to lay down their guns and take the oath of allegiance to the United States. He talked to Ol Shepherd about surrendering his command. The boys received their parole certificates and were able to return home, he told Ol. When Ol took in his command, two were arrested, one of stealing a horse and the other for murder. The rest were paroled.

In Missouri as in Kentucky and elsewhere, men who had not fought in the regular service of the Union had to sign oaths of allegiance. They were provided certificates of parole. The men and boys who did not do so were subject to be shot on sight. On the 8th at the home of Phillip Varner, Jesse Hamlett was attacked by Capt. Arnold's men of the Johnson Co Volunteer Militia. They captured Varner's son.

Back in Kentucky we left Eddyville headed to Louisville to surrender. A late spring rain deluged us in the southern part of Spencer Co. We stopped on May 10th to get out of the weather at the farm of James H. Wakefield. Quantrill headquartered there with about half the boys while the rest of us took shelter at the farm of Alexander Sayers about two miles further down the road. Some of the boys were out near the barn and a nearby shed tending to the horses when Capt. Ed Terrill surprised us. He entered the east gate of the farm on the Bloomfield to Taylorsville road. Wakefield was talking to Dick Glasscock out near the shed when he and Clarke Hockensmith saw them coming from the east. Exhausted and bone tired, Quantrill had retired to the hay loft and was asleep. When Clarke sounded out the alarm, he was immediately awake, climbing down he rushed to a rearing horse but wasn't able to mount it. He joined some of the other boys running for the south west corner of the lot. Clarke Hockinsmith and Dick Glasscock both had mounted their horses and brought up the rear. Quantrill ran to Clarke and was able to mount the horse behind him. Terrill's men shot, killing both Clarke and his horse. Richard Glasscock seeing what had happened reached to get Quantrill's hand to pull him up behind him when Quantrill was shot in the back. The ball entered his left shoulder blade smashing down his spine completely paralyzing him below his arms. Glasscock jumped from his horse and stood over Quantrill protecting him until he himself was shot dead. Isaac Hall escaped on foot and hid in the pond with David Helton. They made their way to the Sayres farm alerting us of what was happening. Robert Hall escaped on foot. Granville Key was killed. Payne Jones was wounded and tried to escape on foot because his horse had been killed. Lee McMurtry was able to mount his horse and escape. He lived in Fort Worth, Texas after the war, married an Indian and became Sheriff. Allen Parmer and Bud Pence were with us at Sayres. Wakefield made it inside the house unharmed. Terrill's men stripped Quantrill of his clothing and took his boots, covering him with a dirty blanket, rolled him on to it and carried him into Wakefield's house.

He insisted he was Capt. Clarke of the 4th Missouri Cav. He wanted very much to stay at Wakefield's. He bribed Terrill by giving him his gold watch and $500. He promised more money if he would leave him at Wakefield's. They called Dr. McClaskey, one of Marion's men who was riding with us to look after him. Dr. McClaskey knew who Quantrill really was and whispered to him that he had a mortal wound. No one knew with certainty who had shot Quantrill. In order to protect the Wakefield's he told Doc to tell them who he was. If Wakefield had knowingly harbored guerillas he could not only lose his farm but his life. Although he was a known southern sympathizer, it no longer matter which side he might have chosen. Terrill was plundering Wakefield's house. He gave him $20 and Lt. Taylor $10 and a jug of whiskey to get them to stop. Terrill and Taylor were steadily drinking when Doc McClaskey told them that the wounded man was none other than William Clarke Quantrill out of Missouri and he was mortally wounded. Lt. Taylor sent some of his men to secure a wagon in which they could transport Quantrill to Louisville.

A few of the boys escaped making their way to the Sayres farm first finding me, William Hulse and JD Hylton. We alerted the rest of the boys telling them to head over to the Thurman house informing the boys with John Barnhill, Tom Harris, John McCorkle and cousin Bud Wigginton of Quantrill's fate and preparing them to move out. JD, Bill and I rode over to Wakefield's but knew there was nothing we could do, the farm was surrounded and heavily guarded. We returned and joined the rest of the boys at Thurman's. We were able to move south undetected.

Taylor's men located a wagon and returned to the farm on Thursday the 11th. They loaded Quantrill into the wagon on the morning of the 12th hauling him to Louisville to the prison hospital there. Terrill reported to Genl. John M. Palmer headquartered at Louisville of the capture. Billy Magruder had been shot in the lung and was at the hospital there recovering when Quantrill arrived and was there when Kate King Clarke arrived. Billy told that a Catholic priest moved Quantrill to a Catholic hospital and baptized him as a Roman Catholic shortly before he died. Quantrill gave Reverend Powers $800 in gold for his burial and left $2,000 to the Catholic priest who attended him. Kate was given the rest. He died June 6 following an operation, he was 27 years old. He was buried at St John's Catholic Church, Portand Cemetery in Louisville. The remaining of us boys escaped. Half of us surrendered in Smiley at Samuel's Depot on July 26th paroled by Capt. Henry Porter. The others went to nearby Bardstown surrendering there to Capt. Young.

Back home in Missouri, Jesse and Arch Clements were going crazy themselves. Early in May, they attacked Holden in Johnson Co, robbing two stores and killing a man. The next day they ransacked Archie's home town of Kingsville killing 8 men. I wasn't there, but Jesse said told Momma he talked to Archie about surrendering but he would have nothing to do with it. He had tried earlier and been shot at. He wasn't trying again. Jesse discussed with some of the boys about going to Lexington to surrender to Provost Marshall J.D. Rodgers. This was the same man Archie had been unwilling to lay down his arms for. Willis King, John Van Meter, Jesse Hamlet, Jack Rupe, and Jesse decided they would avoid Archie's mistake by arriving in town under a white flag. On the 15th of May they made their way toward Lexington having stopped a few miles out affixing their flat to the end of a pole. Riding next to Jesse, Jack Rupe hoisted the flag as they rode in.

Just before reaching town they met a Union regiment under John Jones of the 3rd Wisconsin who began firing on them. Jesse was shot again in the right lung. John Van Meter's horse was shot out from under him. Jack Rupe pulled him up behind him. Turning to flee they saw a Co of around 50 men armed headed their way. Jesse was hanging on to his horse as they fled. Not far down the road he fell from his horse, the horse shied and continued running. Our cousin Dick realized what had happened went back for him, managing to get him onto his horse. They were able to secure another horse from A.P. Lankford. Fearing he would pass out Dick strapped him to the horse's neck and saddle to prevent him from falling. He was unable to draw a deep breath. He knew if he survived his fighting days were over. Our cousin Dick West realized the seriousness of the situation. When Jesse lost consciousness Dick tied his horse to his and continued riding through the night almost 40 miles to Kansas City to get him home to Aunt Lizzie and Uncle Till, Dick's momma and daddy. His little sister Nancy Woodson West had died a month earlier at 15 years old. There was no way Aunt Lizzie was in any shape to care for Jesse very long. And, she and Uncle Till were fearful for his safety as the Union were in control of the city. They ran a business there and had thus far managed to assuage both sides. They convinced Daddy's oldest sister, Aunt Mary and Uncle John Mims who lived across the river to take him in. He was having great difficulty breathing and required almost constant care and watching after. Uncle John had not been too keen on the idea but Aunt Mary, as always was not gonna have her brother's son die because she failed to help him. They hid him in the attic of the house. He was continually watched after by Dick and their daughter, our first cousin Zee, who stayed by Jesse's side.

On June 14, 1865, Joseph Gray, husband of Lou Monday, died. Col. Tom and his command surrendered on June 6, 1865. On June 23, Stand Watie surrendered. A number of Col. Tom's command had contracted measles near the end of the war. Fearing they would infect their families the men chose to hide out in remote areas and caves, a few of the luckier ones stayed in barns. Col. Tom and his men remained in Ark, with camps at Mammoth Springs and Smithville. The vigilantes were worse immediately after the war had been declared over killing both Union and Southern men as they returned home. Another reason for Col. Tom's men to hide out in the weeks before surrendering. Col. Tom ordered his command to band together in groups of men who were neighbors before returning home for increased defense against the vigilantes. The men who were sick with measles, mumps and chicken pox were cared for on the Grimmett farm in northern Izard Co. There were a number of caves and shelters where the women and neighbors could get food to them allowing them time to recover and heal. My friend Bill Lawrence was among the sick, although I'm not certain he had measles, he may have been suffering from exhaustion, malnutrition and summer pneumonia. Unable to make it home he had been among those hiding out while word was taken to his family of his precise whereabouts. His oldest son, seventeen year old James Daniel went to find him. Bill had grown so weak and ill James had to tie his father to his horse to make certain he didn't fall off. I thought of having lashed Jesse to his horse to get him home, traveling for almost two days, and Dick. I shuddered thinking of Bill's young boy being jerked into manhood by the war, faced with getting his daddy home before he died. His son got him safely home and Bill slowly regained his strength. He would live to fish and hunt with me another day.

Capt. Dave Poole successfully which meant safely surrendered over 100 of the boys. Theo Cassell did not want to surrender, not yet. He was thinking on going to Mexico with Genl. Shelby who was refusing to accept the war was over. Before he could round up a few of the boys to go with him on the 24th the White Band Militia killed him, Tom Maupin, John Chatman and Capt. Kelly near Rocheport. One of the militia cut off his finger taking the ring he was wearing. They killed Tom but his brother John severely wounded managed to escape.

Four days later Ol Shepherd, part of Shelby's Brigade surrendered bringing in Milt Dryden, Ling Latton, Frank and Alfred Corum and Ninian Litton "Ning Ling". Jim Anderson was with them but when he was told he would have to surrender unconditionally, laying down his arms, he convinced Clell Shepherd, Henry Akers, Archie Clements, James Hendrix, Ike Berry and William Fell to go to Texas with him to join Shelby. July 7th, Dr. J.M. Angel who had served under George Todd was killed by the Missouri State Militia 3rd Cav.

Facing a three hundred dollar bounty on bushwhackers made it an easy choice for many of the boys to return to Texas. Bill Wilson remained down in Texas hoping for things to settle down back at home. When he heard Dave Poole, Archie, Jim Anderson and over 100 other Partisans, independents and guerillas from Ark and Missouri had arrived at Sherman he joined them. Bill refused to take the oath and eventually chose to abandon his family in Missouri to survive in Texas.

Of those of us who escaped after Wakefield's, we stayed around Kentucky until we learned Quantrill had died. Then many of the boys started making their way home. A group of us remained at the Fristoe's working on their farm and on neighboring farms while Uncle Robert brokered a deal for our surrender. We surrendered on July 26th in two groups, Samuel's Depot at Smiley and the other at Bardstown.

Brigadier Genl. "Col. Jo" Joseph Shelby wanted no part of surrendering. He refused to accept that Genl. Robert E. Lee accepted defeat surrendering at Appomattox. He stated as much to us boys during the last days of Genl. Price's Raid into Missouri, he would not be accepting defeat. He would take whoever would go with him to Texas and on to Mexico. And, that's what he did. There they joined with Emperor Maximilian. Born in Austria, Maximilian was the younger brother of Franz Joseph the Emperor of Austria. These brothers entered into a plan with Napoleon to conquer and rule Mexico, invading in 1861 as we began the War Between the States. Maximillian was to set up a French lead Mexican monarchy and on the 10th of April, 1864 had declared himself Emperor of Mexico. Benito Juarez led the Mexican Republic in defense of the French invasion. Now, the self proclaimed Emperor of Mexico, Maximillian was eager to have Shelby's men join him. Col. Shelby took arms and ammunition with him into Mexico. On July 17th, 1865 at Piedras Negras he negotiated the sale of the largest cannon and ammunition for twenty thousand in gold and some script. Traveling through Texas, he solicited and engaged most of the boys who had gone to Texas to go with him to Mexico. Those choosing not to either remained in Texas making it home, or returned home to Missouri.

Among the boys with Genl. Shelby were Ike Berry, sixteen year old DeKalb Shore, George Cruzen and Joe Macy. One of the Mexican officers had been looking over Ike's fine horse during the sale of ammunition and laid claim to it. Ike laughed at him, enraged the officer forced Ike to swing at him with his sword. He cut the tip of the officer's ear off which erupted into a fight. A number of the Mexican's were killed and the boys took back the artillery they had sold them that morning. Ike had gone with us to Kentucky but when Quantrill offered anyone wanting to go home to leave, Ike and several others headed out. At Paducah they went down the Mississippi River headed south to Mexico. DeKalb Shore was a boy, really, he looked like a baby. No hair on his face and with pretty hair on his head. He was a spunky one though; you didn't want to challenge him. He stayed with Shelby surrendering in July 1865 in Shreveport. George Cruzen he had a baby face himself but a full head of thick black curly hair. Try as he may he mustered up only a little bit of thing on that upper lip, he called it a mustache, we called it peach fuzz.

On the 28th of July on the Salinas River in Mexico, about one hundred and fifty miles south of Eagle Pass, Texas which borders Piedras Negras, Coahuila, Mexico the boys were attacked by Indians and half breed banditos, part Mexican and part Indian, called Comancheros, under Juarez.At Encarnacion de Diaz, near Mexico City, Mexico in Aug, the boys and Col. Shelby nearly had their own internal insurrection when the boys helped 'release' an American woman, Inez Walker. She had been taken by Guaymas Rodriquez who intended to make her his wife. Rodriquez had killed her father. Finally Col. Jo listened to reason and calmed down after hearing Miss Walker tell her story.

Back in Ark in the White River Valley, the Jeffery family of Izard Co lost four boys: Jehoiada Quincy "Suska" and his brother Isaac, and brothers Beniah and Jesse. These boys gave their lives, at home where Isaac was murdered and in service on the battle field. Others both north and south, suffered in the military prison camps. At the Union camp in Rock Island, Illinois, they died of pneumonia, dysentery and other illnesses in the freezing weather. Those that did survive the war, whether free or prisoners of war, then had to face the ordeal of getting home. We began to hear the stories of families who believed their loved one, their husband to be dead having taken another, even bore their children, only to have their loved one return. Or as in the case of Joseph Ward who walked over a 100 miles home from Little Rock to Stone Co in the freezing rain, only to arrive to swollen creeks. Unable to cross, he sat down with his home in sight, leaned against a tree, his gun at his side and died.

Ambrose Jeffery, son of Miles Jeffery and Sarah Williams survived the war. He enlisted as an infantryman, in the Confederacy's First Ark

Mounted Rifles, his horse a sign of his family's wealth. His parents provided him the best of the horses with the hope it would better serve to bring him back home safe. Ambrose served with me at Pea Ridge and Wilson's Creek before the First Ark was dismounted and reorganized as Infantrymen headed into the Western Theatre.

An early disadvantage for the South was seen in its inability to adequately feed both their men and horses leading to 'dismounting' many a unit. The better horses were 'conscripted' into the cavalry with the majority eaten by the soldiers. When the war ended, Ambrose, like most of us had seen horrific battles, men and boys who were his family, friends and neighbors, lose limbs and lives, buried in mass graves, some left to the elements after being scalped by the Union. When the war was over he had to manage to get home. Unlike many who had to walk the entire distance of over 1,000 miles from the East, as far away as Raleigh, Norfork and Charleston, we know from his letters, Ambrose was one of the lucky. He caught a freight car from Loudon, Tennessee to Chattanooga. Then he was able to travel by steamboat from Nashville all the way to Jacksonport. From there, he was left with only 70 miles to walk in order to reach Mount Olive. While Joe Ward died within site of his home, Ambrose arrived safely home. With news of his arrival spreading fast, he was swarmed by upwards of 50 friends and family at his first stop, an aunt's house. News traveled fast and Aunt Lucy, a matriarch in the community, was one of the first to know. Ambrose was the son of Sarah Williams and Miles Jeffery, Mrs Avarilla's own cousin.

President Lincoln ordered the railroads to facilitate returning soldiers home, from both sides, however, with his being assassinated on April 15, 1865 just days after the war was officially over, former Vice President Andrew Johnson, now President had a different plan for reconstruction which included a much less friendly treatment of the rebelling Confederates. Former CSA Soldiers enroute home by rail were put off the trains, required to disembark leading to thousands doing whatever they had to in order to get home. This was for many the beginning of the after the war animosities between the North and South that I believe won't diminish until all of who have served and our children and grandchildren have gone to meet the Lord. We have experienced too much.

The long walk home was a new kind of suffering. Having suffered the loss of the war our boys were now subject to the indignities that accompany that. The boys returned telling stories of encountering good and bad people along the way, dodging folks who didn't want to let go of the war, people who were still fighting small skirmishes even if they did know the war was officially over. They engaged anyone whom they thought might be an enemy, bushwhackers and jayhawkers became synonymous with thievery, and atrocities.

While the numbers vary from three to ten miles a day that an average man can walk, there's no doubt, walking a 1000 miles, crossing rivers and streams, sleeping under the stars, hiding away in a corn crib or barn, seeking shelter with or without permission was all part of the long walk home. If a man could average ten miles a day, it would take over 3 months of foot travel. Perhaps there was luck in finding the benefactor who provided a warm night in a home, barn or shelter of some kind, a bit of food for trade of labor, but it's more likely most of the boys foraged for food along the way. Hunting and gathering in the wilds, gardens and hen houses to keep from starving. The majority of Confederate soldiers conscripted into the army had no shoes or guns. Many of those died of illnesses related to exposure and starvation and those that survived those conditions, fought, and then, if they survived, had to again survive the long walk home. Ambrose was one of the lucky ones.

The atmosphere at home in Missouri remained difficult, in June voters had approved the new Missouri Constitution. It granted Civil Rights to the state's freed slaves and required potential voters take an oath stating that they had not committed any one of 86 disloyal acts against the United States. The result was disenfranchisement of three quarters of Clay Co's white males. Across the board Confederate sympathizers were being removed from political and judicial offices across not only Missouri but the whole of the south being replaced by Unionists.

After surrendering on July 26th to Capt. Young, most of our boys had decided to go home to Missouri. I stayed awhile in Kentucky with family visiting places Momma and Daddy had lived, people they knew and where they had gone to school. No where there or at home was really safe and for some, the War Between the States especially in western Missouri and North Ark will not be forgotten until the grandchildren of the last surviving person having experienced it has died. I knew as I walked the streets of Brandenburg, Kentucky sentiments were being worn on the sleeves of many. I'd had the opportunity to return my state of affairs to some semblance of normalcy while at Uncle Robert Fristoe's. I was enjoying the streets of the historic city perched on the banks of the Ohio River. Having left the river side, heading south, I was near the Brandenburg Bank on Main Street when I encountered four Union soldiers coming towards me along the walk way. There was nothing alarming about me, perhaps they simply wanted to exert their authority over a civilian. I don't know, but when they neared me, it was clear I was to step off the walk way into the muddy street allowing them to pass or the devil would be to pay. I was about to step off when one of the soldiers mouthed off as another one's hand reached down toward his pistol. Instincts, fear, I drew and fired, killing two of them and wounding another. The fourth soldier drew his pistol firing off a few rounds, hitting me in my hip. I fell to the ground but was still in possession of my pistol, the fourth man fled. People came out onto the streets from the businesses. Some men recognizing I must be southern got me to the doctor's office where I was treated. However, soon word was out I was not only a southerner but a guerilla. Southern belle, Isabelle Samuel's came to my rescue. I thought of the kindness and care the women of Batesville had provided us in the winter of 1863. I remained in the home of Wilson and Martha Stoner Samuel's, Belle's parents until Uncle Robert Fristoe came to retrieve me. Of all my wounds, it was this after war injury that would give me the most trouble the rest of my life.

Failing to successfully surrender at Lexington, Jesse had been shot, now a third time in the right side, a second time in his lung. Uncle Till and Aunt Lizzie had gotten him safely across the river to Uncle John and Aunt Mary's but they were becoming increasingly alarmed at the growing relationship between him and their daughter Zee. Susie had stayed behind with Uncle Till and Aunt Lizzie when Momma and Doc had been forced to move. Jesse was insisting he wanted to be with Momma, so Susie and cousin Dick accompanied Jesse by steamer upriver to Rouleau, Nebraska. The July and Aug heat in Nebraska is enough to kill man and beast, but for eight weeks Momma and Doc cared for Jesse. I'm convinced it was Jesse simply pinning for Zee but he insisted he was afraid he was going to die away from home. Momma gave him and in the heat of Aug, they traveled back down river to Kansas City. Jesse was ill, very ill and could have been easily cared for by Uncle Marc Thomason and Doc but he won out again, staying with Aunt Mary and Uncle John where Zee continued to care for him. Momma was dead set against Zee and Jesse's relationship. Gramma Sallie, her momma, had married her own cousin James Cole, momma's daddy. They were the children of siblings, both grand children of Richard Cole and Ann Hubbard. Our families were very closely related and intermarried with the Coles, James, Mims and Poor's. Doc had explained to Momma the growing medical information against marrying so close in a person's family. Momma figured Zee, her namesake, had won out in arguments with Aunt Mary about caring for Jesse in their home. Aunt Mary and Uncle John had taken Daddy and a half dozen of her younger siblings into their home when their parents died. She had always been the head of the family and whatever she said goes. Of course, Momma was furious the family had returned home only to have him play her she said so he could just come home to be with Zee. No one failed to understand Momma's words to Zee, "With my son comes a responsibility." Jesse stayed with them another six weeks before Momma, Uncle Till and Aunt Lizzie went and got him insisting he had recovered enough from his wounds to come home to the farm. I missed all of this but got home shortly after Jesse had been brought home. It didn't take Momma and Susie long to fill me in. Then making my way to Uncle Till's store, I got the rest of the story, Momma's growing concern over Zee and Jesse, much more serious than the wound to his lung was his heart.

Jesse told me Dick Kimberlin was organizing veterans' in the Texas panhandle. He and his brothers had ridden with us with Quantrill. They had joined after their daddy had been tortured then burned to death in the family barn. Dick had been among the boys to leave in Texas joining Genl. Price. He fought in the eastern theatre under Stonewall Jackson.

We heard in Nov Col. John Holt who had been ordered with 140 troops by Genl. Price to accompany us to Lawrence, Kansas had his property and personal belonging confiscated by the U.S. District Court, Western Division, Case Number 45, for siding with the enemy or otherwise aiding the rebellion. Like Cole Younger's daddy and so many other men who rode as irregulars and Partisan Rangers, Col. Holt had begun the War Between the States as a Union man. That is until Jennison and his Kansas Jayhawkers stole his merchandise and burned his property. Genl. Price and Col. Shelby always said, Jennison did more to recruit for the south than any other northerner and a lot of southerners. Now Col. Holt was having his belongings and wealth stolen a second time by the Union.

The war is over, so they say. Southerner's are not allowed to purchase dry goods or staples on credit at the now owned Union stores. Without being able to do that, crops can't get planted and life as we once knew it can't return. It was during the winter of 1865, maybe Jan 1866 we discussed with Momma there had to be a way to get by. Momma now a Union hater of the worst kind was all for anything that would get us by. She had one rule, "No taking from our people," and by that she meant any Southerner who could have possibly suffered one way or another as a result of simply being a Southerner. Momma figured we had a license to take from Union neighbors who had not only survived the war, but prospered.

John Newman Edwards, Col. Shelby's Adjunct during the war had chronicled the events of the war knew many of us. A frequent visitor at the farm, he had returned from Mexico for a few weeks recruiting men to join the Colony of Carlota with Shelby; establishing a new South. We had all survived the war, for better or worse and Momma wanted a photograph of her family. John Newman Edwards and Doc's sister Addie were photographed with us and of course, Jesse's new love our cousin, Zee.

John Newman Edwards, Frank, Jesse, Zee Mims
Sarah Louisa Samuel, Reuben Samuel, Zerelda, Addie Samuel
Fannie Quantrill Samuel, John Thomas Samuel and Susan Lavenia James

The weather was bad and no one wanted to risk Jesse's health. We discussed ideas and with each one who could we trust to be part of it. We'd been betrayed by so many of the boys we'd grown up with. Alvis Dagley and Brantley Bond came to mind. Jesse was adamant about being part of whatever we decided. Momma was pregnant due in the summer and Jesse was still facing infection if he exerted too much. People say lightning never strikes the same place twice, but I'm here to tell you, for all of Jesse's whimpering and whining, always thinking he was dying, having been shot three times on the left side of his body, twice in the lung, had shut him up. He knew he could die if he didn't listen to Momma and the doctors.

The rivers and streams were frozen. When it came time to break the ice so the animals could get water, Jesse was wanted to help but couldn't. As much as he loved being outside any time of the year, I figured he wasn't complaining because he didn't want Momma to know how bad he was. Doc insisted it was just this kind of weather that none of us needed to be out in, especially Jesse. We knew we risked pneumonia so like it or not, we all stayed in except for breaking ice, feeding the animals and bringing in wood. We didn't even venture out hunting. Different ones of the boys would wander by the farm, staying the day sometimes a day or two. I had become especially close to Frank Gregg, the younger brother of Lt. Col. Bill Gregg. He too had a lot of time on his hands and would come by the farm. They lived over near Stoney Valley. His sister Mary Frances married to Samuel Ralston lived between our place and their folks. We'd go over to visit when weather permitted. Jesse was best of friends with John Thrailkill. Older than I am, John was a friend and mentor, replacing Daddy for Jesse. I knew John's plan to move to Mexico was not setting well with him and John Newman Edwards was stepping into John's shoes. Momma sent word to all our family to gather for a celebration of Jan birthdays. Doc, born Jan 12th, 1828. His half brother Fielding, same daddy's different Momma's, was born Jan 28th, 1845. Momma was born Jan. 29th, 1825. Momma's step sister, Aunt Emmy Thomason Garrett was born Jan 12, 1822, Gramps Bob's oldest child. Most of the Thomason's would be coming as would the Samuel clan. The Hudspeth's were invited, Babe was a Jan baby, born a year before me in 1842 on the 12th. His baby brother Joseph Lamartine was seven. We called him Lam, like the baby lamb. His birthday wasn't until May but he'd be coming. He and Sallie and John Thomas were buddies. And of course Zee's Momma, daddy's sister Aunt Mary and Uncle John Mims would be here. Uncle Will James and Aunt Mary weren't coming. Aunt Mary was down sick. Uncle John and Aunt Polly would be here, of course Uncle John would be seeing into everyone's mouth's checking over our teeth. Those refusing got an appointment they best keep. I hoped his son, my cousin Wood would come. We were close in age and always had a good time. Aunt Lizzie and Uncle Till West wouldn't miss it and Uncle Mart and Aunt Susie. We had a gathering almost every month at some one of the family's houses. Most of us lived close to each other, not more than a short ride or a good walk, a few lived closer to the city, like Zee's folks. Momma had said we could invite friends, so I ask Frank Gregg to come bringing another Jan birthday girl, Annie Ralston. She would be 12, Jan 25th. And, born Jan. 10th, 1843, I was about to turn 22.

Any time the men gather, talk turns to politics and making a living. With the women, it was birthing babies, planning weddings and putting out gardens. Life after the war was anything but normal. To be able to vote, people were forced to sign oaths agreeing they had never committed any one of a 100 acts. More than half the people of Missouri were supporters of the Confederacy. Some signed, whether it was the truth or not, others didn't which led to the pro Union and Northerners being elected, obtaining appointments to banking institutions and as postmasters. People who had remained loyal to the South were afraid to put their money in the banks, afraid it would be lost or stolen. Some remembered the crash of 1834 and were simply leery of banks. Most folks we knew put their money in their bedding, buried it in the ground and hid it in caves, crevices and trees. Hiding it was believed safer than a bank, especially a Union run bank.

Jesse's imagination was burning like a wild fire. He had tasted the exciting life, risky and daring, served up riding during the war. He and John Newman Edwards spent a great amount of time telling each other stories of the war. And, each one of them, grander, more daring and exciting than the last. I doubted if John even knew how to shoot a gun, he didn't hold a pistol or a rifle like he knew much. But he was deadly accurate with words when he chose to be, written and spoken. .

Jesse kept insisting he was going along with whatever we decided but Momma put her foot down, as did Zee who had come to stay awhile with us. The hole in Jesse's side was still seeping bloody pus refusing to heal. Momma said, "No" and that was the end of it. Uncle Marc Thomason looked him over cautioning he really wasn't healing up as fast as he should. Even though he was young, he was a wormy sort of boy, always a little on the sickly side or claimed to be, but having been shot three times on the same side of the chest, two puncturing his right lung, that's a hard heal for anyone. In the midst of discussing Jesse's health, a bunch of the little un's run into the house declaring they had found Penny, Susie's dog and her new born puppies. A good animal dog, Penny was a collie and Frank Gregg's old red bone had given her puppies. Momma had been worried the babies might be too big for her, killing her in the birthing process. Susie, Annie, John Thomas, Lam and some of the other youngun's had took a little food into the woods behind the barn coaxing Penny out. Then Lam and John Thomas had inched around to where they could see where she had come from. She had found an old gopher hole under the roots of a felled tree where she had her litter. The boys couldn't see into the hole good enough to see the pups but they declared their must be at least a dozen of them. Momma and Aunt Charlotte eyed each other. I knew that look and hated it. It meant as soon as opportunity presented, they'd be sending us older boys to find the puppies to thump all but maybe two choice ones in the head. I remembered the first time I'd been charged with such an assignment, side by side with Momma we'd looked over the puppies, selected two then Momma had shown me how to thump them in the head just so killing them instantly. I had been horrified realizing the stories they had told us about nature having a way with animals had been at the hands of my Momma. She reassured me it was better than putting them in a toe sack and throwing them in the river. After everyone had gone home, I knew as soon as I saw Momma and Aunt Charlotte turn toward me I had been assigned the task of Penny's puppies. Momma and Zee went out into the yard to do a little practice shooting. Momma was trying to teach Zee how to hold both a rifle and a pistol good enough to hit a target should the occasion arise. Just because the war was over didn't mean warring had stopped. It would also cover any sounds the puppies might make while I was on my assigned task. The kids were lined up watching Momma and Zee when I headed toward the creek to find Penny and the pups.

After the birthday hoedown we still had some hanger on's. We were sitting around discussing the coming of the railroads, be it good or bad, they were coming and with them, change. Momma had been listening each time any of the boys dropped by and rarely was without an opinion of her own. She heard it in our voices and saw it in our faces, life was different and difficult. The farmlands had been devastated through repeated slash and burns. Barns needed rebuilt and homes. We discussed securing work building houses nearer Kansas City. We didn't want to go to work in the cities as our uncles had offered, for the new businesses and stores, or building new homes, all possibilities. We explored our options and while an incapacitated body and idle mind can create all kinds of possibilities, it wasn't Jesse who started us on our path.

The biggest news during the birthday hoedown was talk of the railroads, news Union General's Samuel Curtis and Greenville Dodge having gone to work for the Union Pacific's new Transcontinental Railroad. John Newman Edwards had been hearing more and more talk about the railroads and declared, "The war isn't over." It was simply being fought in a new way. I looked up sensing Momma standing in the doorway. Drying her hands on her apron, "Boys', she said. "Where do Union people put their money?" The room fell silent, she had our attention. "And, how do they get it there?"

About the Author

Freda Cruse Hardison was born and raised in the White River Valley of the Ark Ozarks. After high school, she completed her education at the University of California, San Diego. In addition to work on Creative Interviewing, in 1988, Hardison co-authored Love, Intimacy and Sex, Sage Publications with her university mentor and friend, sociology professor Dr. Jack D. Douglas.

She is the author of Voices of Our People published in 2009 and Places of Our People in 2011. During work on her books of the Ozarks, Hardison realized she was hearing stories of Frank and Jesse James from almost everyone she interviewed. She made notes but hadn't really delved into them when her friend and fellow historian Juanita Stowers was diagnosed with terminal cancer. An avid researcher on Izard Co, Ark, Juanita had boxes of information on the James family. Hardison began working placing their joint research into chronological order. Putting Music of Our People, the third book in her Vanishing Ozarks series on hold, Hardison began pursuing validation of the stories. The process revealed a more involved picture of a never before told story of Frank and Jesse James and their Friends and Family in the White River Valley of Ark.

Hardison, considered one of the primary historians of the Ozarks, has appeared as an expert on a number of documentaries and shows including the Travel Channel's America Declassified and Jesse Ventura's Conspiracy Theory. She is a contributing writer and photographer to the Ark Democrat Gazette, Batesville Guard, Melbourne Times and White River Current. She lectures throughout the United States and has contributed to a number of award winning museum exhibits including Birth of the Ozarks, Calico Rock, Ark. She is married and lives on the White River not far from where she grew up, a place her ancestors have called home for over 200 years.